THIS IS A
SOUVENIR
THE SONGS OF SPEARMINT & SHIRLEY LEE

TRACK LISTING

COVER by James Parsons

BOOK DESIGN & PRODUCTION by Jonathan Chan

IMAGE COMICS, INC.

ROBERT KIRKMAN - chief operating officer
ERIK LARSEN - chief financial officer
TODD McFARLANE - president
MARC SILVESTRI - chief executive officer
JIM VALENTINO - vice-president

ericstephenson - publisher
JOE KEATINGE - pr & marketing coordinator
BRANWYN BIGGLESTONE - accounts manager
TYLER SHAINLINE - administrative assistant
TRACI HUI - traffic manager
ALLEN HUI - production manage
DREW GILL - production artist
JONATHAN CHAN - production artist
MONICA HOWARD - production artist

www.imagecomics.com

INTRODUCTION

The first thing I heard by Spearmint was "Scottish Pop," a summery love song that equated the first blush of romance to the almost transcendental ebullience of, well... Scottish pop. In a brief three minutes and thirty-four seconds, singer and songwriter Shirley Lee managed not only to sum up the altogether amazing feeling of being head over desert-booted heels in love, but also name-checked everyone from Orange Juice's Edwyn Collins to Belle and Sebastian's Stuart Murdoch before concluding, "When I'm with you, I feel like I'm listening to Scottish pop." So what if he somehow managed to skip over Aztec Camera and Roddy Frame? The very second the song stopped, I wanted to hear it again. That, and I wanted to know how I'd never heard of Spearmint before.

See, I love music.

For as long as I can remember, music – especially pop music – has been a huge part of my life. Maybe it's because my father played drums when I was younger: The radio was always on when we were in the car, he and my mother were constantly playing records. They had hundreds of records and their tastes were all over the map, but what really grabbed me were the British bands from the '60s. The Beatles. The Kinks. The Who. The Stones. The Animals. The Zombies. I just couldn't get enough of that stuff, still can't. My tastes changed as I got older, and I got into soul and jazz and folk and so on, but regardless what I was listening to at any given time, I've always viewed discovering new music (which we'll define here as anything we weren't previously aware of) as one of the great joys in life.

And my first exposure to Spearmint made me quite happy indeed.

"Scottish Pop" is on Spearmint's second album, A Different Lifetime, so that was the first one I got after discovering the band. Described on the sleeve notes as "Songs about falling in love... about being in love... about saying goodbye," A Different Lifetime was more or less a concept album tracking a relationship from a couple's first meeting right through to their break-up and beyond. In many ways, it's Spearmint's masterpiece and whenever I'm recommending the band to a friend, A Different Lifetime is always the album I suggest first. Apart from being an amazing collection of songs that actually succeeds in telling a cohesive (as well as brutally honest) story, it highlights all the things Shirley Lee and his band mates do so well.

What is that exactly?

Well, for the uninitiated, Spearmint specialize in what I suppose one might describe as "classic British indie guitar pop." (That's what Wikipedia says, anyway, and they're never wrong, right?) More to the point, though, Spearmint are at their best mixing shimmering, melodic pop with lyrical content that often works on multiple levels, the type of music that sounds quite good on the radio, but also has some real depth to it. So there are guitar riffs that recall everyone from The Smiths to The Style Council, grooves that unmistakably reference Northern Soul and Motown and then lyrics that not only have a bit of meaning, but actually manage to tell concise little stories capturing a variety of emotions, a whole catalogue of different experiences.

Which brings us – and not a moment too soon I might add, since you're probably anxious to move past my long-winded intro – to this very book.

I love comics just as much as I love music, and a few years back, I decided it would be fun to somehow mix the two. A conversation with fellow music addict and Hawaiian Dick scribe B. Clay Moore resulted in the first music-based comics anthology, a collection of short stories based around Belle and Sebastian songs called Put the Book Back on the Shelf, but all along, the band that really fueled my desire to see pop songs reinterpreted as comic book stories was Spearmint. Shirley's songs always have such a strong narrative quality to them that they seemed ideal for adaptation, and even when filtered through some of comics' most unique voices, they retain their meaning. Songs about love, life and loss become stories about the same, and the end result is something really quite special.

Like listening, once again, to "Scottish Pop."

— ericstephenson
Berkeley, CA
2009

SWEEPING THE NATION

featured on **A Week Away**

story by **Kieron Gillen**
art by **Jamie McKelvie**

this song's dedicated to
some of the best bands in the country
some of the bands we never got to hear
bands who never got any records out
give it up
never got played on the radio
never got written about in the press
give it up
this song's dedicated to open up
this song's dedicated to the said liquidator
give it up
this song's deciated to supersaurus
give it up
this song's dedicated to
aaga, kix, the interrogated,
give it up
seize the infidels, chance and
laverne and shirlie

i sometimes feel i'm sweeping the nation
showing my invisible friend
harvey
places where i used to live, well
doesn't your balloon ever land?
the emasculation of a good friend
is nothing i should be singing about
the tattoos all look old and faded
and stupid with a suit

before they took the beach away
you used to walk your brains
right up the coast
but you ended up sweeping the nation
that's such a sad sad loss

an ice sculpture when the summer comes
a butterfly in winter
aaga, kix, the interrogated,
seize the infidels, chance
laverne and shirlie

don't let it land
don't let it land

i, i've been wasting my life
i've finally realised
hey! hey! hey!
i've wasted so much time

are we a happy as when we had no money?
yes we are but that's not why
crippling failure, you get crippling success
well doesn't your balloon ever land?

i've got a red wooden transistor
everything sounds best on that
so just make sure you
sweep the nation
i wanna hear you on that
i wanna hear you on that
i wanna hear you on that
i wanna hear you on that
i wanna hear you on that

well that's my story and i'm sticking to that
i remember standing under byker bridge
in newcastle with michael bradshaw
and mickey turned to me and saying
"shirley, don't worry!

as long as you stick to what you believe in
everything you want will come to you"

give it up
i wanna hear you on that
give it up
i wanna hear you on that
give it up
i wanna hear you on that
give it up
i wanna hear you on that
give it up
i wanna hear you on that

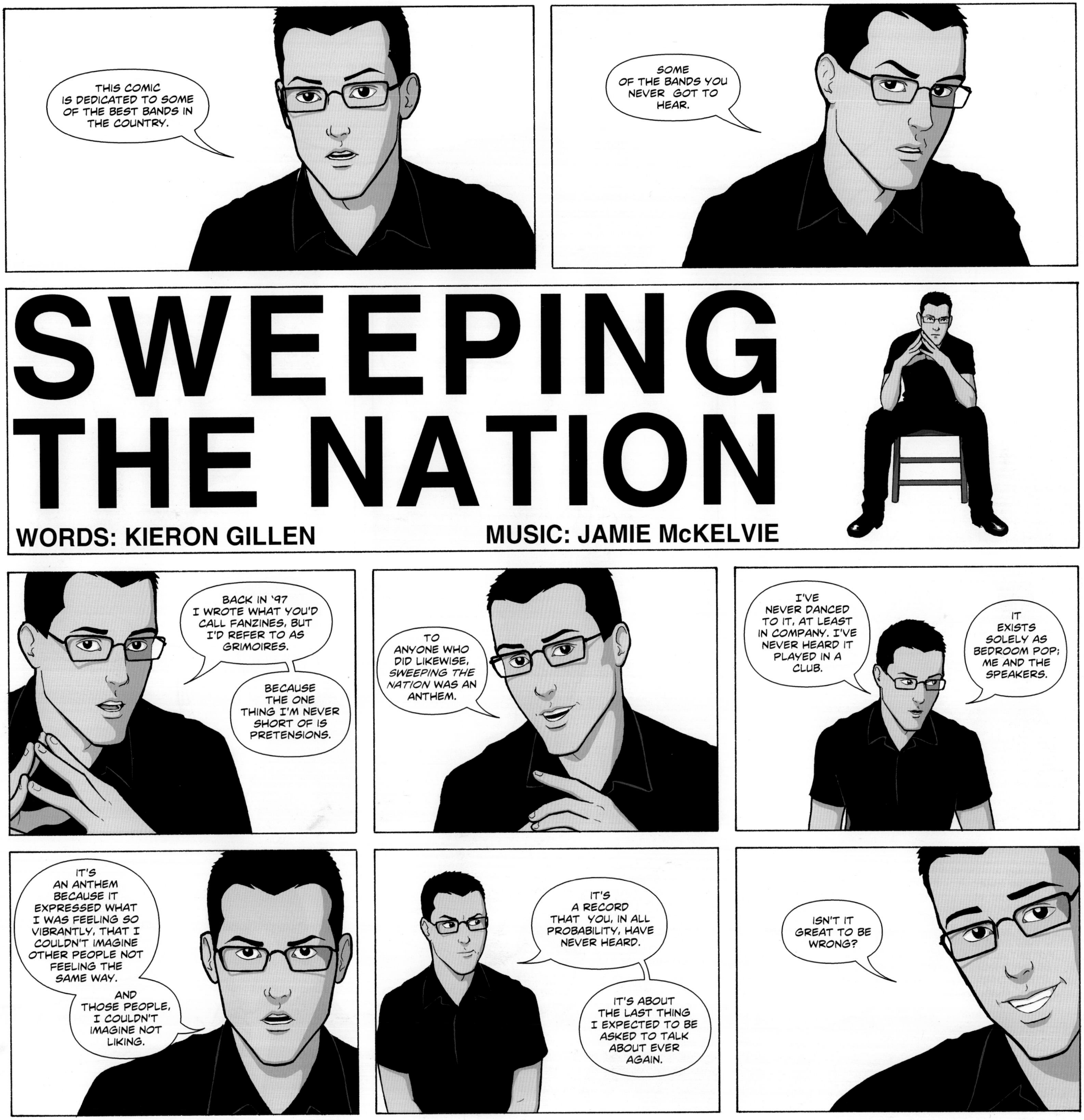
THIS COMIC IS DEDICATED TO SOME OF THE BEST BANDS IN THE COUNTRY.
SOME OF THE BANDS YOU NEVER GOT TO HEAR.
SWEEPING THE NATION
WORDS: KIERON GILLEN
MUSIC: JAMIE McKELVIE
BACK IN '97 I WROTE WHAT YOU'D CALL FANZINES, BUT I'D REFER TO AS GRIMOIRES.
BECAUSE THE ONE THING I'M NEVER SHORT OF IS PRETENSIONS.
TO ANYONE WHO DID LIKEWISE, *SWEEPING THE NATION* WAS AN ANTHEM.
I'VE NEVER DANCED TO IT, AT LEAST IN COMPANY. I'VE NEVER HEARD IT PLAYED IN A CLUB.
IT EXISTS SOLELY AS BEDROOM POP; ME AND THE SPEAKERS.
IT'S AN ANTHEM BECAUSE IT EXPRESSED WHAT I WAS FEELING SO VIBRANTLY, THAT I COULDN'T IMAGINE OTHER PEOPLE NOT FEELING THE SAME WAY.
AND THOSE PEOPLE, I COULDN'T IMAGINE NOT LIKING.
IT'S A RECORD THAT YOU, IN ALL PROBABILITY, HAVE NEVER HEARD.
IT'S ABOUT THE LAST THING I EXPECTED TO BE ASKED TO TALK ABOUT EVER AGAIN.
ISN'T IT GREAT TO BE WRONG?

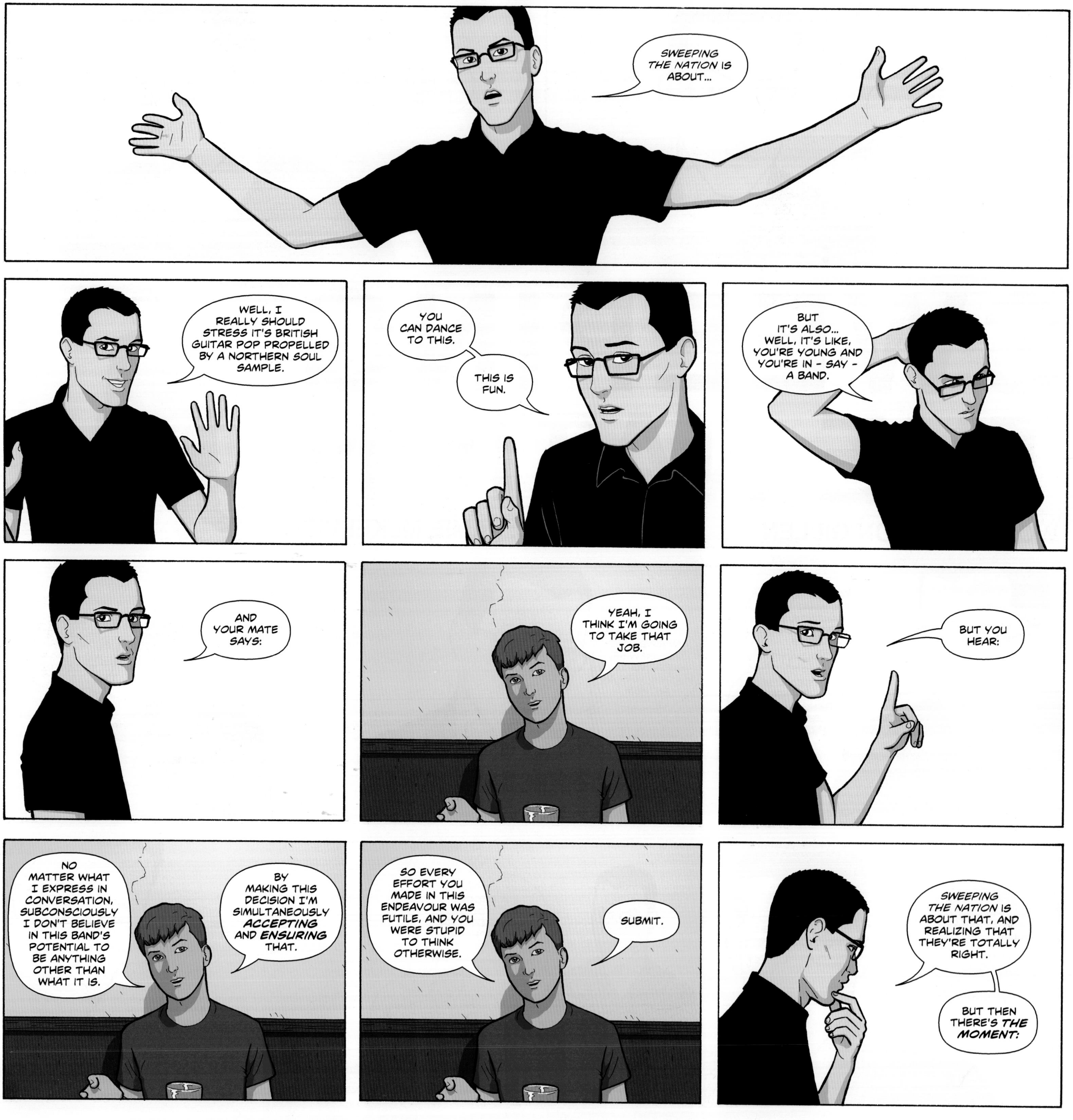

SWEEPING THE NATION IS ABOUT...
WELL, I REALLY SHOULD STRESS IT'S BRITISH GUITAR POP PROPELLED BY A NORTHERN SOUL SAMPLE.
YOU CAN DANCE TO THIS.
THIS IS FUN.
BUT IT'S ALSO... WELL, IT'S LIKE, YOU'RE YOUNG AND YOU'RE IN - SAY - A BAND.
AND YOUR MATE SAYS:
YEAH, I THINK I'M GOING TO TAKE THAT JOB.
BUT YOU HEAR:
NO MATTER WHAT I EXPRESS IN CONVERSATION, SUBCONSCIOUSLY I DON'T BELIEVE IN THIS BAND'S POTENTIAL TO BE ANYTHING OTHER THAN WHAT IT IS.
BY MAKING THIS DECISION I'M SIMULTANEOUSLY ACCEPTING AND ENSURING THAT.
SO EVERY EFFORT YOU MADE IN THIS ENDEAVOUR WAS FUTILE, AND YOU WERE STUPID TO THINK OTHERWISE.
SUBMIT.
SWEEPING THE NATION IS ABOUT THAT, AND REALIZING THAT THEY'RE TOTALLY RIGHT.
BUT THEN THERE'S THE MOMENT:

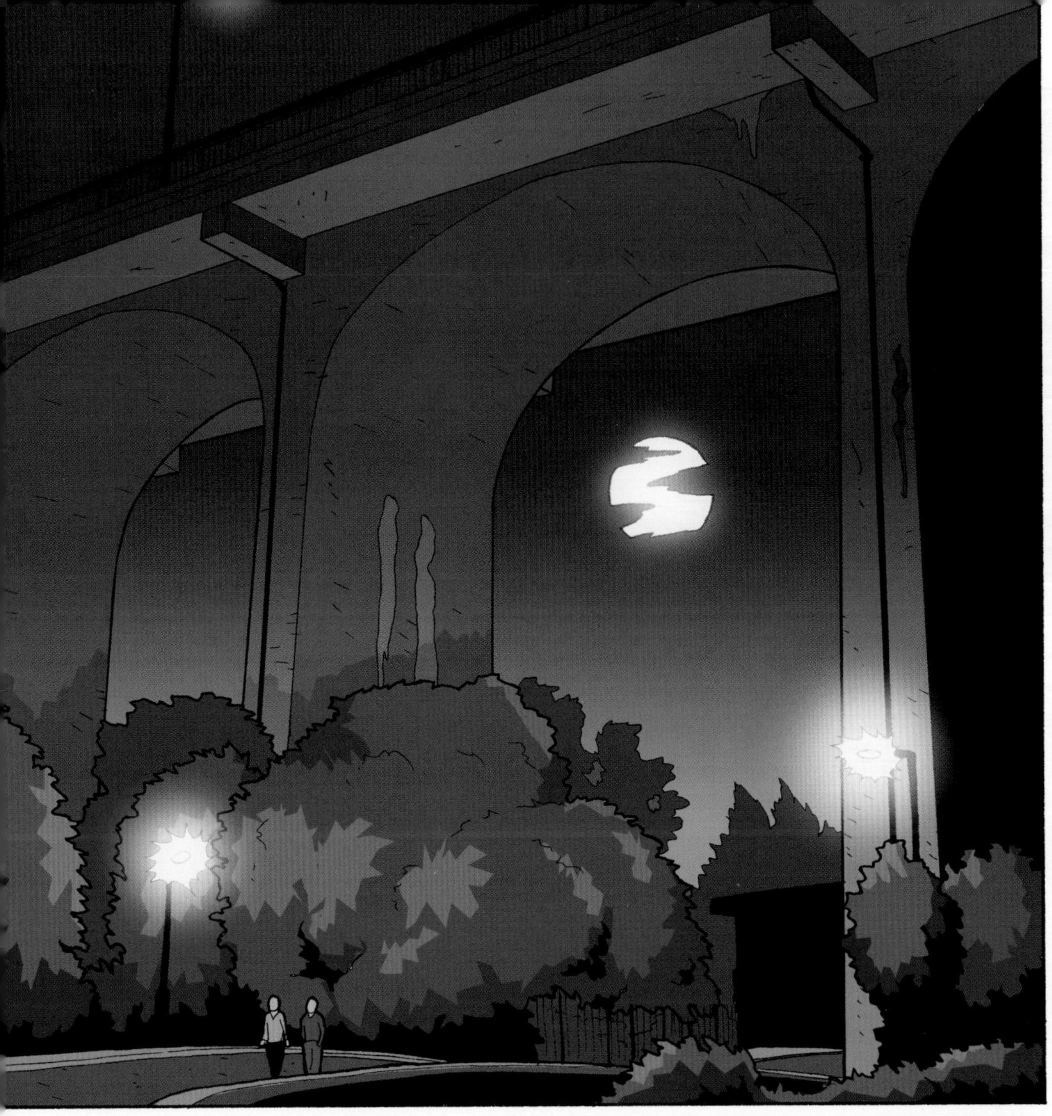

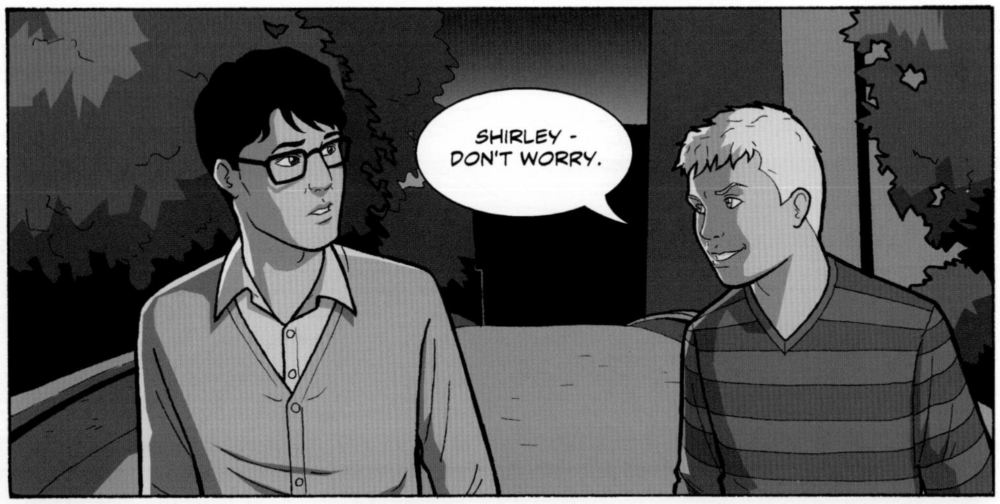
SHIRLEY - DON'T WORRY.

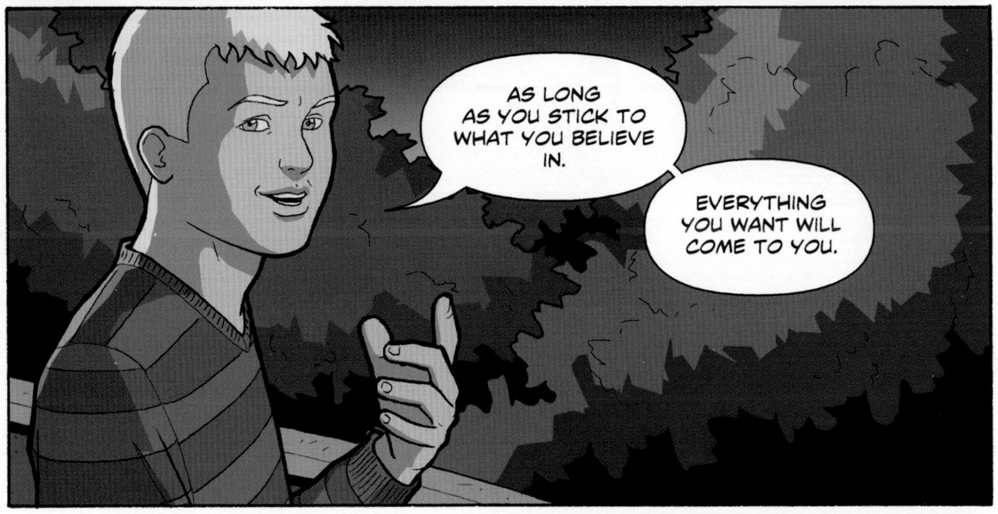
AS LONG AS YOU STICK TO WHAT YOU BELIEVE IN.
EVERYTHING YOU WANT WILL COME TO YOU.

TURN IT UP

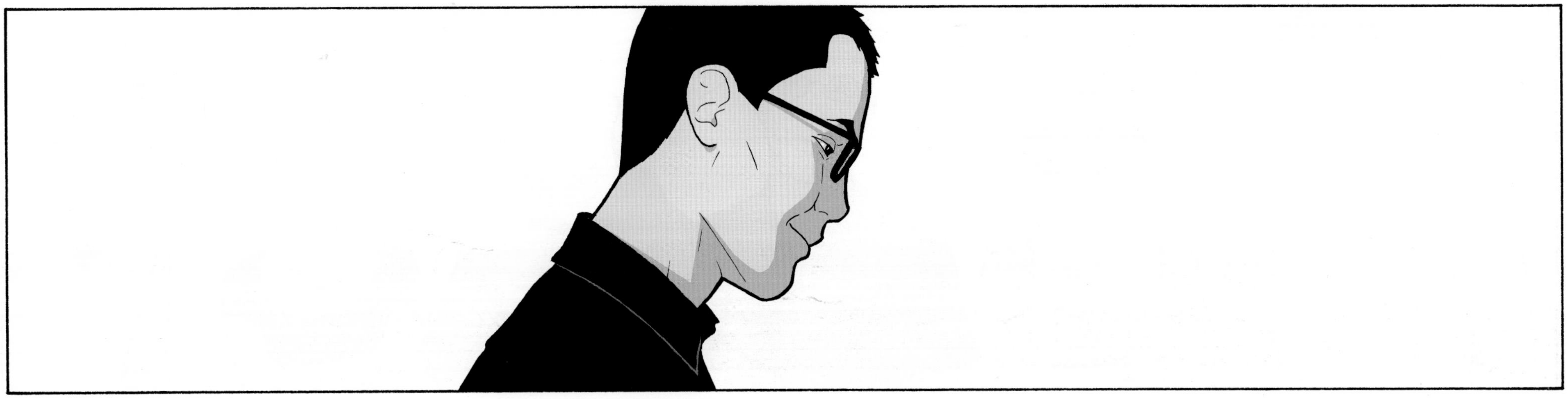

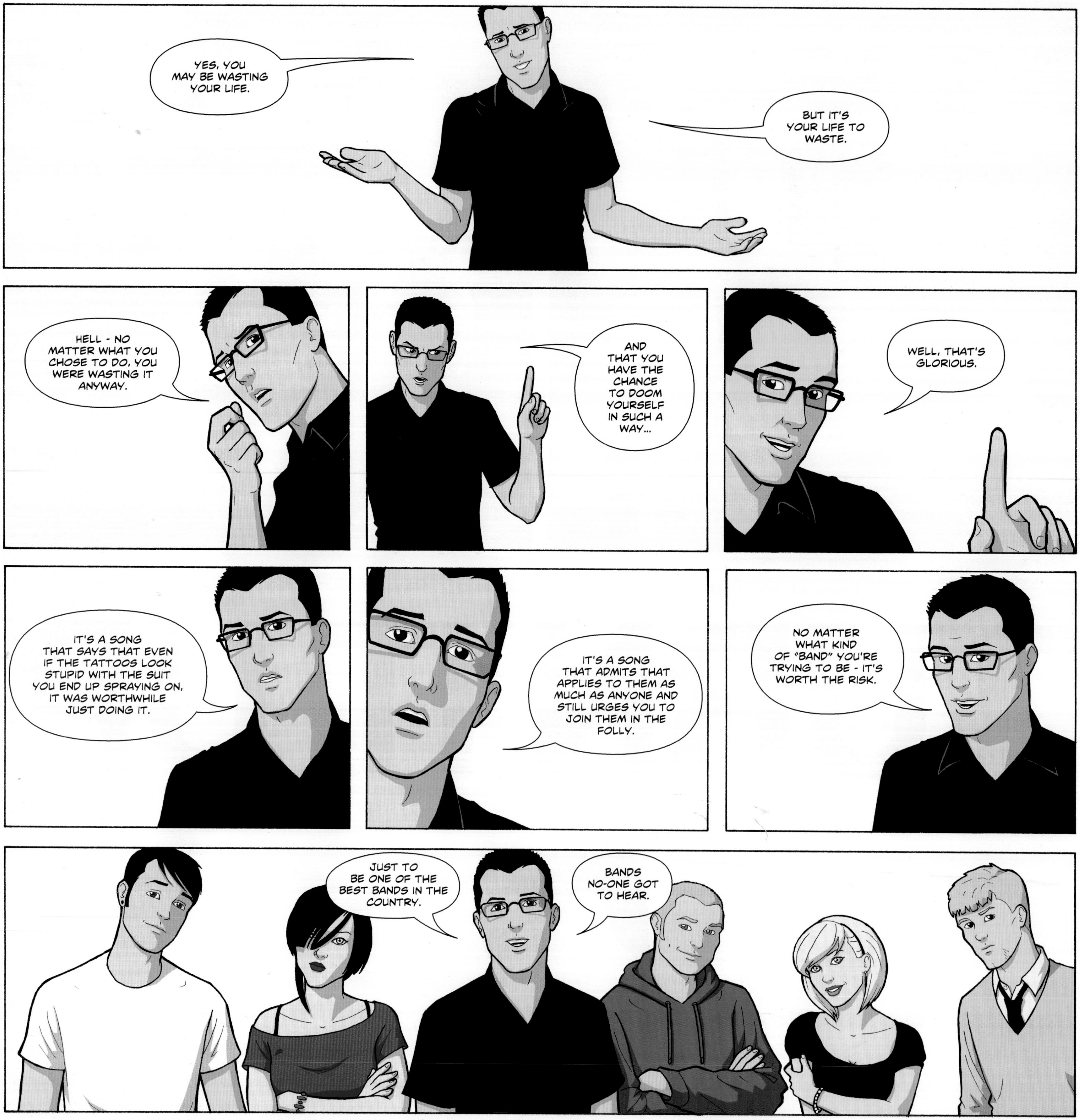

YES, YOU MAY BE WASTING YOUR LIFE.
BUT IT'S YOUR LIFE TO WASTE.
HELL - NO MATTER WHAT YOU CHOSE TO DO, YOU WERE WASTING IT ANYWAY.
AND THAT YOU HAVE THE CHANCE TO DOOM YOURSELF IN SUCH A WAY...
WELL, THAT'S GLORIOUS.
IT'S A SONG THAT SAYS THAT EVEN IF THE TATTOOS LOOK STUPID WITH THE SUIT YOU END UP SPRAYING ON, IT WAS WORTHWHILE JUST DOING IT.
IT'S A SONG THAT ADMITS THAT APPLIES TO THEM AS MUCH AS ANYONE AND STILL URGES YOU TO JOIN THEM IN THE FOLLY.
NO MATTER WHAT KIND OF "BAND" YOU'RE TRYING TO BE - IT'S WORTH THE RISK.
JUST TO BE ONE OF THE BEST BANDS IN THE COUNTRY.
BANDS NO-ONE GOT TO HEAR.

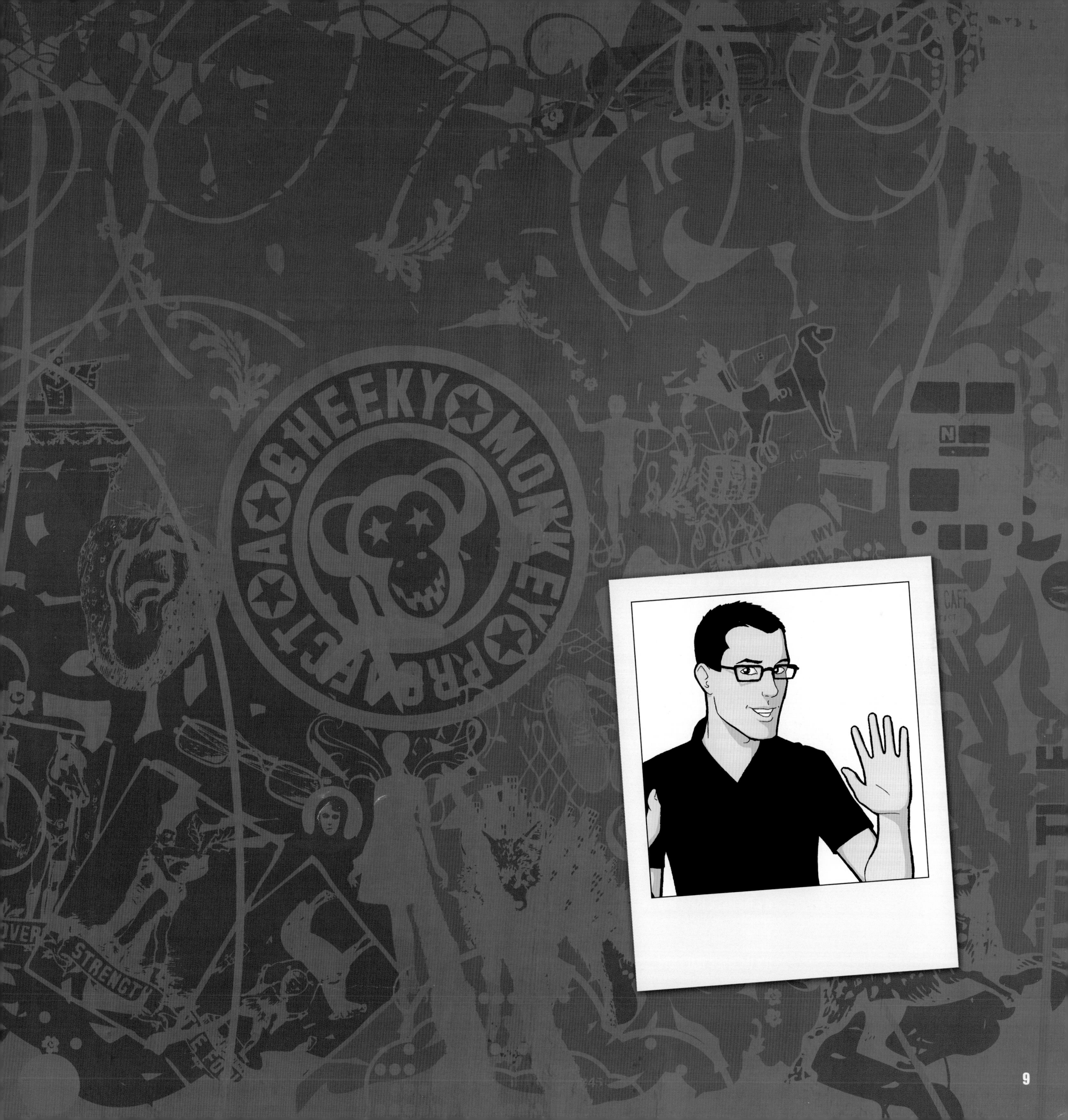
A CHEEKY MONKEY PROJECT

JULIE CHRISTIE!

featured on **A Different Lifetime**

story by **Jamie S. Rich**
art by **Natalie Nourigat**

THANKS, SHAUN!

i didn't want to say out loud
in case it came untrue
but i now know why i'm on this earth
to try to be with you
oh can't you tell i'm different now
by the music that i play
the songs i thought were soppy before
sound wonderful today

alright
alright
it's the music that i love
alright
alright
it's the music that i love

she looks like julie christie
and she's blotted out my past
she had it all laid out for me
i never stood a chance
we took the essence of felt and vic godard
and we blasted into space
and then we showered down on everyone
the whole soppy human race

alright
alright
it's the music that i love
alright
alright
it's the music that i love

i'm lying on the bed
i'm lying on the bed
i'm holding on to you
holding on to you
i'm supposed to be meeting little jim
but why would i be any happier out there
than i am in here?

i've wanted to say this for so long
but i haven't had the nerve
i realise now what i've been missing
you looked like julie christie when i met you
i wanted to laugh out loud
oh can't you tell i'm different now
i'm smiling in the crowd

alright
alright
it's the music that i love
alright
alright
it's the music that i love
alright
alright
it's the music that i love
alright
alright
alright
alright
it's the music that i love

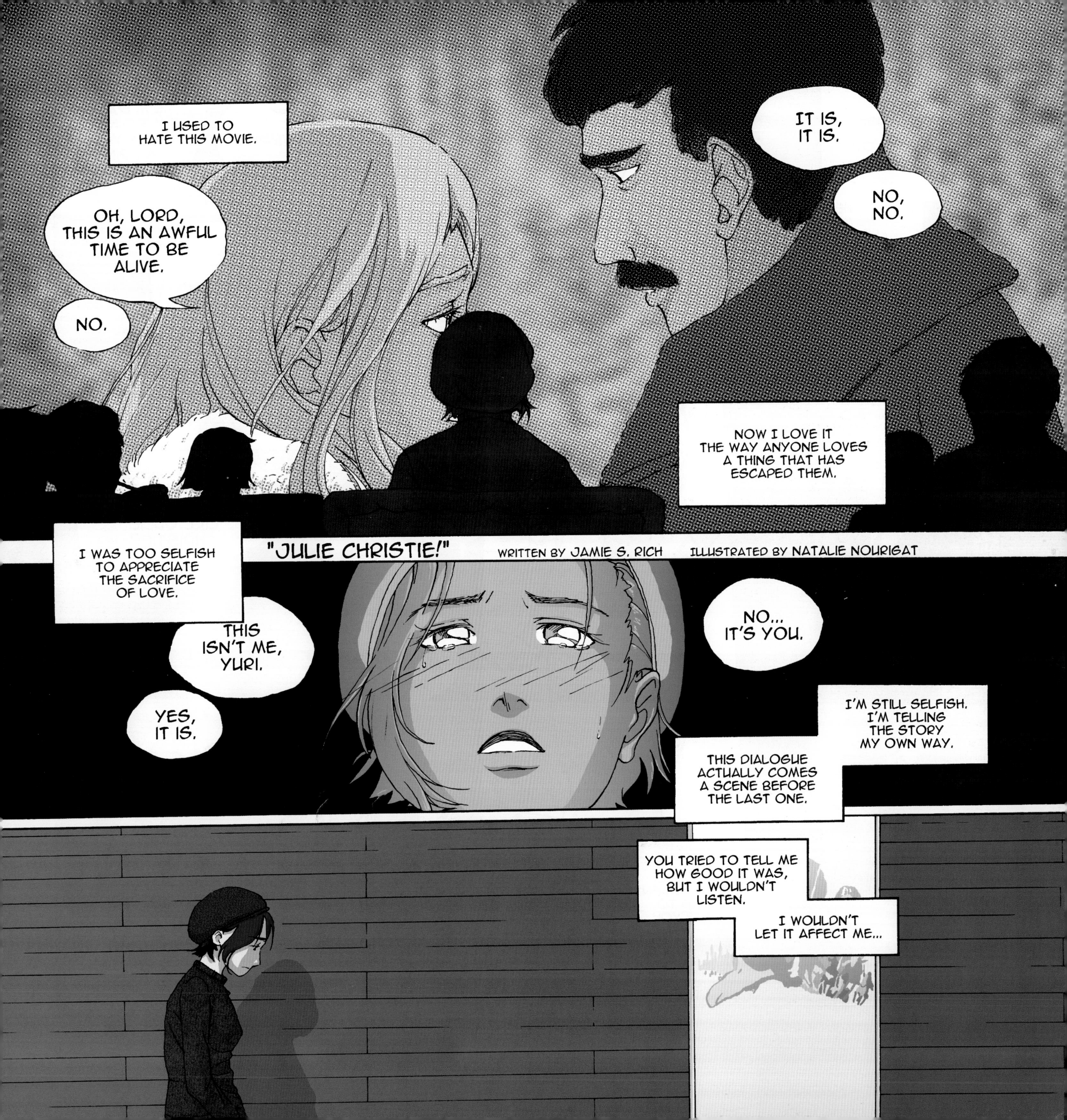
I USED TO HATE THIS MOVIE.
OH, LORD, THIS IS AN AWFUL TIME TO BE ALIVE.
NO.
IT IS, IT IS.
NO, NO.
NOW I LOVE IT THE WAY ANYONE LOVES A THING THAT HAS ESCAPED THEM.
"JULIE CHRISTIE!"
WRITTEN BY JAMIE S. RICH
ILLUSTRATED BY NATALIE NOURIGAT
I WAS TOO SELFISH TO APPRECIATE THE SACRIFICE OF LOVE.
THIS ISN'T ME, YURI.
YES, IT IS.
NO... IT'S YOU.
I'M STILL SELFISH. I'M TELLING THE STORY MY OWN WAY.
THIS DIALOGUE ACTUALLY COMES A SCENE BEFORE THE LAST ONE.
YOU TRIED TO TELL ME HOW GOOD IT WAS, BUT I WOULDN'T LISTEN.
I WOULDN'T LET IT AFFECT ME...

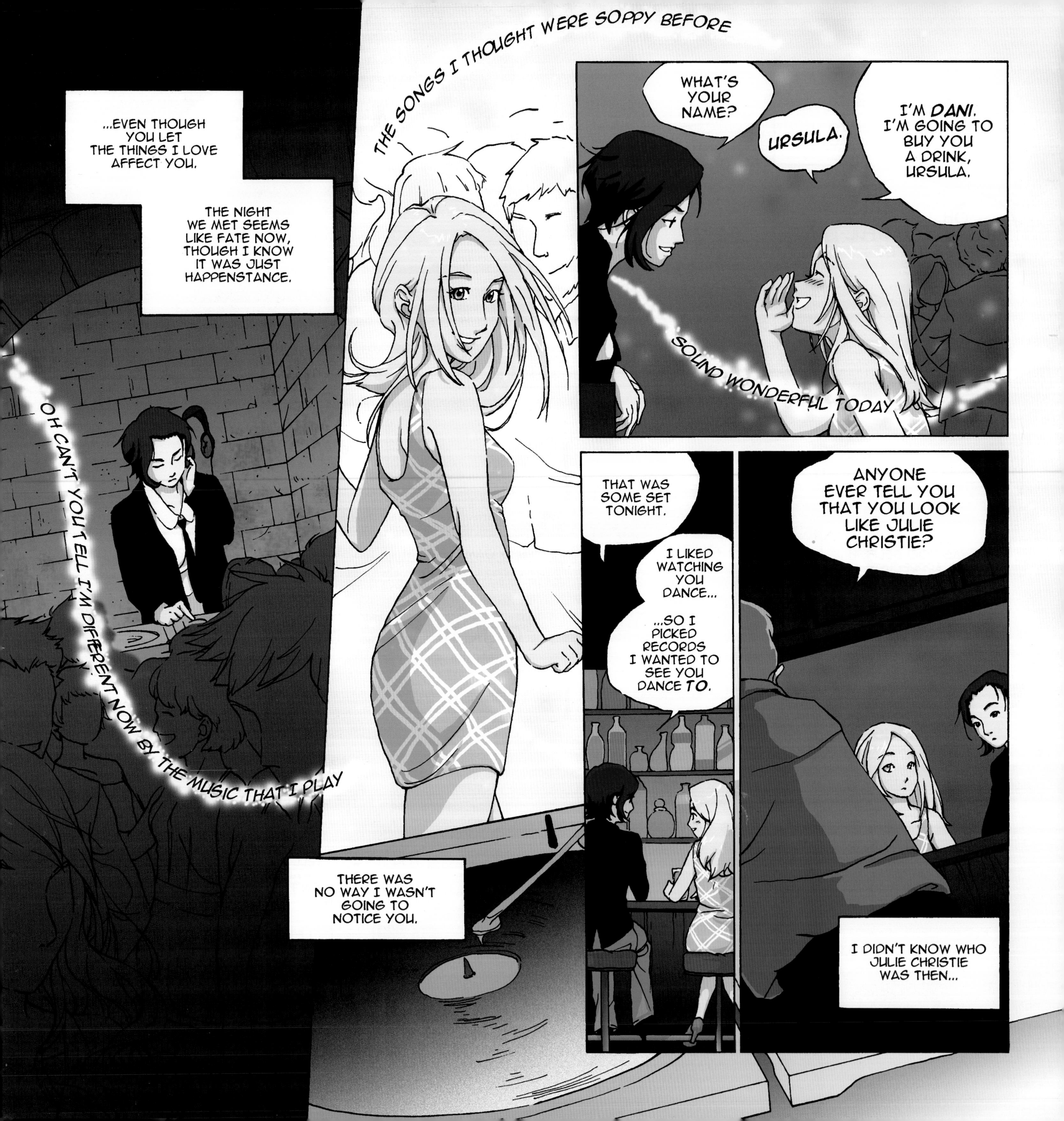
...EVEN THOUGH YOU LET THE THINGS I LOVE AFFECT YOU.
THE NIGHT WE MET SEEMS LIKE FATE NOW, THOUGH I KNOW IT WAS JUST HAPPENSTANCE.
OH CAN'T YOU TELL I'M DIFFERENT NOW BY THE MUSIC THAT I PLAY
THE SONGS I THOUGHT WERE SOPPY BEFORE
WHAT'S YOUR NAME?
URSULA.
I'M DANI. I'M GOING TO BUY YOU A DRINK, URSULA.
SOUND WONDERFUL TODAY
THERE WAS NO WAY I WASN'T GOING TO NOTICE YOU.
THAT WAS SOME SET TONIGHT.
I LIKED WATCHING YOU DANCE...
...SO I PICKED RECORDS I WANTED TO SEE YOU DANCE TO.
ANYONE EVER TELL YOU THAT YOU LOOK LIKE JULIE CHRISTIE?
I DIDN'T KNOW WHO JULIE CHRISTIE WAS THEN...

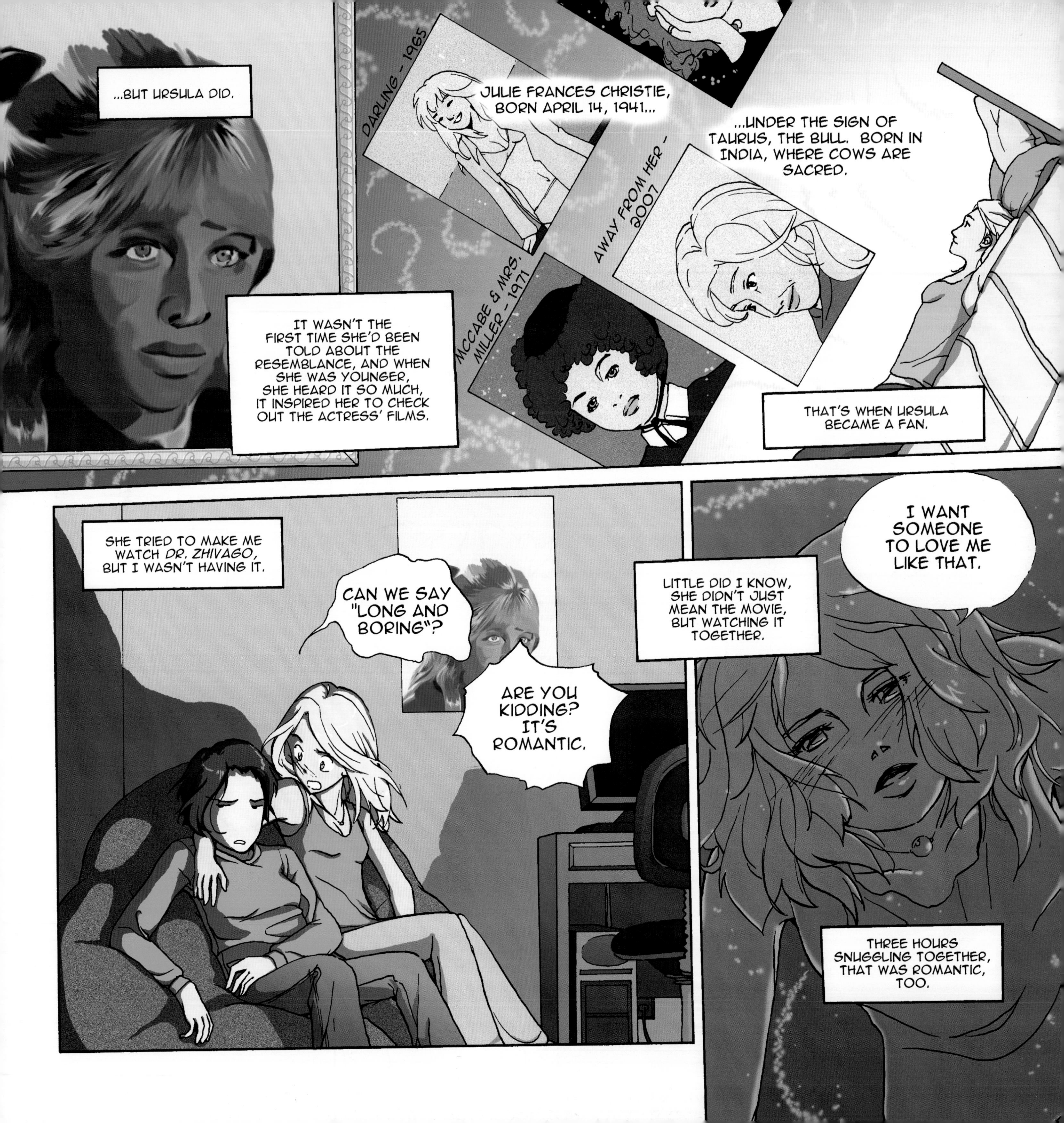

...BUT URSULA DID.
IT WASN'T THE FIRST TIME SHE'D BEEN TOLD ABOUT THE RESEMBLANCE, AND WHEN SHE WAS YOUNGER, SHE HEARD IT SO MUCH, IT INSPIRED HER TO CHECK OUT THE ACTRESS' FILMS.
DARLING – 1965
JULIE FRANCES CHRISTIE, BORN APRIL 14, 1941...
MCCABE & MRS. MILLER – 1971
AWAY FROM HER – 2007
...UNDER THE SIGN OF TAURUS, THE BULL. BORN IN INDIA, WHERE COWS ARE SACRED.
THAT'S WHEN URSULA BECAME A FAN.
SHE TRIED TO MAKE ME WATCH *DR. ZHIVAGO*, BUT I WASN'T HAVING IT.
CAN WE SAY "LONG AND BORING"?
ARE YOU KIDDING? IT'S ROMANTIC.
LITTLE DID I KNOW, SHE DIDN'T JUST MEAN THE MOVIE, BUT WATCHING IT TOGETHER.
I WANT SOMEONE TO LOVE ME LIKE THAT.
THREE HOURS SNUGGLING TOGETHER, THAT WAS ROMANTIC, TOO.

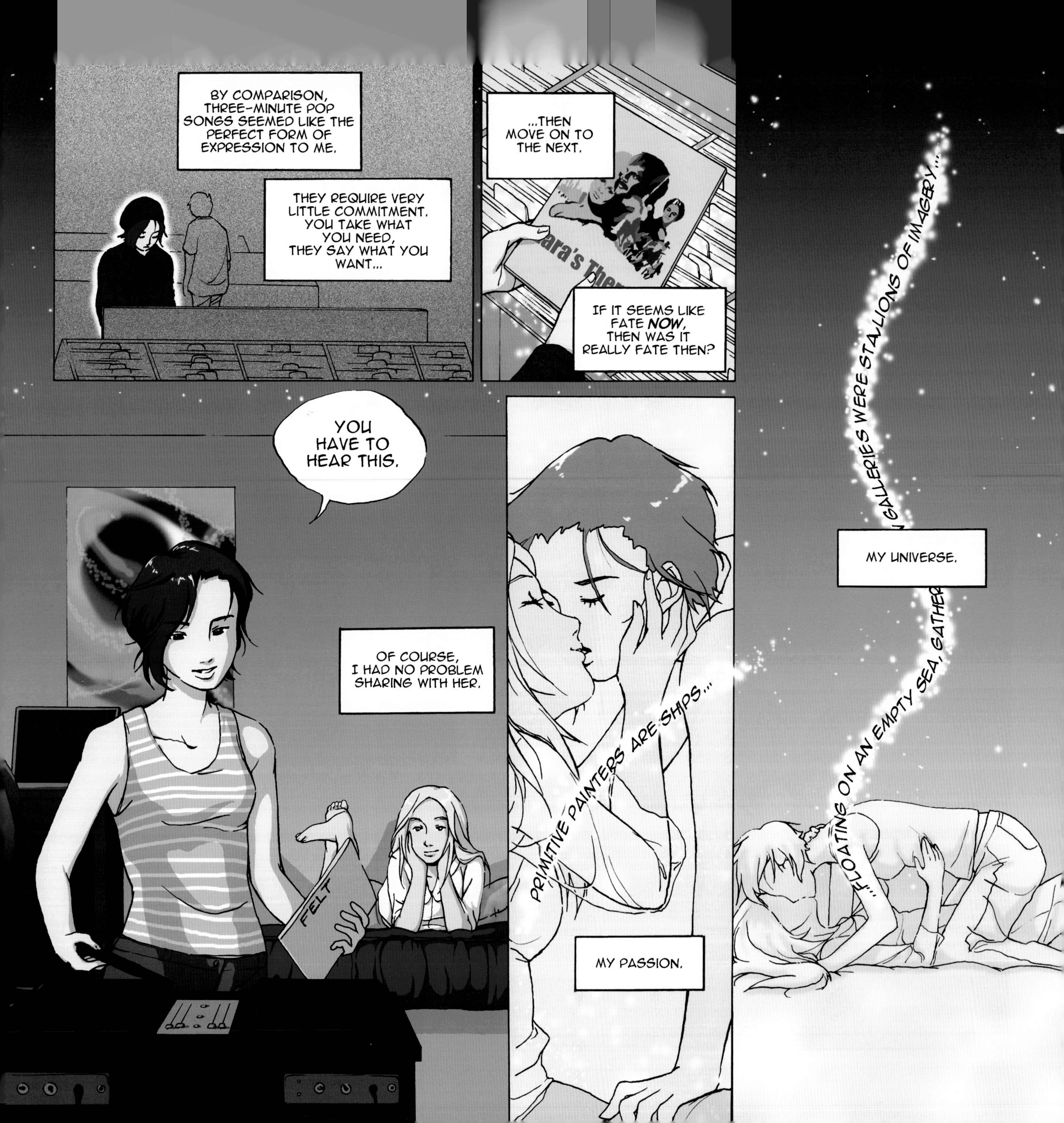

BY COMPARISON, THREE-MINUTE POP SONGS SEEMED LIKE THE PERFECT FORM OF EXPRESSION TO ME.
THEY REQUIRE VERY LITTLE COMMITMENT. YOU TAKE WHAT YOU NEED, THEY SAY WHAT YOU WANT...
...THEN MOVE ON TO THE NEXT.
IF IT SEEMS LIKE FATE **NOW**, THEN WAS IT REALLY FATE THEN?
YOU HAVE TO HEAR THIS.
OF COURSE, I HAD NO PROBLEM SHARING WITH HER.
FELT
PRIMITIVE PAINTERS ARE SHIPS...
MY PASSION.
...FLOATING ON AN EMPTY SEA, GATHER
MY UNIVERSE.
GALLERIES WERE STATIONS OF IMAGERY...

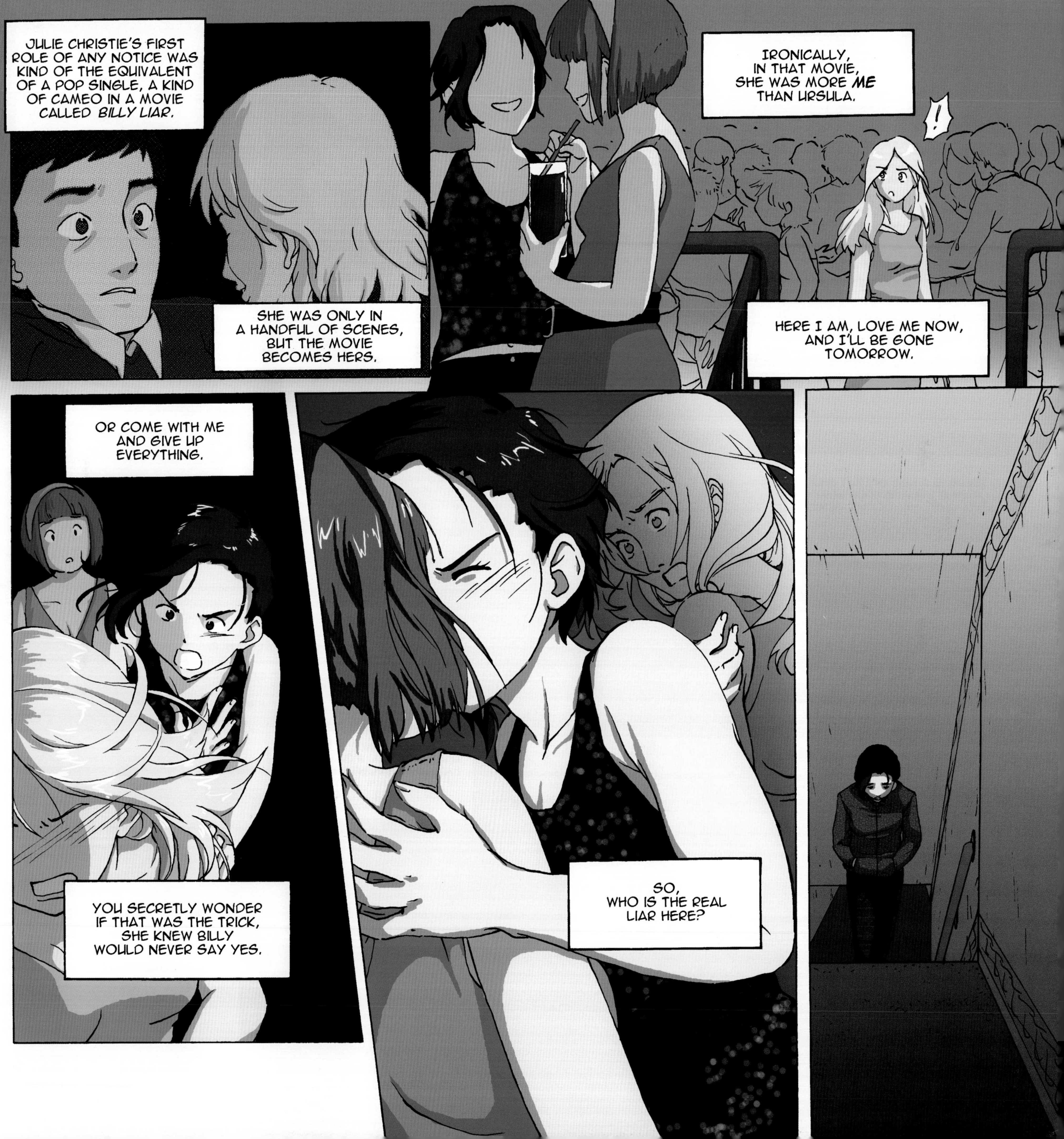
JULIE CHRISTIE'S FIRST ROLE OF ANY NOTICE WAS KIND OF THE EQUIVALENT OF A POP SINGLE, A KIND OF CAMEO IN A MOVIE CALLED *BILLY LIAR*.
SHE WAS ONLY IN A HANDFUL OF SCENES, BUT THE MOVIE BECOMES HERS.
IRONICALLY, IN THAT MOVIE, SHE WAS MORE *ME* THAN URSULA.
!
HERE I AM, LOVE ME NOW, AND I'LL BE GONE TOMORROW.
OR COME WITH ME AND GIVE UP EVERYTHING.
YOU SECRETLY WONDER IF THAT WAS THE TRICK, SHE KNEW BILLY WOULD NEVER SAY YES.
SO, WHO IS THE REAL LIAR HERE?

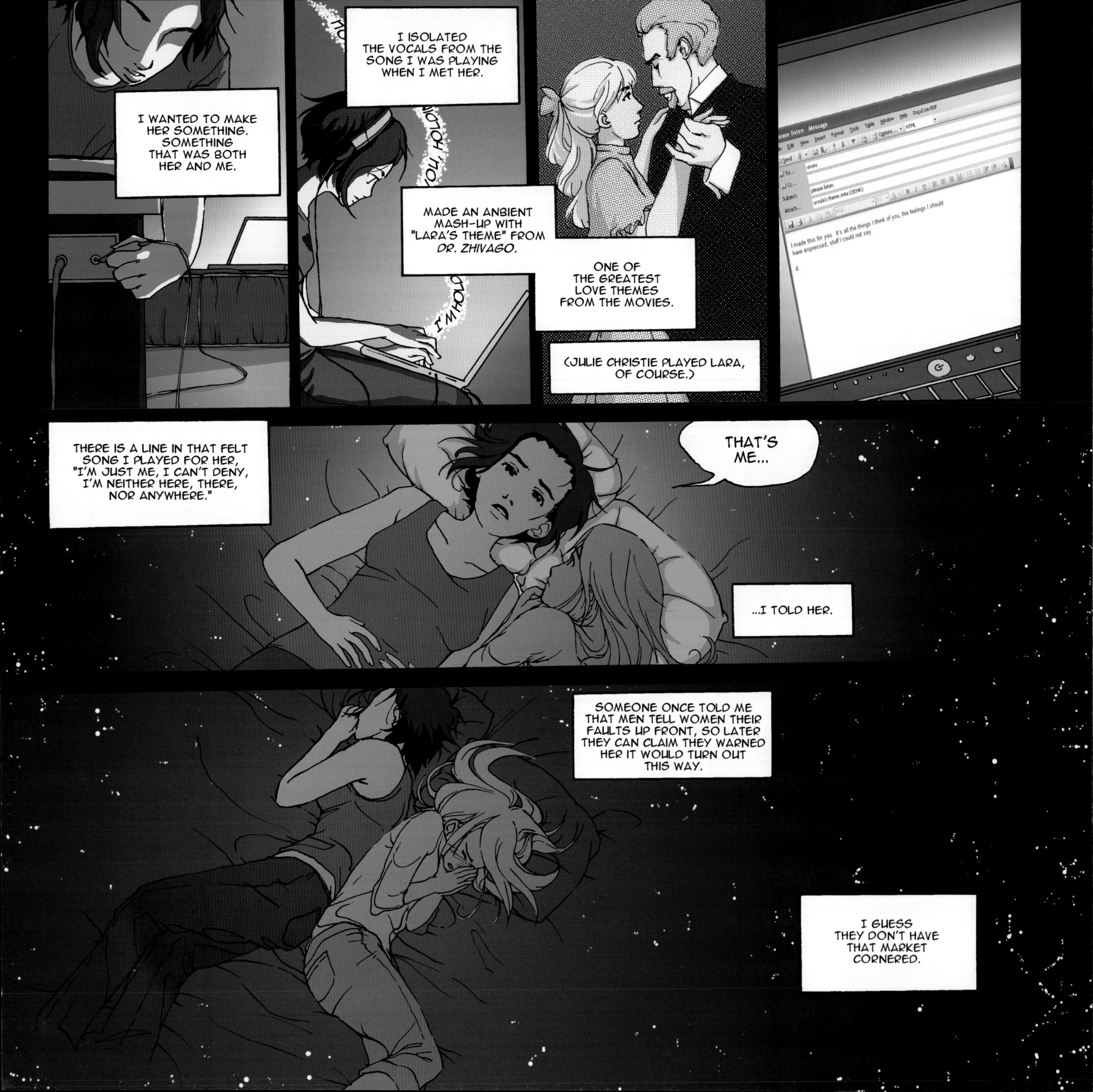
I WANTED TO MAKE HER SOMETHING. SOMETHING THAT WAS BOTH HER AND ME.
I ISOLATED THE VOCALS FROM THE SONG I WAS PLAYING WHEN I MET HER.
MADE AN ANBIENT MASH-UP WITH "LARA'S THEME" FROM DR. ZHIVAGO.
ONE OF THE GREATEST LOVE THEMES FROM THE MOVIES.
(JULIE CHRISTIE PLAYED LARA, OF COURSE.)
please listen - Message
To... urusu
Subject: please listen
Attach... ursula's theme.m4a (2834K)
I made this for you. It's all the things I think of you, the feelings I should have expressed, stuff I could not say.
d.
THERE IS A LINE IN THAT FELT SONG I PLAYED FOR HER, "I'M JUST ME, I CAN'T DENY, I'M NEITHER HERE, THERE, NOR ANYWHERE."
THAT'S ME...
...I TOLD HER.
SOMEONE ONCE TOLD ME THAT MEN TELL WOMEN THEIR FAULTS UP FRONT, SO LATER THEY CAN CLAIM THEY WARNED HER IT WOULD TURN OUT THIS WAY.
I GUESS THEY DON'T HAVE THAT MARKET CORNERED.

I DIDN'T REALIZE THAT THE FEELING OF EMPTINESS I HAD ALMOST IMMEDIATELY AFTER WE SPLIT WAS REGRET.

REMINDERS OF HER WERE EVERYWHERE, IN PLACES EXPECTED...

Shampoo, 1975

...AND PLACES NOT SO EXPECTED.

I WENT BACK TO THE VIDEO STORE TO START RENTING JULIE CHRISTIE MOVIES, HOPING MAYBE I'D START TO UNDERSTAND.

MAYBE I WOULDN'T MISS URSULA SO MUCH.

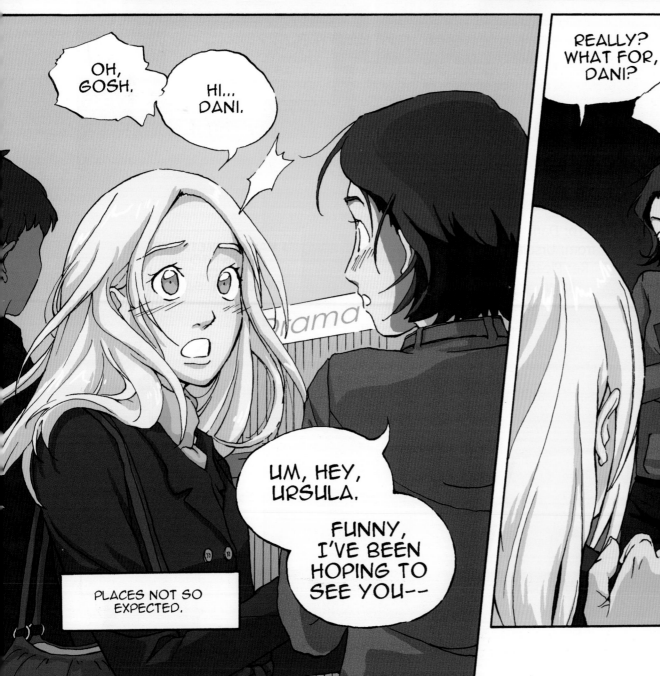

OH, GOSH.

HI... DANI.

UM, HEY, URSULA.

FUNNY, I'VE BEEN HOPING TO SEE YOU--

PLACES NOT SO EXPECTED.

REALLY? WHAT FOR, DANI?

NEVER MIND.

THERE IS A LINE THAT JULIE CHRISTIE SAYS IN THE NARRATION OF *DARLING*...

"LIFE'S FULL OF 'IF ONLYS.' YOU KNOW, IF ONLY, IF ONLY..."

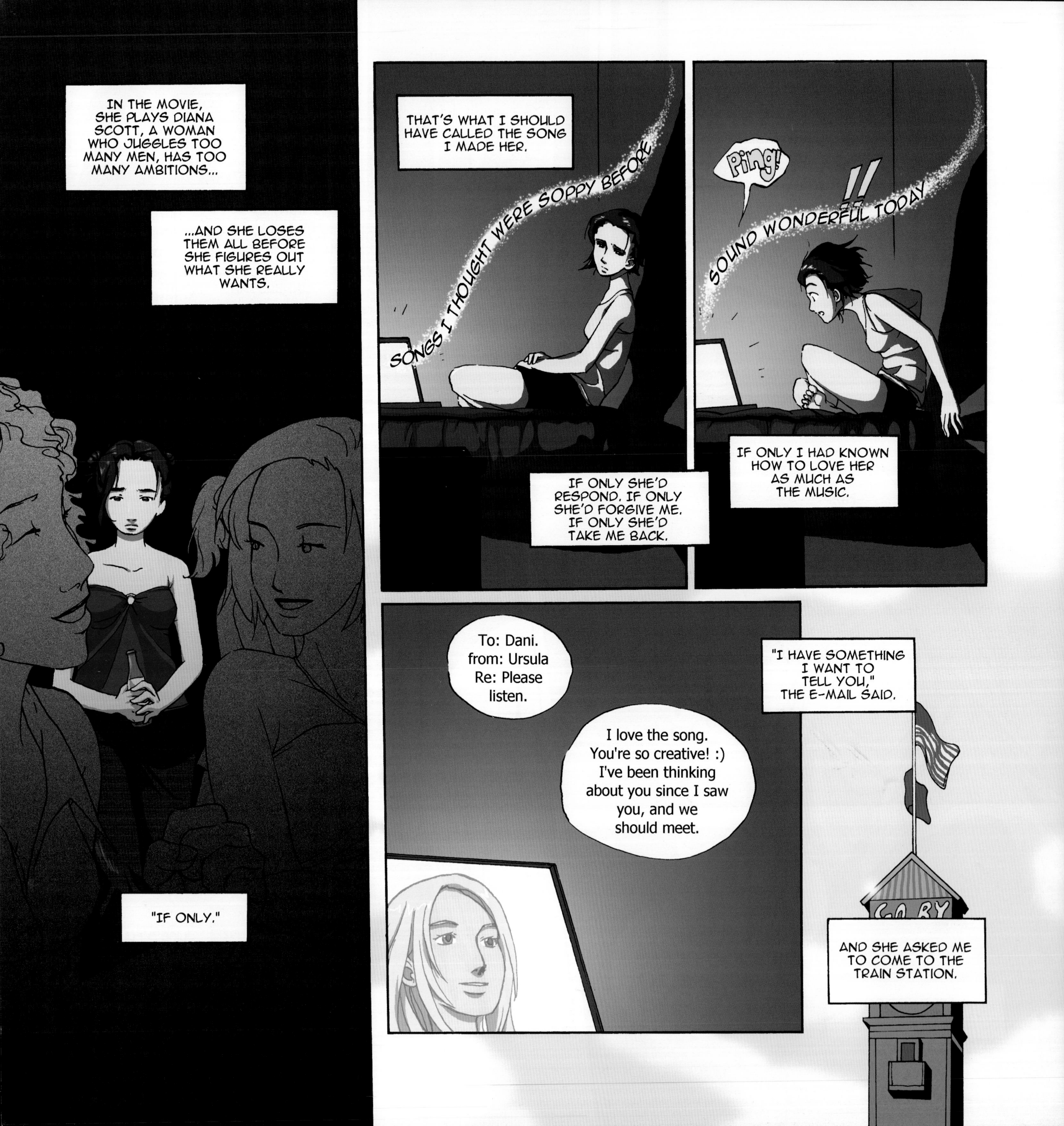
IN THE MOVIE, SHE PLAYS DIANA SCOTT, A WOMAN WHO JUGGLES TOO MANY MEN, HAS TOO MANY AMBITIONS...
...AND SHE LOSES THEM ALL BEFORE SHE FIGURES OUT WHAT SHE REALLY WANTS.
"IF ONLY."
THAT'S WHAT I SHOULD HAVE CALLED THE SONG I MADE HER.
SONGS I THOUGHT WERE SOPPY BEFORE
IF ONLY SHE'D RESPOND. IF ONLY SHE'D FORGIVE ME. IF ONLY SHE'D TAKE ME BACK.
PING!
!!
SOUND WONDERFUL TODAY
IF ONLY I HAD KNOWN HOW TO LOVE HER AS MUCH AS THE MUSIC.
To: Dani.
from: Ursula
Re: Please listen.
I love the song. You're so creative! :) I've been thinking about you since I saw you, and we should meet.
"I HAVE SOMETHING I WANT TO TELL YOU," THE E-MAIL SAID.
AND SHE ASKED ME TO COME TO THE TRAIN STATION.

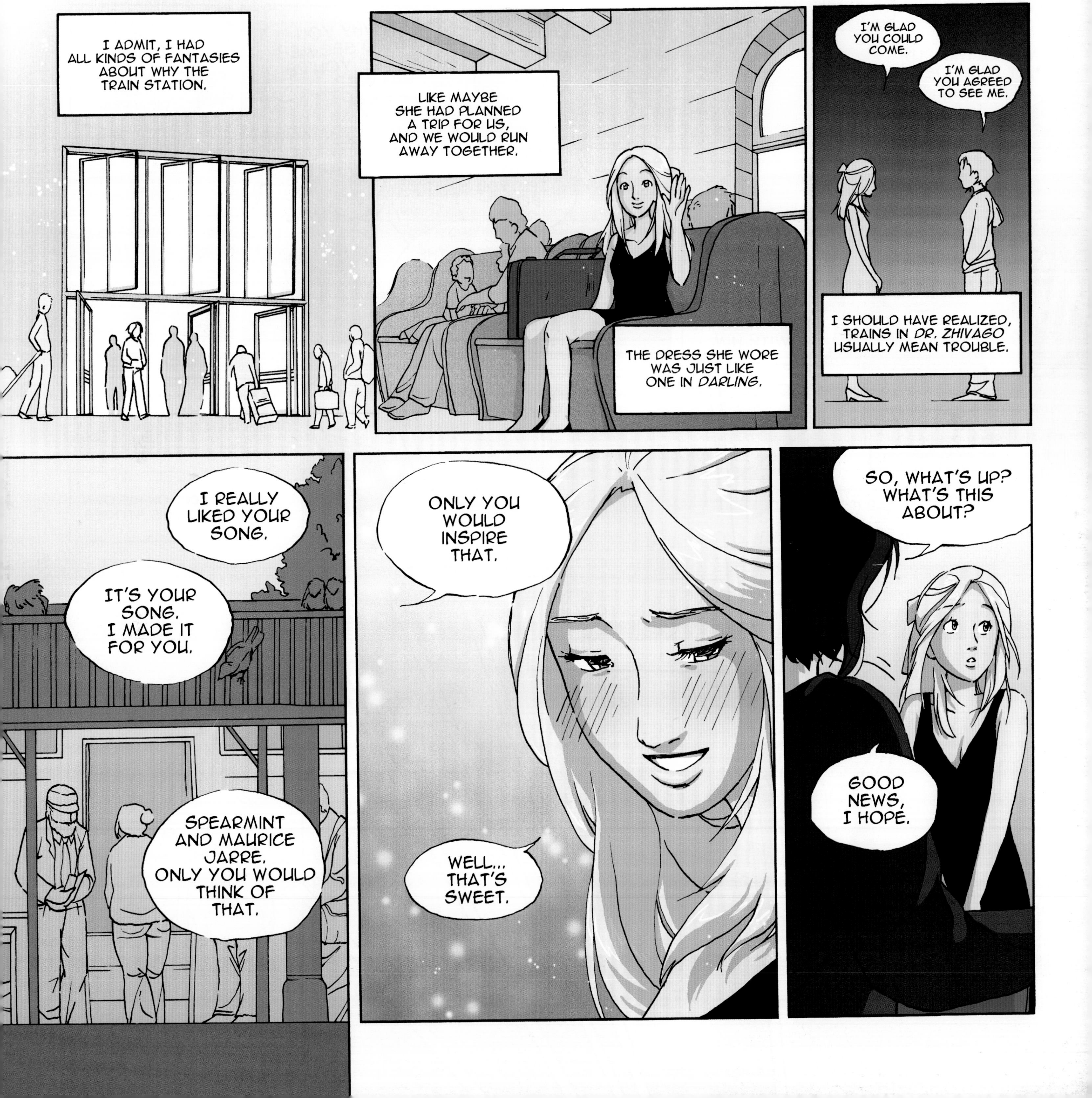
I ADMIT, I HAD ALL KINDS OF FANTASIES ABOUT WHY THE TRAIN STATION.
LIKE MAYBE SHE HAD PLANNED A TRIP FOR US, AND WE WOULD RUN AWAY TOGETHER.
THE DRESS SHE WORE WAS JUST LIKE ONE IN *DARLING*.
I'M GLAD YOU COULD COME.
I'M GLAD YOU AGREED TO SEE ME.
I SHOULD HAVE REALIZED, TRAINS IN *DR. ZHIVAGO* USUALLY MEAN TROUBLE.
I REALLY LIKED YOUR SONG.
IT'S YOUR SONG. I MADE IT FOR YOU.
SPEARMINT AND MAURICE JARRE. ONLY YOU WOULD THINK OF THAT.
ONLY YOU WOULD INSPIRE THAT.
WELL... THAT'S SWEET.
SO, WHAT'S UP? WHAT'S THIS ABOUT?
GOOD NEWS, I HOPE.

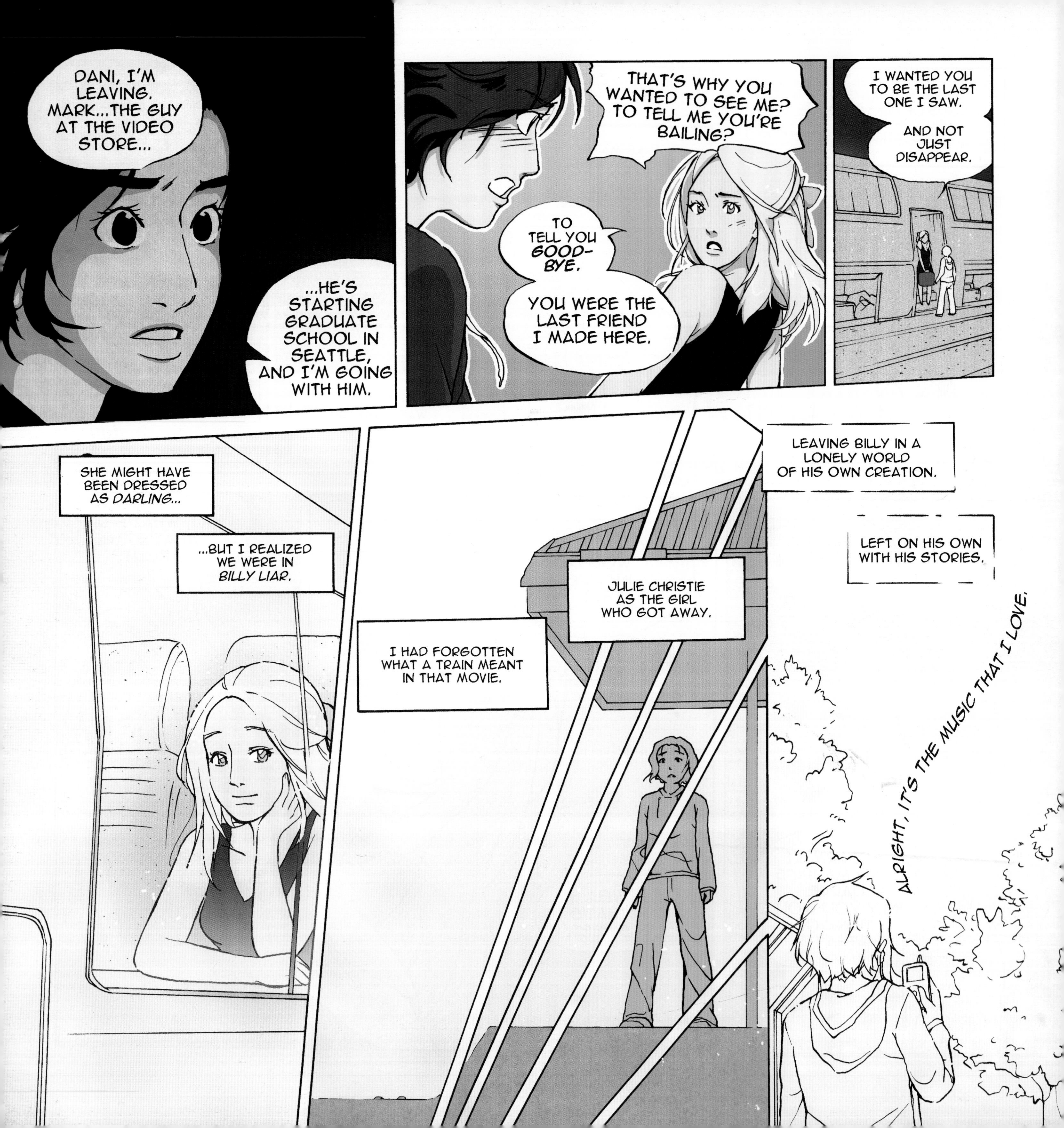
DANI, I'M LEAVING. MARK...THE GUY AT THE VIDEO STORE...
...HE'S STARTING GRADUATE SCHOOL IN SEATTLE, AND I'M GOING WITH HIM.
THAT'S WHY YOU WANTED TO SEE ME? TO TELL ME YOU'RE BAILING?
TO TELL YOU *GOOD-BYE.*
YOU WERE THE LAST FRIEND I MADE HERE.
I WANTED YOU TO BE THE LAST ONE I SAW.
AND NOT JUST DISAPPEAR.
SHE MIGHT HAVE BEEN DRESSED AS *DARLING*...
...BUT I REALIZED WE WERE IN *BILLY LIAR.*
I HAD FORGOTTEN WHAT A TRAIN MEANT IN THAT MOVIE.
JULIE CHRISTIE AS THE GIRL WHO GOT AWAY.
LEAVING BILLY IN A LONELY WORLD OF HIS OWN CREATION.
LEFT ON HIS OWN WITH HIS STORIES.
ALRIGHT, IT'S THE MUSIC THAT I LOVE.

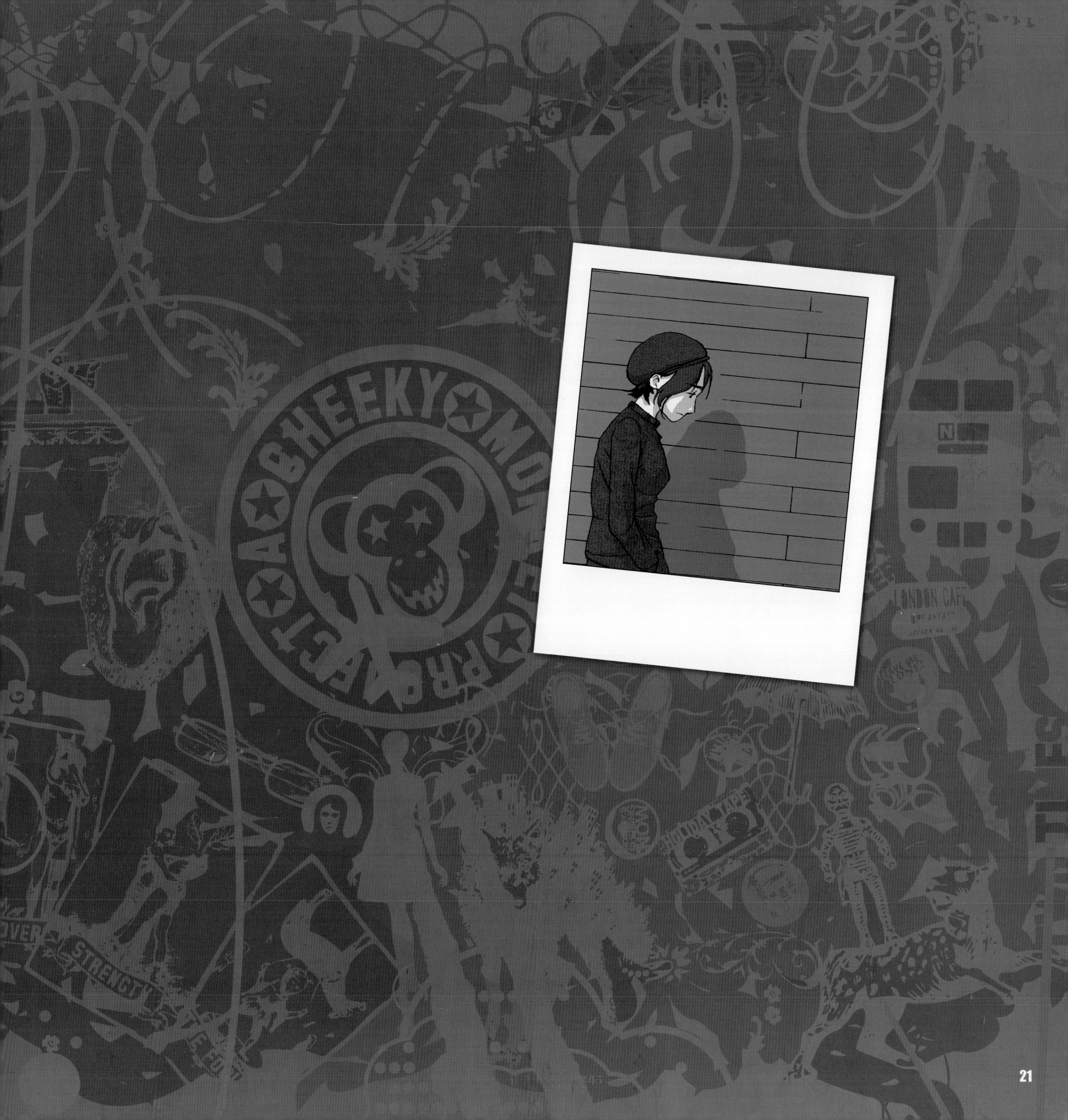
A CHEEKY MO
LONDON CAFE
BREAKFAST
HOLIDAY TAPE
STRENGT
OVER

I INVENTED SOMEONE

featured on **A Leopard and Other Stories**

by **Salgood Sam**

i watched "the red shoes"
i went to the opera
two galleries a week
i gave up smoking
i started learning italian
i stopped seeing my friends
i changed my politics
went to poetry readings
stopped eating certain foods
i cut my hair short
i had it darkened
i watched your favourite soap
i watched the films you love
but they all seem so slow
i don't know

i learned of your religion
the five books of moses
and moshe dayan
i considered converting
ah ah
the circumcision
it put me off a bit
no milk with meat
no meat with milk
in your dietry laws
i invented someone
i invented someone
i invented someone

you always said that
men always pushed you
they always pushed you for sex
so i pretended

ah ah
that was purely surface
it didn't matter to me
i'm lying on the floor
doing sit-ups in the morning light
i invented someone
i invented someone
the ideal man
i shaped myself
into someone you really want
until you warmed to me
i invented someone
and once i'd won you totally
i gradually changed back to me
'cos you see
i invented someone
i invented someone

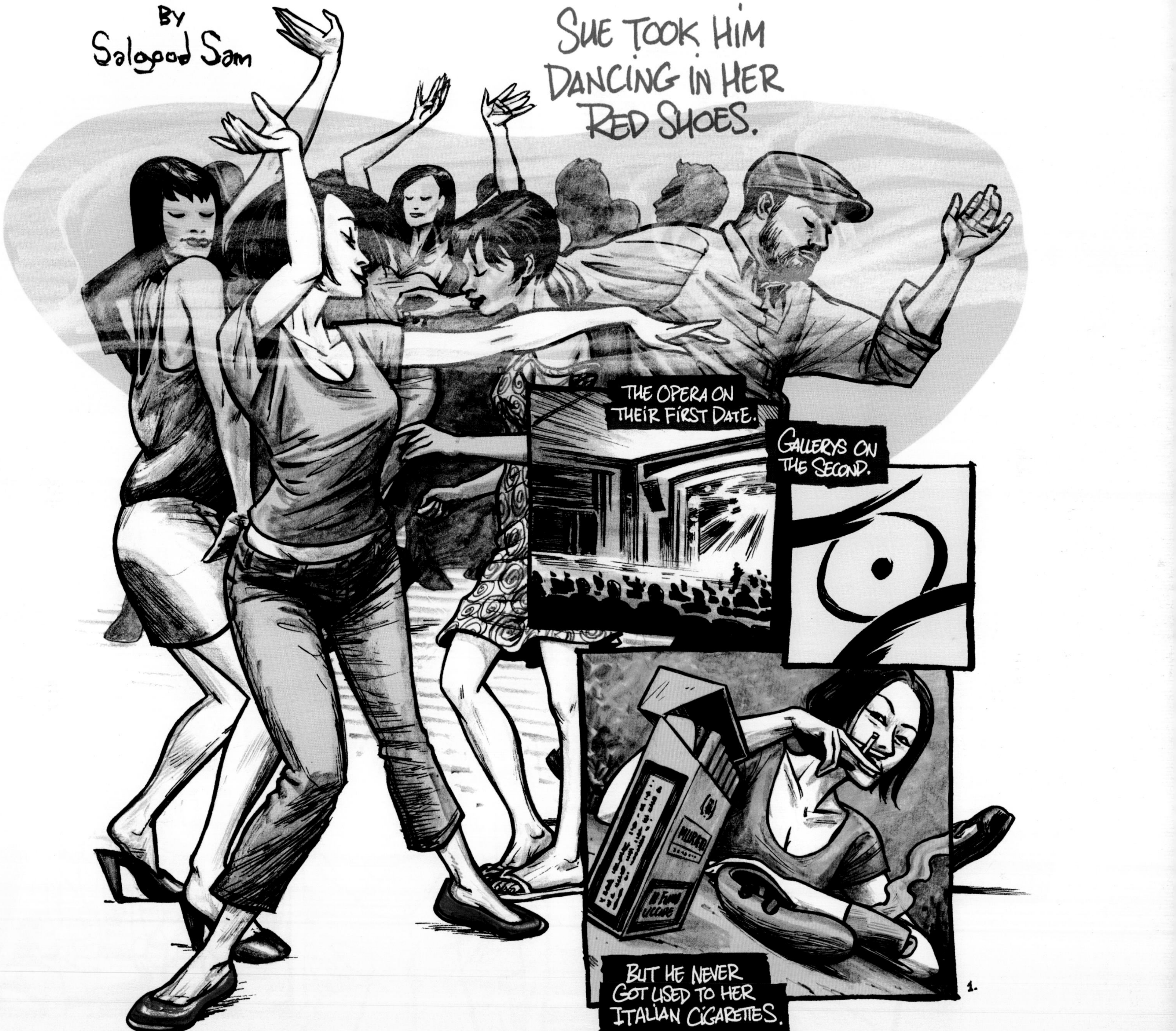
By
Salgood Sam
SUE TOOK HIM DANCING IN HER RED SHOES.
THE OPERA ON THEIR FIRST DATE.
GALLERYS ON THE SECOND.
BUT HE NEVER GOT USED TO HER ITALIAN CIGARETTES.
1.

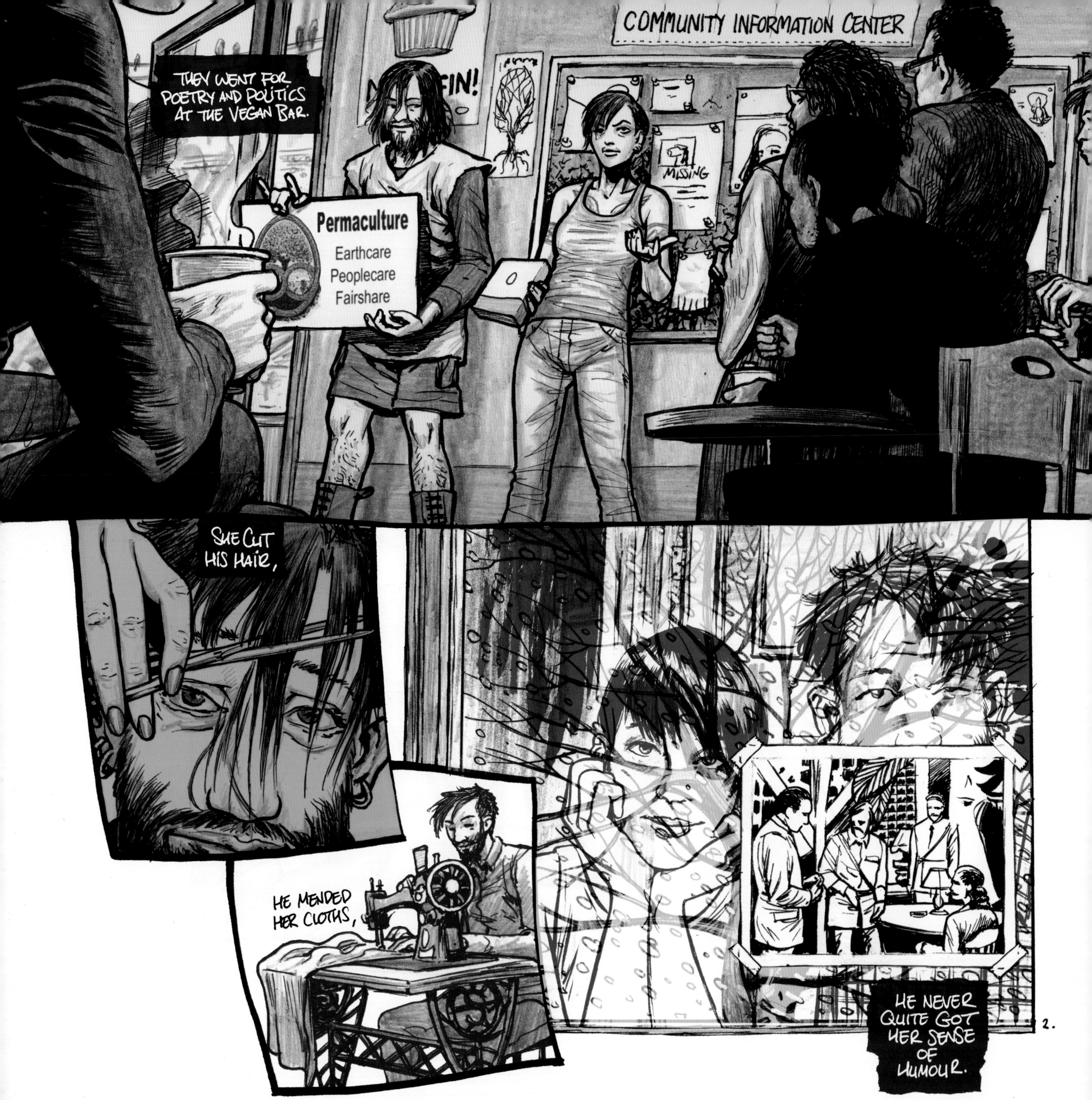
THEY WENT FOR POETRY AND POLITICS AT THE VEGAN BAR.
COMMUNITY INFORMATION CENTER
Permaculture
Earthcare
Peoplecare
Fairshare
MISSING
SHE CUT HIS HAIR,
HE MENDED HER CLOTHS,
HE NEVER QUITE GOT HER SENSE OF HUMOUR.
2.

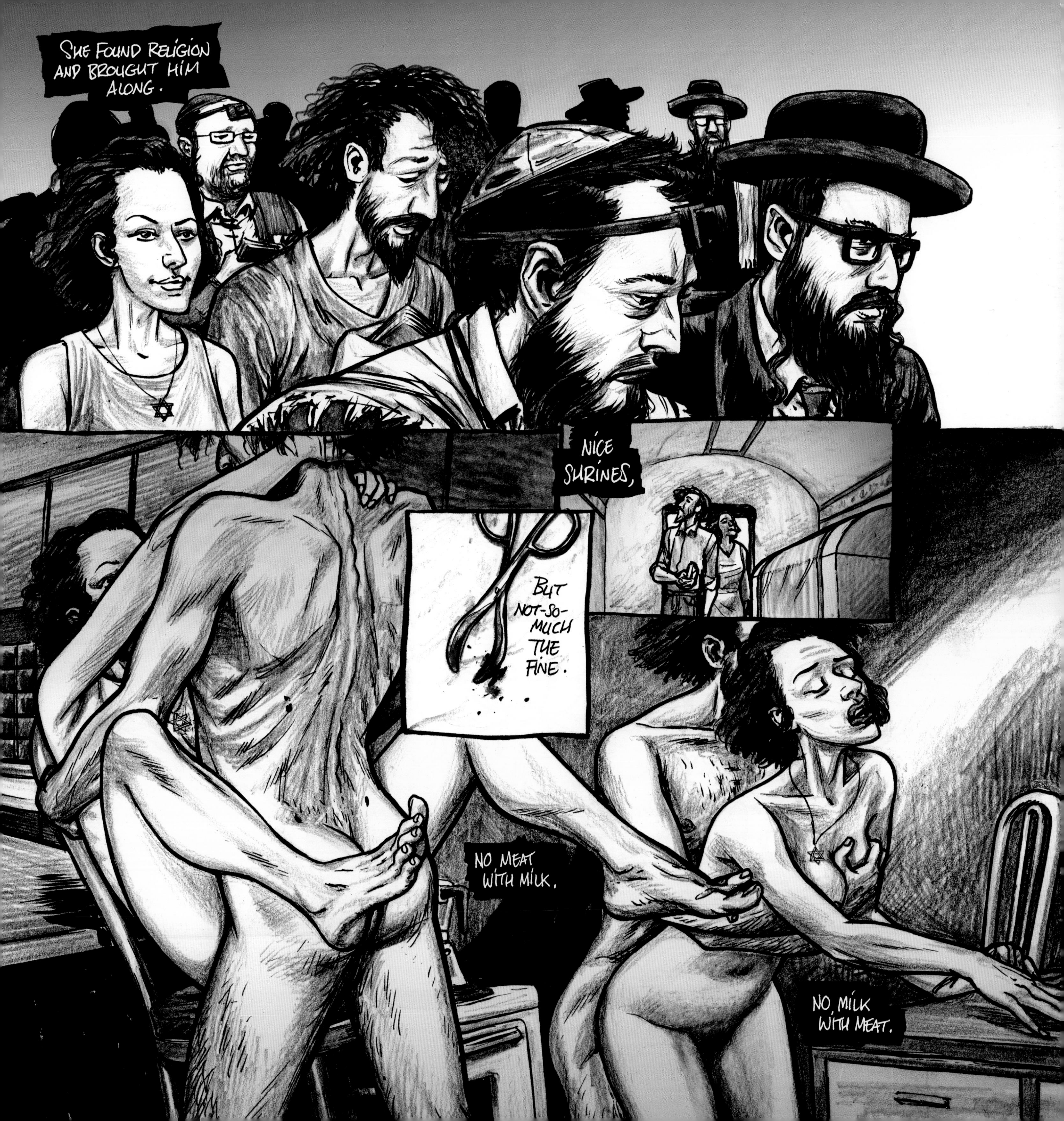
SHE FOUND RELIGION AND BROUGHT HIM ALONG.
NICE SHRINES,
BUT NOT-SO-MUCH THE FINE.
NO MEAT WITH MILK.
NO, MILK WITH MEAT.

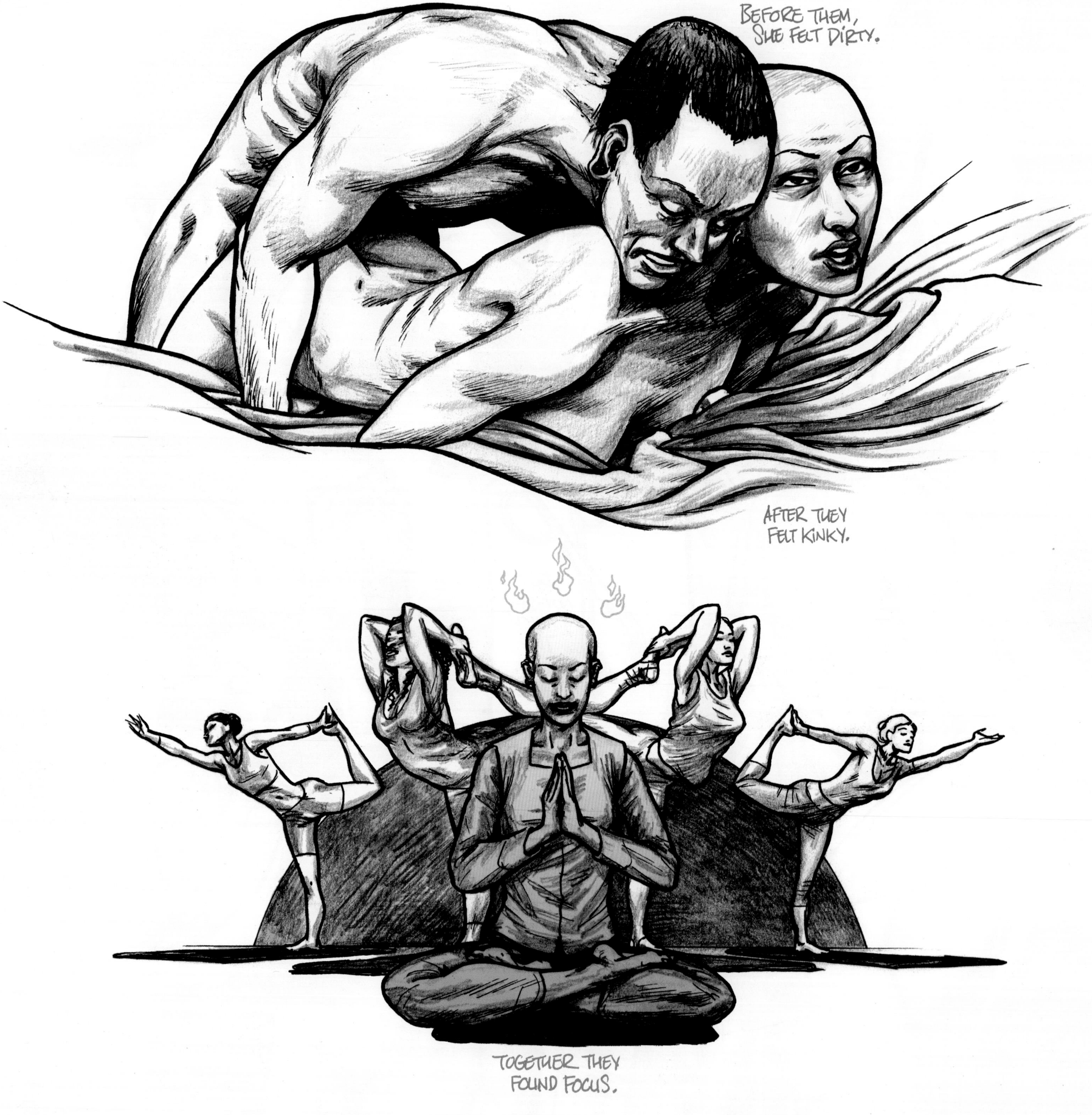
BEFORE THEM, SHE FELT DIRTY.
AFTER THEY FELT KINKY.
TOGETHER THEY FOUND FOCUS.

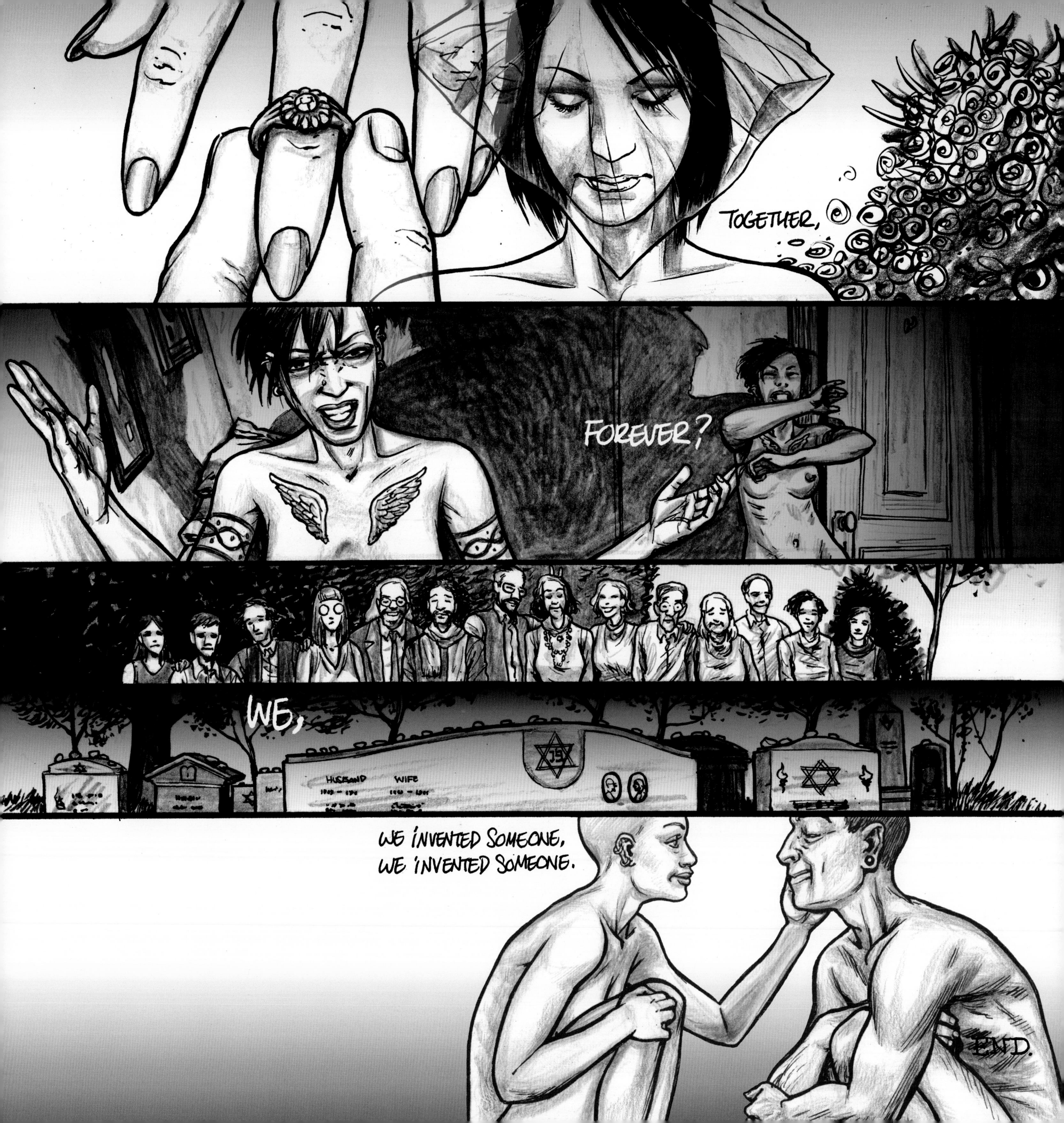
TOGETHER,
FOREVER?
WE,
HUSBAND
WIFE
WE INVENTED SOMEONE,
WE INVENTED SOMEONE.
END.

MY GIRLFRIEND IS A KILLER

featured on **Paris in a Bottle**

story by **Frank Beaton**
art by **Ryan Stark &**
Bill Crabtree
lettering by **Jill Beaton**

late in the night
i wonder if she's ok
my girlfriend is a killer
my girlfriend is a killer

four, lonely weeks
i've been waiting here
with no word from her
brown, were her eyes
when i last saw her
and her hair was black...

acid in the bathroom
five passports in the drawer
my girlfriend is a killer
my girlfriend is a killer
parcels in the freezer
that i just ignore
my girlfriend is a killer
my girlfriend is a killer

but it keeps her calm
it keeps her sane
oh and the money's good
she gets to travel round the world
for payment or revenge
it doesn't matter to her
it makes no difference
so long as the job is clean
the job is good

i don't ask where she's going
i don't ask where she's been
my girlfriend is a killer
my girlfriend is a killer
i'm trusted to say nothing
about all the things i've seen
my girlfriend is a killer
my girlfriend is a killer

this is what i wanted
this is what i got
to be the house husband
for a killing machine
they're saying on the news
a diplomat's been shot
two bullets in this head
and one in his heart
as he slept on his yacht

but late in the night
I'm washing out her clothes
my girlfriend is a killer
my girlfriend is a killer
hmm hmmm...

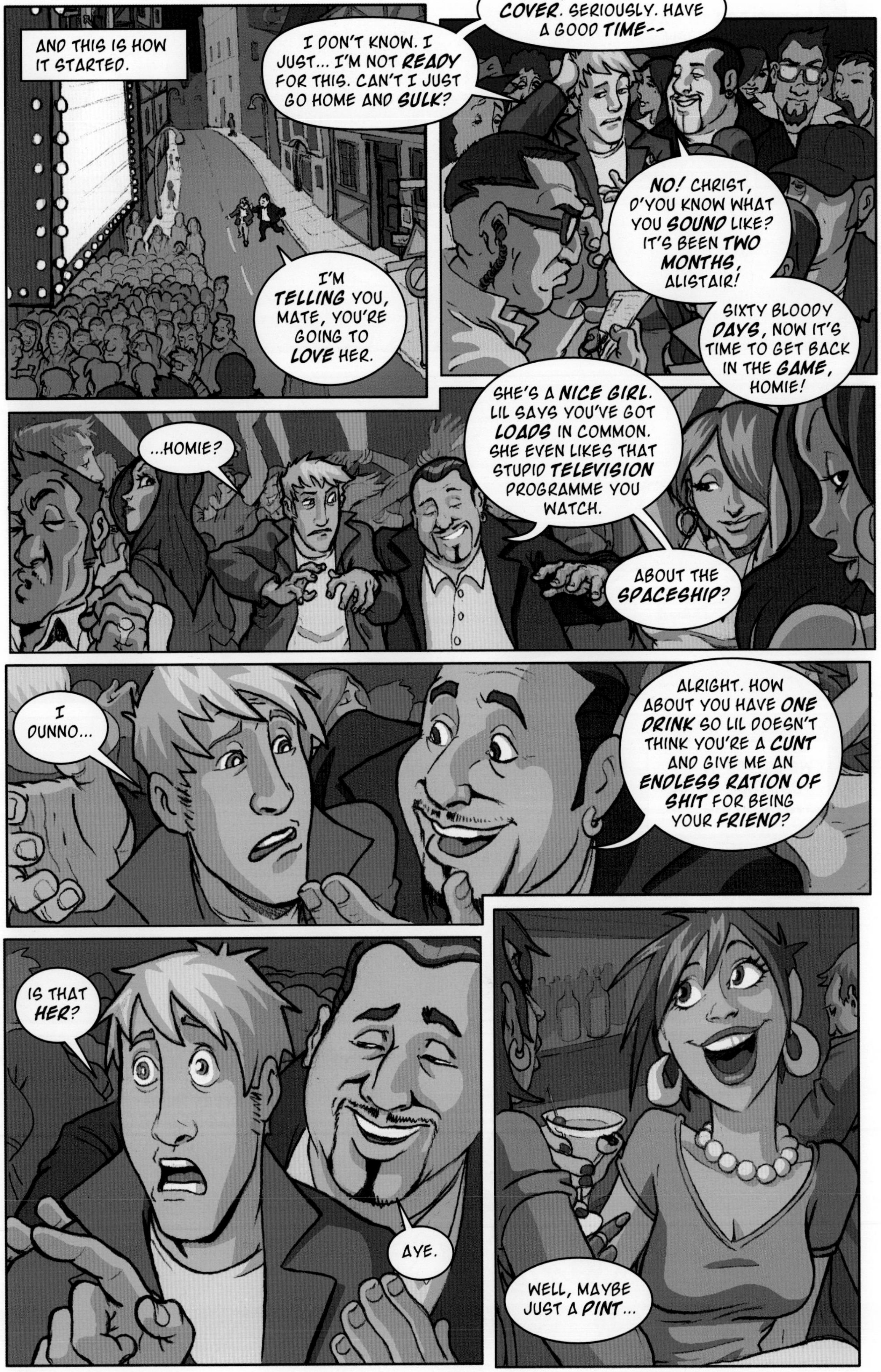
AND THIS IS HOW IT STARTED.
I'M TELLING YOU, MATE, YOU'RE GOING TO LOVE HER.
I DON'T KNOW. I JUST... I'M NOT READY FOR THIS. CAN'T I JUST GO HOME AND SULK?
LOOK, I'LL PAY YOUR COVER. SERIOUSLY. HAVE A GOOD TIME--
NO! CHRIST, D'YOU KNOW WHAT YOU SOUND LIKE? IT'S BEEN TWO MONTHS, ALISTAIR!
SIXTY BLOODY DAYS, NOW IT'S TIME TO GET BACK IN THE GAME, HOMIE!
...HOMIE?
SHE'S A NICE GIRL. LIL SAYS YOU'VE GOT LOADS IN COMMON. SHE EVEN LIKES THAT STUPID TELEVISION PROGRAMME YOU WATCH.
ABOUT THE SPACESHIP?
I DUNNO...
ALRIGHT. HOW ABOUT YOU HAVE ONE DRINK SO LIL DOESN'T THINK YOU'RE A CUNT AND GIVE ME AN ENDLESS RATION OF SHIT FOR BEING YOUR FRIEND?
IS THAT HER?
AYE.
WELL, MAYBE JUST A PINT...

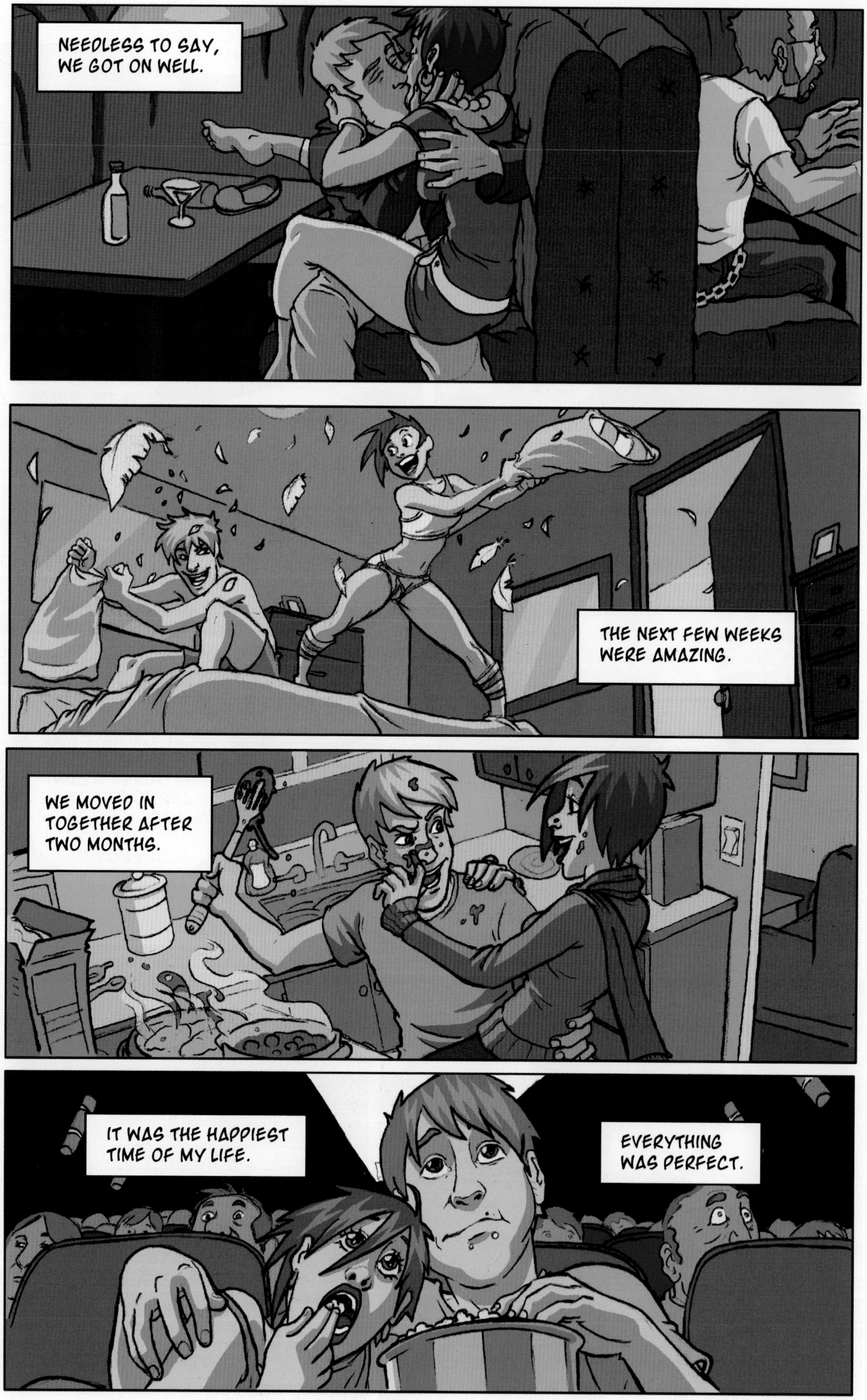
NEEDLESS TO SAY, WE GOT ON WELL.
THE NEXT FEW WEEKS WERE AMAZING.
WE MOVED IN TOGETHER AFTER TWO MONTHS.
IT WAS THE HAPPIEST TIME OF MY LIFE.
EVERYTHING WAS PERFECT.

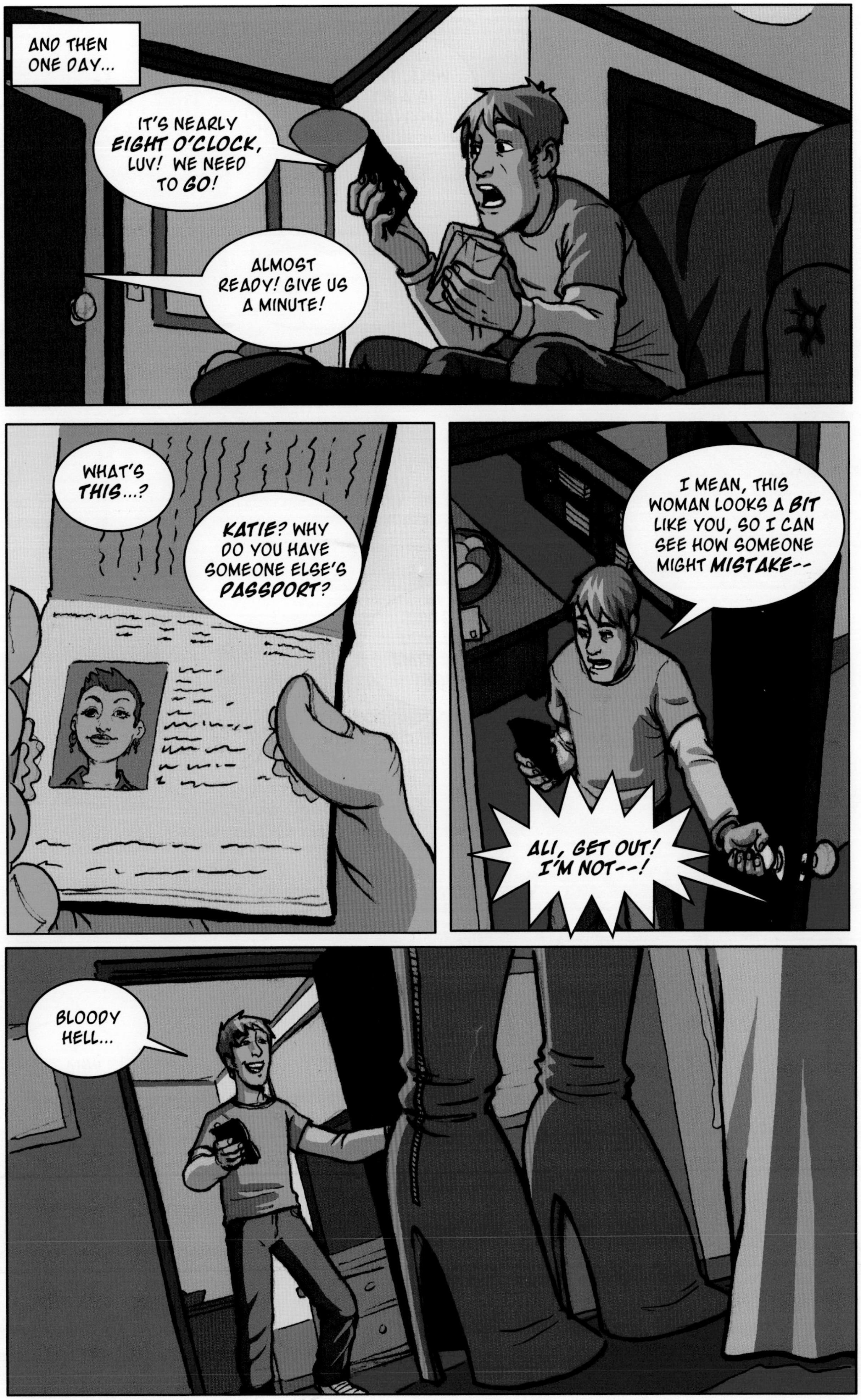
AND THEN ONE DAY...
IT'S NEARLY EIGHT O'CLOCK, LUV! WE NEED TO GO!
ALMOST READY! GIVE US A MINUTE!
WHAT'S THIS...?
KATIE? WHY DO YOU HAVE SOMEONE ELSE'S PASSPORT?
I MEAN, THIS WOMAN LOOKS A BIT LIKE YOU, SO I CAN SEE HOW SOMEONE MIGHT MISTAKE--
ALI, GET OUT! I'M NOT--!
BLOODY HELL...

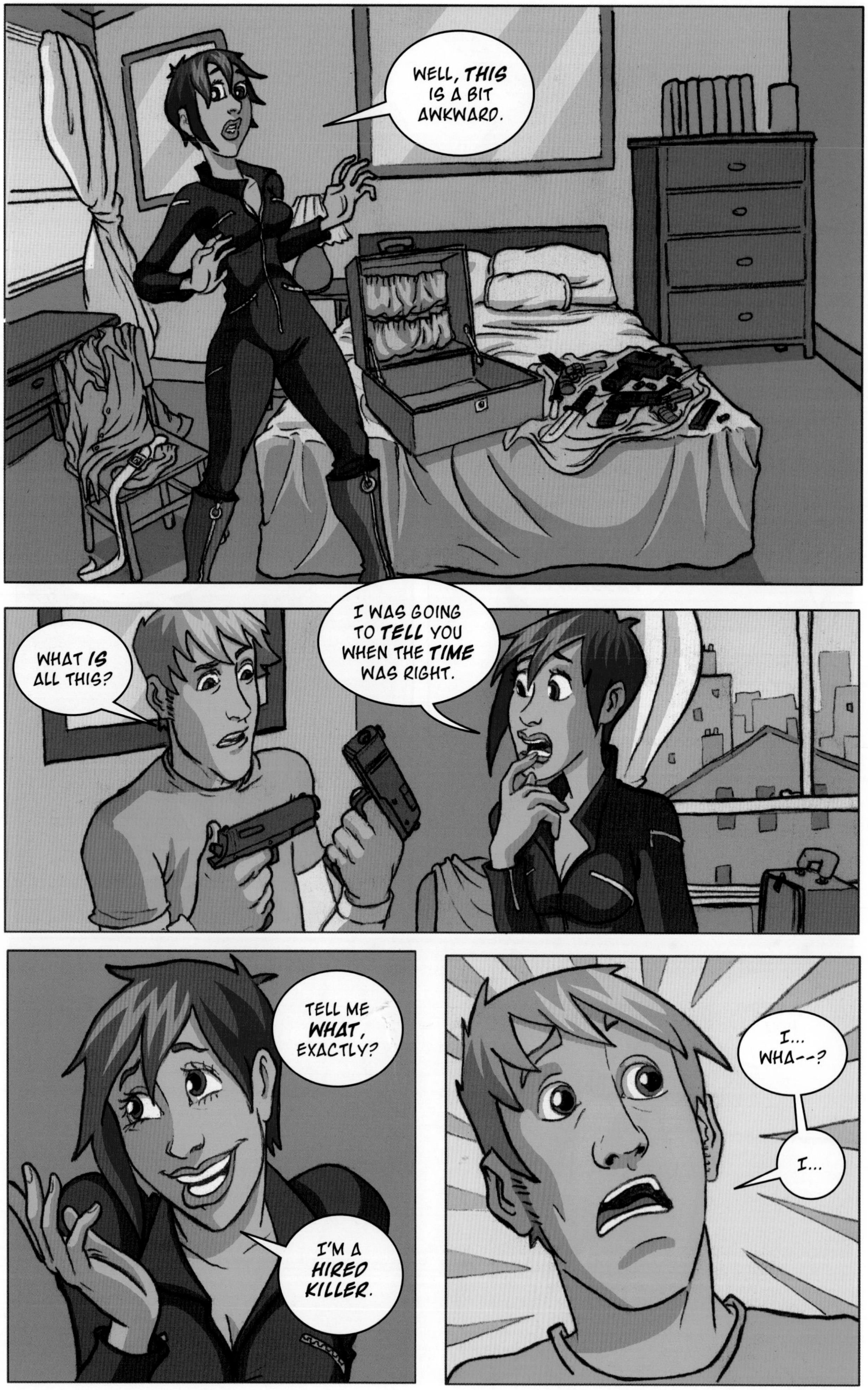
WELL, THIS IS A BIT AWKWARD.
WHAT IS ALL THIS?
I WAS GOING TO TELL YOU WHEN THE TIME WAS RIGHT.
TELL ME WHAT, EXACTLY?
I'M A HIRED KILLER.
I... WHA--?
I...

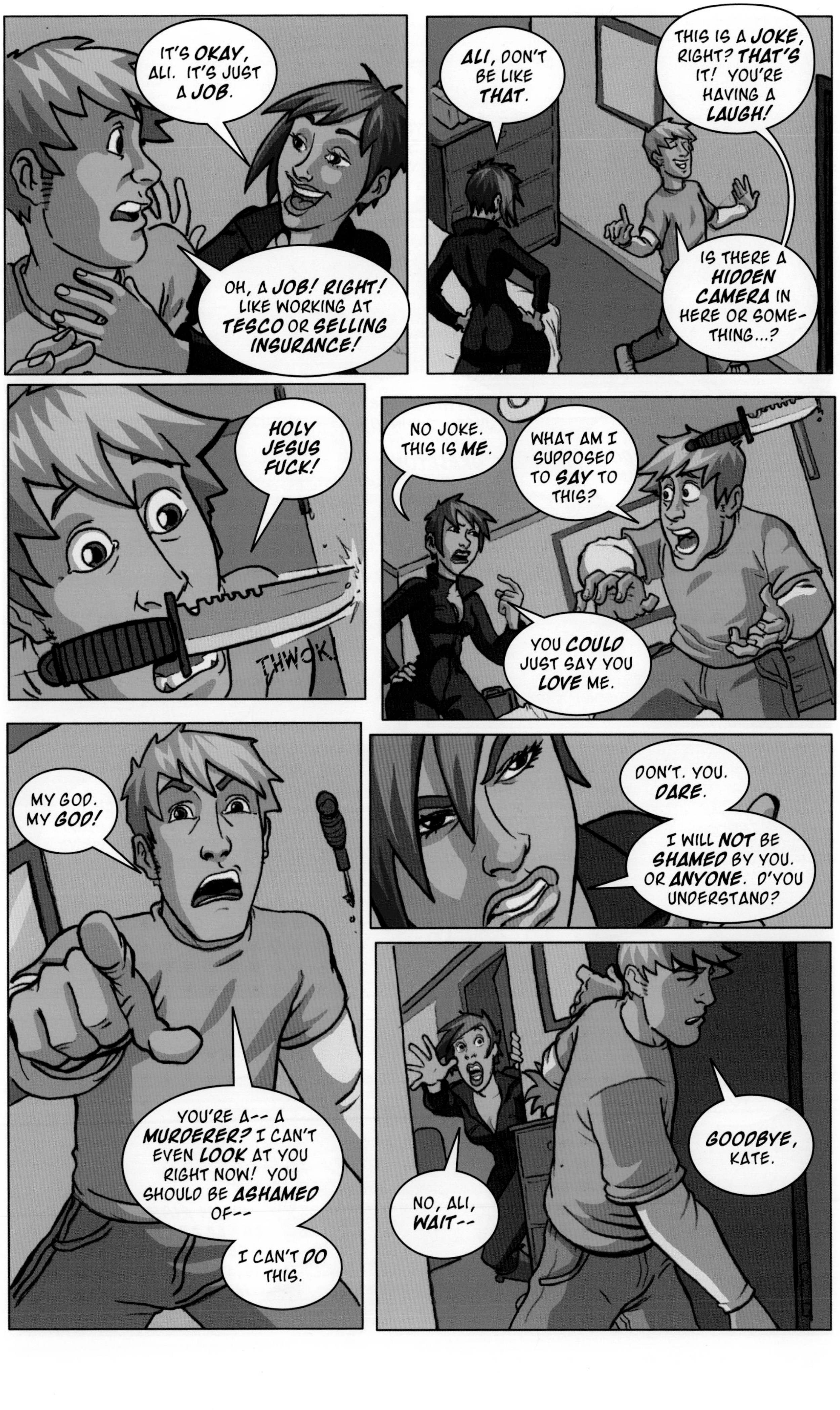
IT'S OKAY, ALI. IT'S JUST A JOB.
OH, A JOB! RIGHT! LIKE WORKING AT TESCO OR SELLING INSURANCE!
ALI, DON'T BE LIKE THAT.
THIS IS A JOKE, RIGHT? THAT'S IT! YOU'RE HAVING A LAUGH!
IS THERE A HIDDEN CAMERA IN HERE OR SOME-THING...?
HOLY JESUS FUCK!
THWOK!
NO JOKE. THIS IS ME.
WHAT AM I SUPPOSED TO SAY TO THIS?
YOU COULD JUST SAY YOU LOVE ME.
MY GOD. MY GOD!
YOU'RE A-- A MURDERER? I CAN'T EVEN LOOK AT YOU RIGHT NOW! YOU SHOULD BE ASHAMED OF--
I CAN'T DO THIS.
DON'T. YOU. DARE.
I WILL NOT BE SHAMED BY YOU. OR ANYONE. D'YOU UNDERSTAND?
GOODBYE, KATE.
NO, ALI, WAIT--

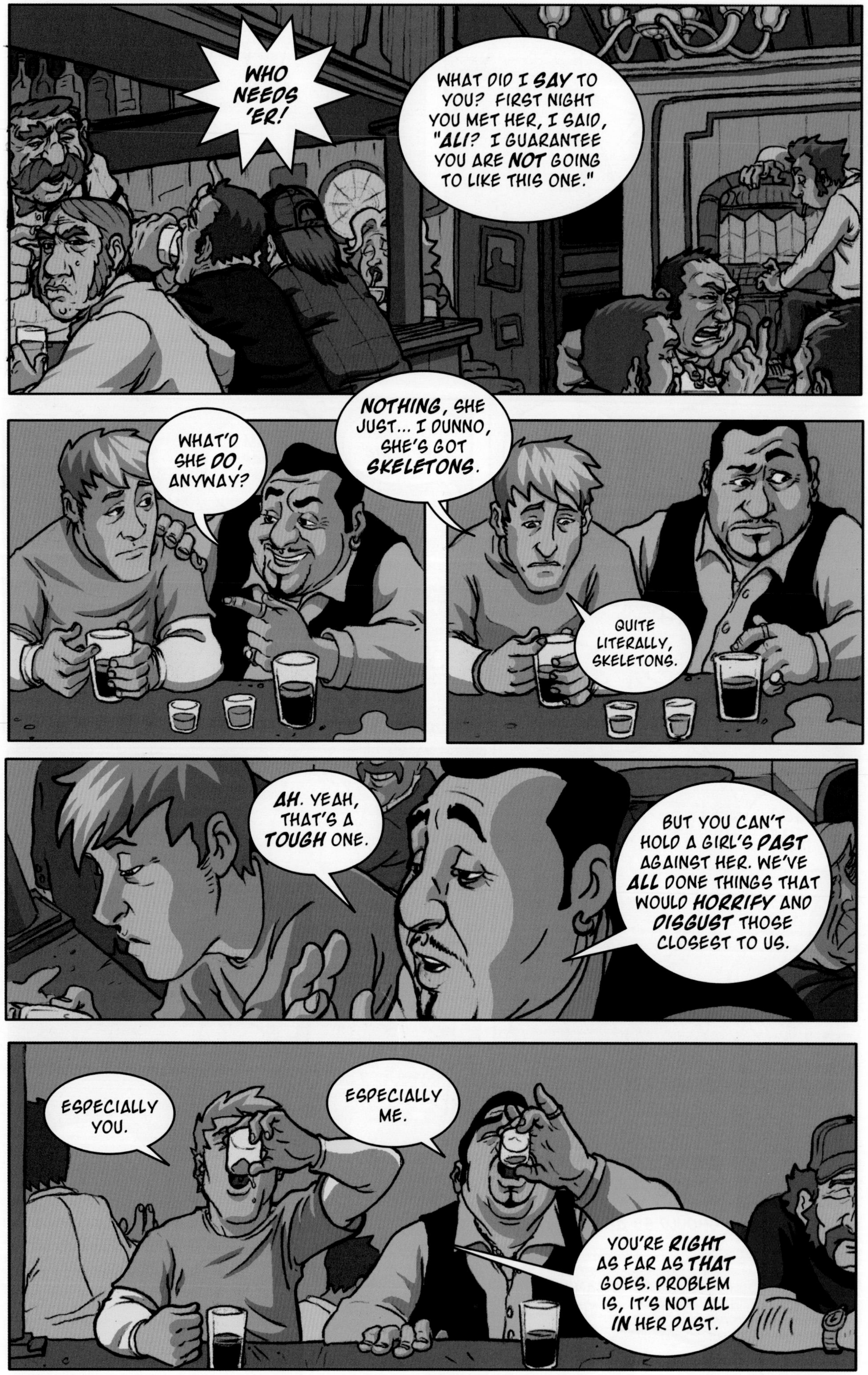

WHO NEEDS 'ER!
WHAT DID I SAY TO YOU? FIRST NIGHT YOU MET HER, I SAID, "ALI? I GUARANTEE YOU ARE NOT GOING TO LIKE THIS ONE."
WHAT'D SHE DO, ANYWAY?
NOTHING, SHE JUST... I DUNNO, SHE'S GOT SKELETONS.
QUITE LITERALLY, SKELETONS.
AH. YEAH, THAT'S A TOUGH ONE.
BUT YOU CAN'T HOLD A GIRL'S PAST AGAINST HER. WE'VE ALL DONE THINGS THAT WOULD HORRIFY AND DISGUST THOSE CLOSEST TO US.
ESPECIALLY YOU.
ESPECIALLY ME.
YOU'RE RIGHT AS FAR AS THAT GOES. PROBLEM IS, IT'S NOT ALL IN HER PAST.

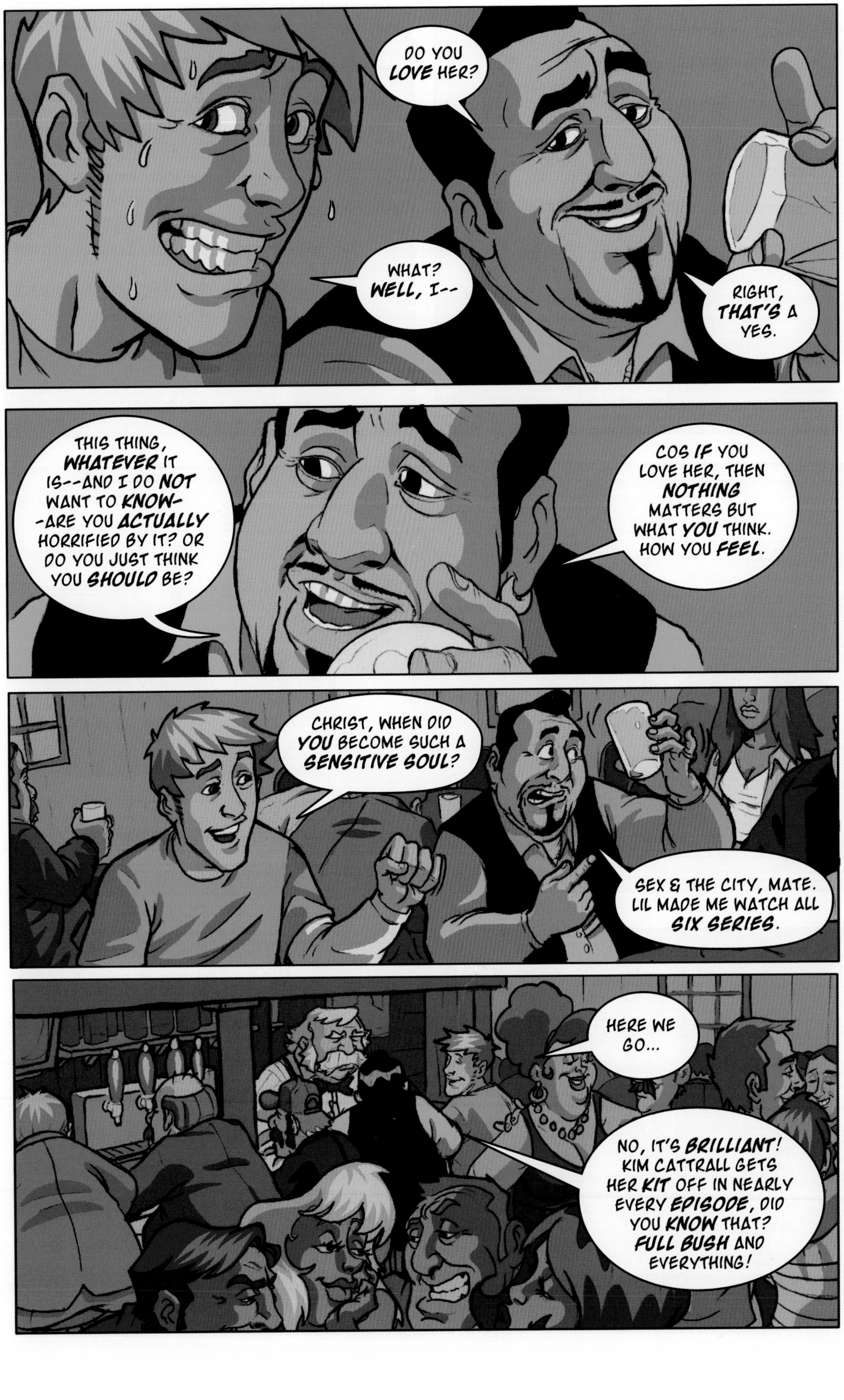
DO YOU LOVE HER?
WHAT? WELL, I--
RIGHT, THAT'S A YES.
THIS THING, WHATEVER IT IS--AND I DO NOT WANT TO KNOW--ARE YOU ACTUALLY HORRIFIED BY IT? OR DO YOU JUST THINK YOU SHOULD BE?
COS IF YOU LOVE HER, THEN NOTHING MATTERS BUT WHAT YOU THINK. HOW YOU FEEL.
CHRIST, WHEN DID YOU BECOME SUCH A SENSITIVE SOUL?
SEX & THE CITY, MATE. LIL MADE ME WATCH ALL SIX SERIES.
HERE WE GO...
NO, IT'S BRILLIANT! KIM CATTRALL GETS HER KIT OFF IN NEARLY EVERY EPISODE, DID YOU KNOW THAT? FULL BUSH AND EVERYTHING!

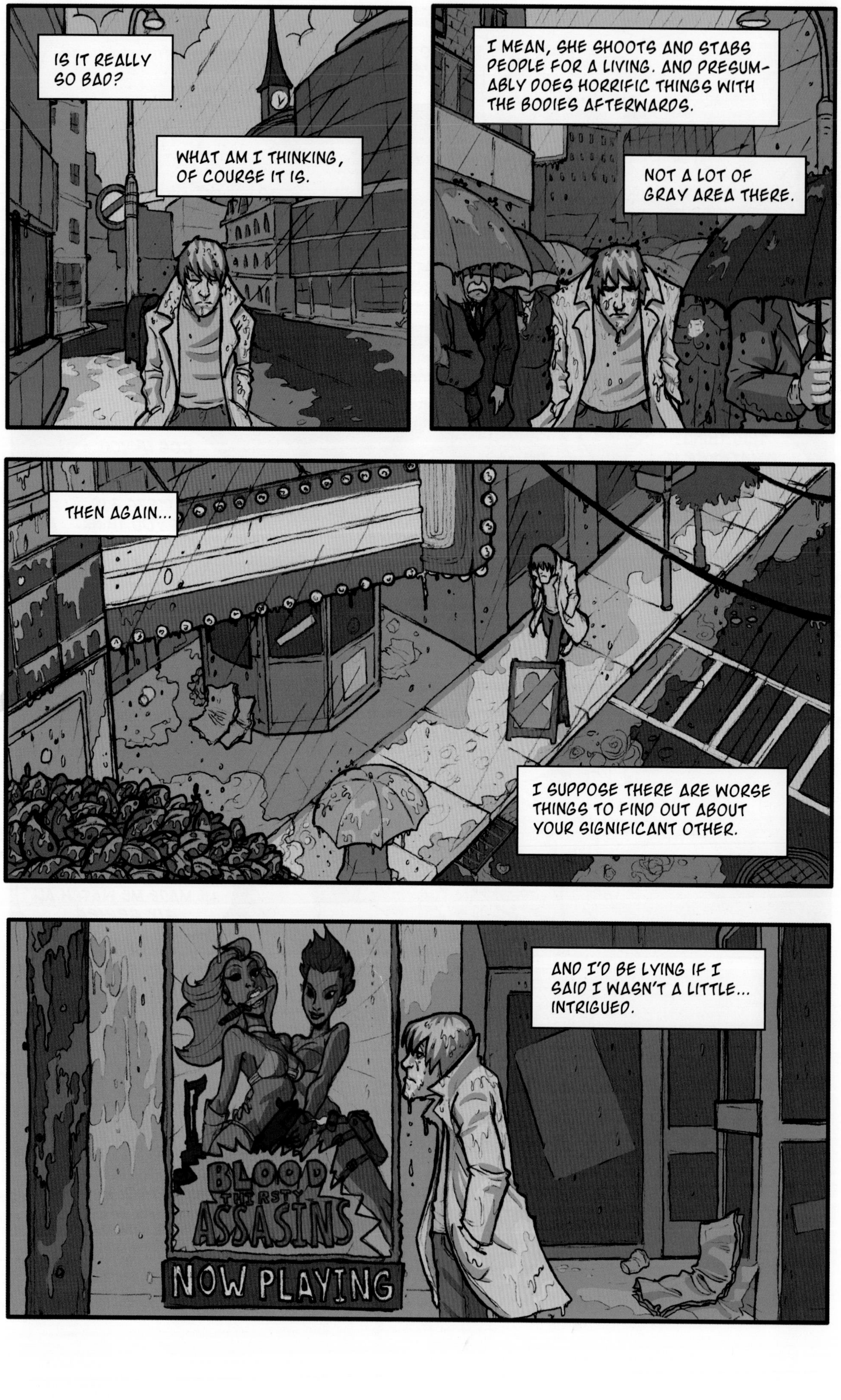
IS IT REALLY SO BAD?
WHAT AM I THINKING, OF COURSE IT IS.
I MEAN, SHE SHOOTS AND STABS PEOPLE FOR A LIVING. AND PRESUMABLY DOES HORRIFIC THINGS WITH THE BODIES AFTERWARDS.
NOT A LOT OF GRAY AREA THERE.
THEN AGAIN...
I SUPPOSE THERE ARE WORSE THINGS TO FIND OUT ABOUT YOUR SIGNIFICANT OTHER.
BLOOD THIRSTY ASSASINS
NOW PLAYING
AND I'D BE LYING IF I SAID I WASN'T A LITTLE... INTRIGUED.

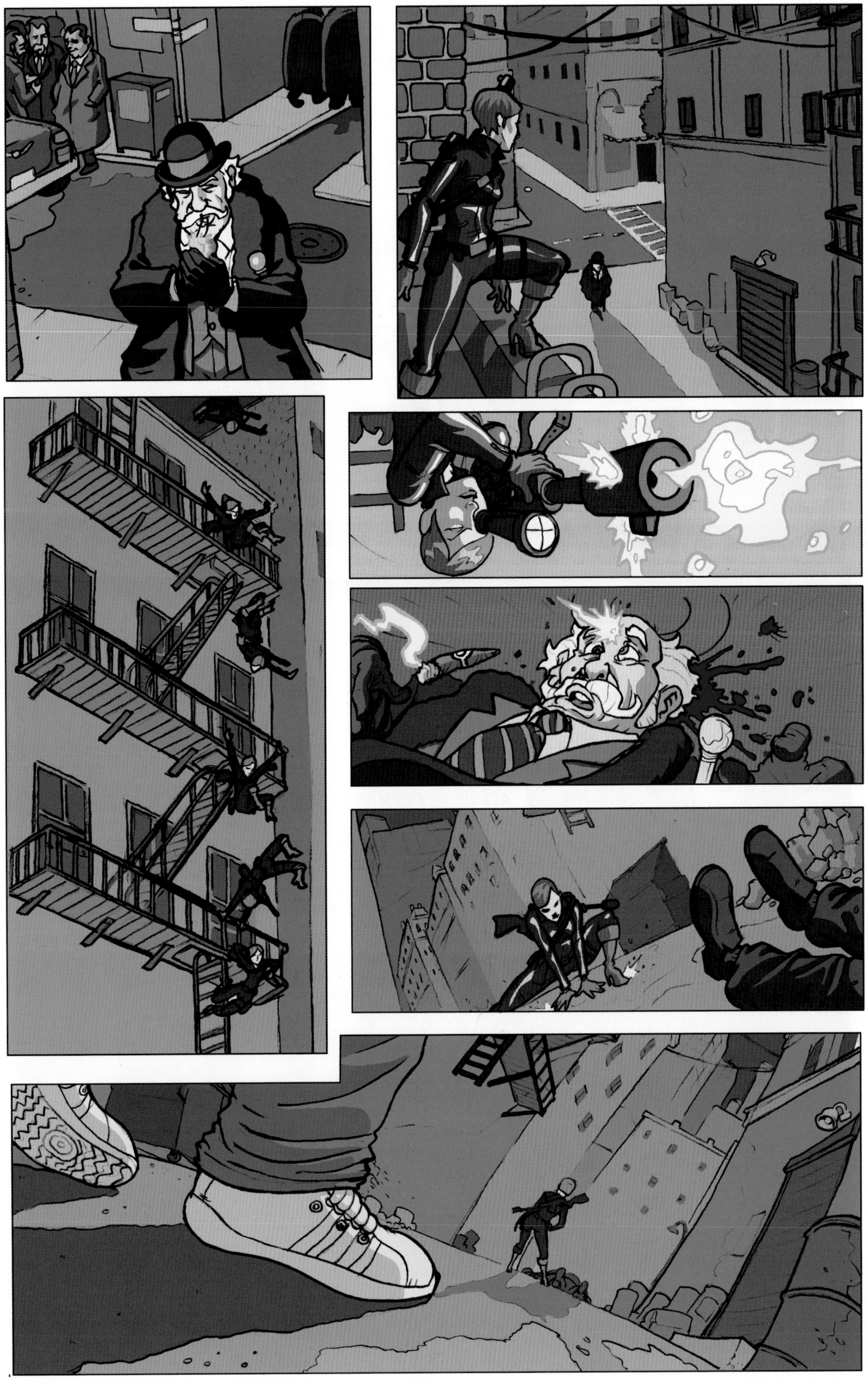

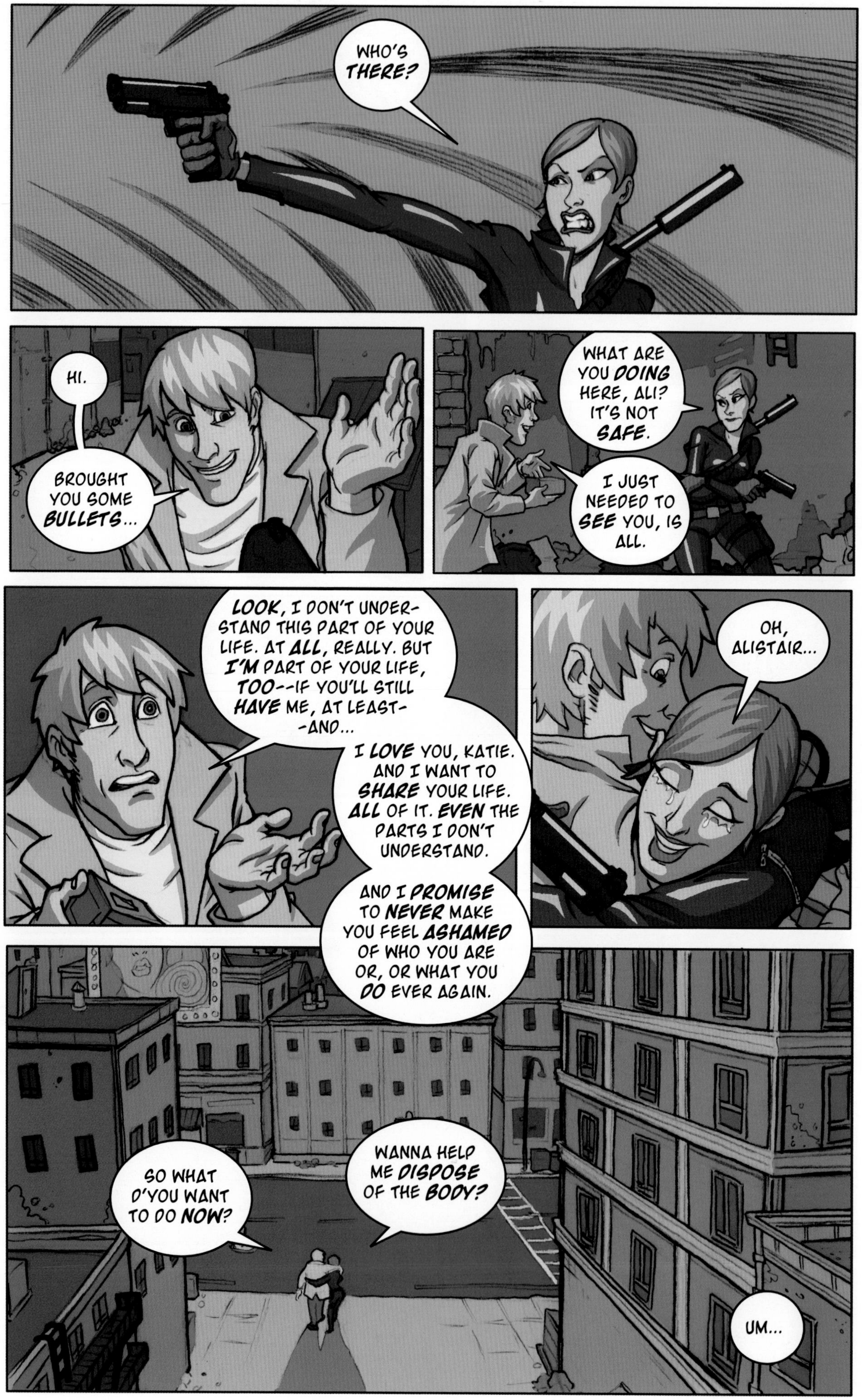
WHO'S THERE?
HI.
BROUGHT YOU SOME BULLETS...
WHAT ARE YOU DOING HERE, ALI? IT'S NOT SAFE.
I JUST NEEDED TO SEE YOU, IS ALL.
LOOK, I DON'T UNDER-STAND THIS PART OF YOUR LIFE. AT ALL, REALLY. BUT I'M PART OF YOUR LIFE, TOO--IF YOU'LL STILL HAVE ME, AT LEAST- -AND...
I LOVE YOU, KATIE. AND I WANT TO SHARE YOUR LIFE. ALL OF IT. EVEN THE PARTS I DON'T UNDERSTAND.
AND I PROMISE TO NEVER MAKE YOU FEEL ASHAMED OF WHO YOU ARE OR, OR WHAT YOU DO EVER AGAIN.
OH, ALISTAIR...
SO WHAT D'YOU WANT TO DO NOW?
WANNA HELP ME DISPOSE OF THE BODY?
UM...

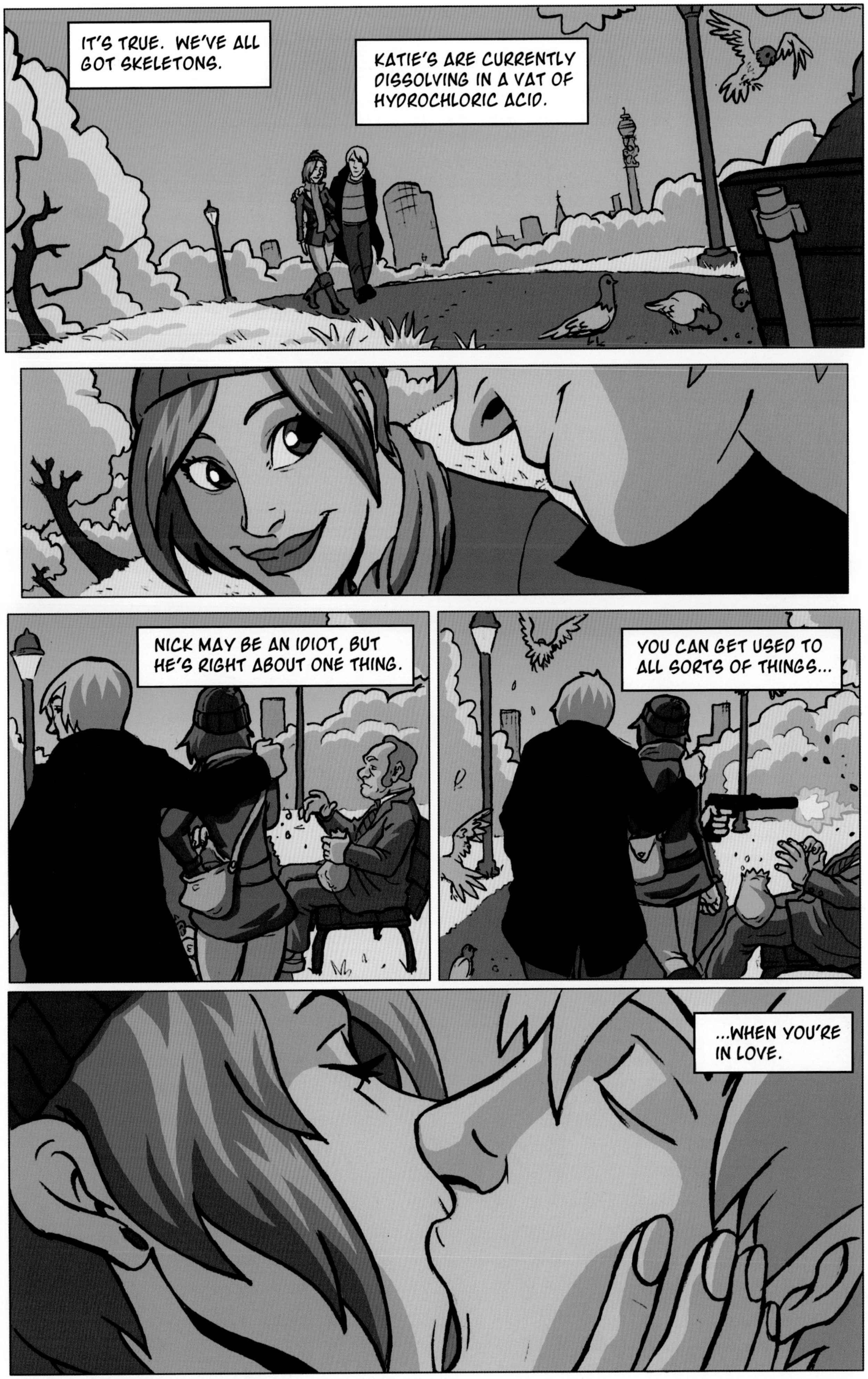
IT'S TRUE. WE'VE ALL GOT SKELETONS.
KATIE'S ARE CURRENTLY DISSOLVING IN A VAT OF HYDROCHLORIC ACID.
NICK MAY BE AN IDIOT, BUT HE'S RIGHT ABOUT ONE THING.
YOU CAN GET USED TO ALL SORTS OF THINGS...
...WHEN YOU'RE IN LOVE.

"My Girlfriend is a Killer"
Story: Frank Beaton ~ Art: Ryan Stark ~ Colors: Bill Crabtree ~ Letters: Jill Beaton

A DIFFERENT LIFETIME

featured on **A Different Lifetime**

story by **B. Clay Moore**
art by **Kevin Mellon**
colors by **Kevin Mellon & Eric White**
letters by **Crank!**

this may be over for now
but it's not over for ever
i have to believe that
one day we will have our time together

i will kiss you again
undress you again
i will sleep with you again
and again
i will be there when you wake
i promise you
i have to believe that

and the time i spent with you
is the most perfect i have known
it already seems like it was stolen
from a different lifetime

i will keep you warm
i will show you stars
i will touch you every way i now
over again
i will drink you in
i will fill you up
i have to believe that

and all these things will be
and one day you will be mine
even if it has to be
even if it has to be
in a different lifetime

trying to live a second life
in your first
when even your friends say
"right person, wrong lifetime"
i will take care of you
i will cook for you
we will do the things that we cannot do
i will marry you
i'll make it easy for you
you won't even have to try
so sad
i have to believe that

and all these things will be
all these things will be
and one day you will be mine
one day you will be mine
even if it has to be
even if it
even if it has to be
in a different lifetime

i have to believe that
even if it has to be
even if it
even if it has to be
in a different lifetime

years go fast, weeks go slow
one day we will be together
years go fast, weeks go slow
one day we will be together

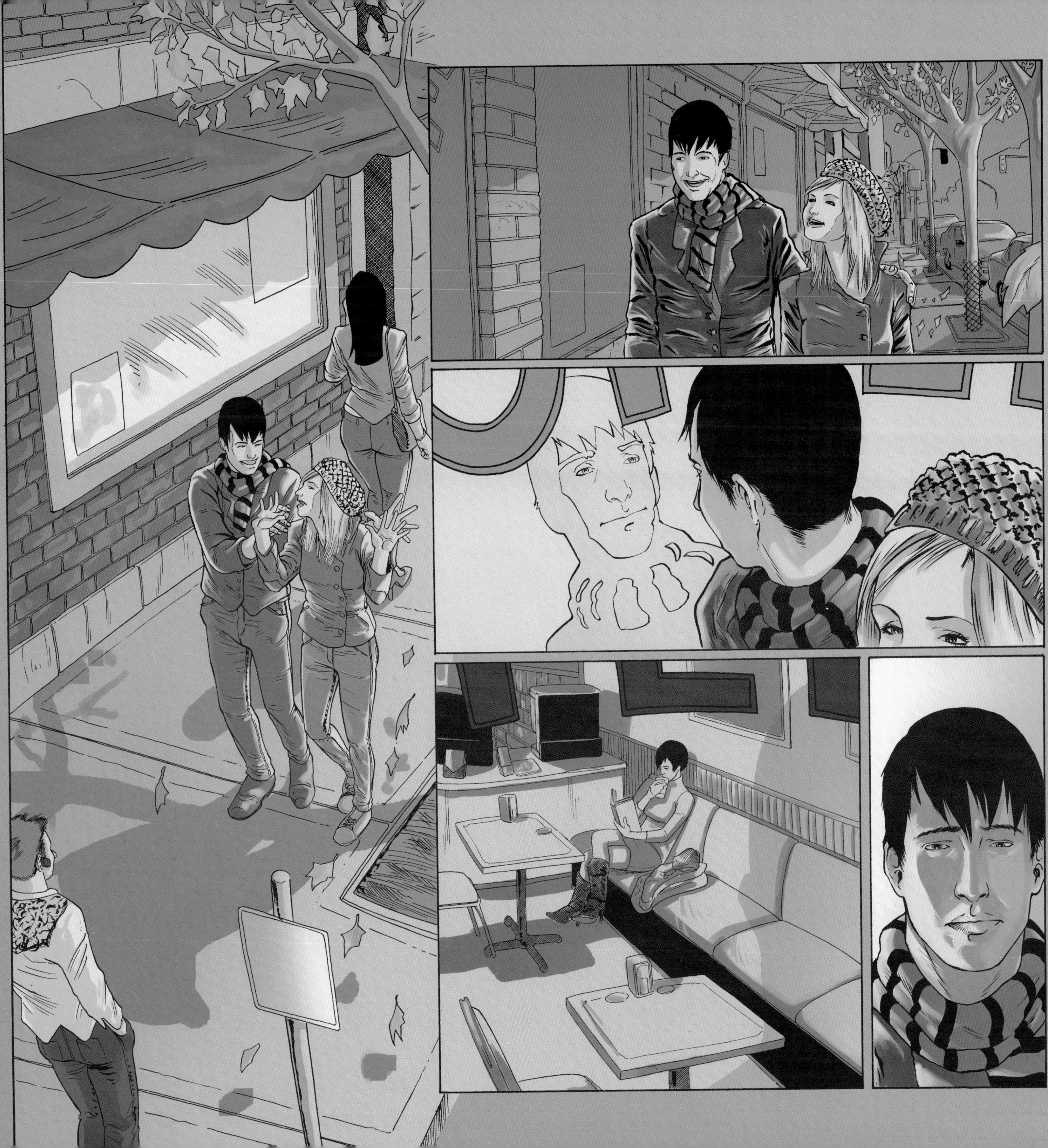

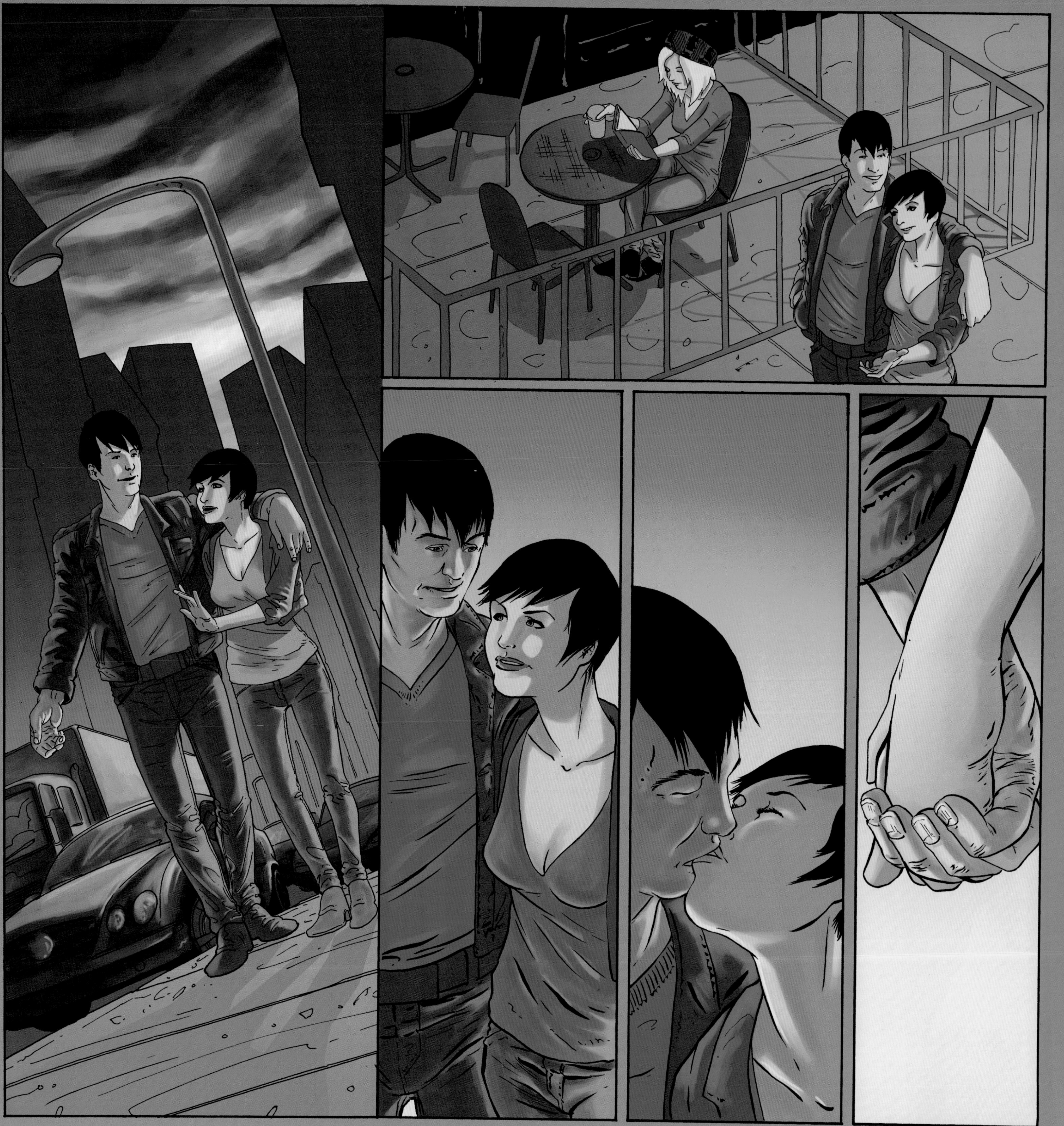

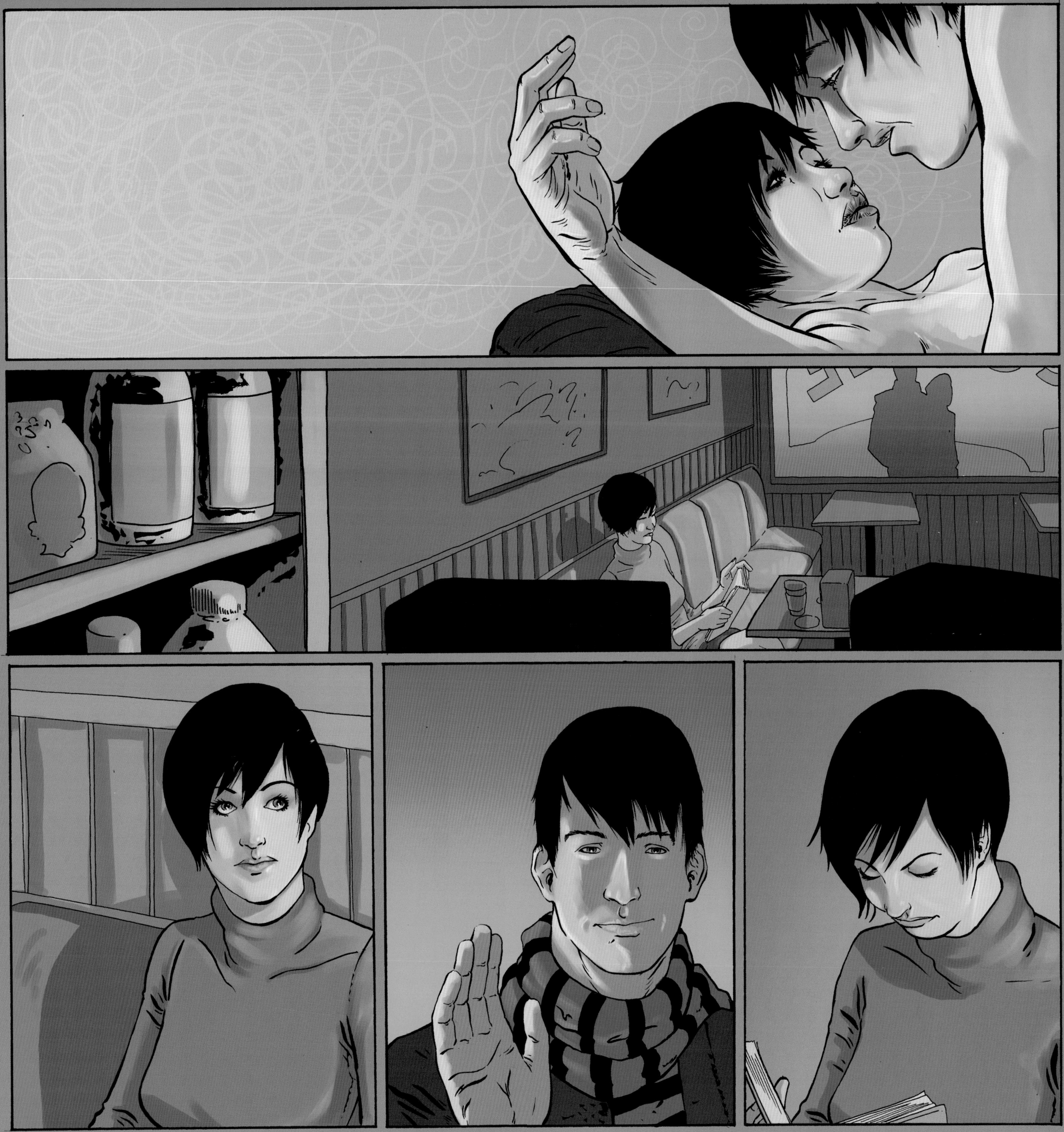

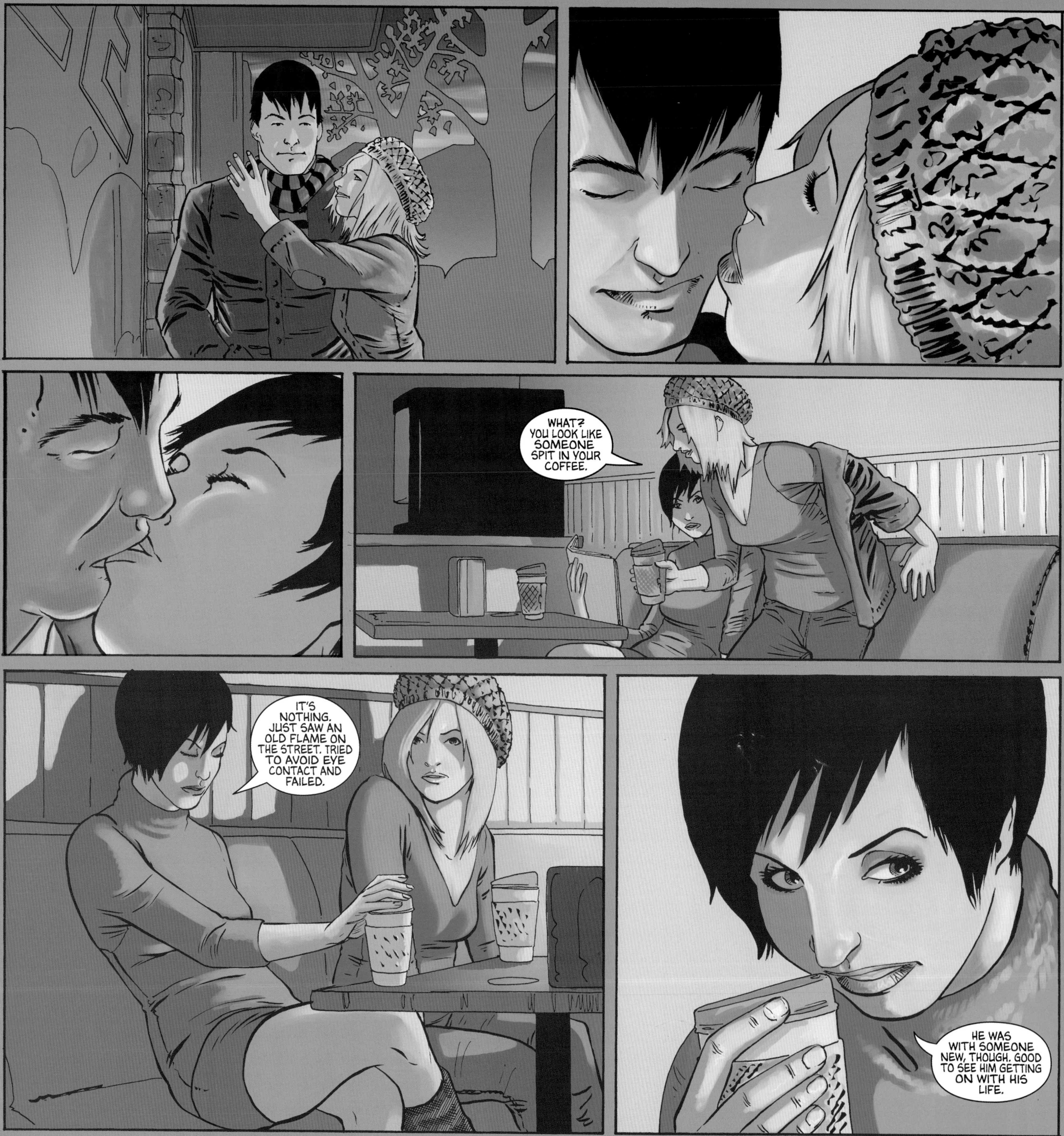
WHAT? YOU LOOK LIKE SOMEONE SPIT IN YOUR COFFEE.
IT'S NOTHING. JUST SAW AN OLD FLAME ON THE STREET. TRIED TO AVOID EYE CONTACT AND FAILED.
HE WAS WITH SOMEONE NEW, THOUGH. GOOD TO SEE HIM GETTING ON WITH HIS LIFE.

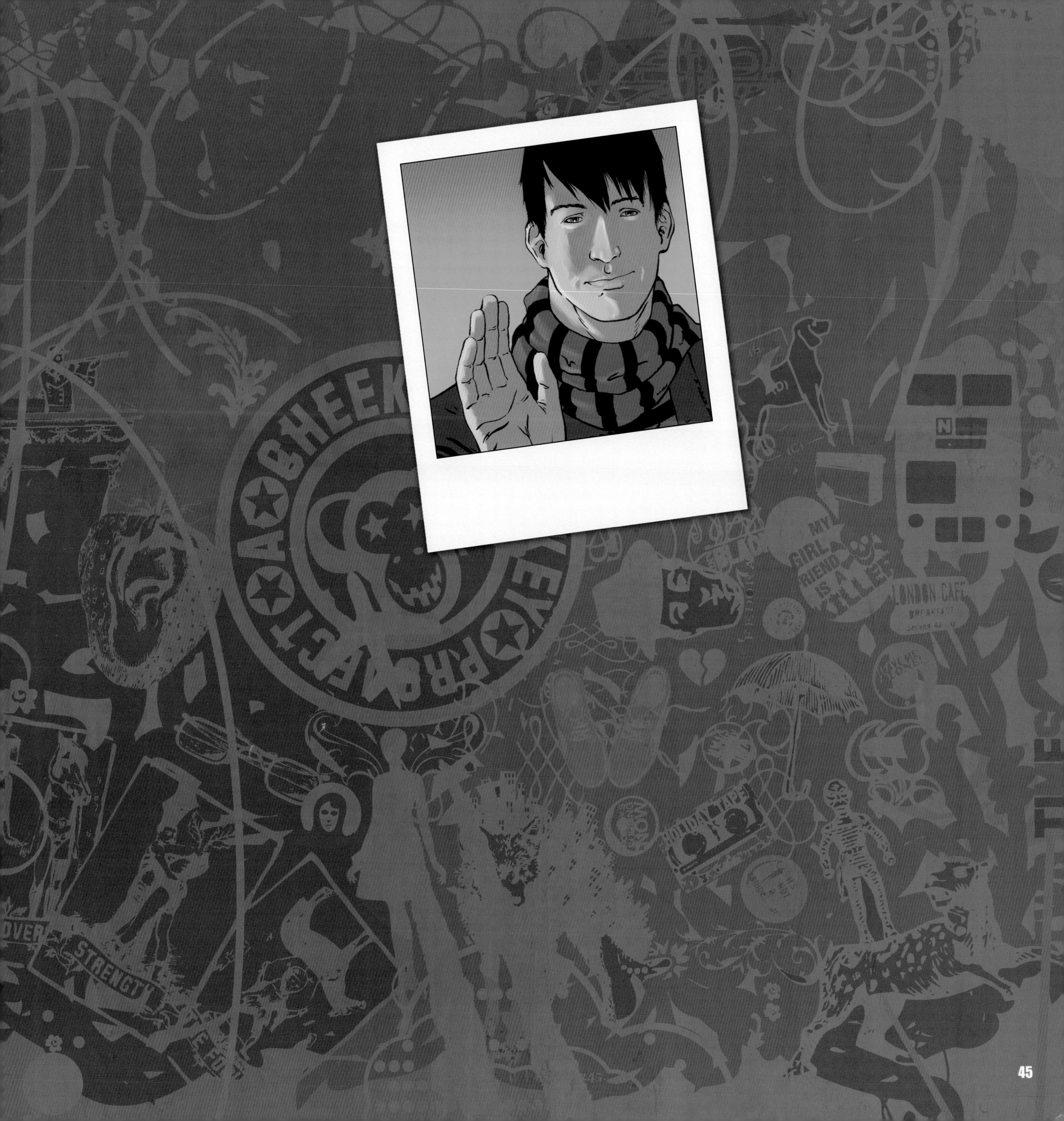
LONDON CAFÉ
BREAKFAST
HOLIDAY TAPE

THIS IS A SOUVENIR

featured on **A Leopard and Other Stories**

by **Mike Holmes**

i remember somebody saying
that one of the things about music
is that it's got the power to make you remember
exactly how you felt at a certain point in your life
and it's true
sometimes when you hear a song coming out of a shop
or on the radio
and it doesn't even have to be something you particularly like
it can make you feel things
even taste things you'd completely forgotten about
like when i hear "the onion song"
i can feel warm bath water around me on a hot summer's day
or "shady lane"
i can see gary going up an escalator
in a shop on oxford street
at about 3 o'clock on a friday afternoon
or "she's a waterfall"
i can feel my jeans sticking to my legs
in the heat in a room above a shop in waterloo station
or "range life"
i can smell a dark rehearsal studio
on a wednesday night in greenwich
or "spit on a stranger"
i can remember lying to a friend
and i still regret that
or "the man whose head expanded"
i can see a flying saucer
above a dundee street at 4.30 on a winter's afternoon
or "out come the freaks"
i can taste the taste of peanut butter on toast for breakfast

when you hear this
you remember

where you were
in the summer
when you hear this
you remember
the night we finally brought
the government down
a comet appeared
and my stars were told
we walked for miles
and miles around this town
to a new art café riot
and your hair was cold
this is a souvenir
of a cinema that's impossible to get into
and you remember where you were

see when i hear "stereo"
i can smell fine white plaster dust covering the living room
or "major league"
i can see sand all over the floor
in a hall of residence
or "the girl from ipanema"
i can hear the sound of shagging in the flat above
or "born a woman"
i can hear the sound of dave
practising his trumpet in a flat below
or "cut your hair"
i can smell the smell of brand new vinyl in my hands
or "passionate friend"
i can remember my first proper kiss
or "jam kids"
or "jam kids"
i remember you

when you hear this
you remember
where you were
in the summer
when you hear this
you remember
where you were
you were with me

if you ever walk through these streets again
you remember me
you'll forever associate this scent
with this place on this day
if anybody mentions this film again
you remember me
you'll forever associate this taste
with the meal we ate here in this place
some things can take me back in time
and when they do
i want to be there

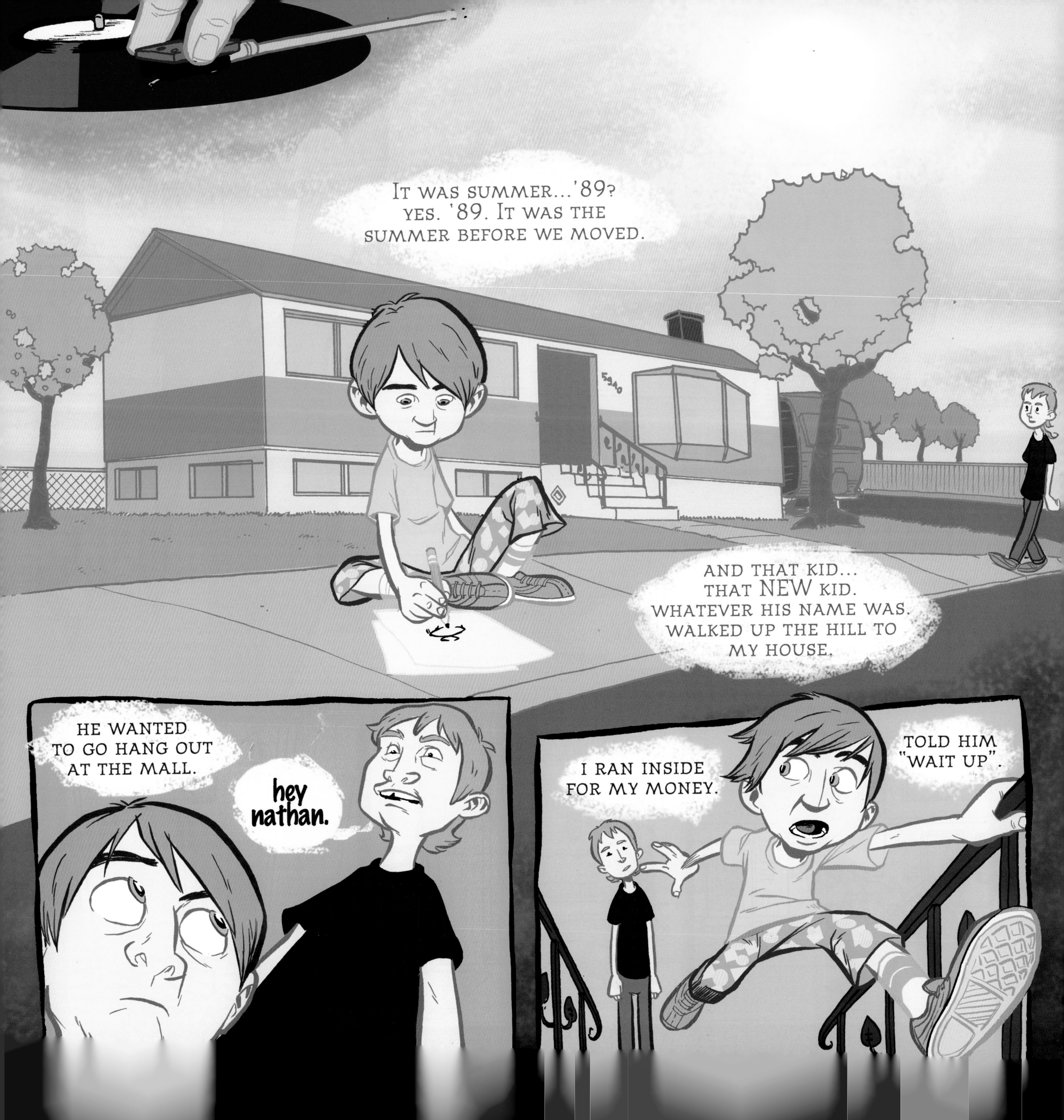
It was summer...'89? yes. '89. It was the summer before we moved.
5940
And that kid... that NEW kid. Whatever his name was. Walked up the hill to my house.
He wanted to go hang out at the mall.
hey nathan.
I ran inside for my money.
Told him "wait up".

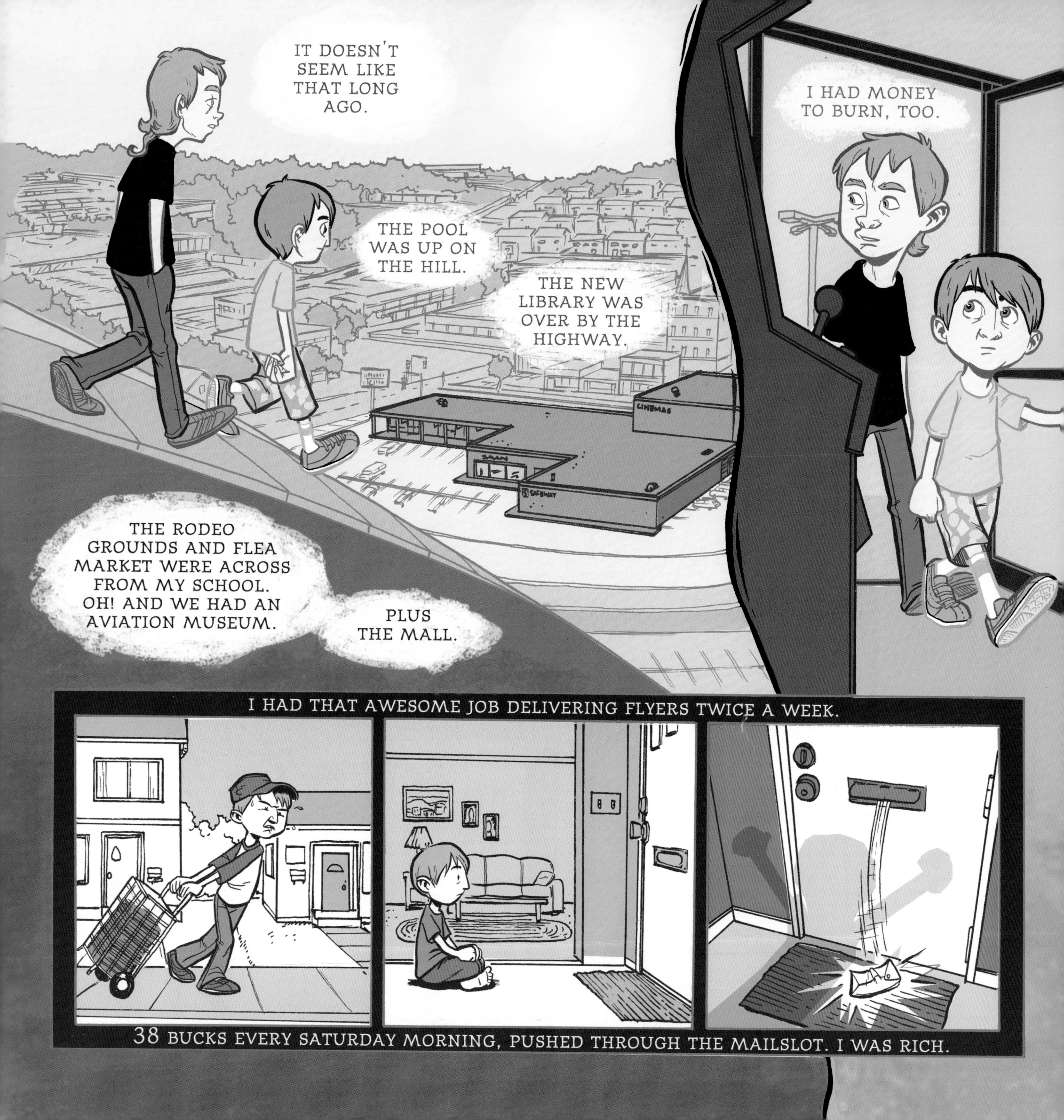

IT DOESN'T SEEM LIKE THAT LONG AGO.
THE POOL WAS UP ON THE HILL.
THE NEW LIBRARY WAS OVER BY THE HIGHWAY.
THE RODEO GROUNDS AND FLEA MARKET WERE ACROSS FROM MY SCHOOL. OH! AND WE HAD AN AVIATION MUSEUM.
PLUS THE MALL.
I HAD MONEY TO BURN, TOO.
I HAD THAT AWESOME JOB DELIVERING FLYERS TWICE A WEEK.
38 BUCKS EVERY SATURDAY MORNING, PUSHED THROUGH THE MAILSLOT. I WAS RICH.

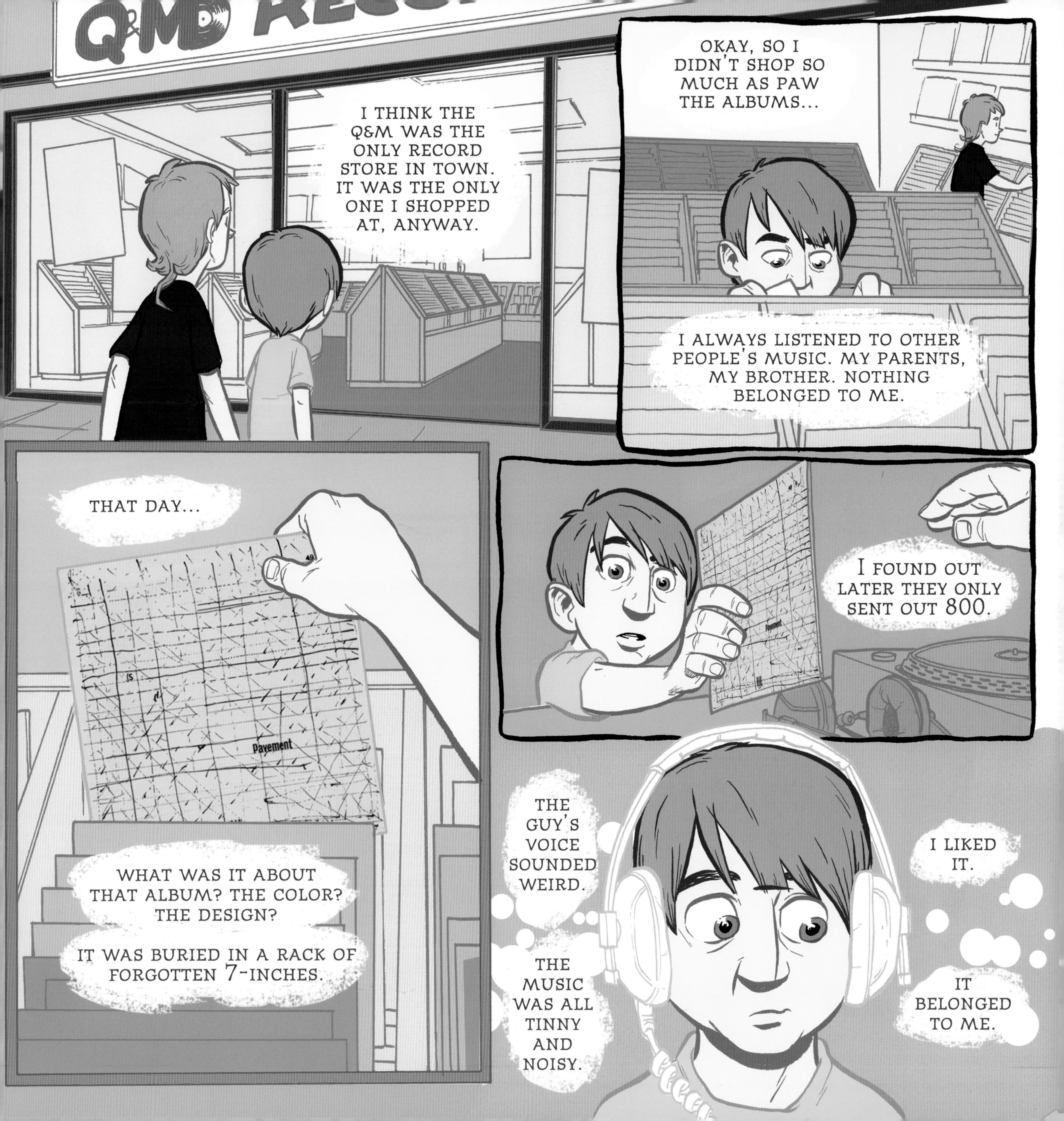
Q&MD RECO
I THINK THE Q&M WAS THE ONLY RECORD STORE IN TOWN. IT WAS THE ONLY ONE I SHOPPED AT, ANYWAY.
OKAY, SO I DIDN'T SHOP SO MUCH AS PAW THE ALBUMS...
I ALWAYS LISTENED TO OTHER PEOPLE'S MUSIC. MY PARENTS, MY BROTHER. NOTHING BELONGED TO ME.
THAT DAY...
Pavement
WHAT WAS IT ABOUT THAT ALBUM? THE COLOR? THE DESIGN?
IT WAS BURIED IN A RACK OF FORGOTTEN 7-INCHES.
I FOUND OUT LATER THEY ONLY SENT OUT 800.
Pavement
THE GUY'S VOICE SOUNDED WEIRD.
THE MUSIC WAS ALL TINNY AND NOISY.
I LIKED IT.
IT BELONGED TO ME.

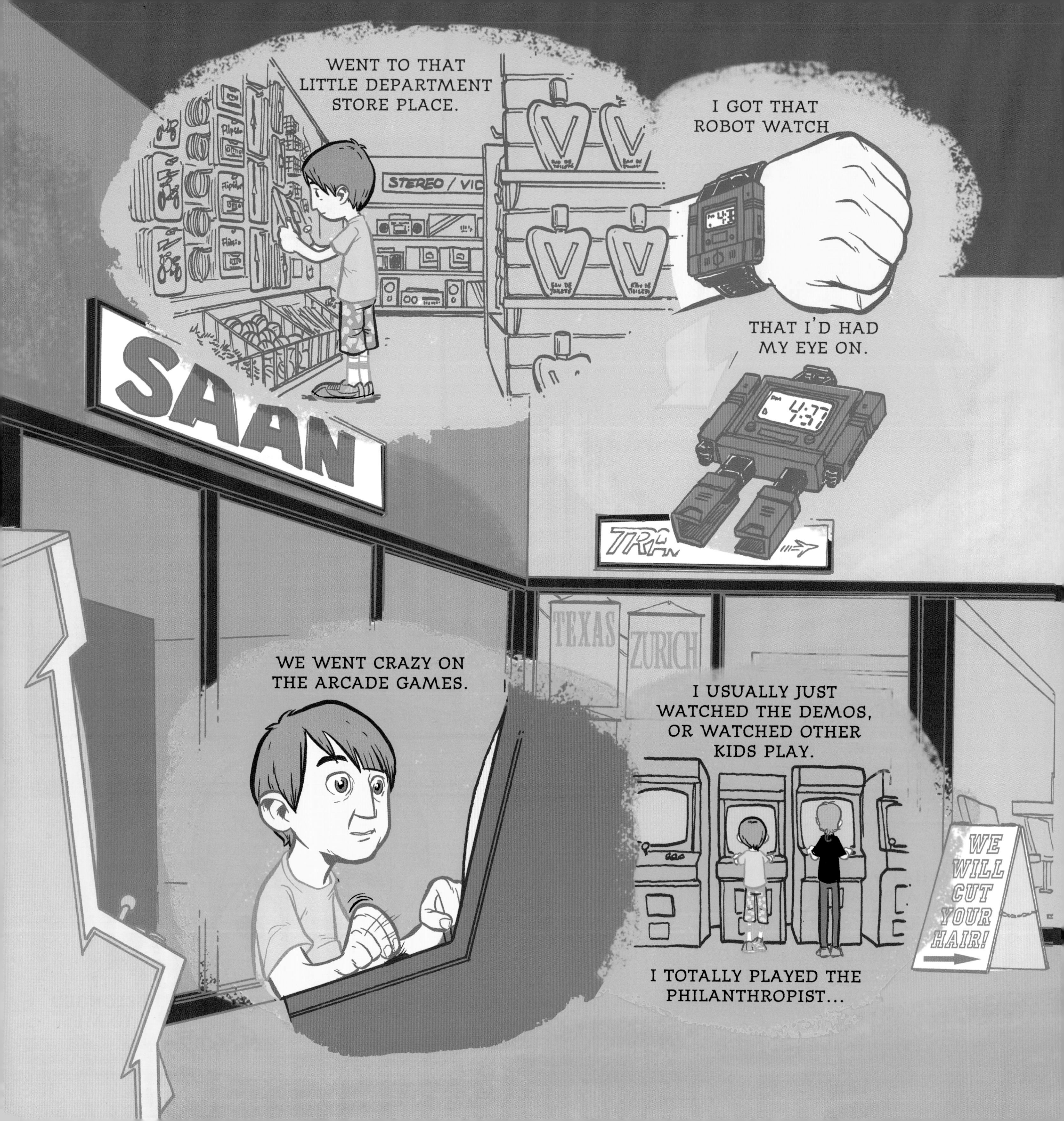

WENT TO THAT LITTLE DEPARTMENT STORE PLACE.
STEREO / VIC
SAAN
I GOT THAT ROBOT WATCH
THAT I'D HAD MY EYE ON.
WE WENT CRAZY ON THE ARCADE GAMES.
TEXAS
ZURICH
I USUALLY JUST WATCHED THE DEMOS, OR WATCHED OTHER KIDS PLAY.
WE WILL CUT YOUR HAIR!
I TOTALLY PLAYED THE PHILANTHROPIST...

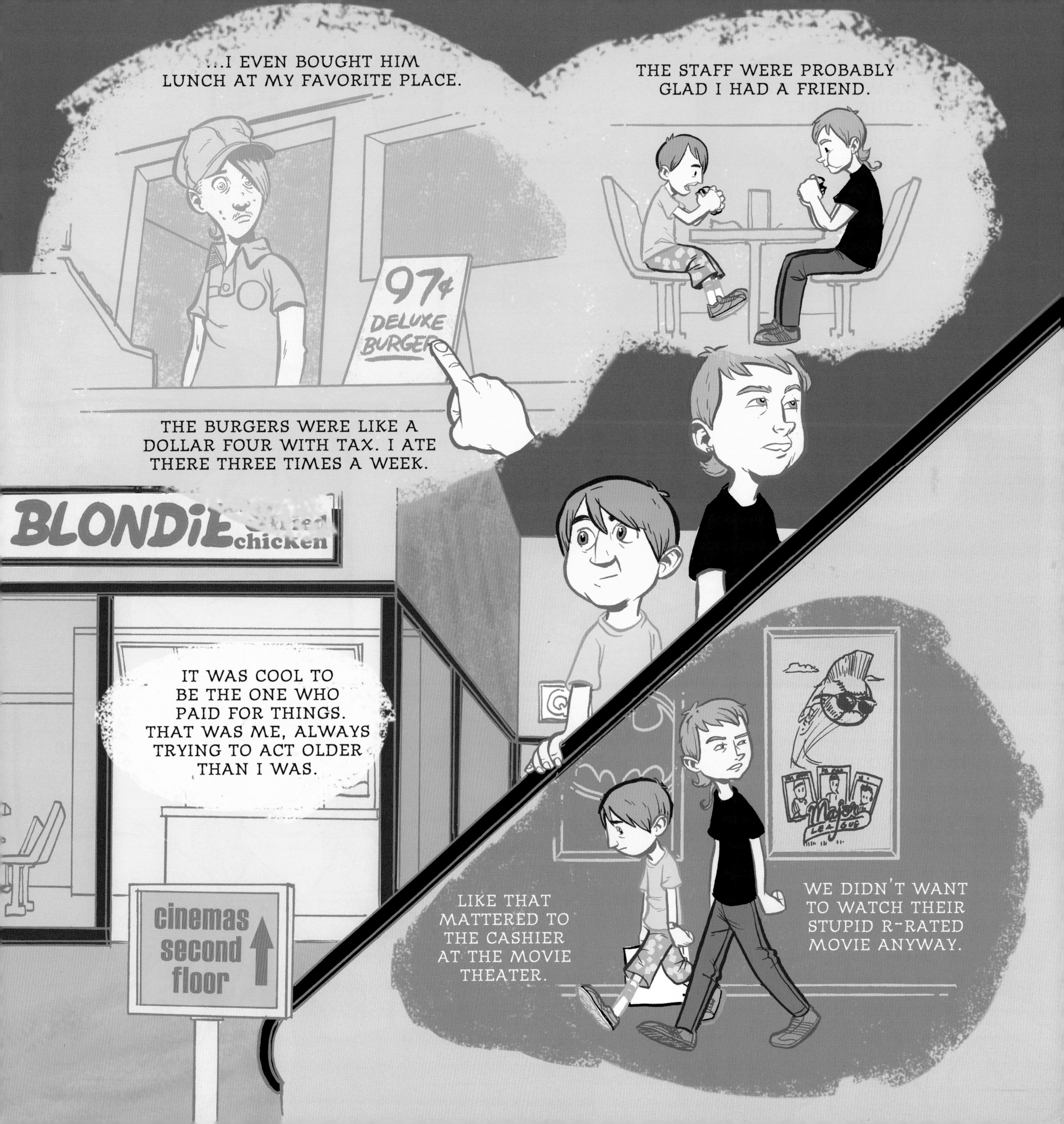
...I EVEN BOUGHT HIM LUNCH AT MY FAVORITE PLACE.
97¢ DELUXE BURGER
THE STAFF WERE PROBABLY GLAD I HAD A FRIEND.
THE BURGERS WERE LIKE A DOLLAR FOUR WITH TAX. I ATE THERE THREE TIMES A WEEK.
BLONDIE chicken
IT WAS COOL TO BE THE ONE WHO PAID FOR THINGS. THAT WAS ME, ALWAYS TRYING TO ACT OLDER THAN I WAS.
cinemas second floor
Major League
LIKE THAT MATTERED TO THE CASHIER AT THE MOVIE THEATER.
WE DIDN'T WANT TO WATCH THEIR STUPID R-RATED MOVIE ANYWAY.

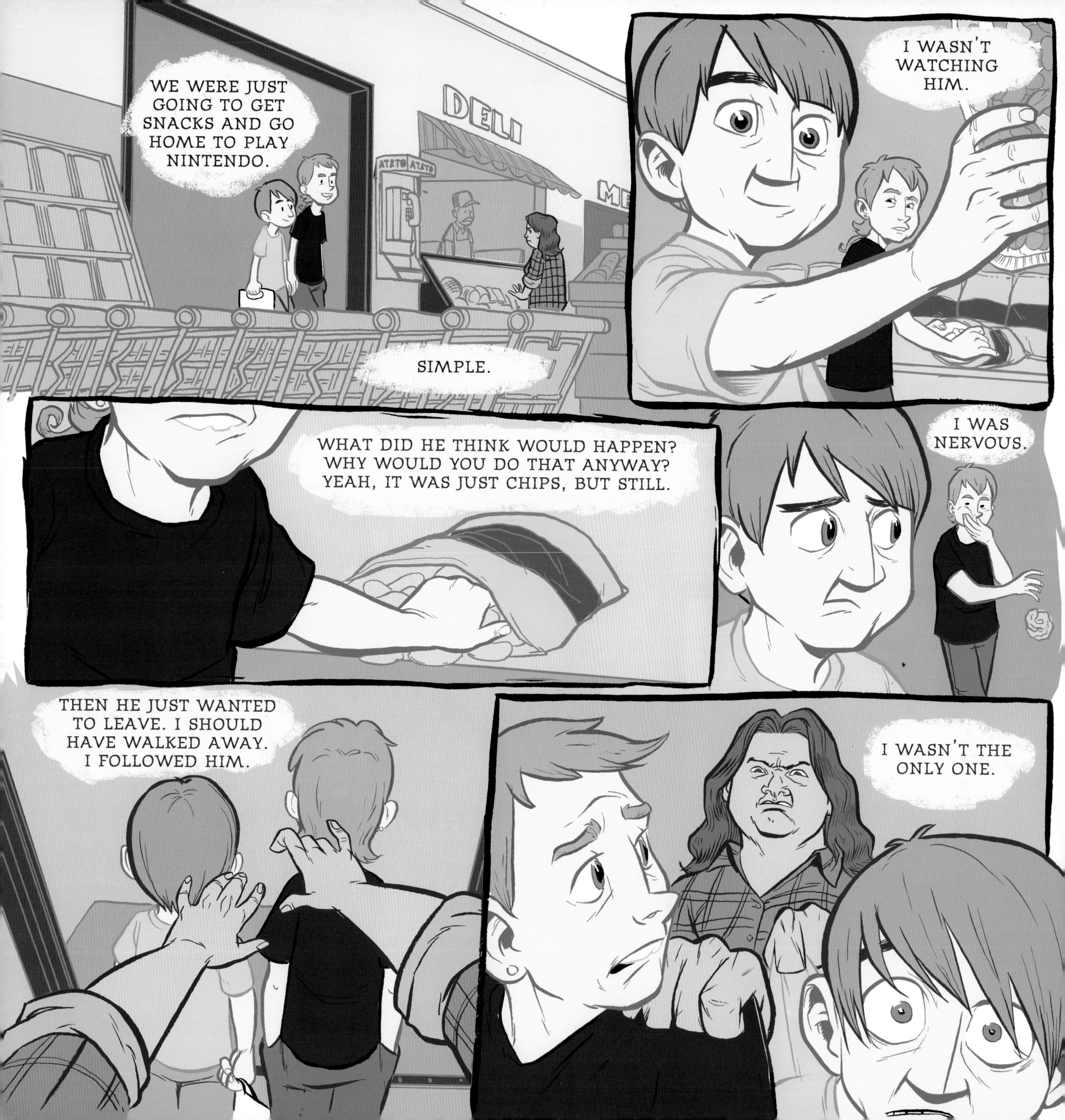
WE WERE JUST GOING TO GET SNACKS AND GO HOME TO PLAY NINTENDO.
DELI
SIMPLE.
I WASN'T WATCHING HIM.
WHAT DID HE THINK WOULD HAPPEN? WHY WOULD YOU DO THAT ANYWAY? YEAH, IT WAS JUST CHIPS, BUT STILL.
I WAS NERVOUS.
THEN HE JUST WANTED TO LEAVE. I SHOULD HAVE WALKED AWAY. I FOLLOWED HIM.
I WASN'T THE ONLY ONE.

I'D NEVER BEEN IN THE BACK OF A GROCERY STORE BEFORE. IT WAS DANK AND IT SMELLED LIKE ROTTEN PRODUCE. THE STORE DETECTIVE, AS SHE CALLED HERSELF, SAT US AT A TABLE.

I ASSUME IT WAS RESERVED FOR THIEVES AND OTHER FORMS OF LOWLIFE SCUM.

SHE WENT ON ABOUT NOBODY STEALS FROM MY STORE, BUSTER.

HE CRIED AND WAILED.

HE SAID HE WAS SORRY AND THAT HE DIDN'T DO IT ANYWAY.

I STONEWALLED. I WASN'T IN TROUBLE.

I'M CLEAN, LADY.

SHE PUT THE SCREWS TO ME. I DIDN'T BREAK.

SOMEHOW, SHE GOT OUR HOME NUMBERS OUT OF US.

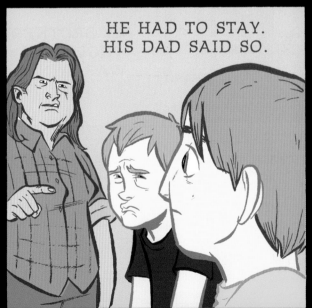

HE HAD TO STAY. HIS DAD SAID SO.

I WAS FREE TO GO.

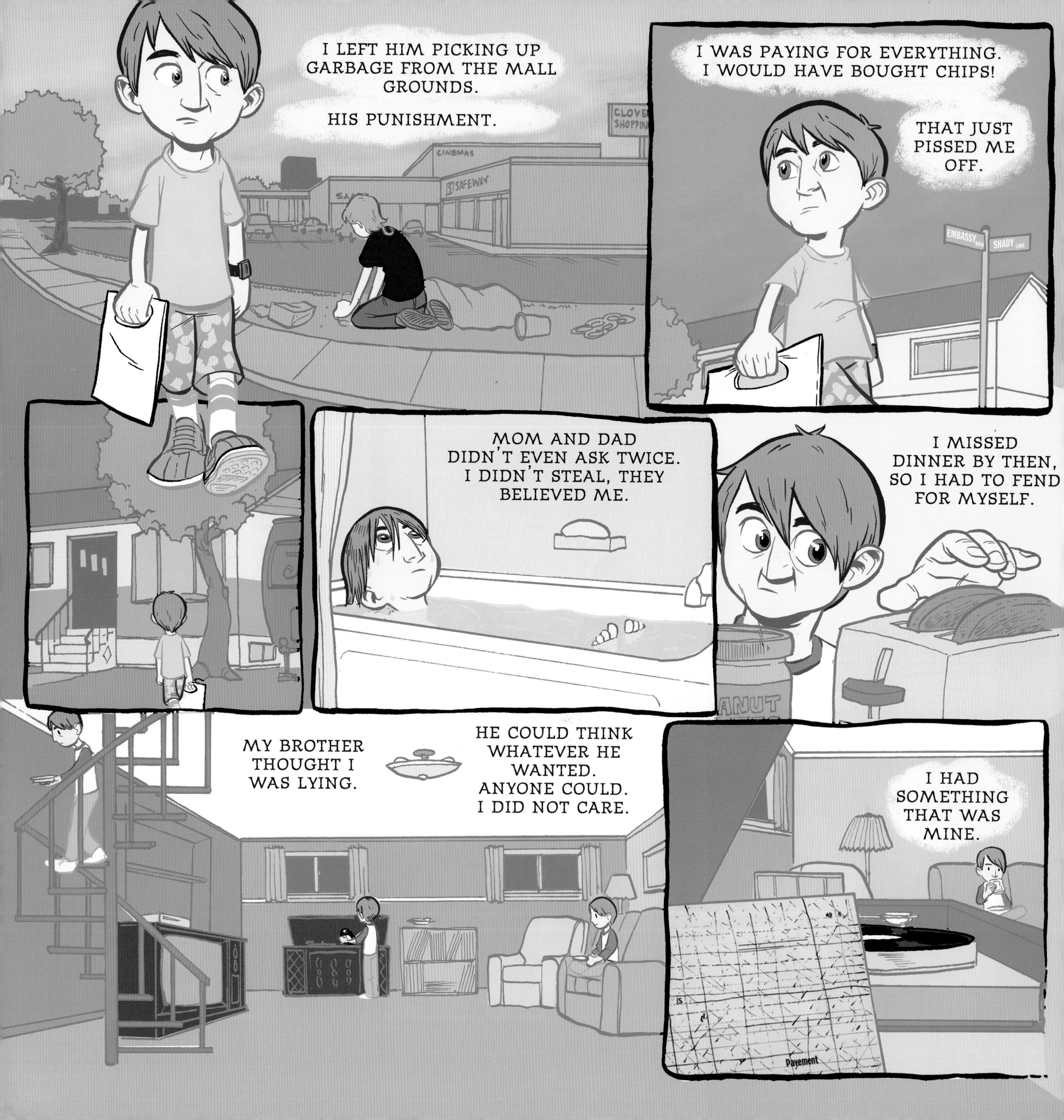
I LEFT HIM PICKING UP GARBAGE FROM THE MALL GROUNDS.
HIS PUNISHMENT.
CLOVER SHOPPING
CINEMAS
SAFEWAY
I WAS PAYING FOR EVERYTHING. I WOULD HAVE BOUGHT CHIPS!
THAT JUST PISSED ME OFF.
EMBASSY ROW
SHADY LANE
MOM AND DAD DIDN'T EVEN ASK TWICE. I DIDN'T STEAL, THEY BELIEVED ME.
I MISSED DINNER BY THEN, SO I HAD TO FEND FOR MYSELF.
ANUT
MY BROTHER THOUGHT I WAS LYING.
HE COULD THINK WHATEVER HE WANTED. ANYONE COULD. I DID NOT CARE.
I HAD SOMETHING THAT WAS MINE.
Pavement

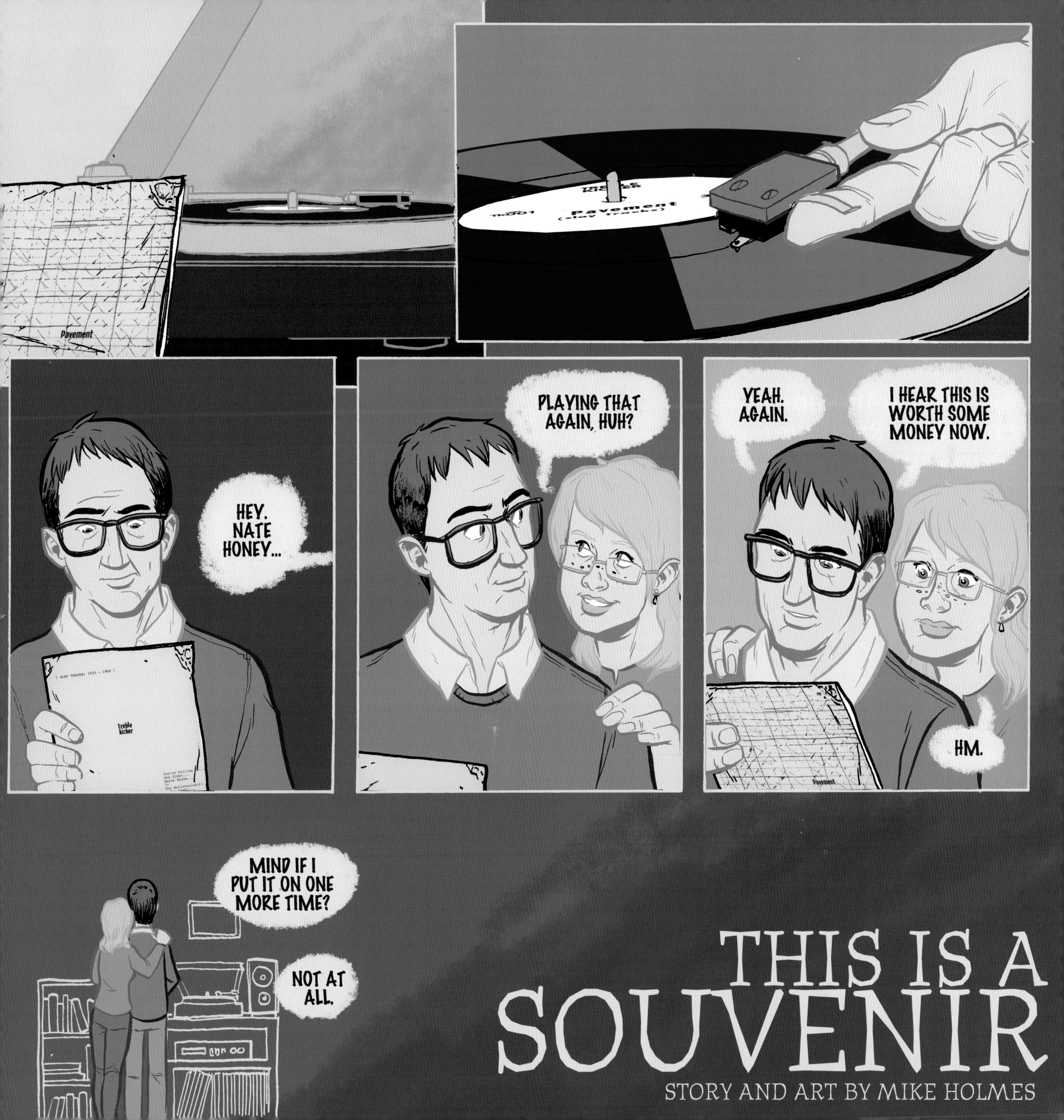
Pavement
Pavement
(slay tracks)
HEY. NATE HONEY...
treble kicker
PLAYING THAT AGAIN, HUH?
YEAH. AGAIN.
I HEAR THIS IS WORTH SOME MONEY NOW.
HM.
Pavement
MIND IF I PUT IT ON ONE MORE TIME?
NOT AT ALL.
THIS IS A SOUVENIR
STORY AND ART BY MIKE HOLMES

OKLAHOMA!

featured on **Oklahoma**

story by **Greg Thompson**
art by **Robbi Rodriguez**
colors by **Russ Lowery**

he will sleep outside tonight
he caused a stir in town earlier
up to his antics
dressed as a cowboy
oklahoma!
oklahoma!
oklahoma!
oklahoma!
and singing his songs
they prefer not to talk about him

wandering and wandering around
until you finally feel invisible

hey, everybody knew you
but nobody knew your name
hey, everybody knew you
but nobody spoke to you
and this is why

you were the only black man in this town
this lovely boring northern town
this is where the people they look right through you
this is where the people can gradually convince you
that you're not really there
until you're not really there

standing
in the middle of woolworths
in the middle of christmas
singing oklahoma at the top of your voice

hey, i never spoke to you
oh but i remember you

so how far can you go
and still be ignored
hey, there's a ghost in the centre of town

standing
outside boots dressed as a cowboy
shouting at the top of your voice
and brandishing your gun
bang!

wandering and wandering around
until you finally feel invisible

oklahoma!
oklahoma!

and then someone always pipes up and says
you chose that lifestyle
what? chose to sleep outside in the winter
i don't think so

oklahoma!
oklahoma!

and the strange thing is that now you're gone
people almost seem tosee you even more
than when you were around
it's the guilt that does that

oklahoma!
oklahoma!

merry christmas everybody!

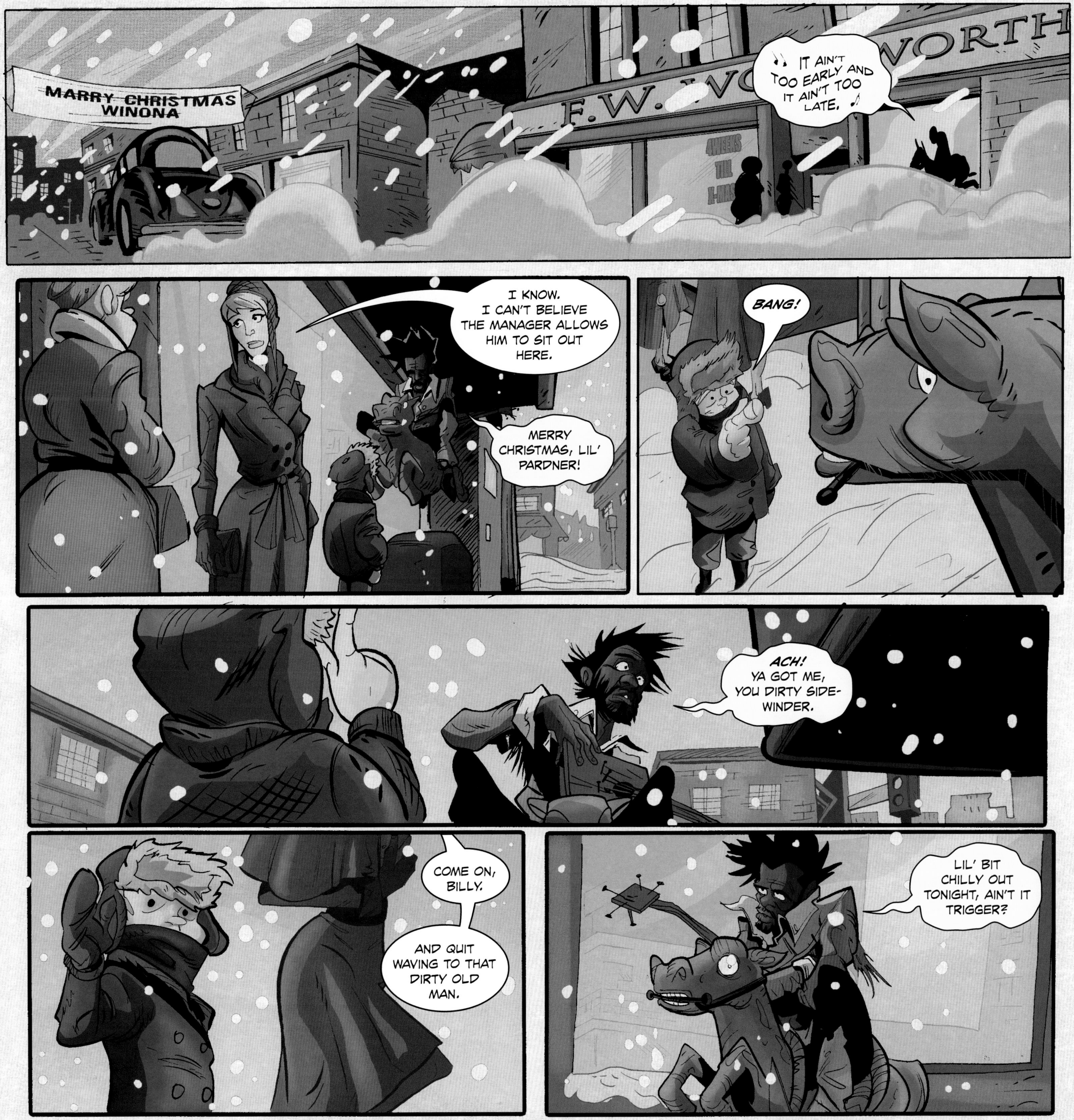
MARRY CHRISTMAS WINONA
F.W. WO WORTH
4 WEEKS TIL X-MAS
IT AIN'T TOO EARLY AND IT AIN'T TOO LATE.
I KNOW. I CAN'T BELIEVE THE MANAGER ALLOWS HIM TO SIT OUT HERE.
MERRY CHRISTMAS, LIL' PARDNER!
BANG!
ACH! YA GOT ME, YOU DIRTY SIDE-WINDER.
COME ON, BILLY.
AND QUIT WAVING TO THAT DIRTY OLD MAN.
LIL' BIT CHILLY OUT TONIGHT, AIN'T IT TRIGGER?

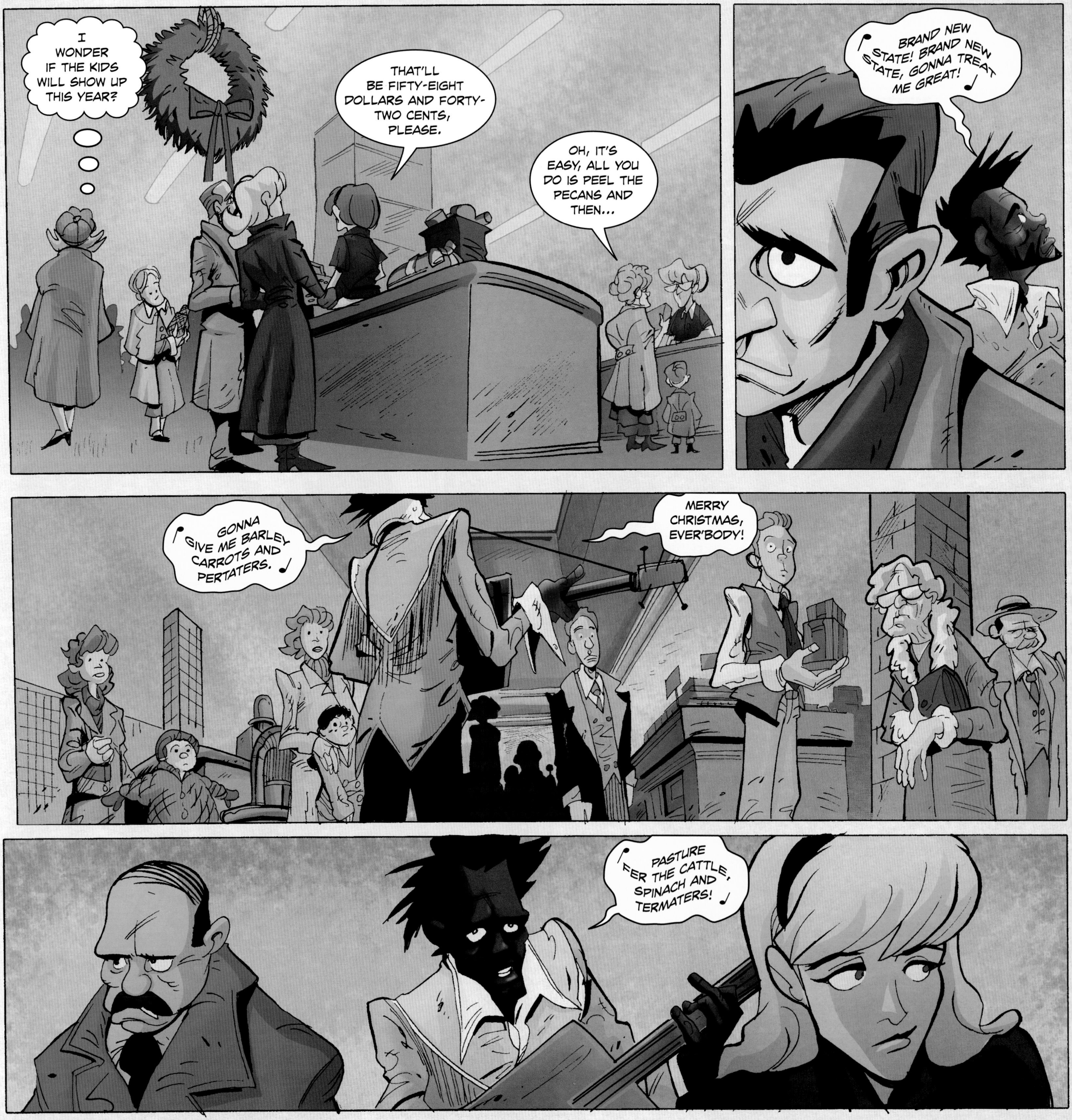
I WONDER IF THE KIDS WILL SHOW UP THIS YEAR?
THAT'LL BE FIFTY-EIGHT DOLLARS AND FORTY-TWO CENTS, PLEASE.
OH, IT'S EASY, ALL YOU DO IS PEEL THE PECANS AND THEN...
BRAND NEW STATE! BRAND NEW STATE, GONNA TREAT ME GREAT!
GONNA GIVE ME BARLEY CARROTS AND PERTATERS.
MERRY CHRISTMAS, EVER'BODY!
PASTURE FER THE CATTLE, SPINACH AND TERMATERS!

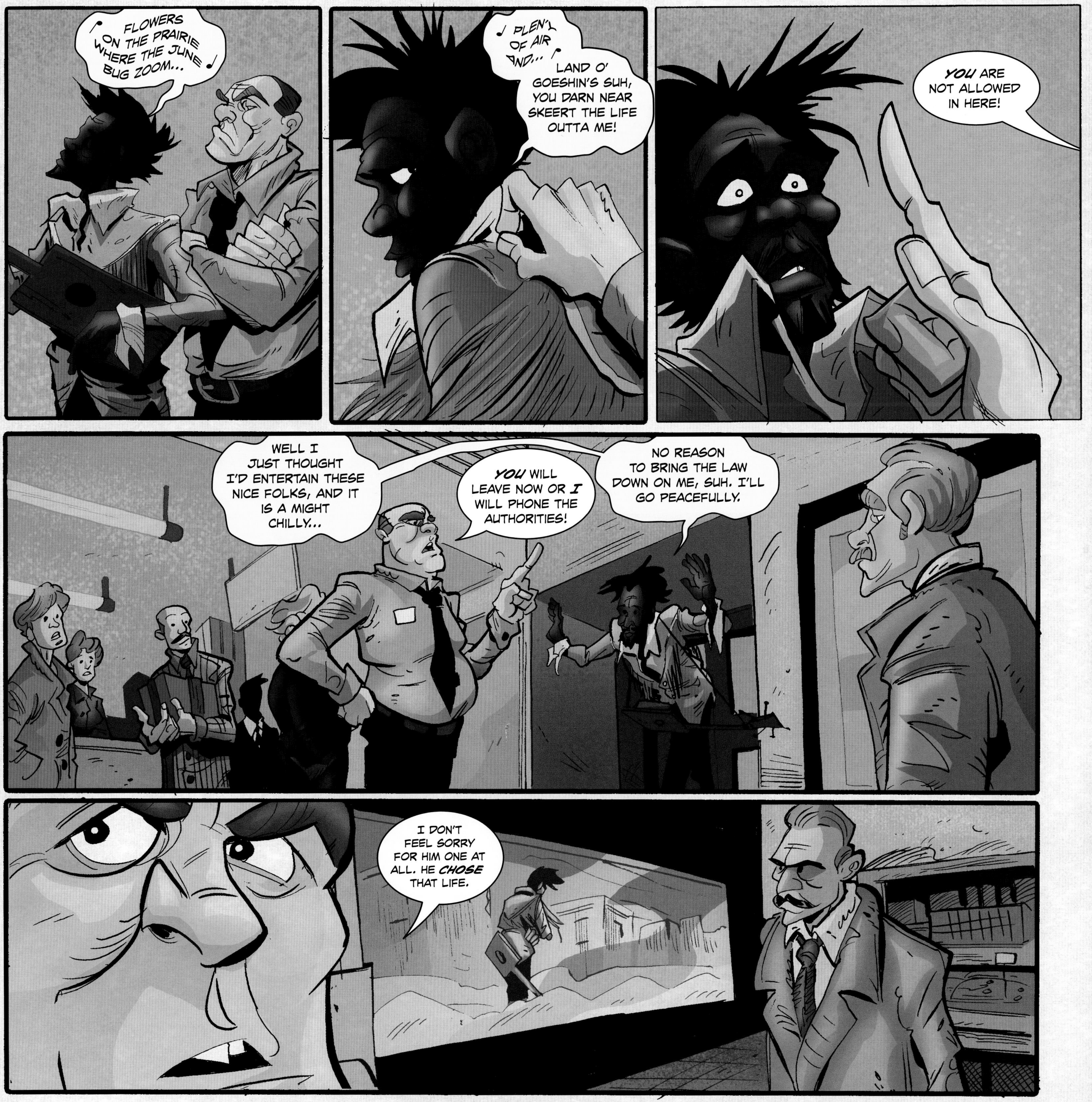
♪ FLOWERS ON THE PRAIRIE WHERE THE JUNE BUG ZOOM... ♪
♪ PLEN'Y OF AIR AND... ♪
LAND O' GOESHIN'S SUH, YOU DARN NEAR SKEERT THE LIFE OUTTA ME!
YOU ARE NOT ALLOWED IN HERE!
WELL I JUST THOUGHT I'D ENTERTAIN THESE NICE FOLKS, AND IT IS A MIGHT CHILLY...
YOU WILL LEAVE NOW OR I WILL PHONE THE AUTHORITIES!
NO REASON TO BRING THE LAW DOWN ON ME, SUH. I'LL GO PEACEFULLY.
I DON'T FEEL SORRY FOR HIM ONE AT ALL. HE CHOSE THAT LIFE.

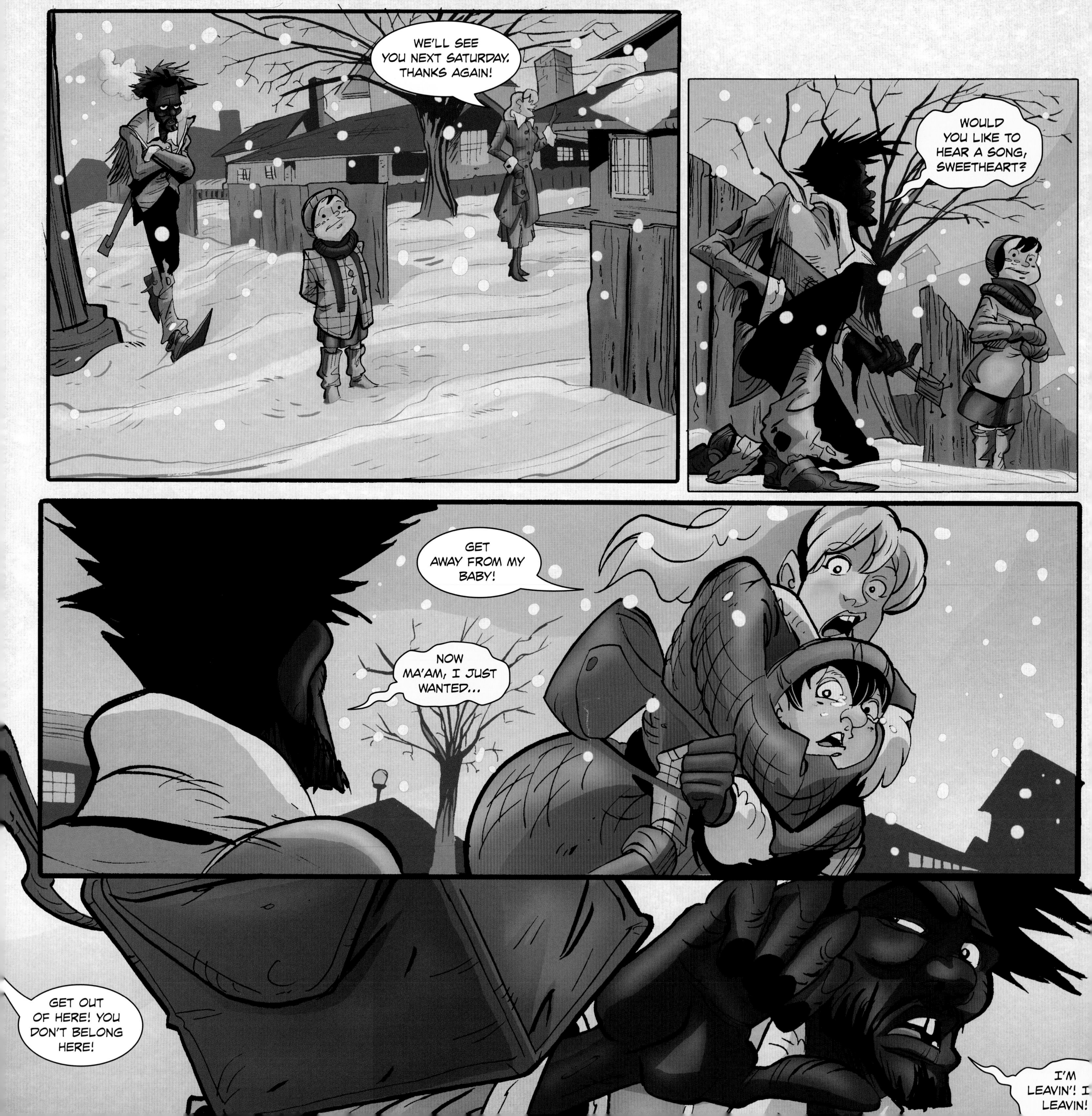
WE'LL SEE YOU NEXT SATURDAY. THANKS AGAIN!
WOULD YOU LIKE TO HEAR A SONG, SWEETHEART?
GET AWAY FROM MY BABY!
NOW MA'AM, I JUST WANTED...
GET OUT OF HERE! YOU DON'T BELONG HERE!
I'M LEAVIN'! I LEAVIN!

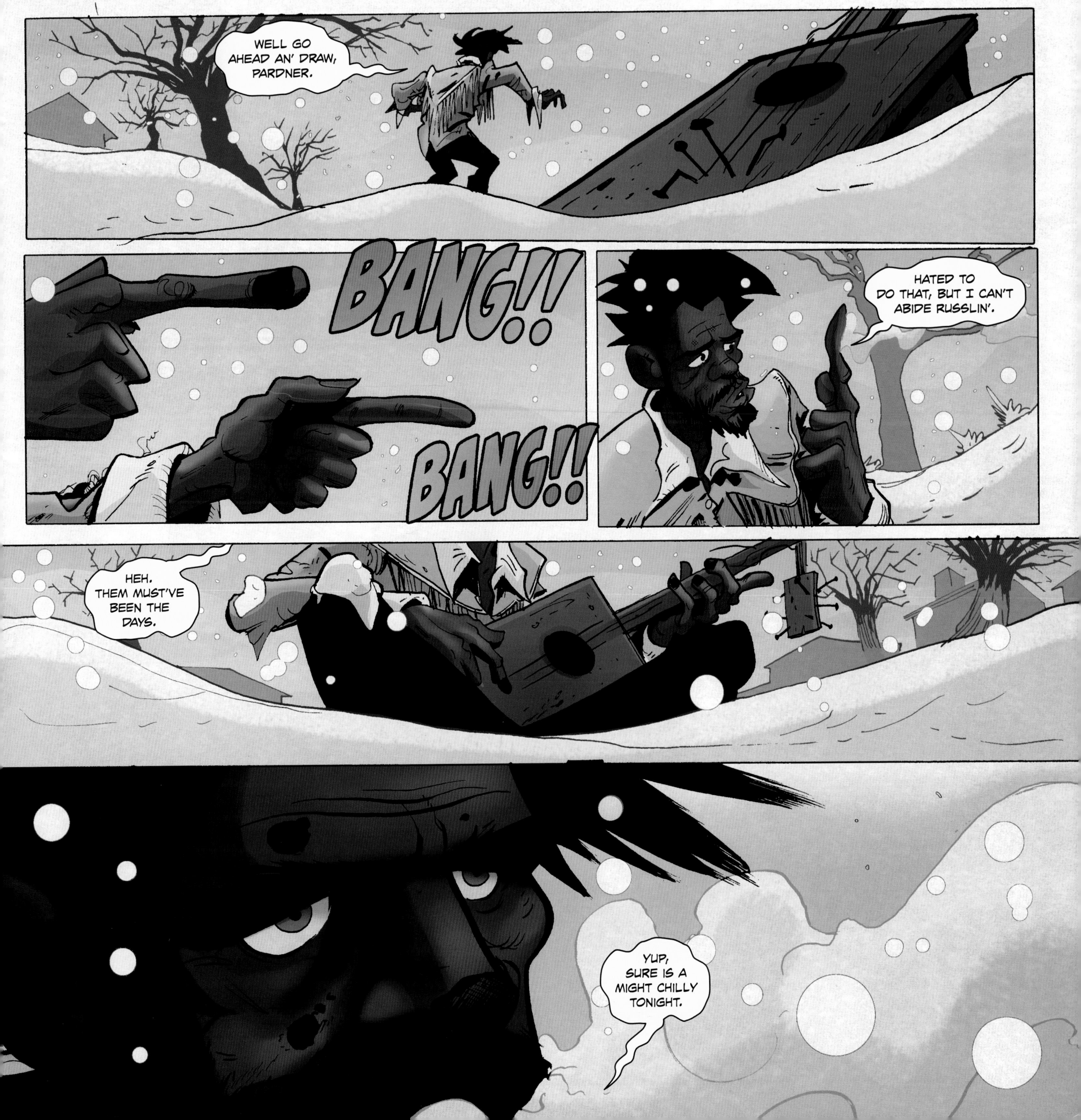

WELL GO AHEAD AN' DRAW, PARDNER.
BANG!!
BANG!!
HATED TO DO THAT, BUT I CAN'T ABIDE RUSSLIN'.
HEH. THEM MUST'VE BEEN THE DAYS.
YUP, SURE IS A MIGHT CHILLY TONIGHT.

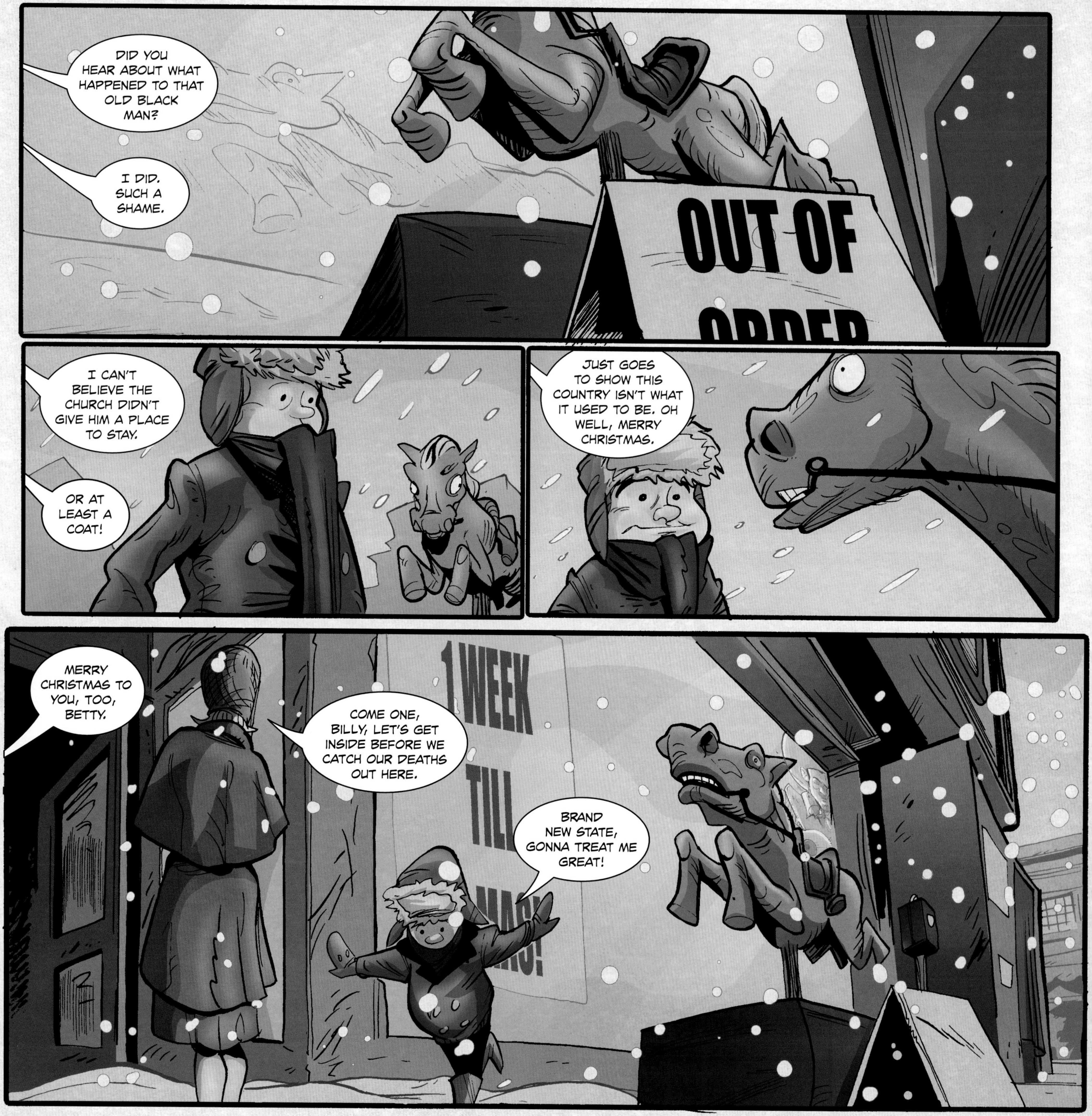
DID YOU HEAR ABOUT WHAT HAPPENED TO THAT OLD BLACK MAN?
I DID. SUCH A SHAME.
OUT OF ORDER
I CAN'T BELIEVE THE CHURCH DIDN'T GIVE HIM A PLACE TO STAY.
OR AT LEAST A COAT!
JUST GOES TO SHOW THIS COUNTRY ISN'T WHAT IT USED TO BE. OH WELL, MERRY CHRISTMAS.
MERRY CHRISTMAS TO YOU, TOO, BETTY.
1 WEEK TILL
COME ONE, BILLY, LET'S GET INSIDE BEFORE WE CATCH OUR DEATHS OUT HERE.
BRAND NEW STATE, GONNA TREAT ME GREAT!

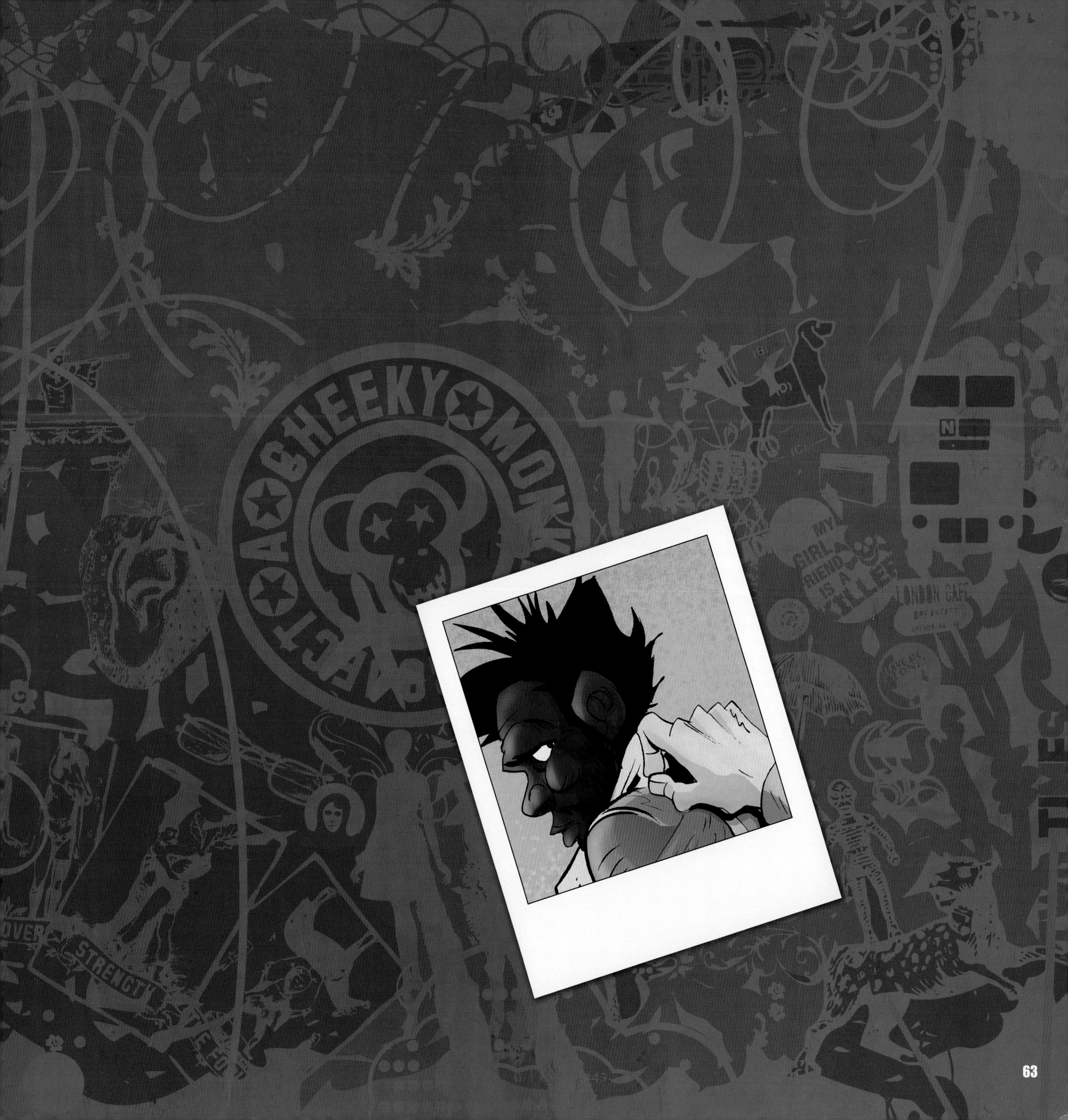
CHEEKY
MY GIRL FRIEND IS A

ISN'T IT GREAT TO BE ALIVE

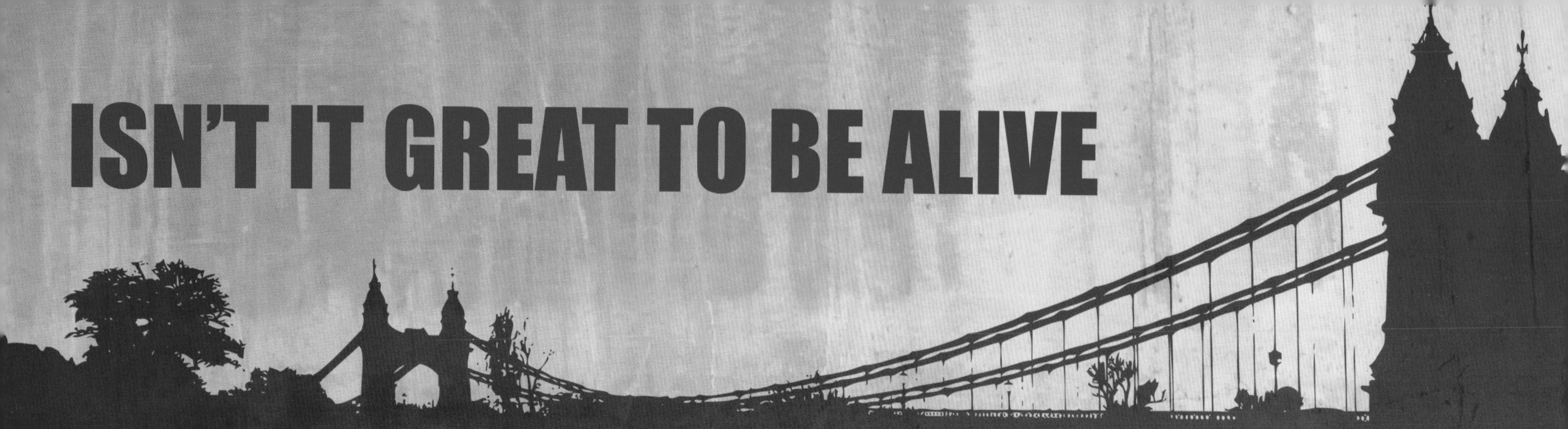

featured on **A Week Away**

by **Scott Mills**

came out of the gig
scooped some snow off a car
rubbed it into my face
isn't it great to be alive
isn't it great to be alive
11 o'clock
a woman came out
told you to get off
john steele stepped to the front
and kissed her full on the mouth
and martin said
"isn't it great to be alive
isn't it great to be alive"

hollow and sad
drifting like ghosts through the crowds
how can we come to terms
with ordinary life again now
now that we've tasted something more?
and if i can't be with you
this is the best my body can do
lying in a haze of you
it's the closest thing to "being with you"

showaddywaddy at the royal hall
i had a crush on you
waiting with you by the phones
so you could ring your man
sometimes it's, it's not that great to be alive
meeting you in the carmello
to discuss my musical
drinking skol at the fair
and yes you were there
you were the first song that i ever wrote

isn't it great to be alive
isn't it great to be alive

we hardly said a word on the way home
when you feel like this
you might as well be alone
tonight i don't want a train or a bus
i need to walk across this town
feel the rain on my face
sort these feelings out
'cos if i can't be with you
i don't know what i'm going to do

except fill myself with thoughts of you
it's the closest thing to being with you
standing in the drizzle
skimming stones across the sea
salt water ruined my shoes
and you laughed at me

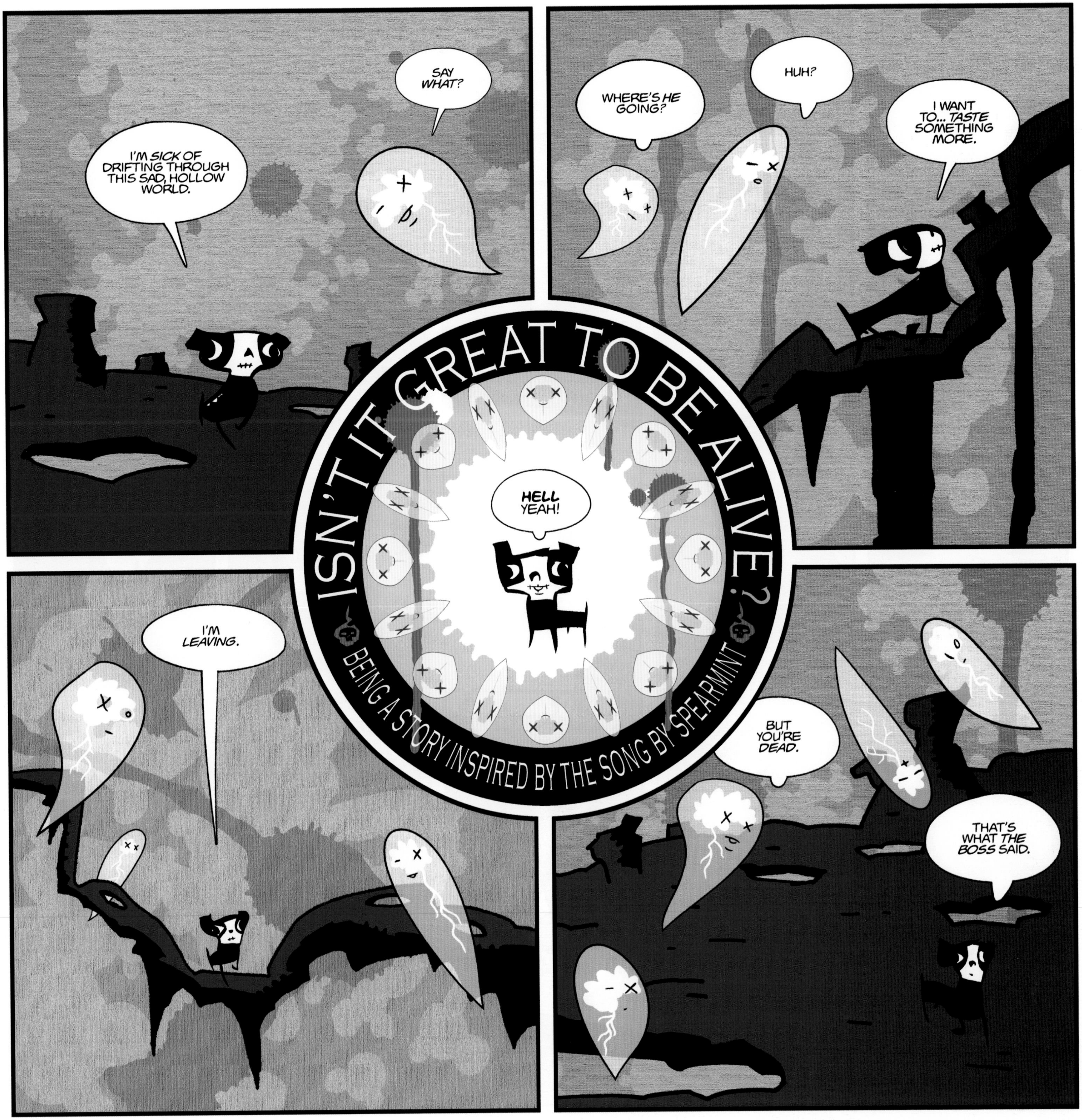

ISN'T IT GREAT TO BE ALIVE?
BEING A STORY INSPIRED BY THE SONG BY SPEARMINT
I'M SICK OF DRIFTING THROUGH THIS SAD, HOLLOW WORLD.
SAY WHAT?
WHERE'S HE GOING?
HUH?
I WANT TO... TASTE SOMETHING MORE.
HELL YEAH!
I'M LEAVING.
BUT YOU'RE DEAD.
THAT'S WHAT THE BOSS SAID.

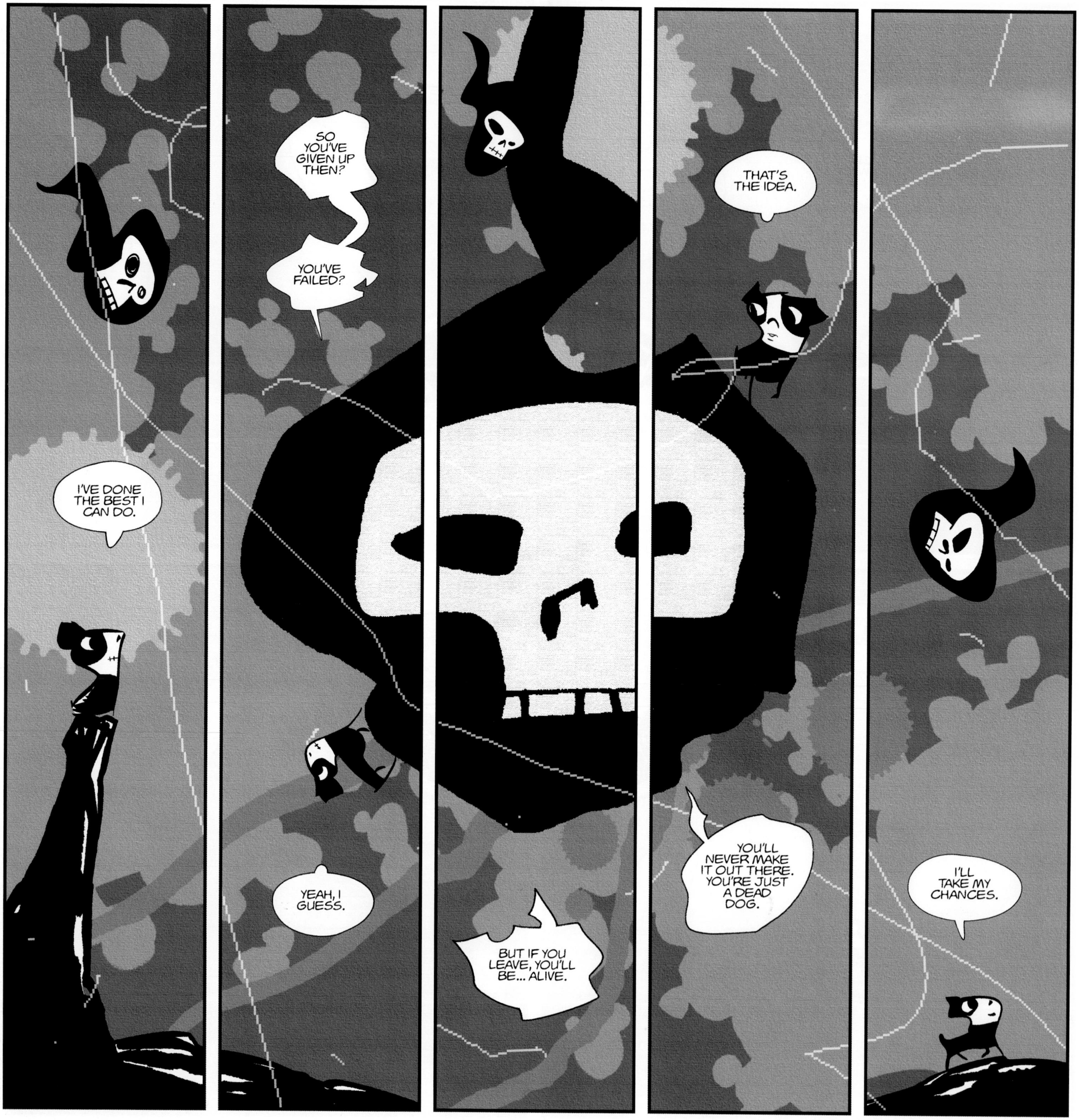
I'VE DONE THE BEST I CAN DO.
SO YOU'VE GIVEN UP THEN?
YOU'VE FAILED?
YEAH, I GUESS.
BUT IF YOU LEAVE, YOU'LL BE... ALIVE.
THAT'S THE IDEA.
YOU'LL NEVER MAKE IT OUT THERE. YOU'RE JUST A DEAD DOG.
I'LL TAKE MY CHANCES.

YOU'RE CRAZY!
I SEE LIGHT UP AHEAD.
I WANT TO FEEL RAIN ON MY FACE.
WHAT'S RAIN?
I WANNA SKIM STONES ACROSS WATER.
YIKES!
IS THAT... THE SKY?
SWEET!
I ADMIT IT. YOU WERE RIGHT.
YEAH...

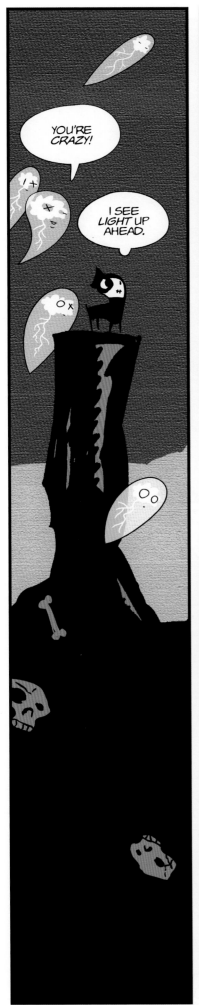

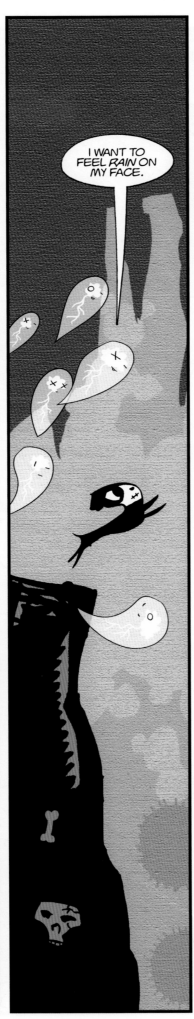

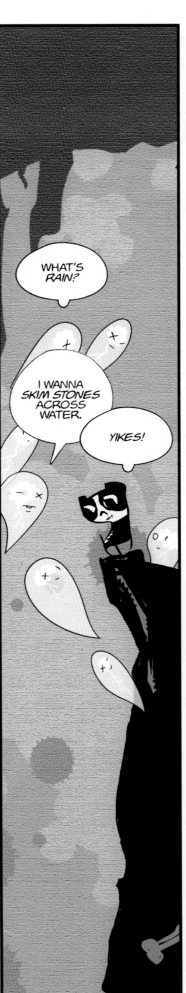

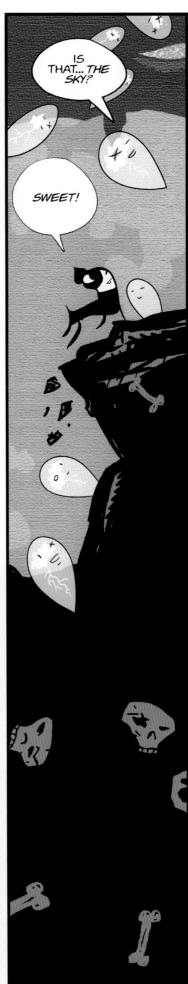

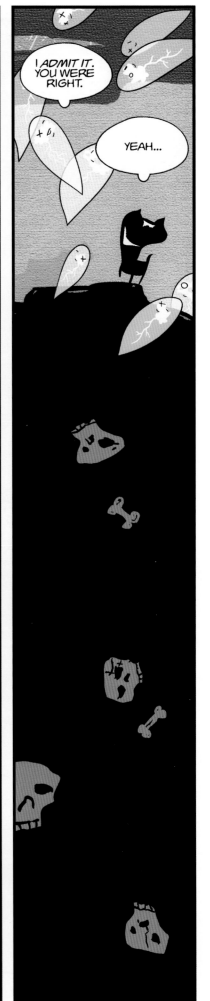

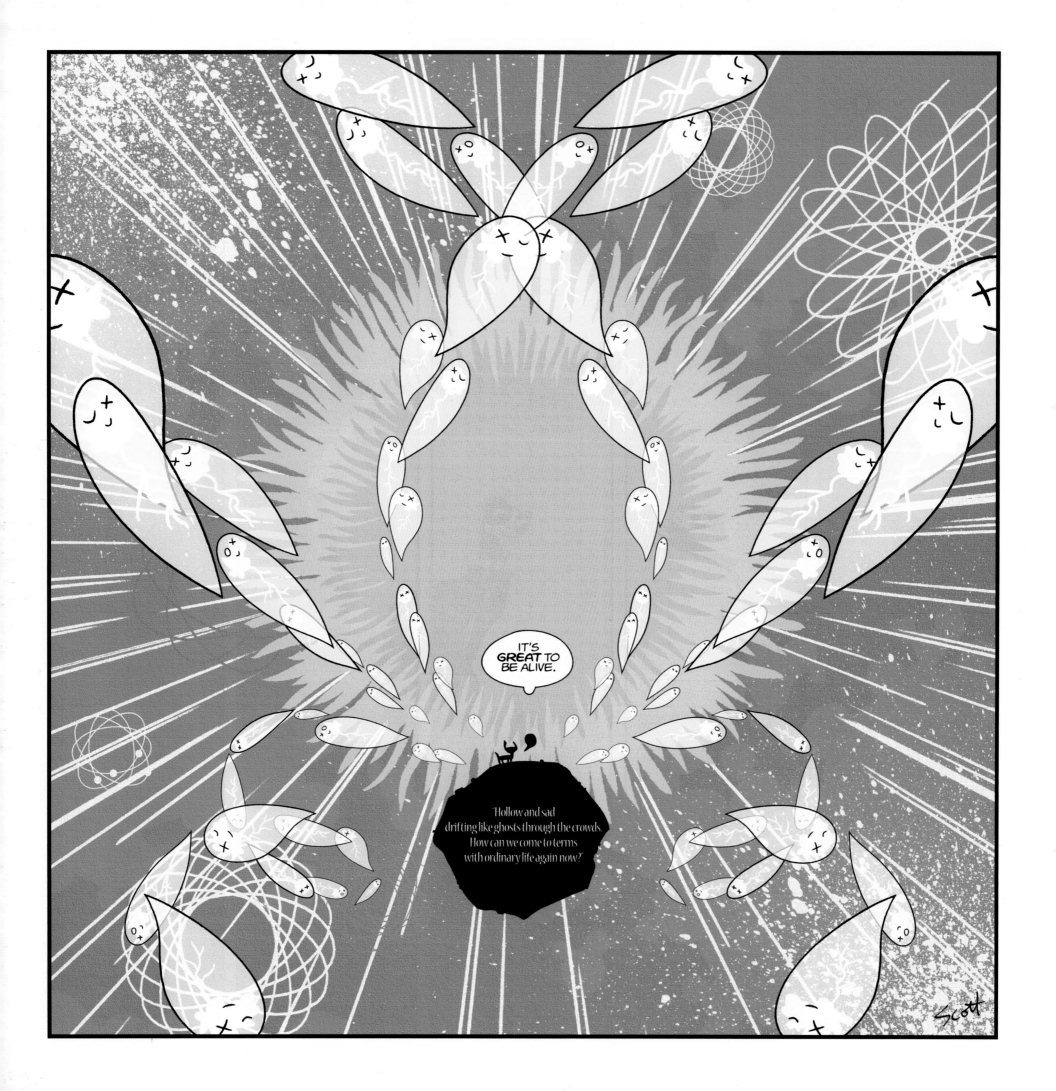

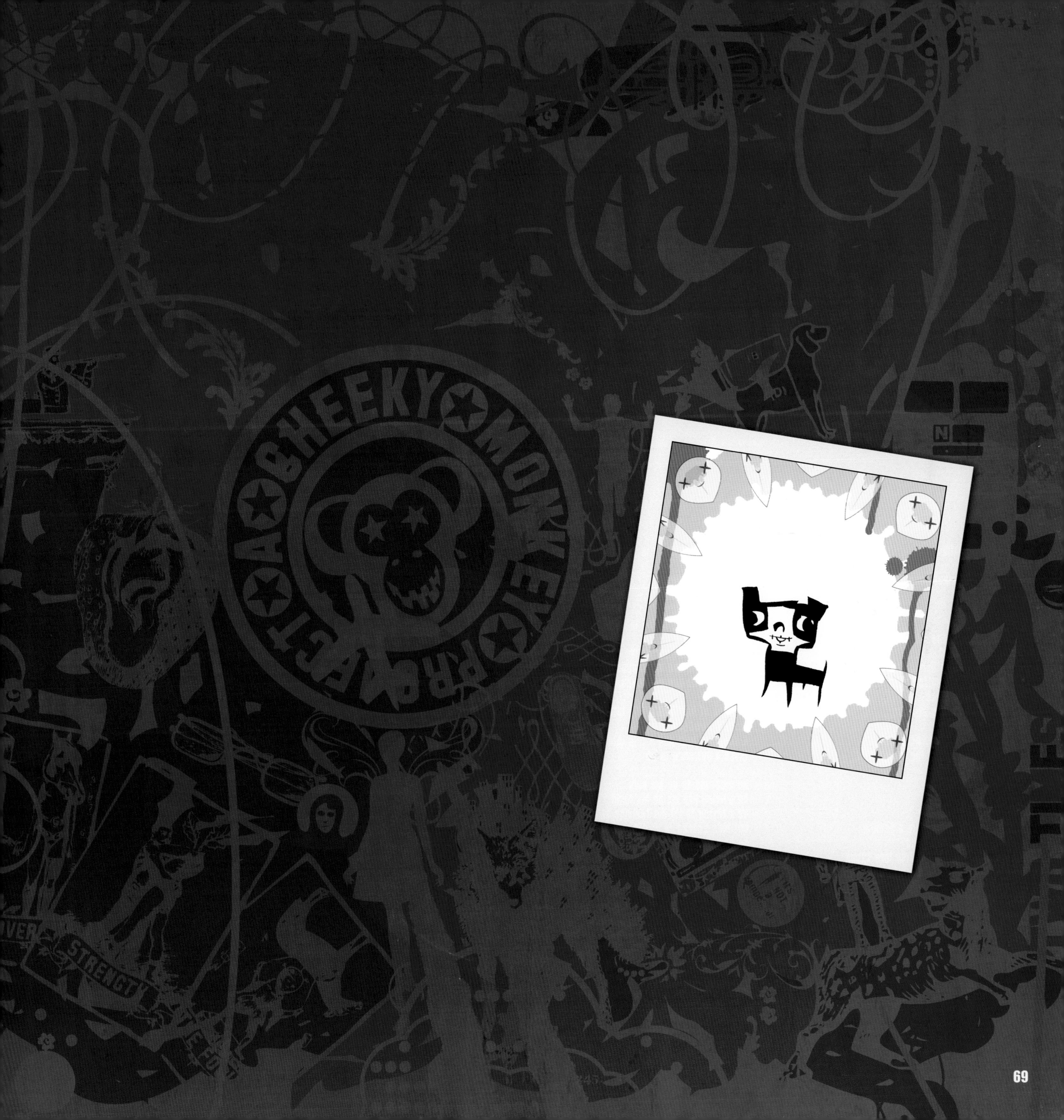
A CHEEKY MONKEY PROJECT

A TRIP INTO SPACE

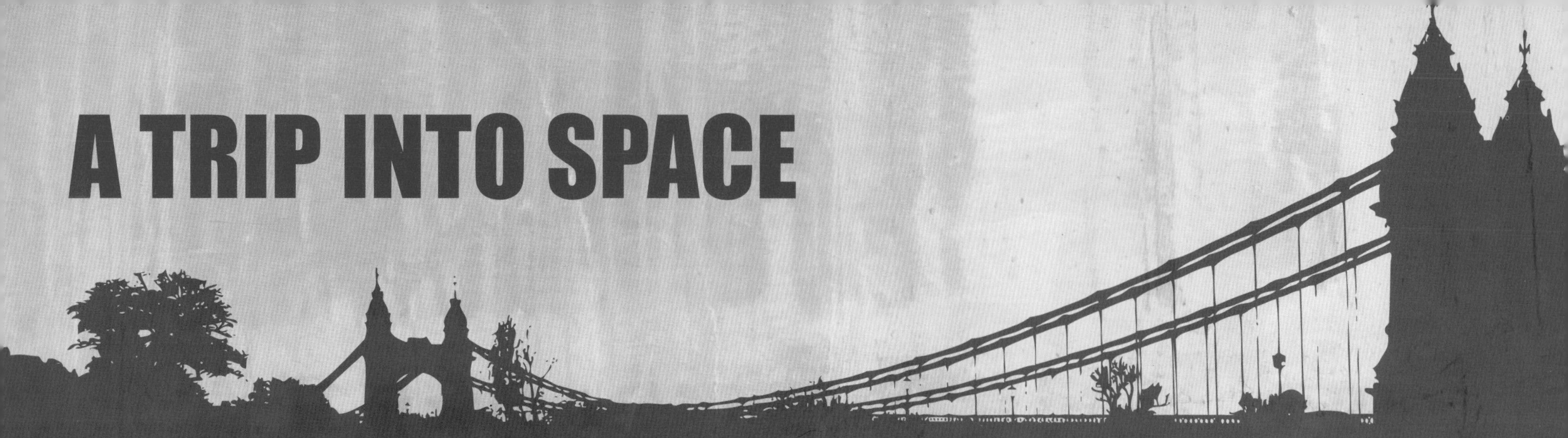

featured on **A Week Away**

story by **Rich Johnston**
art by **Terry Wiley**

aaaaaaaaaahhhhhh
i met myself
where'd you meet yourself shirley?
i met myself
coming back
from the grave
by then it was too late
aaaaaaaaaahhhhhh
they were all gathered round
i hadn't seen them for ages
i was in the ground
but by then it was too late

you can see he was beautiful
cigarette, he stops for a cigarette
you can't move him
he thinks a lot
writes it down
stops for a cigarette
all the world carried in a handbag
levitating above the bed
a shock of hair and a trip into space
the handbag drops and rolls away
oh how on earth are we supposed to help him?
how on earth are we supposed to help him?

he had the chance
to go into space
he had the chance
to know himself
he traded it for a guaranteed
place on earth
no
you can't move him
he won't let anybody in
even us
we're left outside
he's inside smoking
we're left outside
the rain comes pouring in
he's inside
the rain comes pouring in
how on earth are we supposed to help him?
how on earth are we supposed to help him?

a shock of hair and a trip into space
there's nowhere to go
a shock of hair and a trip into space
there's nowhere to go

he's sat inside on his own
he's living life inside his head
he's trying to let his feelings show
but he's scared to really open up
he had the chance to go into space
he had the chance to know himself
he dreams of getting off the floor
but he can't get up, he can't get up

you see
he was beautiful
you see
he was beautiful

a shock of hair and a trip into space
there's nowhere to go
a shock of hair and a trip into space
there's nowhere to go

you see
he was beautiful
he's sat inside his bedroom with nothing to do
and you see
he was so full of promise
and you see
when you look at him now
you can barely recognise him
just lying there
looking at the air
looking inside his head
to think what he'd do today

a head of hair and a trip into space
the back end of your dreams and thoughts
a winkle-picking day out
with a lost love and forgotten friends
oh how on earth are we supposed to help him?

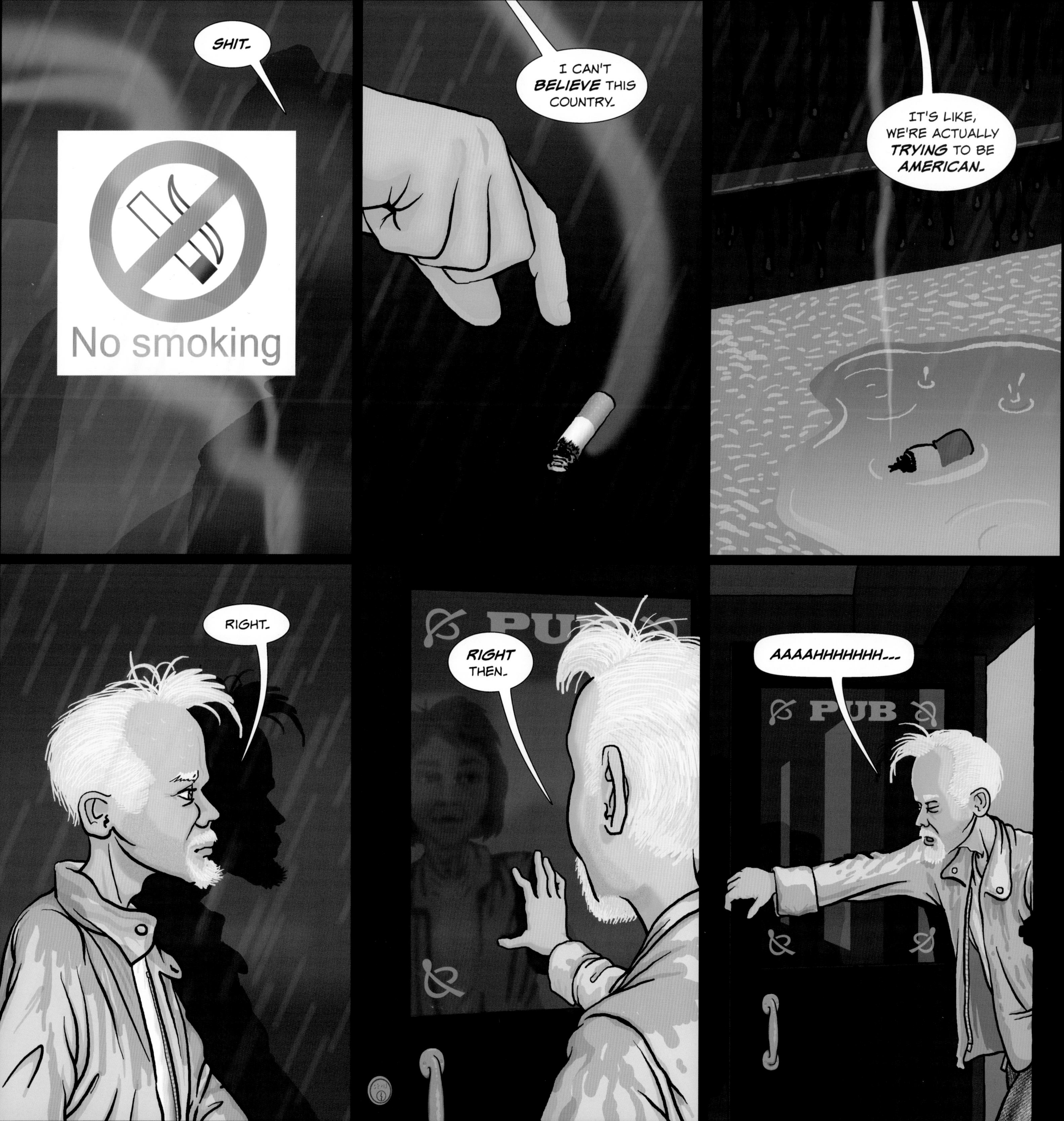
SHIT.
No smoking
I CAN'T *BELIEVE* THIS COUNTRY.
IT'S LIKE, WE'RE ACTUALLY *TRYING* TO BE *AMERICAN*.
RIGHT.
PUB
RIGHT THEN.
AAAAHHHHHHH...
PUB

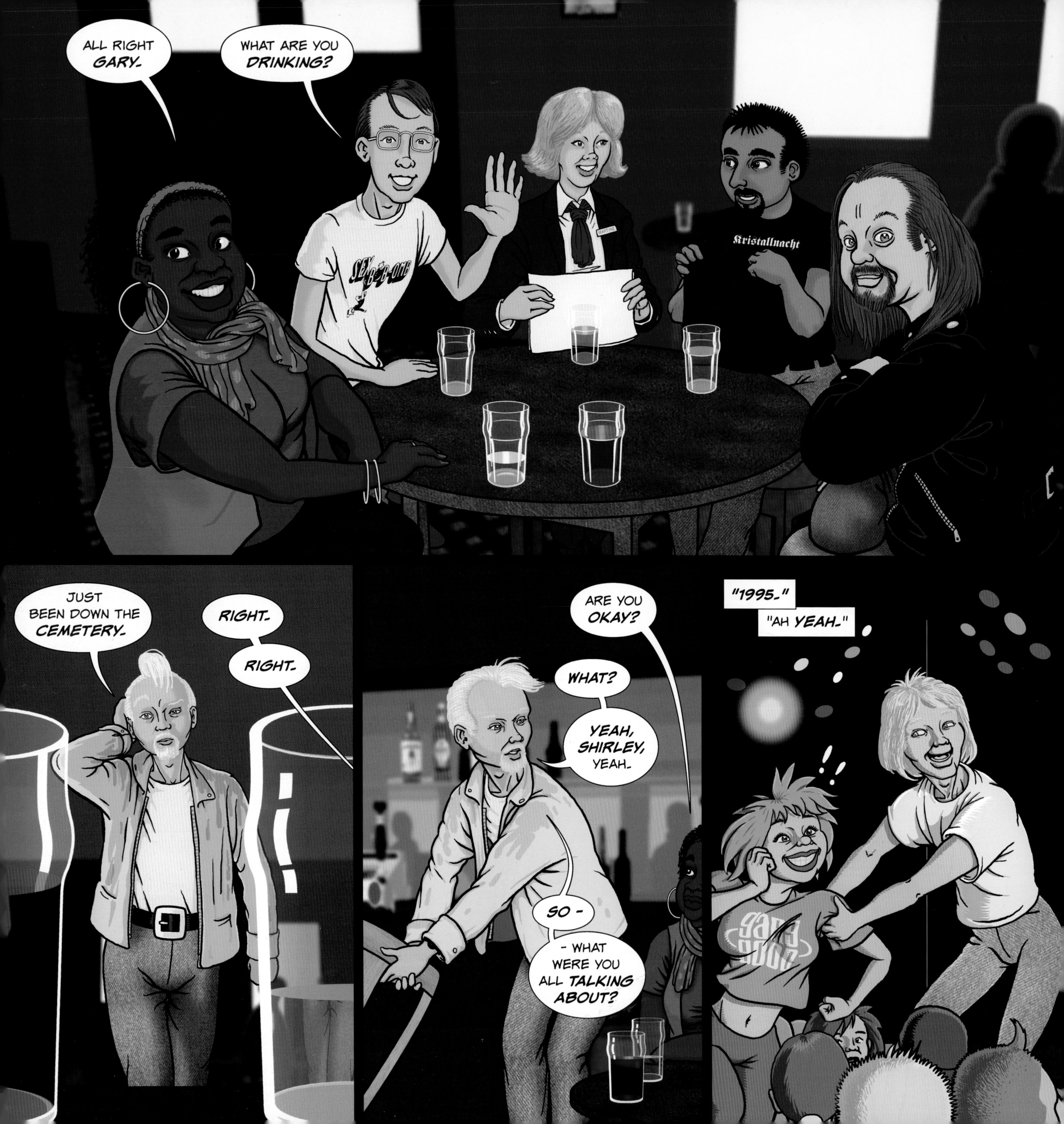

ALL RIGHT GARY.
WHAT ARE YOU DRINKING?
MARTINE
Kristallnacht
SEX BOB-OMB
JUST BEEN DOWN THE CEMETERY.
RIGHT.
RIGHT.
ARE YOU OKAY?
WHAT?
YEAH, SHIRLEY, YEAH.
SO -
- WHAT WERE YOU ALL TALKING ABOUT?
"1995."
"AH YEAH."
!!

TRIP INTO SPACE

SCRIPT BY
RICH JOHNSTON

ART BY
TERRY WILEY

BASED ON LYRICS AND MUSIC
PERFORMED BY
SPEARMINT

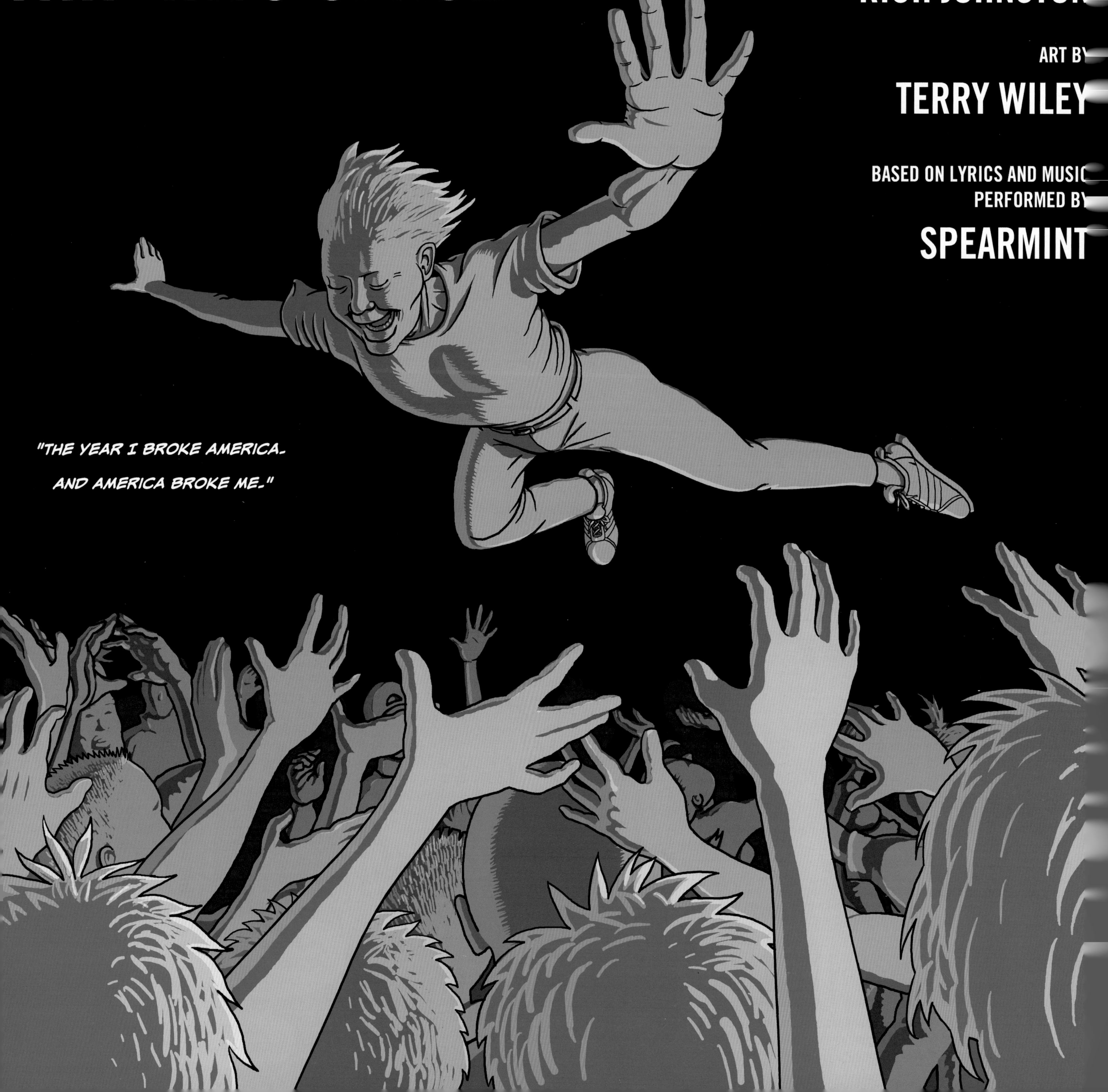
"THE YEAR I BROKE AMERICA.
AND AMERICA BROKE ME."

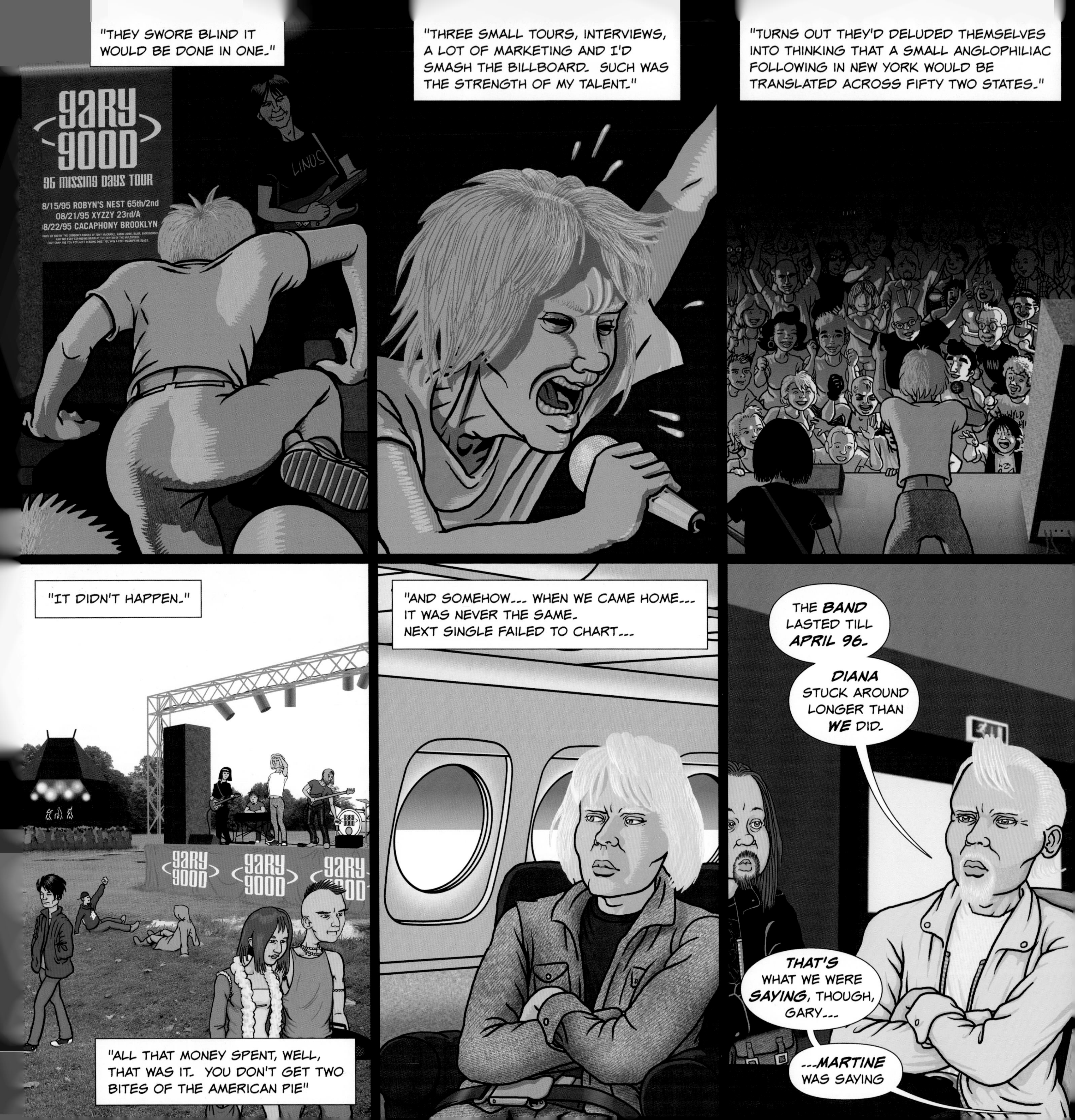
"THEY SWORE BLIND IT WOULD BE DONE IN ONE."
gary good
95 missing days TOUR
8/15/95 ROBYN'S NEST 65th/2nd
08/21/95 XYZZY 23rd/A
8/22/95 CACAPHONY BROOKLYN
AND THE EVER EXPANDING BRAIN AT THE CENTER OF THE MULTIVERSE.
HOLY CRAP ARE YOU ACTUALLY READING THIS? YOU WIN A FREE MAGNIFYING GLASS.
LINUS
"THREE SMALL TOURS, INTERVIEWS, A LOT OF MARKETING AND I'D SMASH THE BILLBOARD. SUCH WAS THE STRENGTH OF MY TALENT."
"TURNS OUT THEY'D DELUDED THEMSELVES INTO THINKING THAT A SMALL ANGLOPHILIAC FOLLOWING IN NEW YORK WOULD BE TRANSLATED ACROSS FIFTY TWO STATES."
"IT DIDN'T HAPPEN."
gary good
gary good
gary good
"ALL THAT MONEY SPENT, WELL, THAT WAS IT. YOU DON'T GET TWO BITES OF THE AMERICAN PIE"
"AND SOMEHOW... WHEN WE CAME HOME... IT WAS NEVER THE SAME. NEXT SINGLE FAILED TO CHART..."
THE **BAND** LASTED TILL **APRIL 96.**
DIANA STUCK AROUND LONGER THAN **WE** DID.
THAT'S WHAT WE WERE **SAYING**, THOUGH, GARY...
...**MARTINE** WAS SAYING

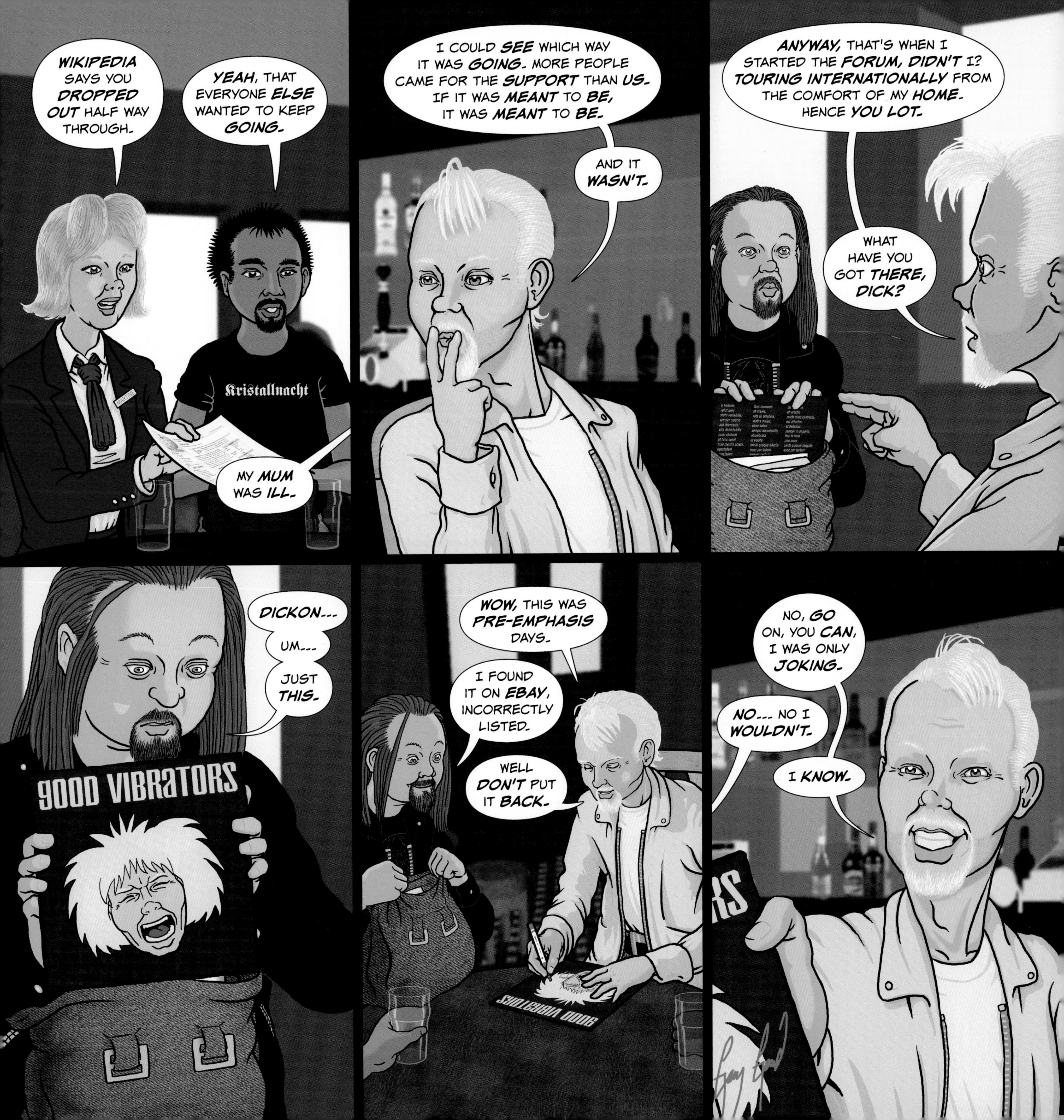
WIKIPEDIA SAYS YOU DROPPED OUT HALF WAY THROUGH.
YEAH, THAT EVERYONE ELSE WANTED TO KEEP GOING.
Kristallnacht
MY MUM WAS ILL.
I COULD SEE WHICH WAY IT WAS GOING. MORE PEOPLE CAME FOR THE SUPPORT THAN US. IF IT WAS MEANT TO BE, IT WAS MEANT TO BE.
AND IT WASN'T.
ANYWAY, THAT'S WHEN I STARTED THE FORUM, DIDN'T I? TOURING INTERNATIONALLY FROM THE COMFORT OF MY HOME. HENCE YOU LOT.
WHAT HAVE YOU GOT THERE, DICK?
DICKON...
UM...
JUST THIS.
GOOD VIBRATORS
WOW, THIS WAS PRE-EMPHASIS DAYS.
I FOUND IT ON EBAY, INCORRECTLY LISTED.
WELL DON'T PUT IT BACK.
GOOD VIBRATORS
NO, GO ON, YOU CAN, I WAS ONLY JOKING.
NO... NO I WOULDN'T.
I KNOW.

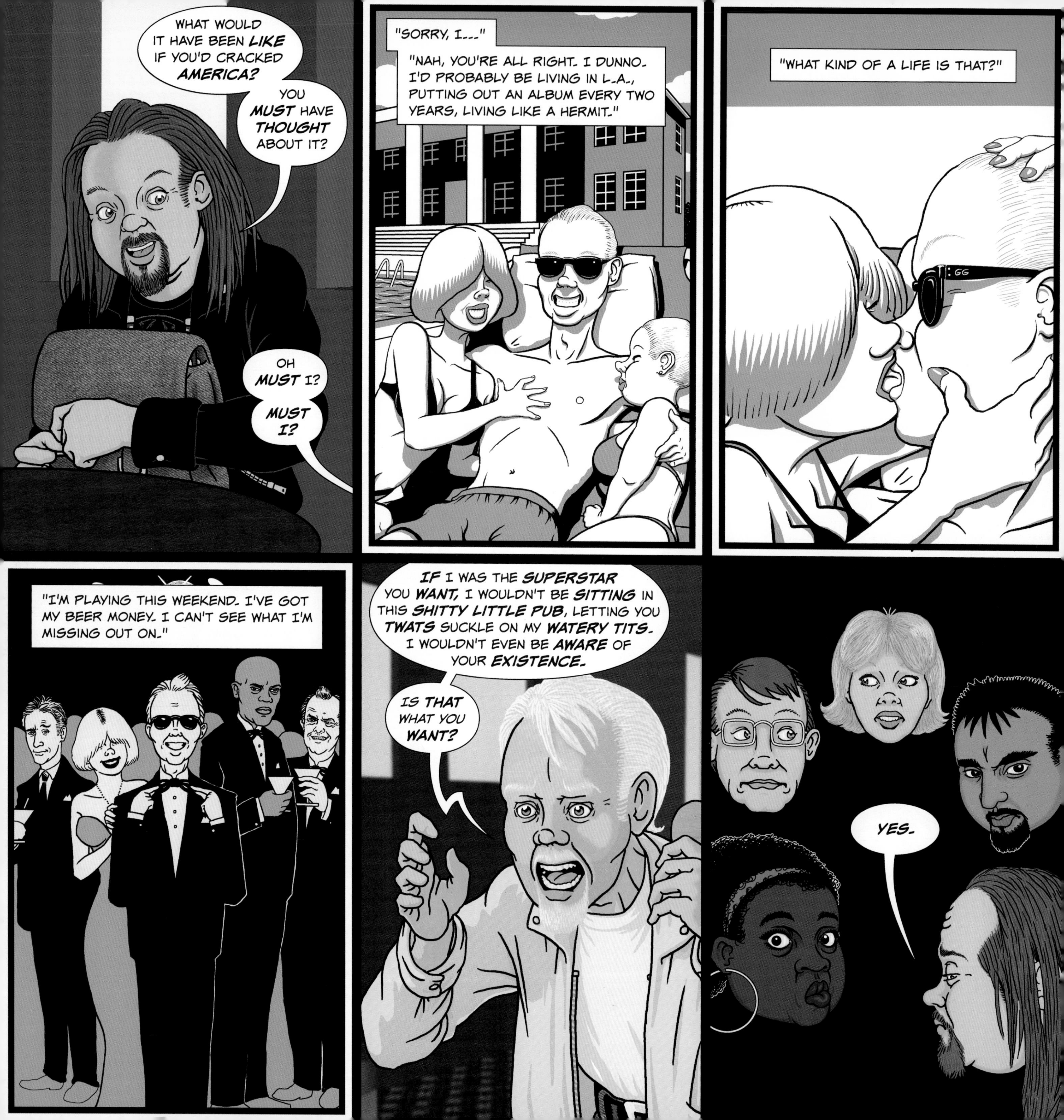
WHAT WOULD IT HAVE BEEN LIKE IF YOU'D CRACKED AMERICA?
YOU MUST HAVE THOUGHT ABOUT IT?
OH MUST I?
MUST I?
"SORRY, I..."
"NAH, YOU'RE ALL RIGHT. I DUNNO. I'D PROBABLY BE LIVING IN L.A., PUTTING OUT AN ALBUM EVERY TWO YEARS, LIVING LIKE A HERMIT."
"WHAT KIND OF A LIFE IS THAT?"
GG
"I'M PLAYING THIS WEEKEND. I'VE GOT MY BEER MONEY. I CAN'T SEE WHAT I'M MISSING OUT ON."
IF I WAS THE SUPERSTAR YOU WANT, I WOULDN'T BE SITTING IN THIS SHITTY LITTLE PUB, LETTING YOU TWATS SUCKLE ON MY WATERY TITS. I WOULDN'T EVEN BE AWARE OF YOUR EXISTENCE.
IS THAT WHAT YOU WANT?
YES.

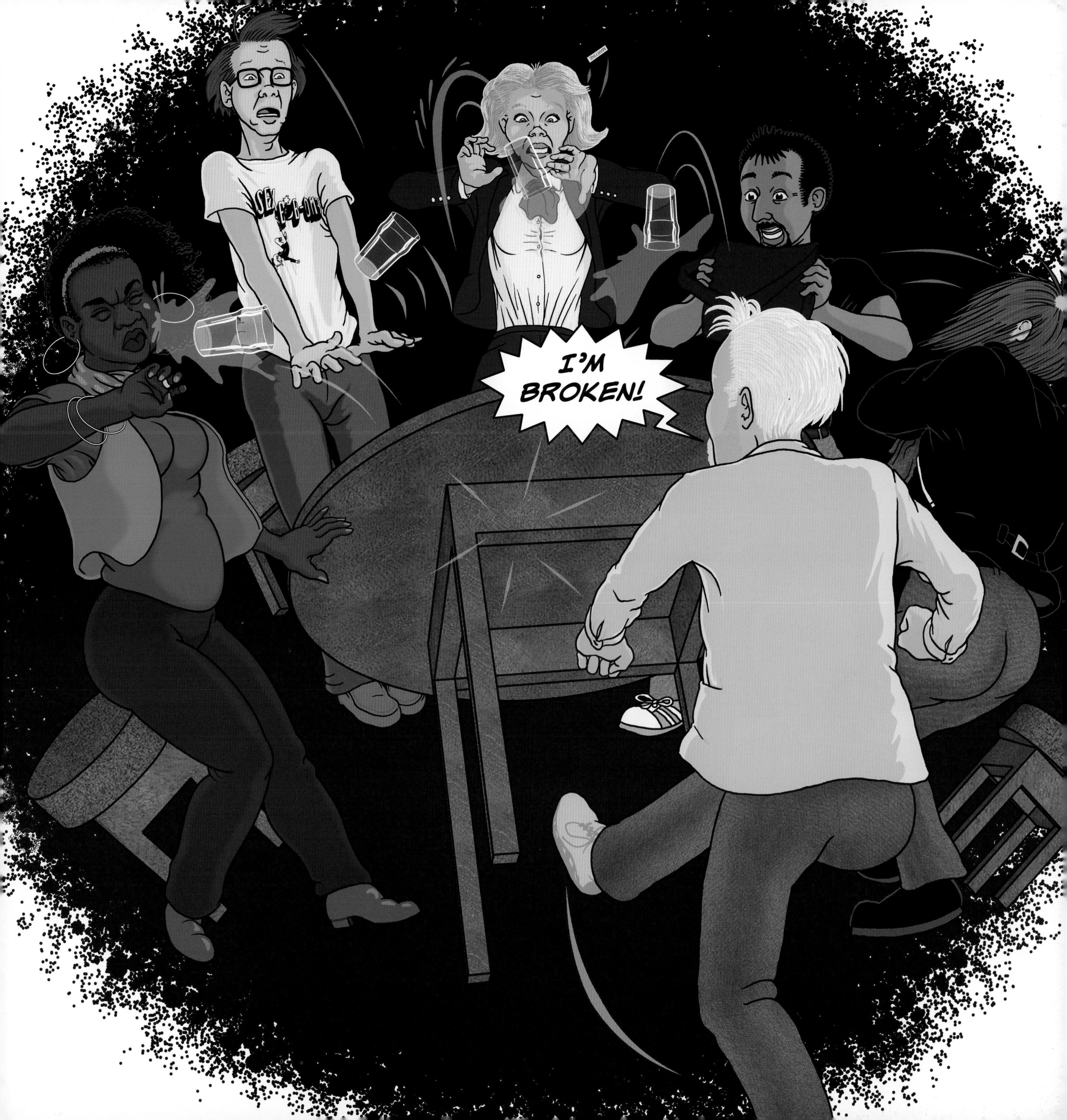
I'M BROKEN!

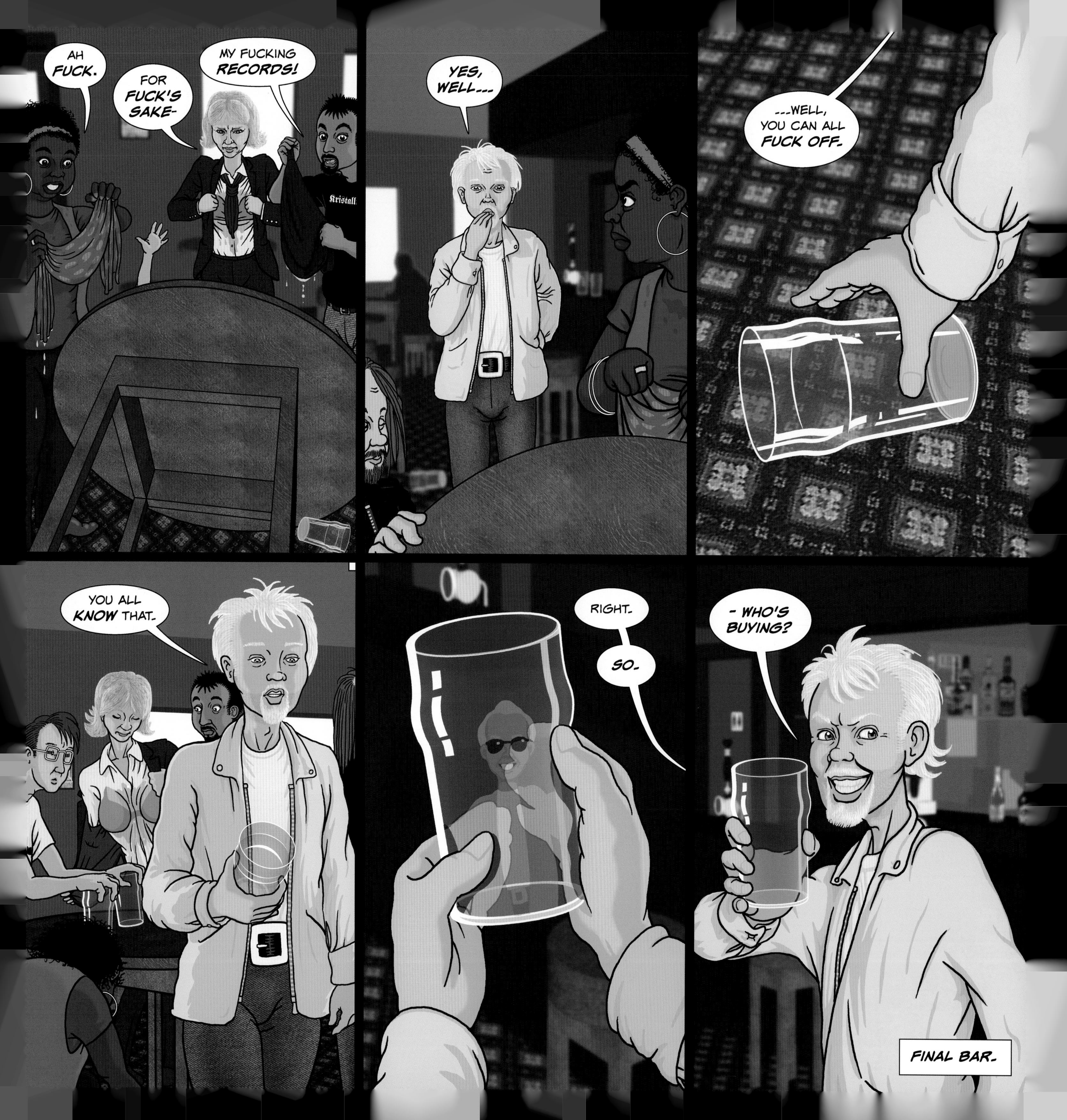
AH FUCK.
FOR FUCK'S SAKE-
MY FUCKING RECORDS!
YES, WELL...
...WELL, YOU CAN ALL FUCK OFF.
YOU ALL KNOW THAT.
RIGHT.
SO.
- WHO'S BUYING?
FINAL BAR.

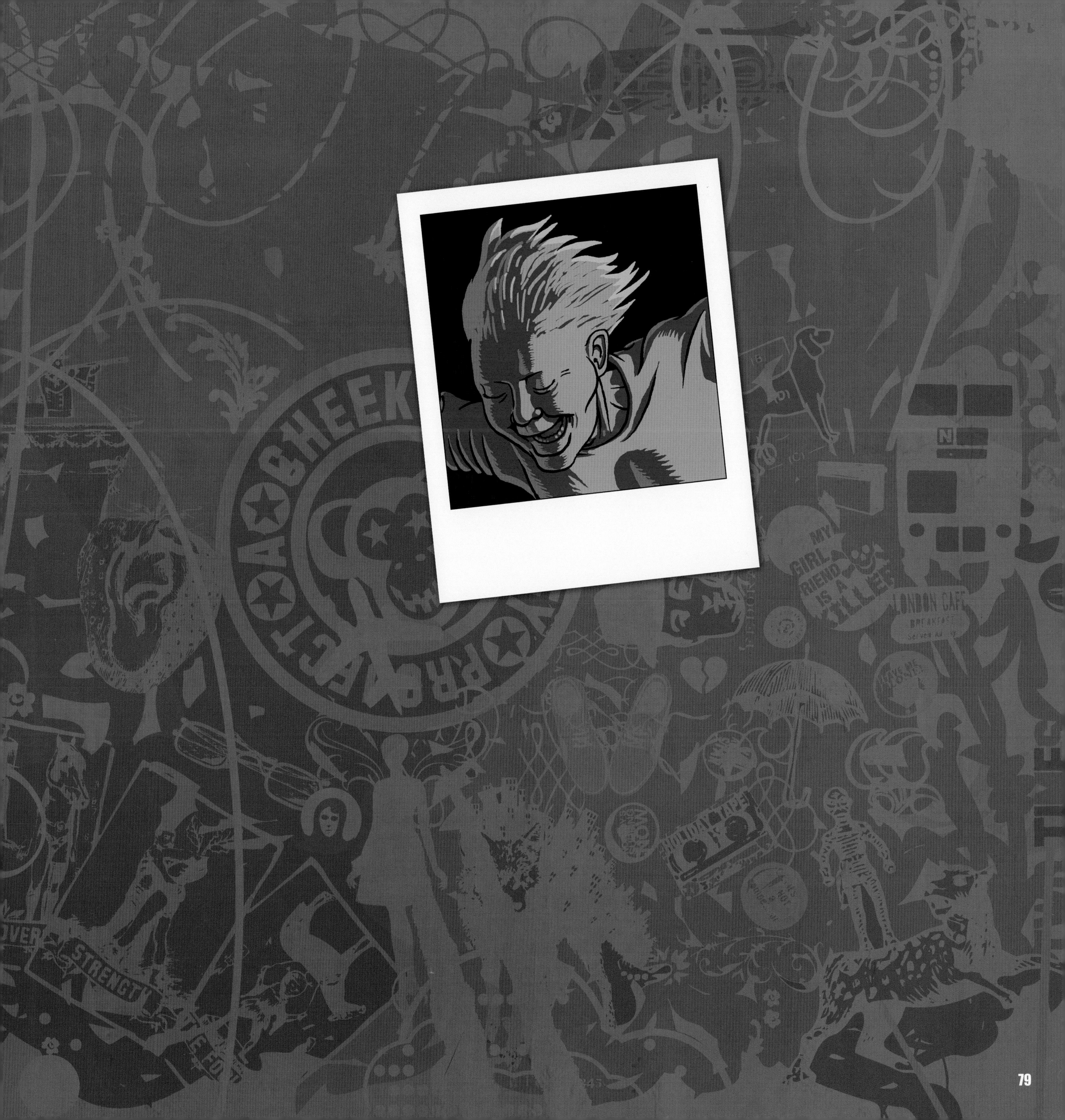
MY GIRL FRIEND IS A KILLER
LONDON CAFE
BREAKFAST
HOLIDAY TAPE

WEDNESDAY NIGHT

featured on **Paris in a Bottle**

story by **Harold Sipe**
art by **Buster Moody**

wednesday night
eight o'clock
i wish that i'd been late

maybe i'll
have a drink
if i'm going to have to wait

some people would
be comfortable
sitting here
on their own
me i sit
playing with my phone...

wednesday night
eight o'clock
i'm sure that's what we said

i've tried to ring
there's no reply...

it seems to me
they stare at me
it seems to me
they pity me
watching me
sat on my own

i wish i knew for sure
that i'd been stood up
at least then i'd know
that i could go...

wednesday night
nine o'clock
fifteen minutes more...

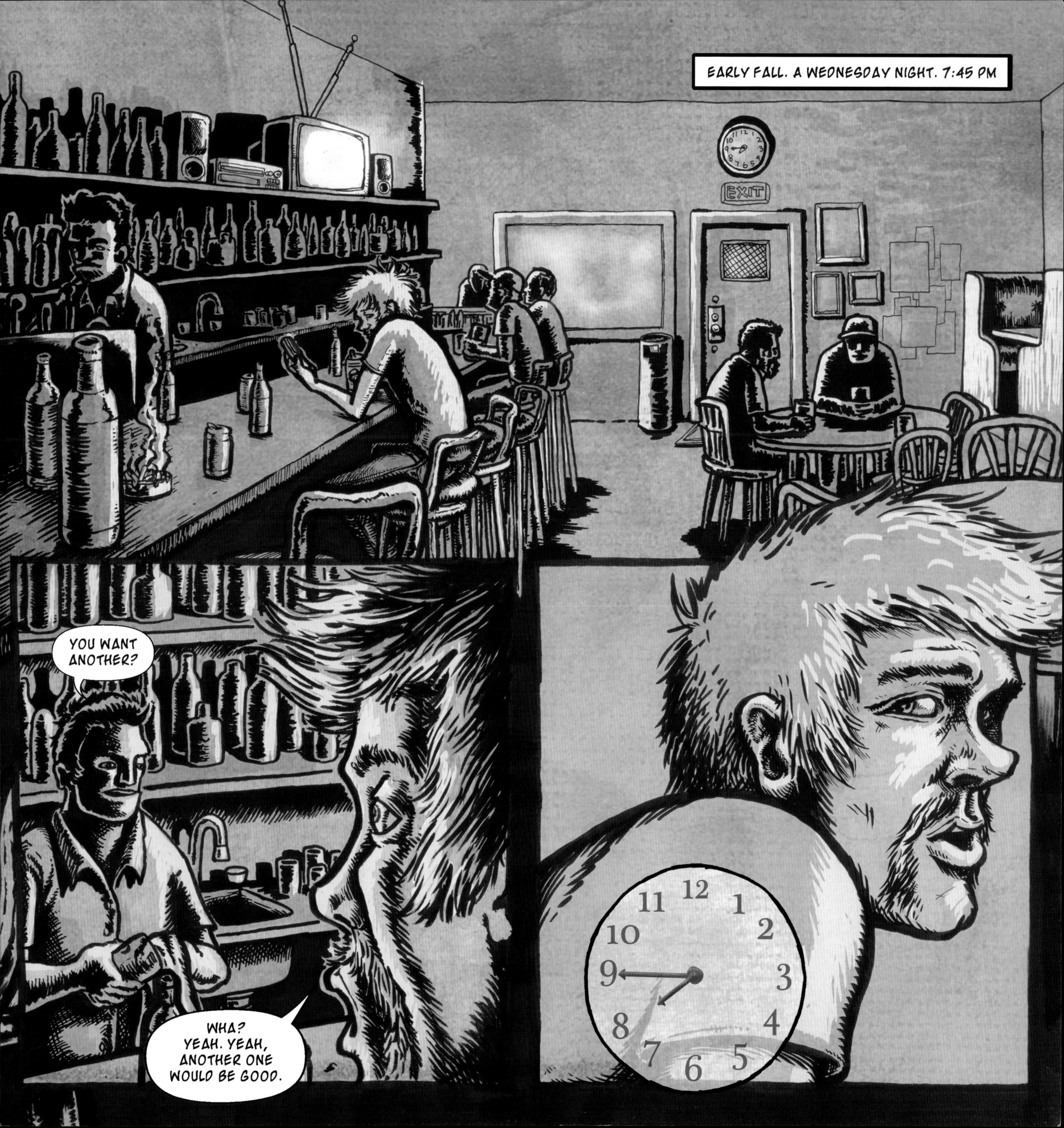
EARLY FALL. A WEDNESDAY NIGHT. 7:45 PM
EXIT
YOU WANT ANOTHER?
WHA? YEAH. YEAH, ANOTHER ONE WOULD BE GOOD.

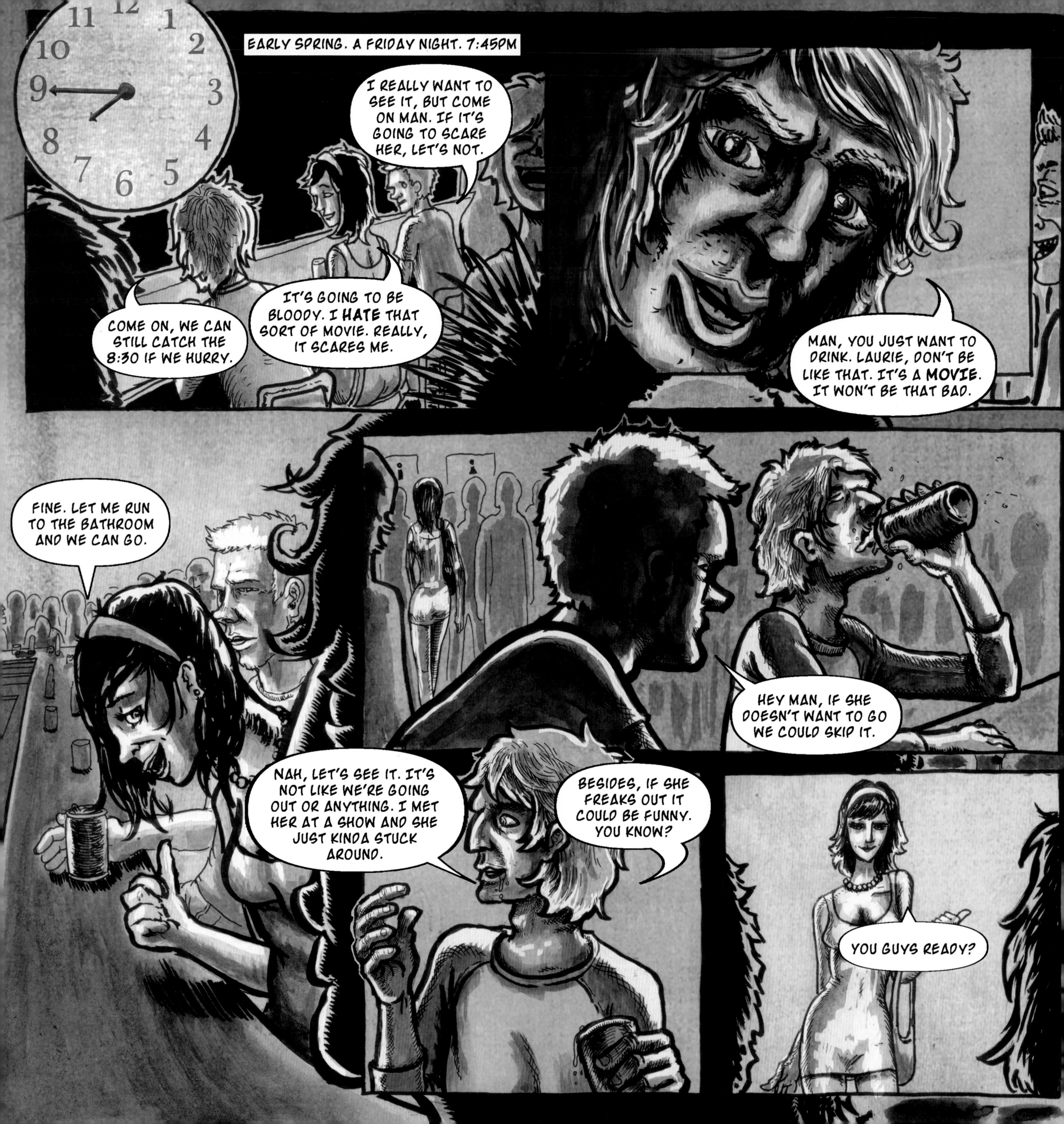

EARLY SPRING. A FRIDAY NIGHT. 7:45PM
I REALLY WANT TO SEE IT, BUT COME ON MAN. IF IT'S GOING TO SCARE HER, LET'S NOT.
COME ON, WE CAN STILL CATCH THE 8:30 IF WE HURRY.
IT'S GOING TO BE BLOODY. I **HATE** THAT SORT OF MOVIE. REALLY, IT SCARES ME.
MAN, YOU JUST WANT TO DRINK. LAURIE, DON'T BE LIKE THAT. IT'S A **MOVIE**. IT WON'T BE THAT BAD.
FINE. LET ME RUN TO THE BATHROOM AND WE CAN GO.
HEY MAN, IF SHE DOESN'T WANT TO GO WE COULD SKIP IT.
NAH, LET'S SEE IT. IT'S NOT LIKE WE'RE GOING OUT OR ANYTHING. I MET HER AT A SHOW AND SHE JUST KINDA STUCK AROUND.
BESIDES, IF SHE FREAKS OUT IT COULD BE FUNNY. YOU KNOW?
YOU GUYS READY?

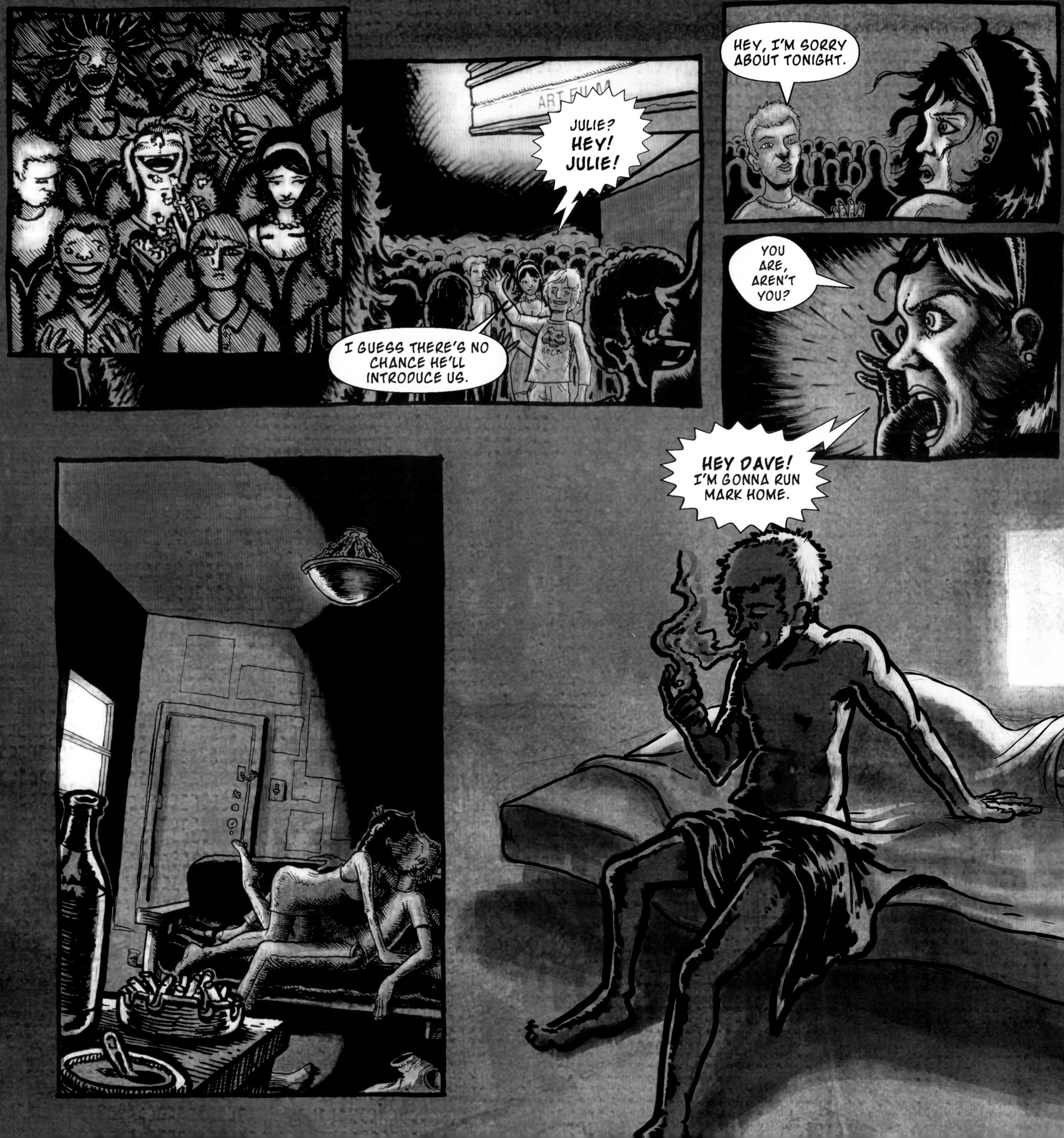
ART FILM
JULIE? HEY! JULIE!
I GUESS THERE'S NO CHANCE HE'LL INTRODUCE US.
ROCK
HEY, I'M SORRY ABOUT TONIGHT.
YOU ARE, AREN'T YOU?
HEY DAVE! I'M GONNA RUN MARK HOME.

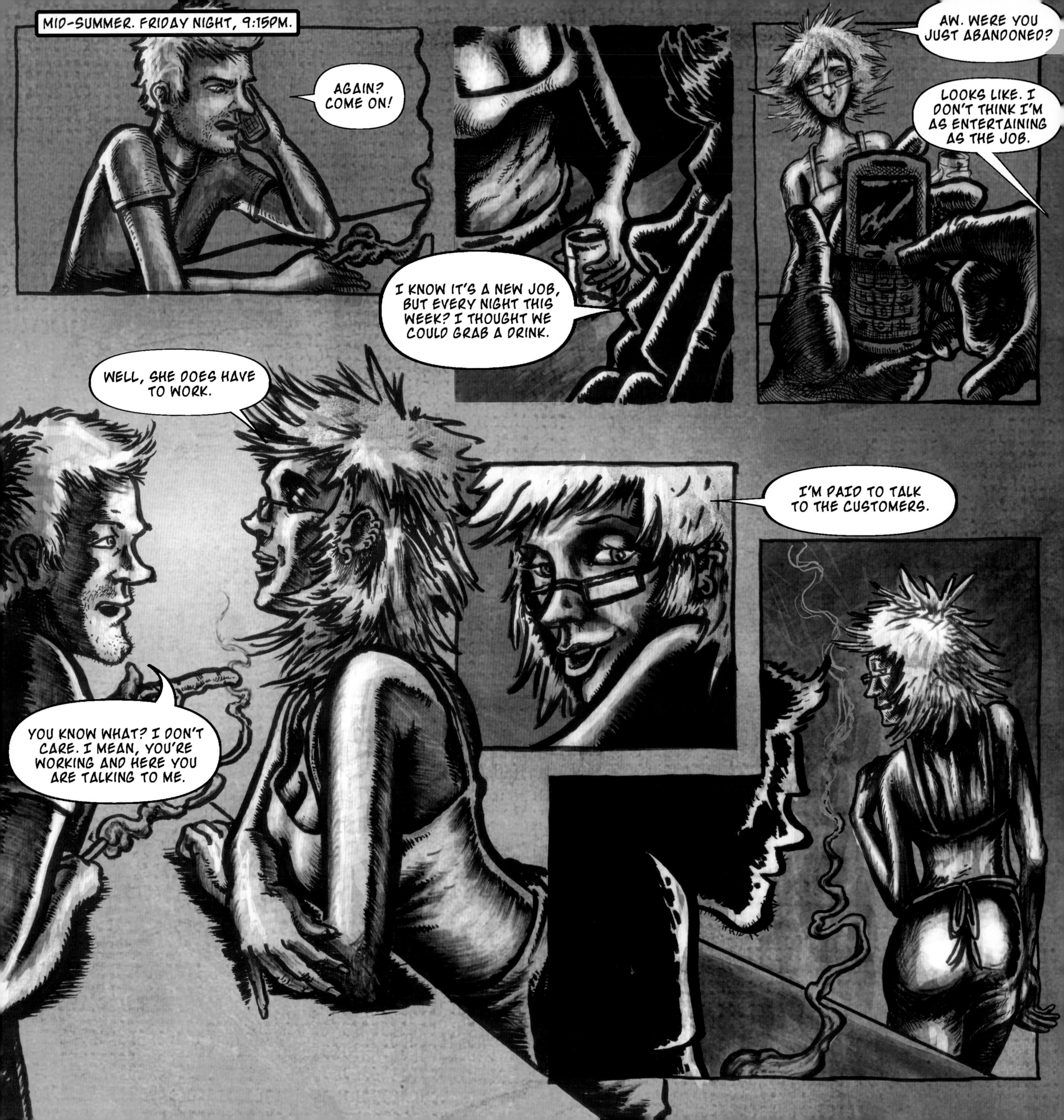
MID-SUMMER. FRIDAY NIGHT, 9:15PM.
AGAIN? COME ON!
I KNOW IT'S A NEW JOB, BUT EVERY NIGHT THIS WEEK? I THOUGHT WE COULD GRAB A DRINK.
AW. WERE YOU JUST ABANDONED?
LOOKS LIKE. I DON'T THINK I'M AS ENTERTAINING AS THE JOB.
WELL, SHE DOES HAVE TO WORK.
YOU KNOW WHAT? I DON'T CARE. I MEAN, YOU'RE WORKING AND HERE YOU ARE TALKING TO ME.
I'M PAID TO TALK TO THE CUSTOMERS.

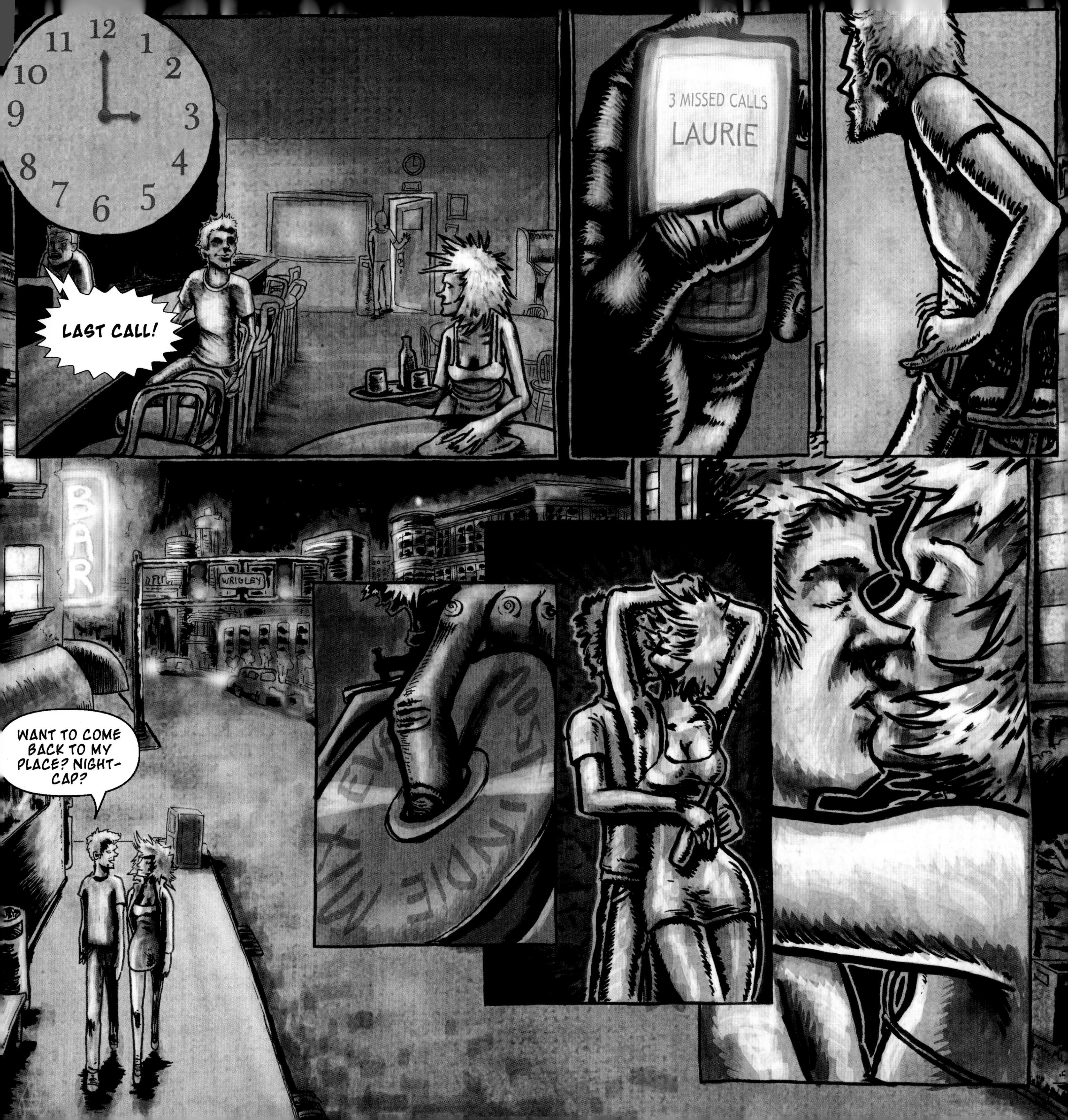
12
11
1
10
2
9
3
8
4
7
5
6
LAST CALL!
3 MISSED CALLS
LAURIE
BAR
WRIGLEY
WANT TO COME BACK TO MY PLACE? NIGHT-CAP?

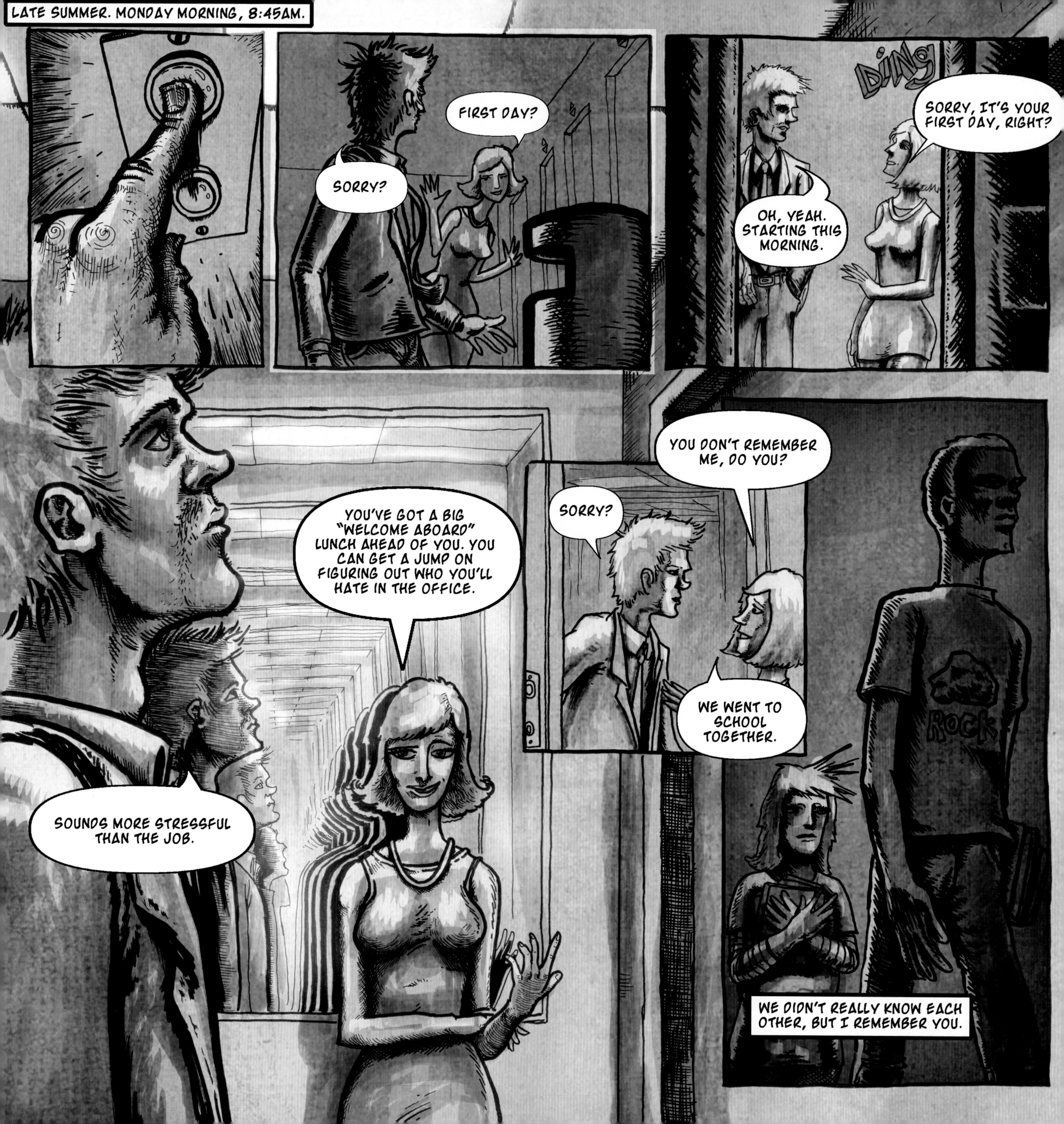
LATE SUMMER. MONDAY MORNING, 8:45AM.
FIRST DAY?
SORRY?
DING
SORRY, IT'S YOUR FIRST DAY, RIGHT?
OH, YEAH. STARTING THIS MORNING.
YOU'VE GOT A BIG "WELCOME ABOARD" LUNCH AHEAD OF YOU. YOU CAN GET A JUMP ON FIGURING OUT WHO YOU'LL HATE IN THE OFFICE.
SOUNDS MORE STRESSFUL THAN THE JOB.
SORRY?
YOU DON'T REMEMBER ME, DO YOU?
WE WENT TO SCHOOL TOGETHER.
ROCK
WE DIDN'T REALLY KNOW EACH OTHER, BUT I REMEMBER YOU.

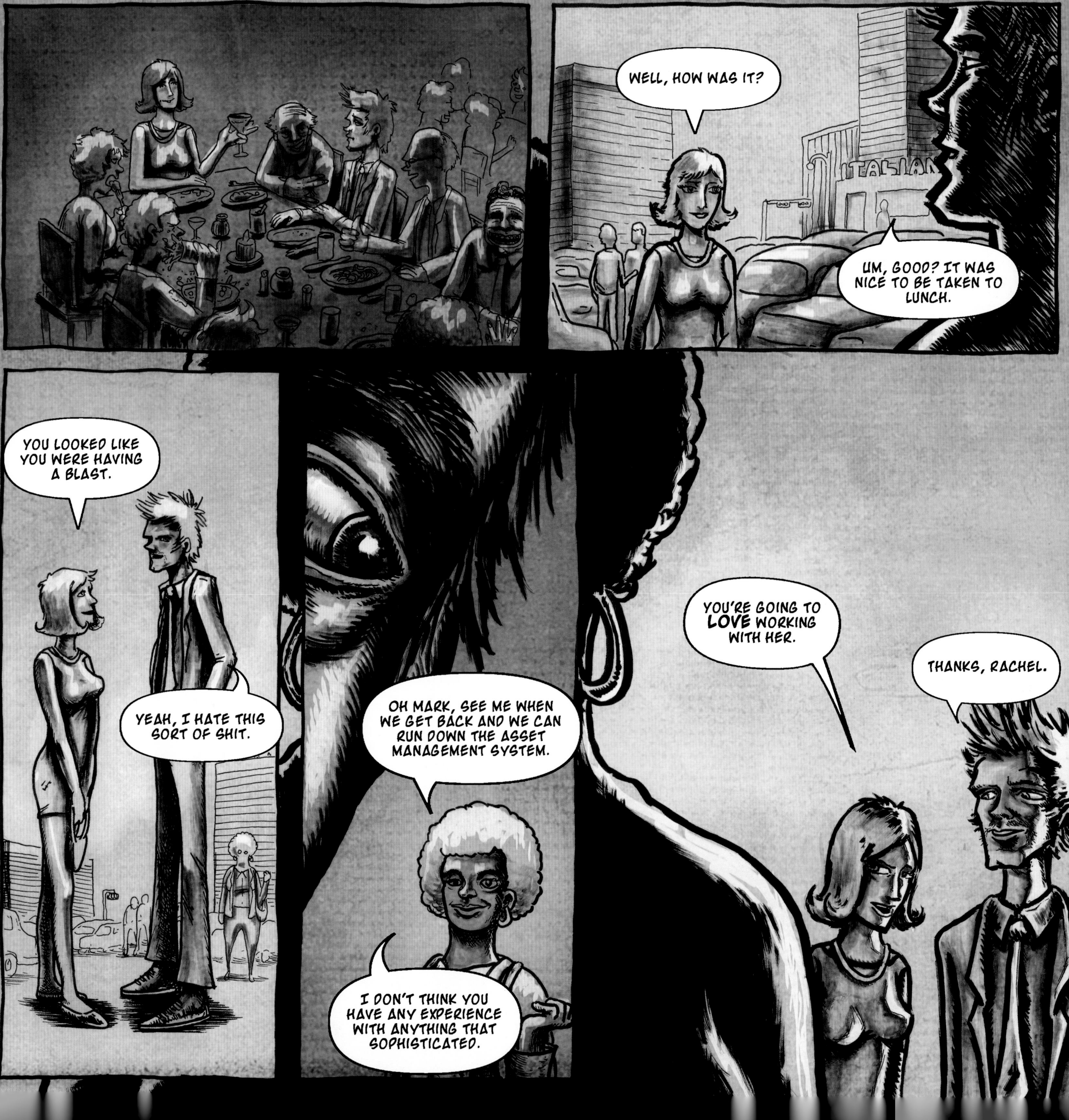
WELL, HOW WAS IT?
UM, GOOD? IT WAS NICE TO BE TAKEN TO LUNCH.
YOU LOOKED LIKE YOU WERE HAVING A BLAST.
YEAH, I HATE THIS SORT OF SHIT.
OH MARK, SEE ME WHEN WE GET BACK AND WE CAN RUN DOWN THE ASSET MANAGEMENT SYSTEM.
I DON'T THINK YOU HAVE ANY EXPERIENCE WITH ANYTHING THAT SOPHISTICATED.
YOU'RE GOING TO LOVE WORKING WITH HER.
THANKS, RACHEL.
ITALIAN

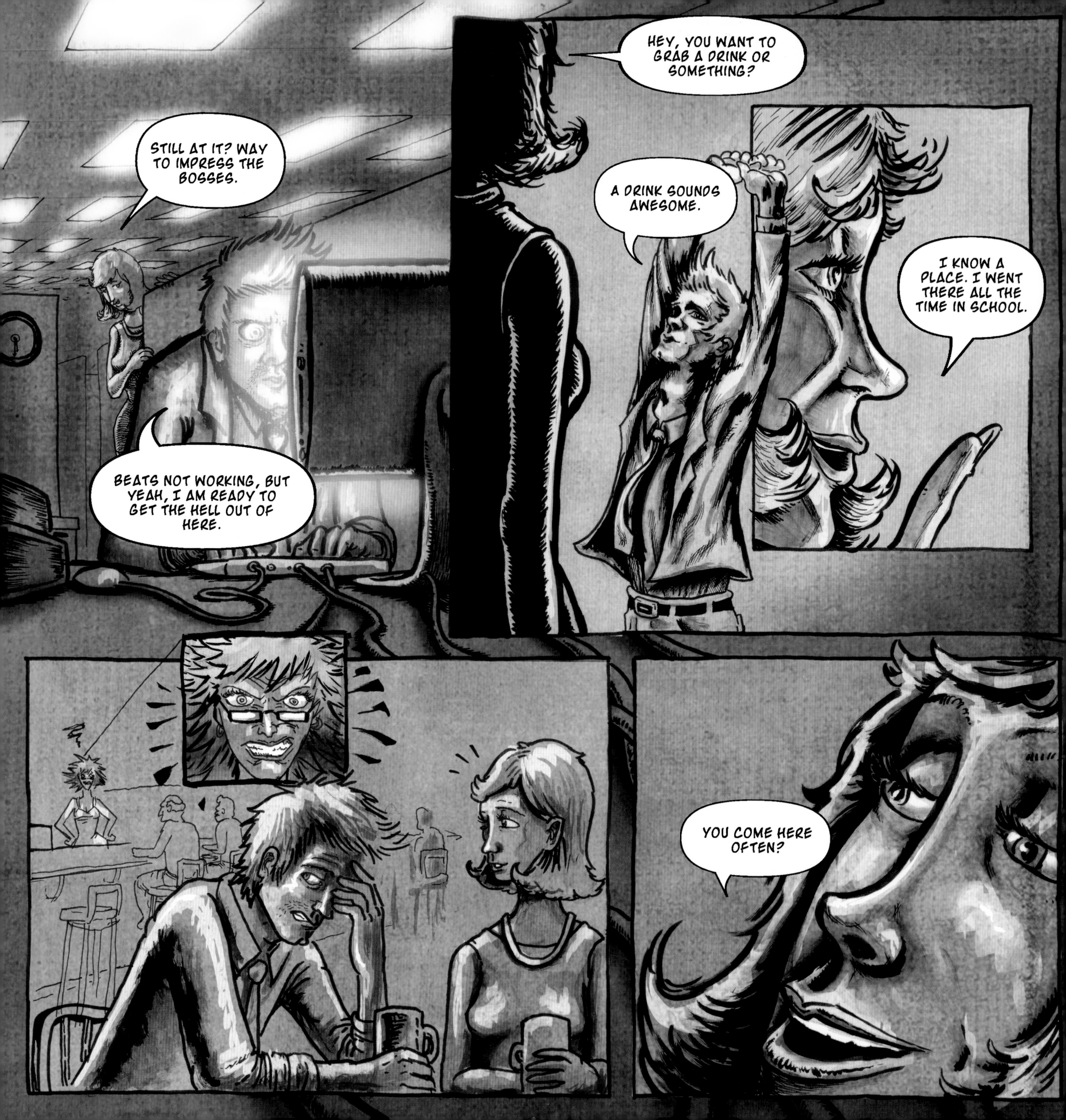
STILL AT IT? WAY TO IMPRESS THE BOSSES.
BEATS NOT WORKING, BUT YEAH, I AM READY TO GET THE HELL OUT OF HERE.
HEY, YOU WANT TO GRAB A DRINK OR SOMETHING?
A DRINK SOUNDS AWESOME.
I KNOW A PLACE. I WENT THERE ALL THE TIME IN SCHOOL.
YOU COME HERE OFTEN?

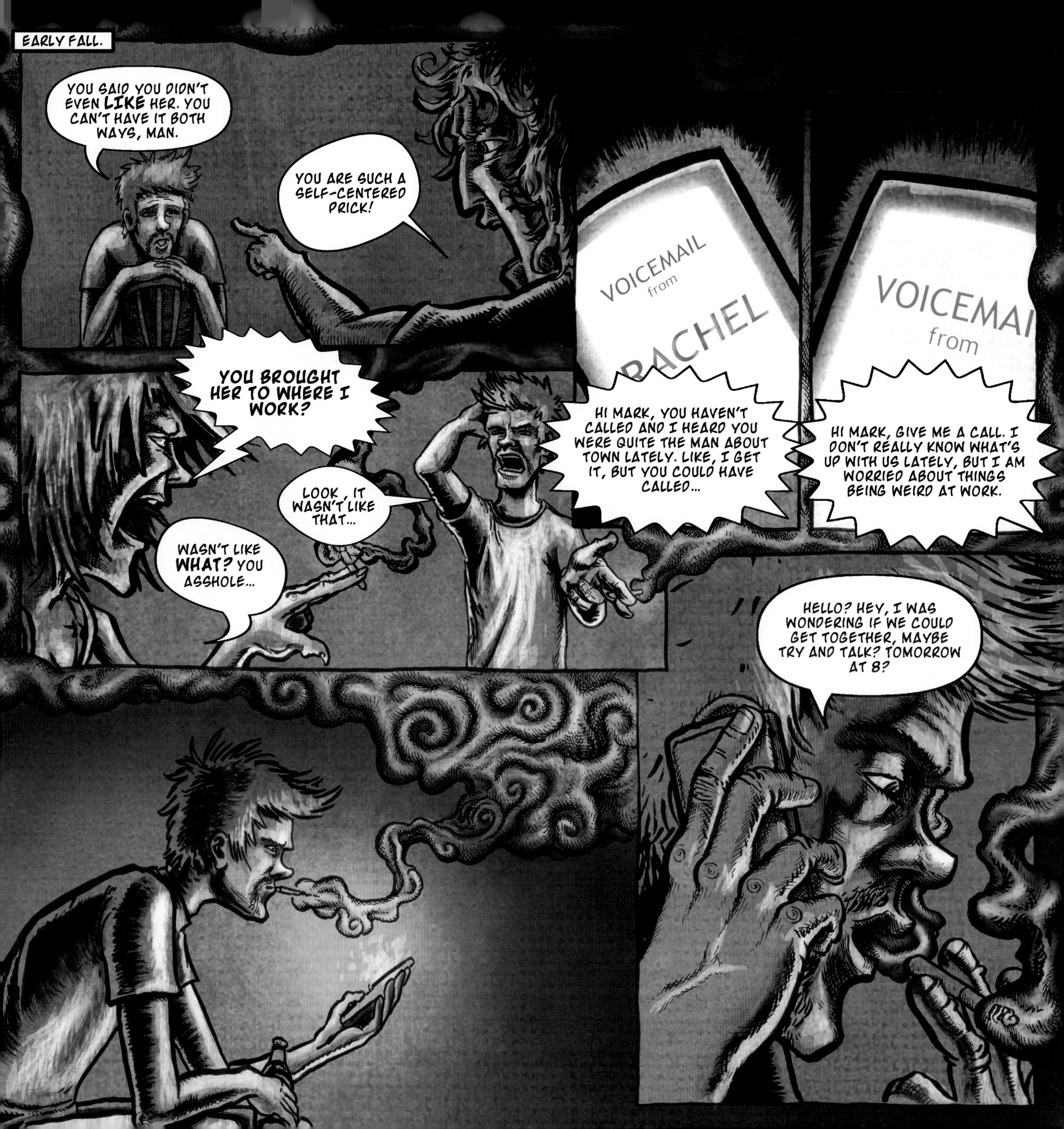
EARLY FALL.
YOU SAID YOU DIDN'T EVEN LIKE HER. YOU CAN'T HAVE IT BOTH WAYS, MAN.
YOU ARE SUCH A SELF-CENTERED PRICK!
VOICEMAIL from RACHEL
VOICEMAIL from
YOU BROUGHT HER TO WHERE I WORK?
LOOK , IT WASN'T LIKE THAT...
WASN'T LIKE WHAT? YOU ASSHOLE...
HI MARK, YOU HAVEN'T CALLED AND I HEARD YOU WERE QUITE THE MAN ABOUT TOWN LATELY. LIKE, I GET IT, BUT YOU COULD HAVE CALLED...
HI MARK, GIVE ME A CALL. I DON'T REALLY KNOW WHAT'S UP WITH US LATELY, BUT I AM WORRIED ABOUT THINGS BEING WEIRD AT WORK.
HELLO? HEY, I WAS WONDERING IF WE COULD GET TOGETHER, MAYBE TRY AND TALK? TOMORROW AT 8?

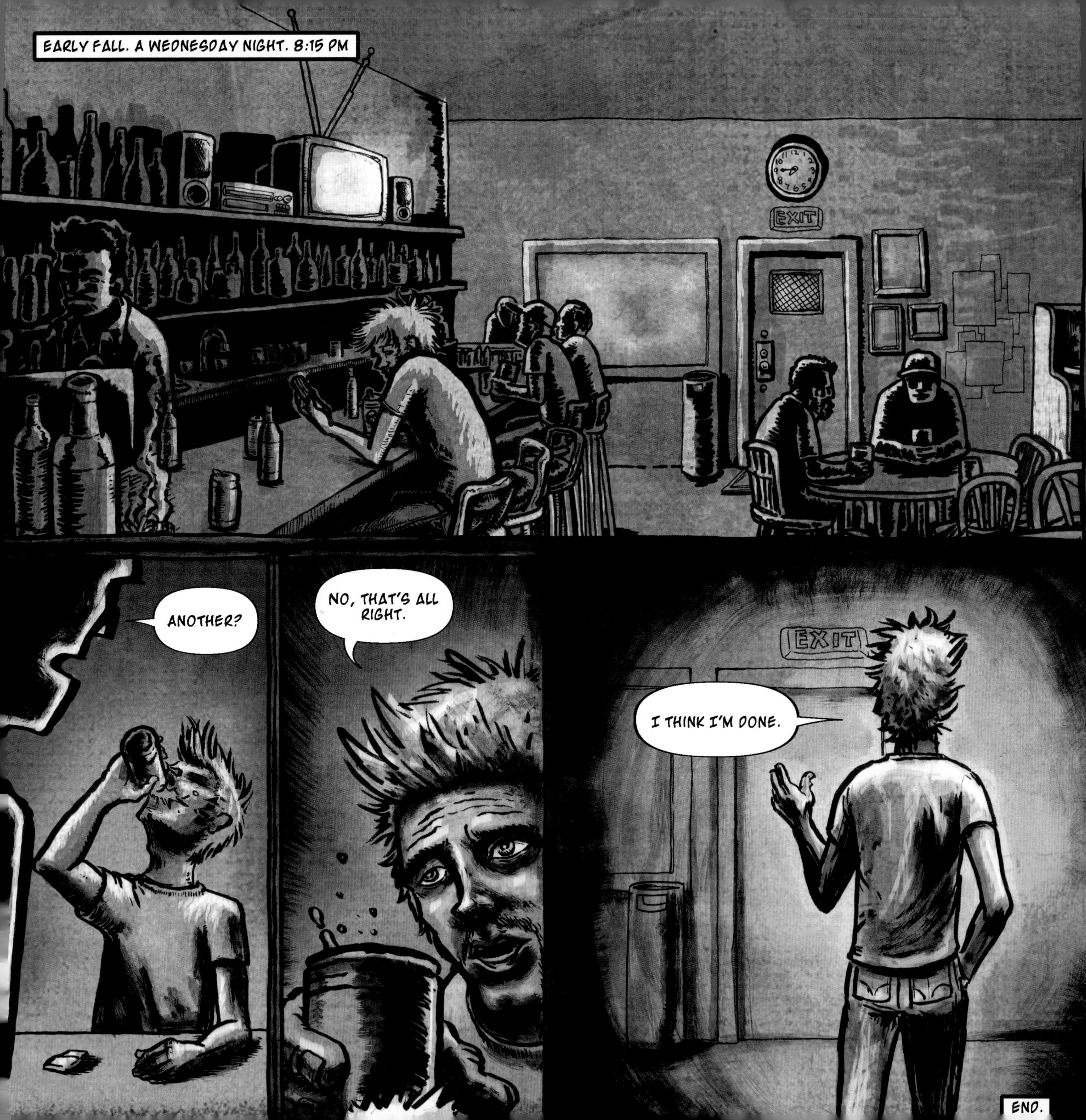
EARLY FALL. A WEDNESDAY NIGHT. 8:15 PM
EXIT
ANOTHER?
NO, THAT'S ALL RIGHT.
EXIT
I THINK I'M DONE.
END.

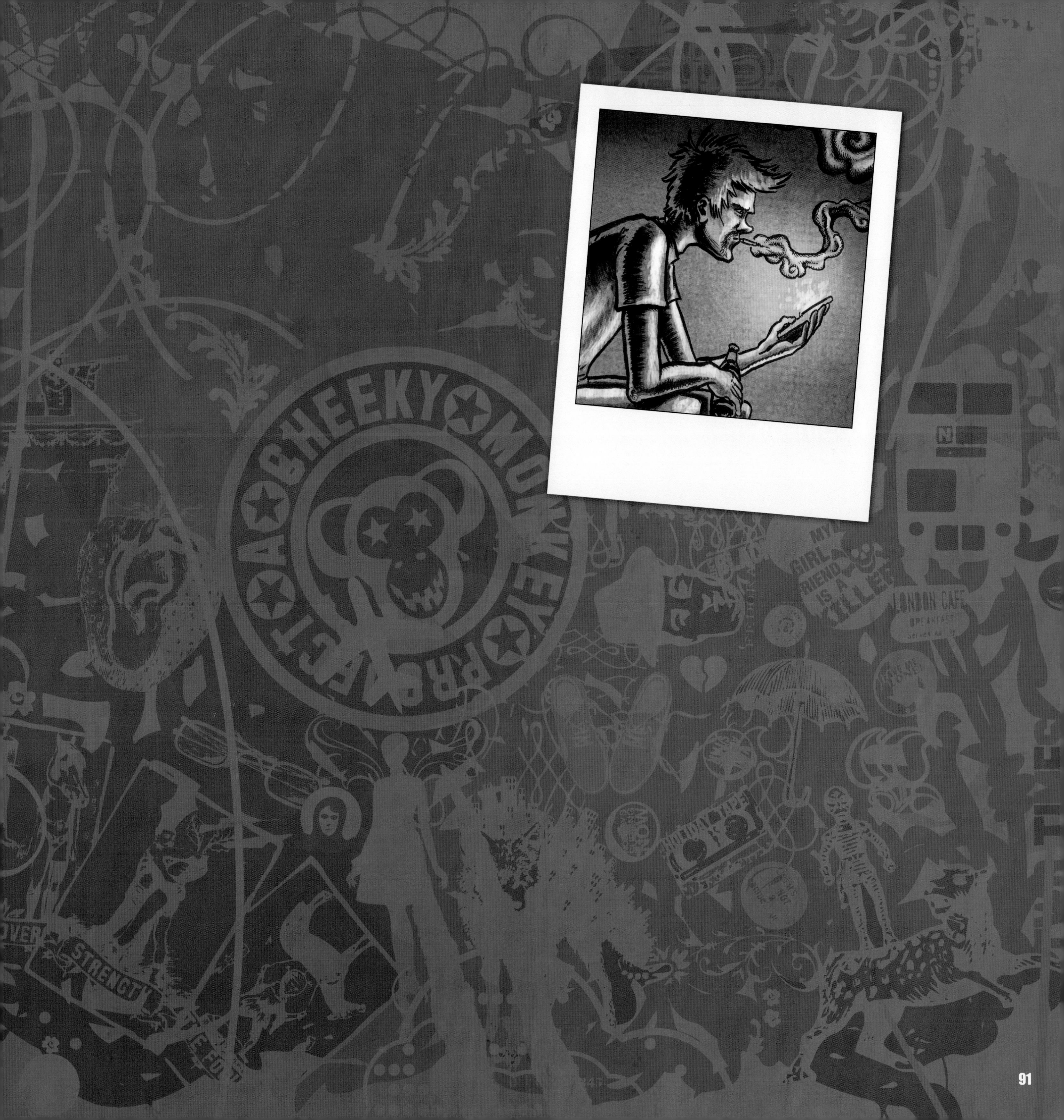
A CHEEKY MONKEY PROJECT
LONDON CAFE
BREAKFAST
STRENGTH
HOLIDAY TAPE

THE LAST BUS HOME

featured on **A Leopard and Other Stories**

story by **Derek McCulloch**
art by **Jimmie Robinson**

the wrong bus comes i stand near it anyway
feel the warm air from the engine
twenty people shivering, waiting
for the last bus home

top deck on the left so you get the heater
sit in silence and sway around
i've got a lot of thinking to do
on the last bus home

find a bottle in my bag
cold water running down my throat
down down into my belly
on the last bus home

his lovely large leering mouth
he leans across to his friend josie
he leans towards me and he's sick on the floor
on the last bus home

stirring up the dust, stirring up the memories
i catch a glimpse of my reflection
it is my father staring back at me

flowers taped to the railings
a photograph in a plastic folder
stuck in traffic at 4am
on the last bus home

trying to look inside people's windows
probably catch glimpses of three-way sex
all i see is people watching tv
and someone watching me

dad drove up on the pavement
on his way to the hospital
i say "you're not steve mcqueen you know"
though inside i thought "maybe you are
maybe you are"

it's pitch black and it's pouring down
somebody's washing is still out on the line
i'm thinking about living out of london
on the last bus home

josie nods, falls, sleeps, dreams of travel
the eiffel tower and a sea of colour
mr city fox slips into an alleyway
he's going home

i don't believe in destiny
i don't believe in fate
i don't believe that you and i
were meant to be together
but love is great when it's this easy
all you've got to do is stick around

she thinks that david thewlis is ian hart
she thinks when the clock goes back
you have to change the timers
she lost my stereolab cd

shuddering against the glass
falling asleep still thinking of allison
waking up and i've missed my stop
and now i'm all alone

a bus pass and a pair of specs
a black scarf and a record bag
all left, lost, forgotten
on the last bus home

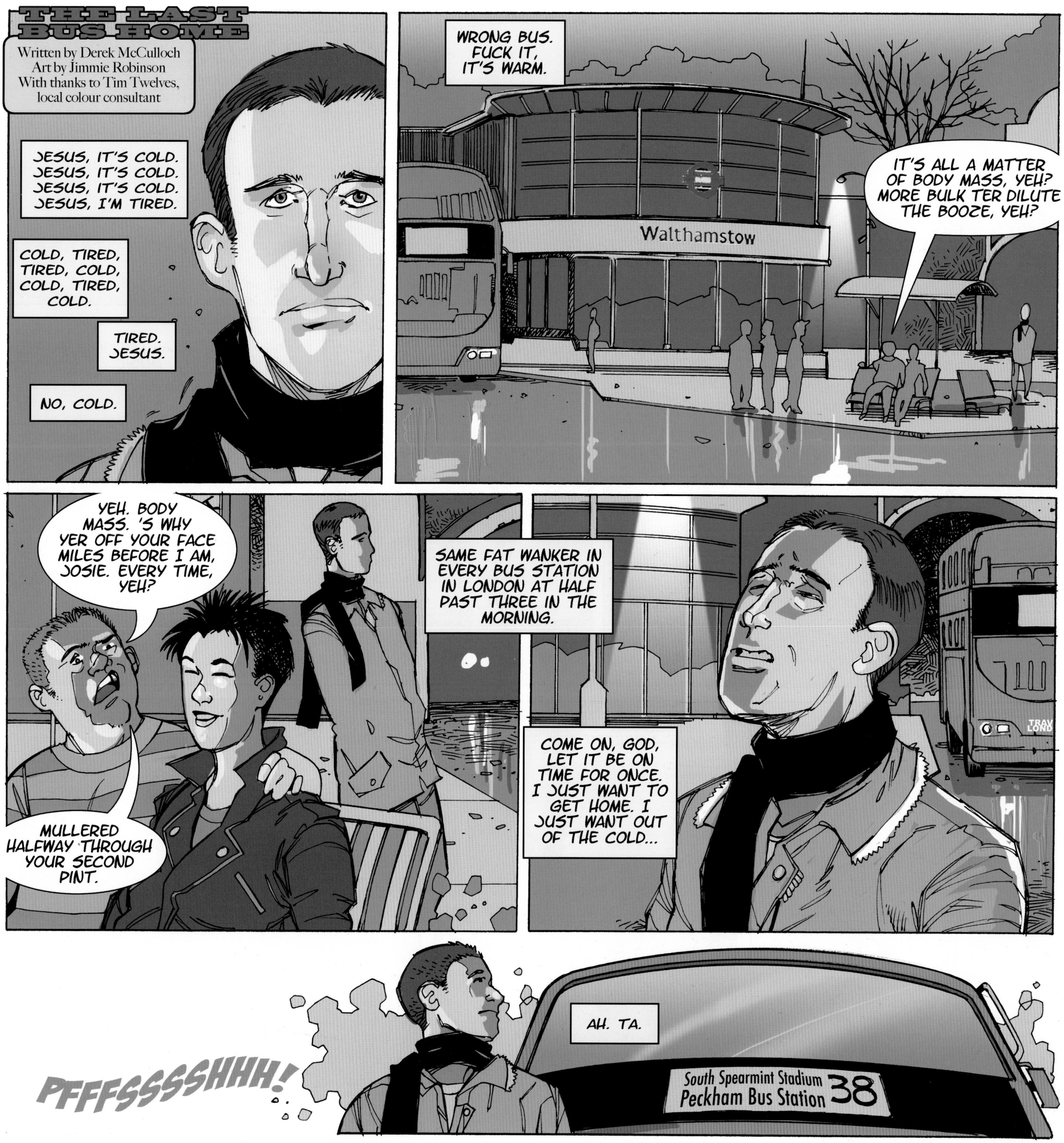
THE LAST BUS HOME
Written by Derek McCulloch
Art by Jimmie Robinson
With thanks to Tim Twelves, local colour consultant
JESUS, IT'S COLD. JESUS, IT'S COLD. JESUS, IT'S COLD. JESUS, I'M TIRED.
COLD, TIRED, TIRED, COLD, COLD, TIRED, COLD.
TIRED. JESUS.
NO, COLD.
WRONG BUS. FUCK IT, IT'S WARM.
Walthamstow
IT'S ALL A MATTER OF BODY MASS, YEH? MORE BULK TER DILUTE THE BOOZE, YEH?
YEH. BODY MASS. 'S WHY YER OFF YOUR FACE MILES BEFORE I AM, JOSIE. EVERY TIME, YEH?
MULLERED HALFWAY THROUGH YOUR SECOND PINT.
SAME FAT WANKER IN EVERY BUS STATION IN LONDON AT HALF PAST THREE IN THE MORNING.
COME ON, GOD, LET IT BE ON TIME FOR ONCE. I JUST WANT TO GET HOME. I JUST WANT OUT OF THE COLD...
PFFFSSSSHHH!
AH. TA.
South Spearmint Stadium
Peckham Bus Station 38

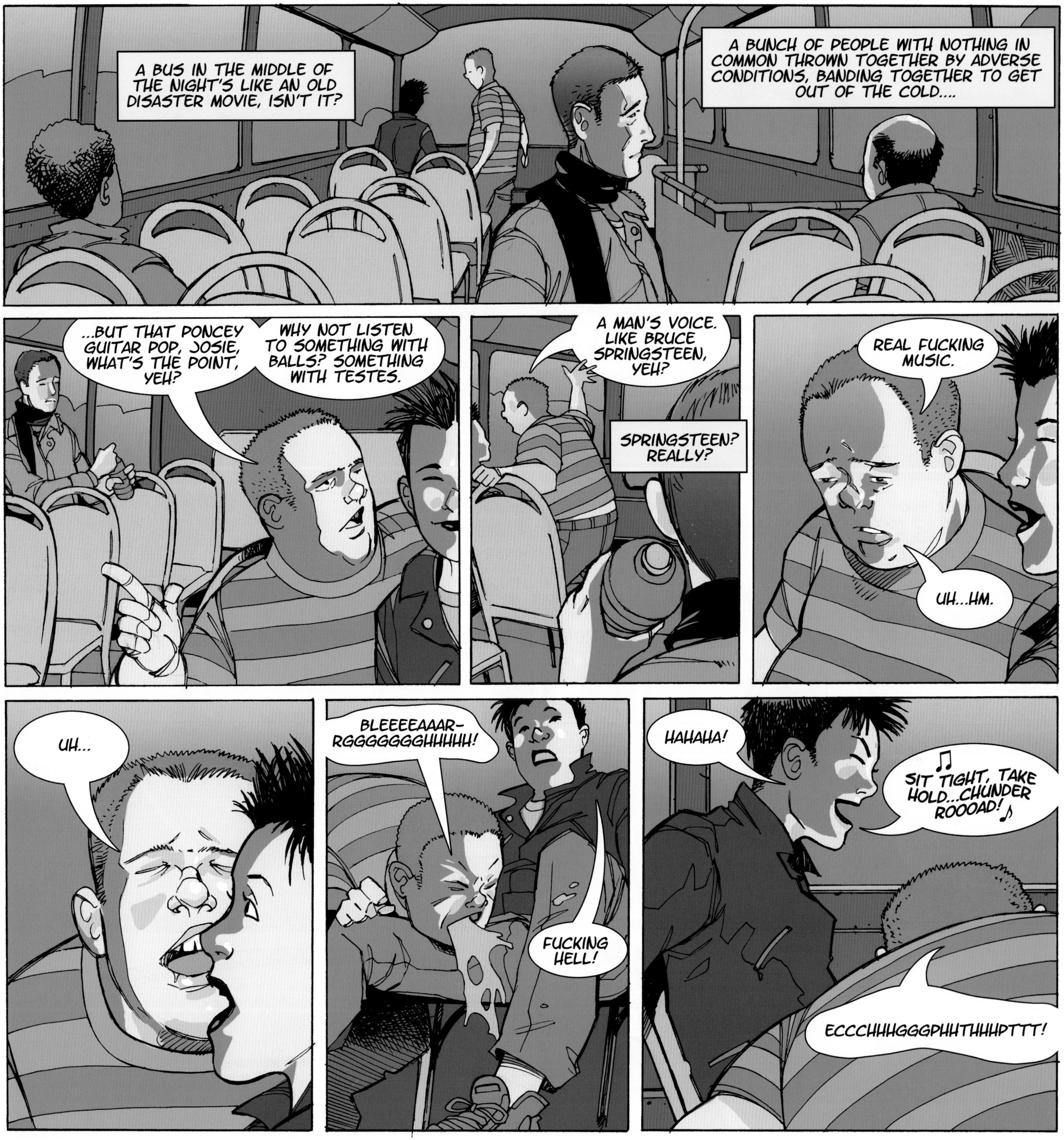
A BUS IN THE MIDDLE OF THE NIGHT'S LIKE AN OLD DISASTER MOVIE, ISN'T IT?
A BUNCH OF PEOPLE WITH NOTHING IN COMMON THROWN TOGETHER BY ADVERSE CONDITIONS, BANDING TOGETHER TO GET OUT OF THE COLD....
...BUT THAT PONCEY GUITAR POP, JOSIE, WHAT'S THE POINT, YEH?
WHY NOT LISTEN TO SOMETHING WITH BALLS? SOMETHING WITH TESTES.
A MAN'S VOICE. LIKE BRUCE SPRINGSTEEN, YEH?
SPRINGSTEEN? REALLY?
REAL FUCKING MUSIC.
UH...HM.
UH...
BLEEEEAAAR-RGGGGGGGHHHHH!
FUCKING HELL!
HAHAHA!
SIT TIGHT, TAKE HOLD...CHUNDER ROOOAD!
ECCCHHHGGGPHHTHHHPTTT!

HATE TO BE THE POOR BUGGER HAS TO CLEAN THAT UP, YEH?

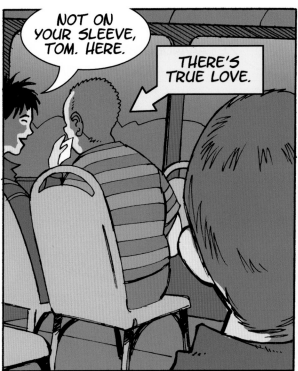

NOT ON YOUR SLEEVE, TOM. HERE.

THERE'S TRUE LOVE.

EVERYWHERE YOU LOOK, WHEN YOU START THINKING ABOUT IT.

DIRTY THREE-WAY, MAYBE?

granola granny yoga

RECORDS

38

MM. TAKING A BREAK BEFORE THEY PUT THE KUNDALINI YOGA VIDEO BACK ON, MORE LIKE.

OH. HULLO, DAD.

RIGHT. NOW YOU KNOW WHAT I MEAN BY "KEEP YOUR HANDS AWAY FROM THE BLOODY BAND SAW," DON'T YOU?

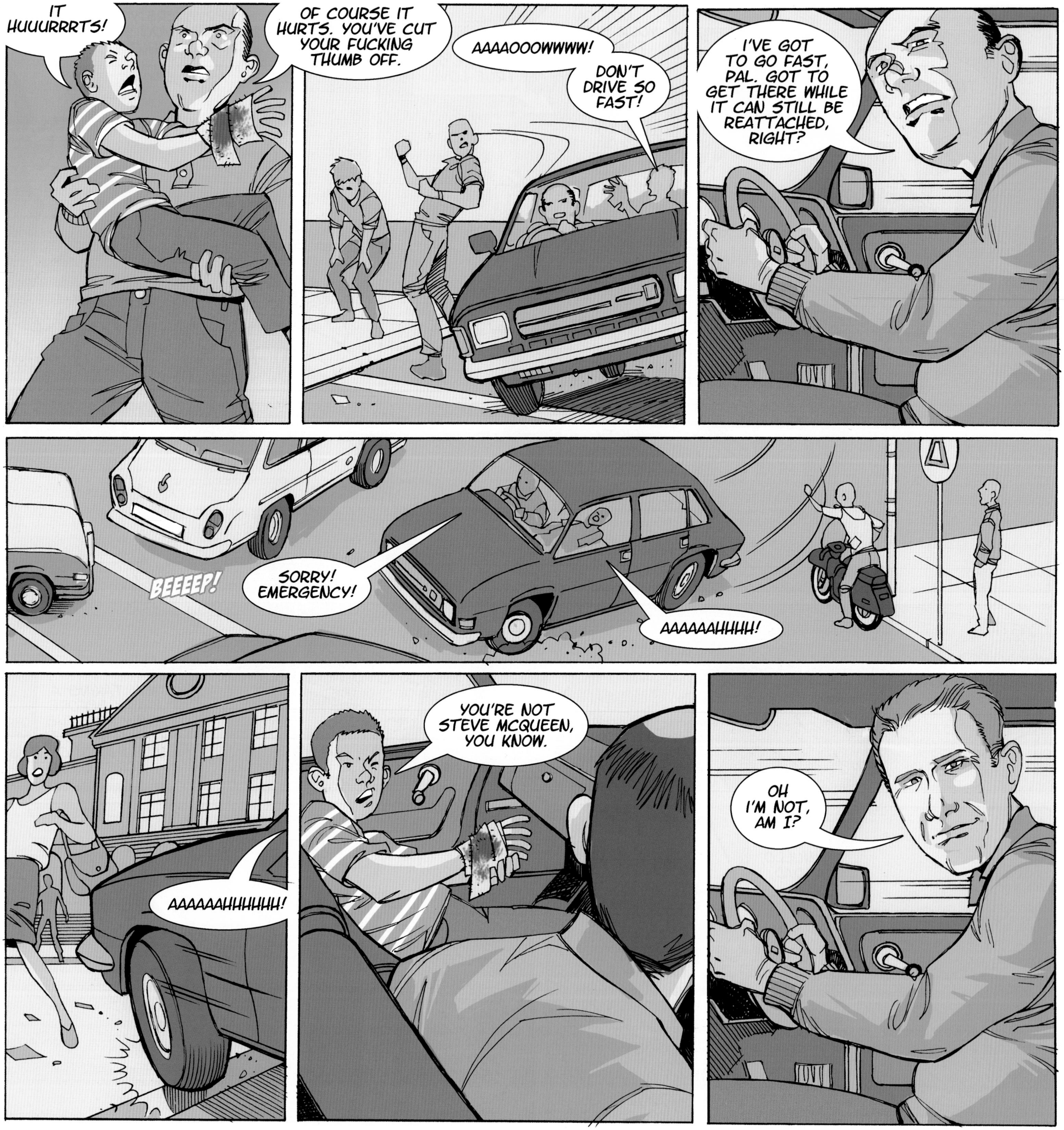
IT HUUURRRTS!
OF COURSE IT HURTS. YOU'VE CUT YOUR FUCKING THUMB OFF.
AAAAOOOWWWW!
DON'T DRIVE SO FAST!
I'VE GOT TO GO FAST, PAL. GOT TO GET THERE WHILE IT CAN STILL BE REATTACHED, RIGHT?
BEEEEP!
SORRY! EMERGENCY!
AAAAAAHHHH!
AAAAAAHHHHHH!
YOU'RE NOT STEVE MCQUEEN, YOU KNOW.
OH I'M NOT, AM I?

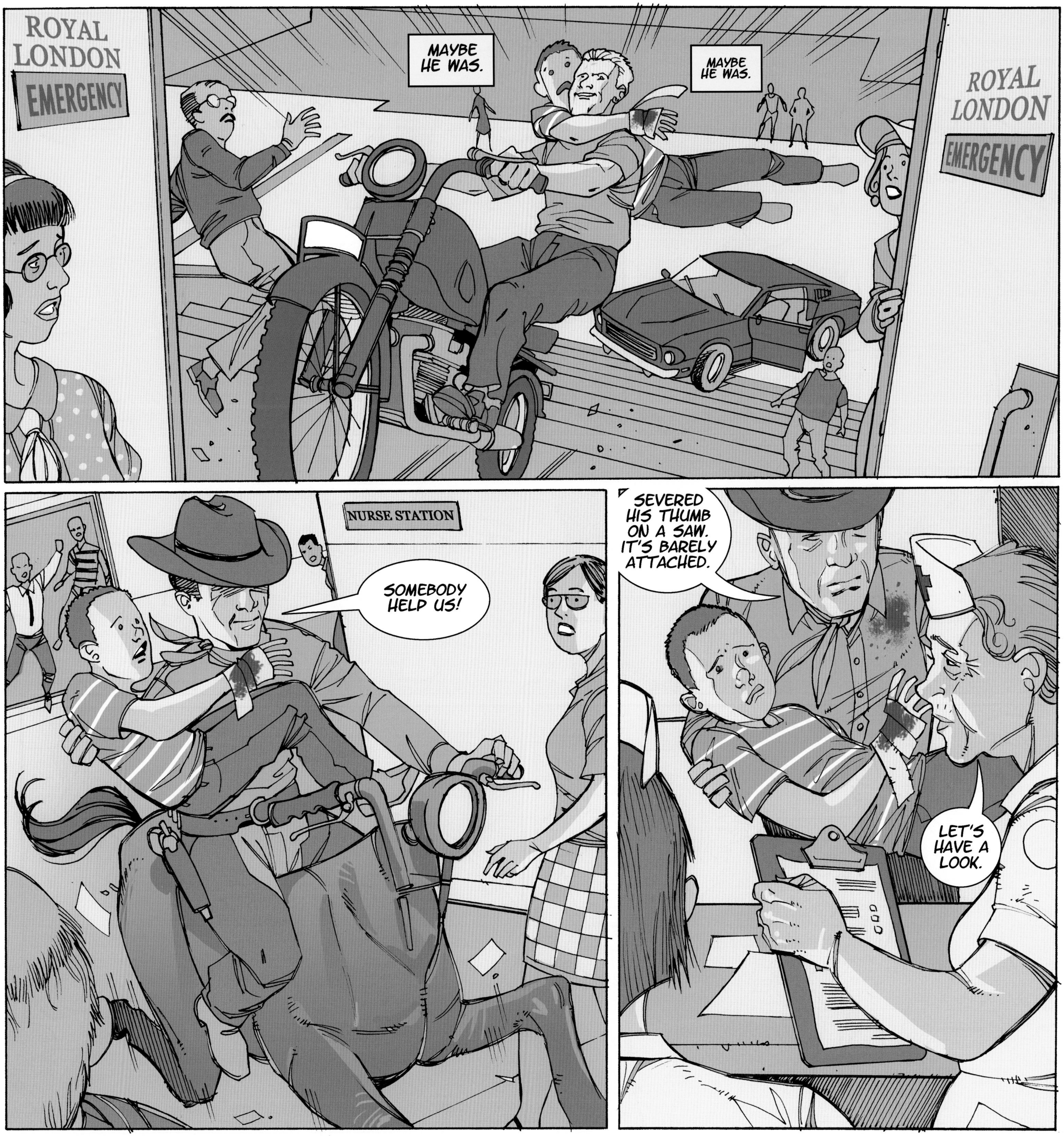
ROYAL LONDON
EMERGENCY
MAYBE HE WAS.
MAYBE HE WAS.
ROYAL LONDON
EMERGENCY
NURSE STATION
SOMEBODY HELP US!
SEVERED HIS THUMB ON A SAW. IT'S BARELY ATTACHED.
LET'S HAVE A LOOK.

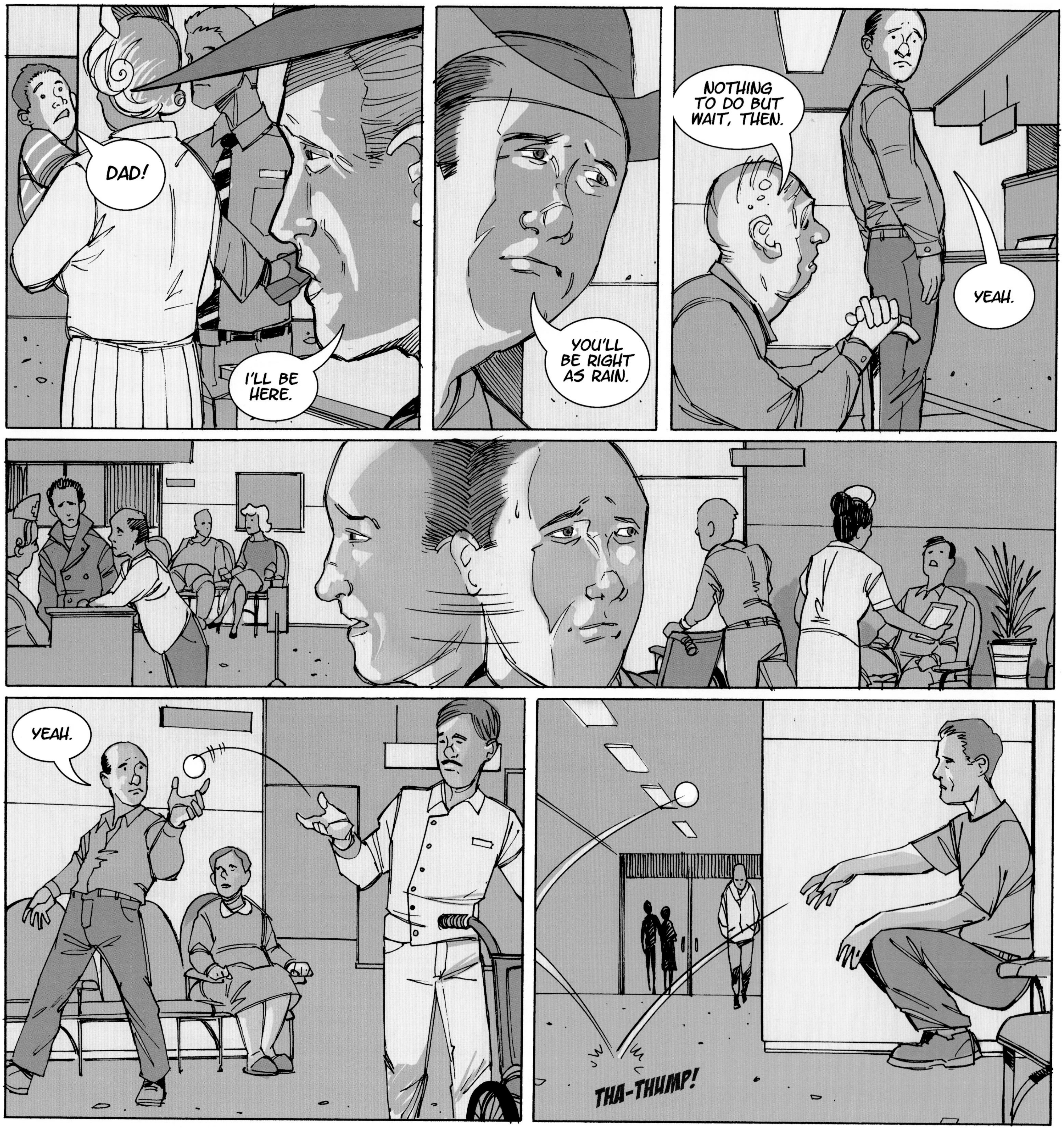
DAD!
I'LL BE HERE.
YOU'LL BE RIGHT AS RAIN.
NOTHING TO DO BUT WAIT, THEN.
YEAH.
YEAH.
THA-THUMP!

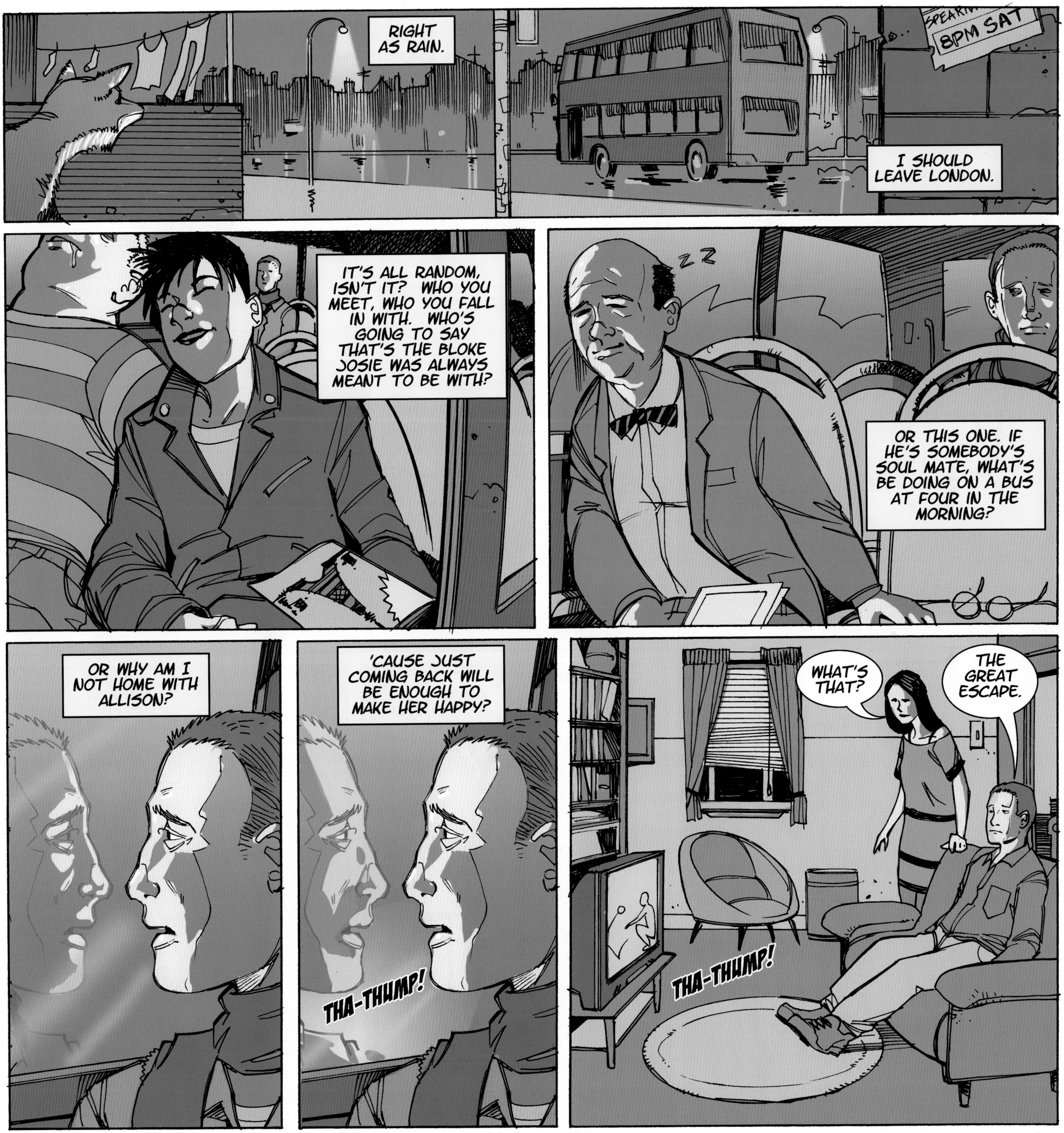

SPEARM
8PM SAT
RIGHT AS RAIN.
I SHOULD LEAVE LONDON.
IT'S ALL RANDOM, ISN'T IT? WHO YOU MEET, WHO YOU FALL IN WITH. WHO'S GOING TO SAY THAT'S THE BLOKE JOSIE WAS ALWAYS MEANT TO BE WITH?
Z Z
OR THIS ONE. IF HE'S SOMEBODY'S SOUL MATE, WHAT'S BE DOING ON A BUS AT FOUR IN THE MORNING?
OR WHY AM I NOT HOME WITH ALLISON?
'CAUSE JUST COMING BACK WILL BE ENOUGH TO MAKE HER HAPPY?
THA-THUMP!
WHAT'S THAT?
THE GREAT ESCAPE.
THA-THUMP!

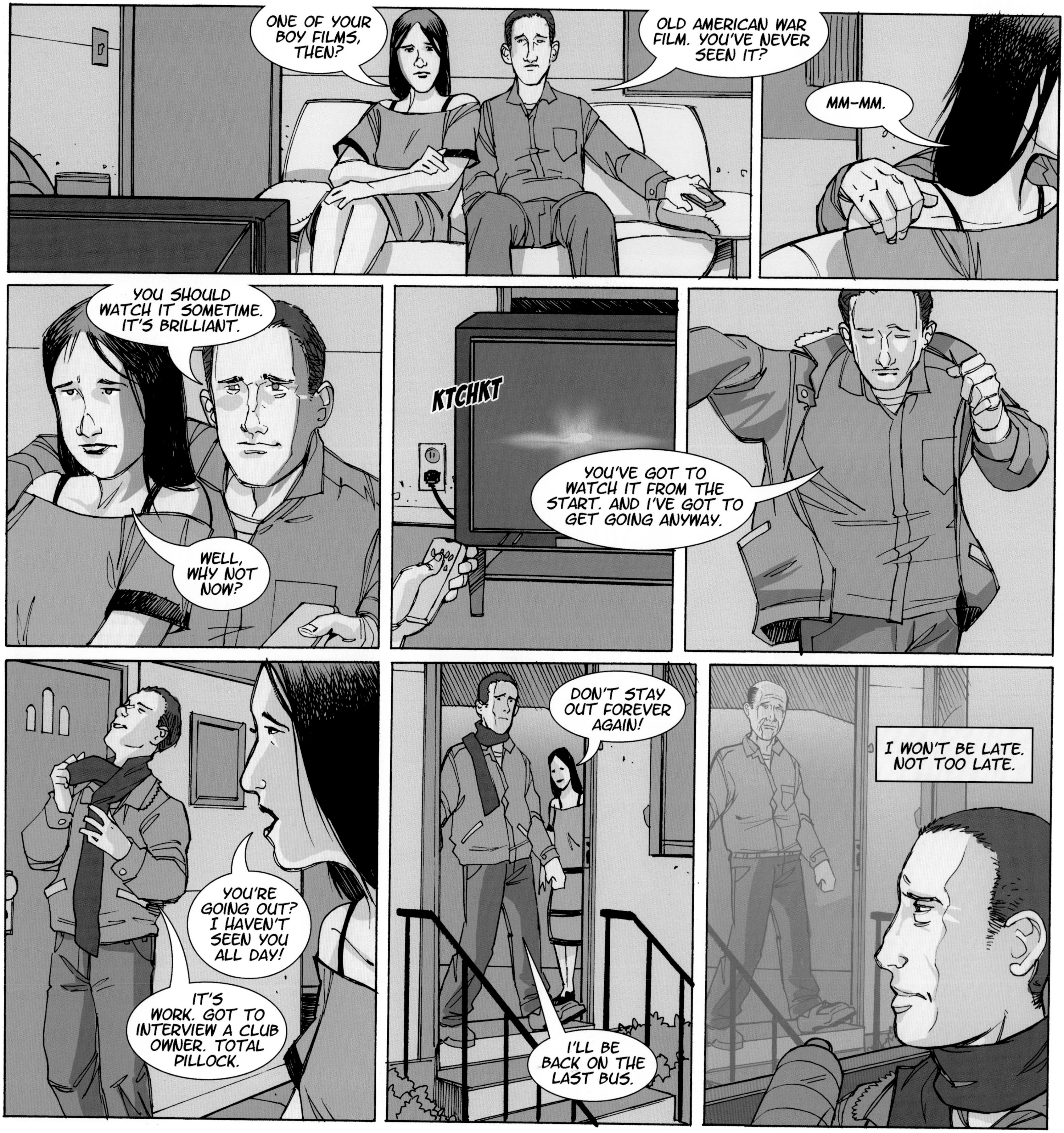
ONE OF YOUR BOY FILMS, THEN?
OLD AMERICAN WAR FILM. YOU'VE NEVER SEEN IT?
MM-MM.
YOU SHOULD WATCH IT SOMETIME. IT'S BRILLIANT.
WELL, WHY NOT NOW?
KTCHKT
YOU'VE GOT TO WATCH IT FROM THE START. AND I'VE GOT TO GET GOING ANYWAY.
YOU'RE GOING OUT? I HAVEN'T SEEN YOU ALL DAY!
IT'S WORK. GOT TO INTERVIEW A CLUB OWNER. TOTAL PILLOCK.
DON'T STAY OUT FOREVER AGAIN!
I'LL BE BACK ON THE LAST BUS.
I WON'T BE LATE. NOT TOO LATE.

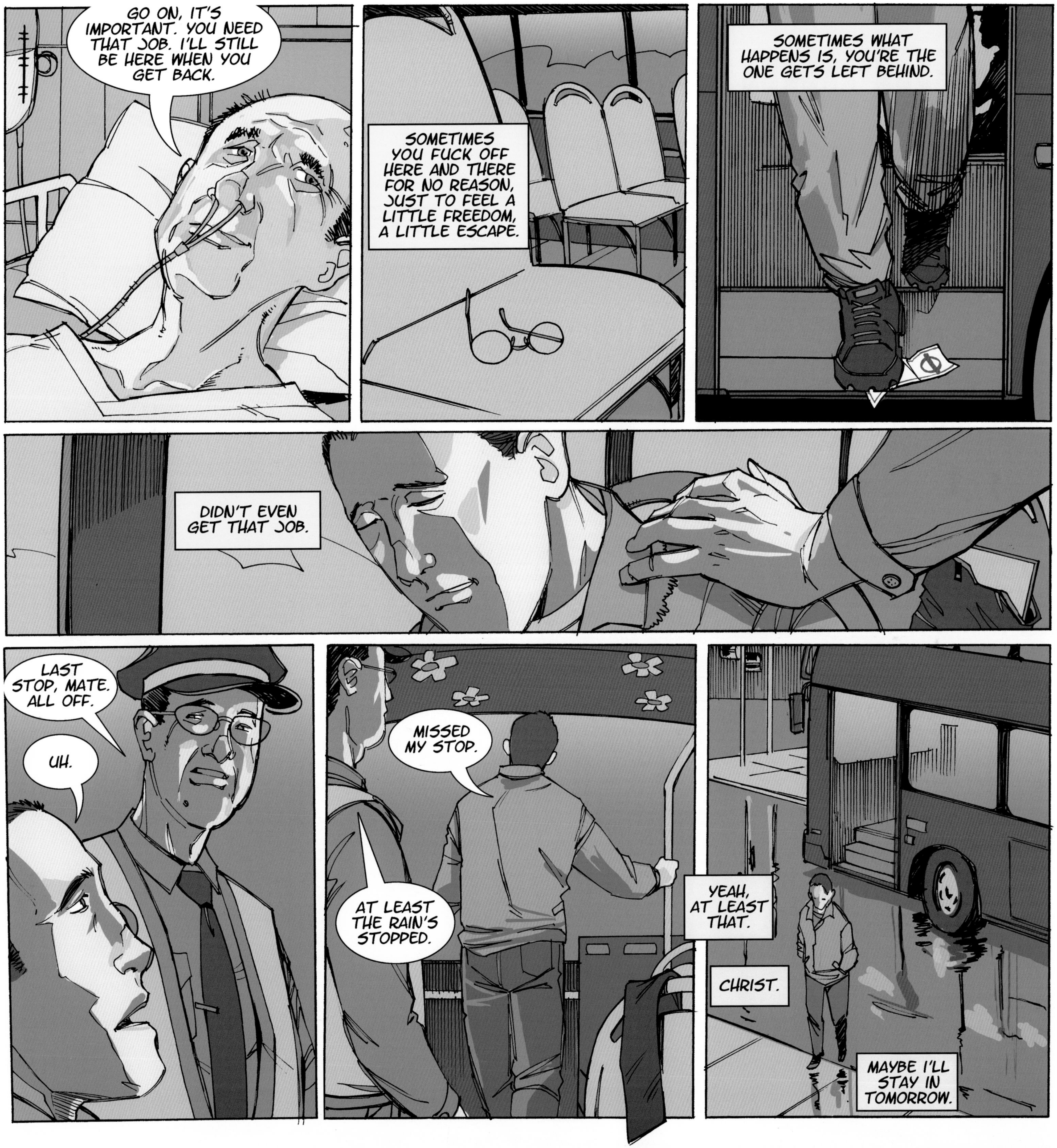
GO ON, IT'S IMPORTANT. YOU NEED THAT JOB. I'LL STILL BE HERE WHEN YOU GET BACK.
SOMETIMES YOU FUCK OFF HERE AND THERE FOR NO REASON, JUST TO FEEL A LITTLE FREEDOM, A LITTLE ESCAPE.
SOMETIMES WHAT HAPPENS IS, YOU'RE THE ONE GETS LEFT BEHIND.
DIDN'T EVEN GET THAT JOB.
LAST STOP, MATE. ALL OFF.
UH.
MISSED MY STOP.
AT LEAST THE RAIN'S STOPPED.
YEAH, AT LEAST THAT.
CHRIST.
MAYBE I'LL STAY IN TOMORROW.

A LEOPARD

featured on **A Leopard and Other Stories**

story by **Jennifer DeGuzman**
art by **Brian Belew**

frayed and tattered and the blinds are drawn down low
the sweet smell of rotting
heat and decay now the summer is over
an echo of something
the tennis courts are overgrown
our old friends have all grown up and gone

a curve of glass, a deep red carpet in the hall
dust in the sunshine
three kids are crawling up the stairs
absolutely terrified
a fortune-teller sits there still
she's turning cards and waiting for us to come

and it's all gone
a leopard is gone
those days are over
a leopard is gone
a leopard is gone now

a white-haired man, fedora hat and overcoat
we hide in the garden
in the basement we'd pretend to be at sea
swallows and amazons
the biggest house i ever saw
adventures and clues behind every door

i used to cause havoc with my friends
running round breaking and taking
and smashing and climbing
spending my days outside
and it's all gone
and it was clear to me that i wasn't doing anything wrong
in fact it was my absolute right

those days are over now
and when adults came out and tried to stop me
i had a righteous, bewildered expression
and it's all gone

and then 5 years later on i was an anaesthetized 16 year old
spending my days inside
those days are over now
i remember telling my mother not to get so wound up
about some boys outside kicking a football against the gate
and it's all gone
and then the other day
there were some kids outside climbing on the fence
a leopard is gone
i got more and more angry until eventually
those days are over now
i stormed outside and confronted them
a leopard is gone
and saw that same, righteous, bewildered expression

and it's all gone
a leopard is gone
those days are over
a leopard is gone
a leopard is gone
a leopard is gone now

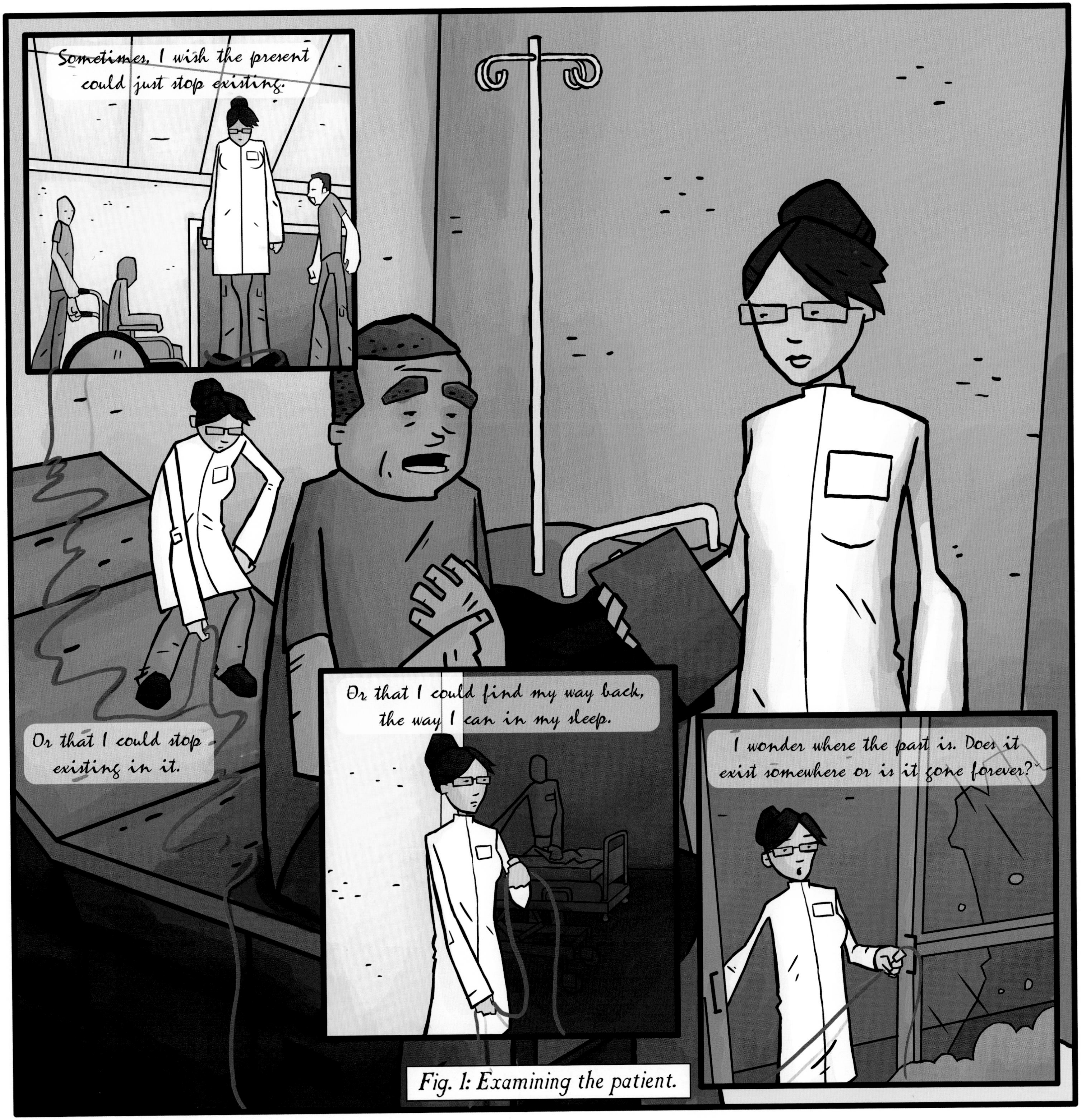
Sometimes, I wish the present could just stop existing.
Or that I could stop existing in it.
Or that I could find my way back, the way I can in my sleep.
I wonder where the past is. Does it exist somewhere or is it gone forever?

Fig. 1: Examining the patient.

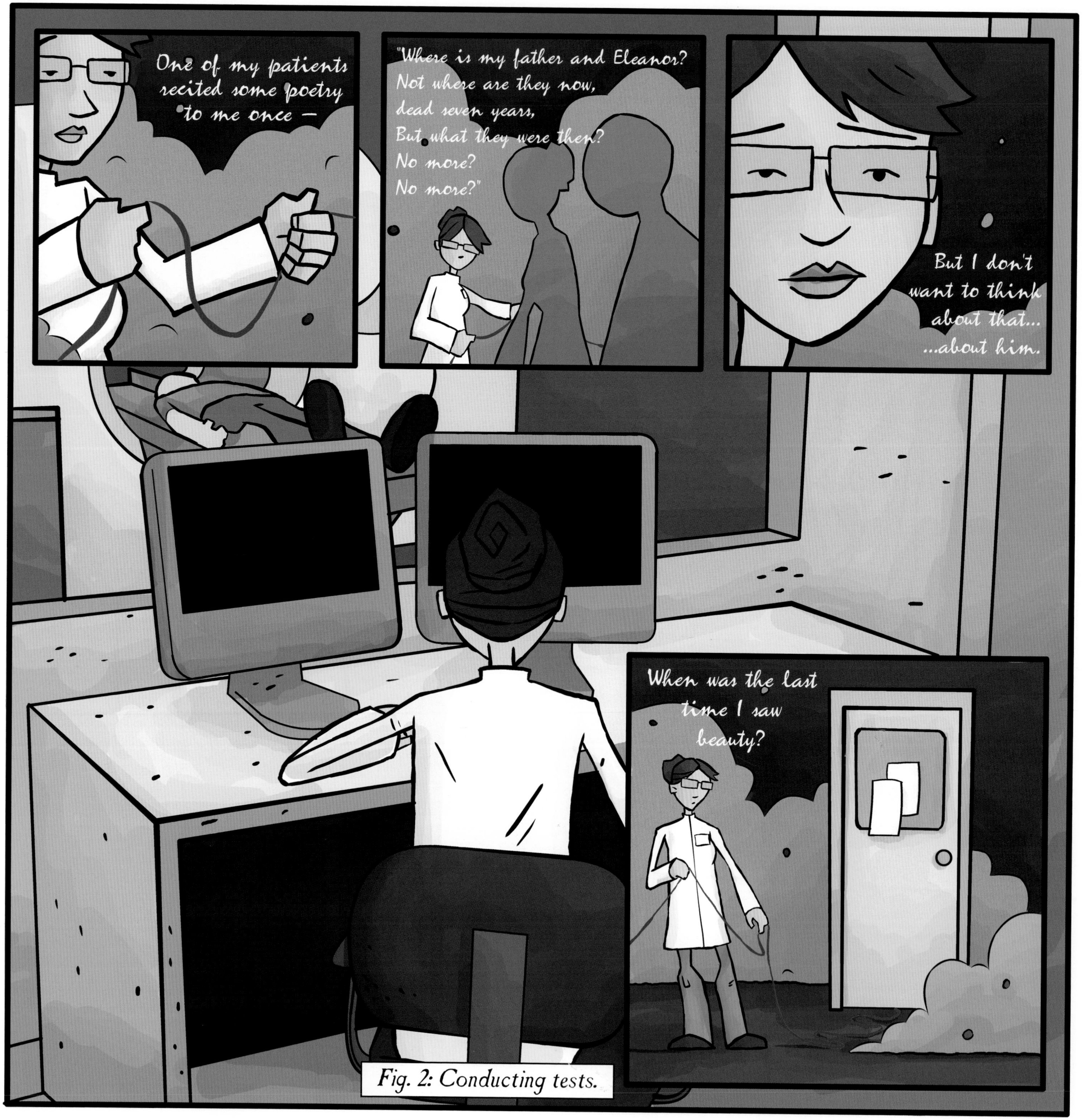
One of my patients recited some poetry to me once —
"Where is my father and Eleanor? Not where are they now, dead seven years, But what they were then? No more? No more?"
But I don't want to think about that... ...about him.
When was the last time I saw beauty?
Fig. 2: Conducting tests.

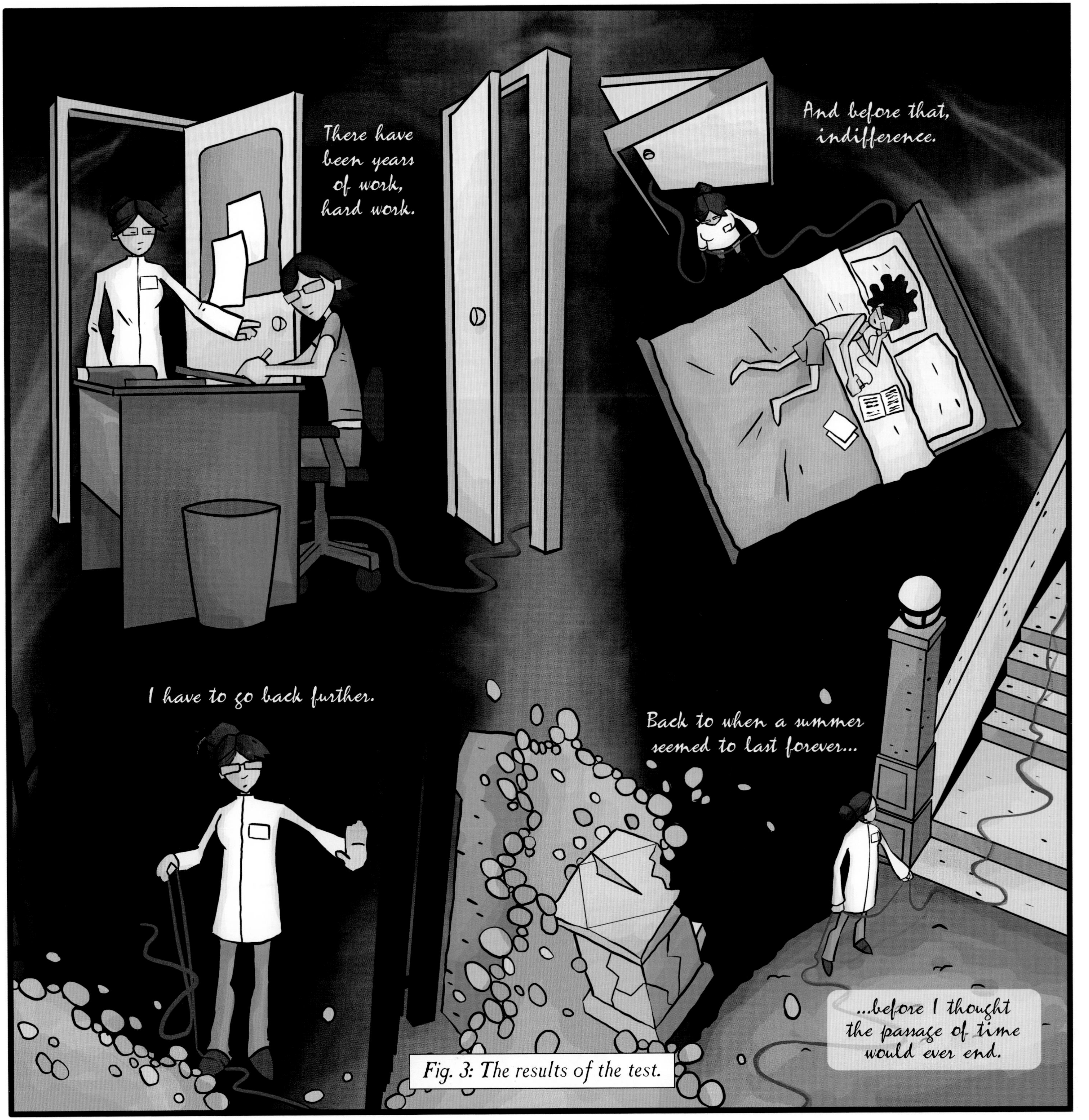
There have been years of work, hard work.
And before that, indifference.
I have to go back further.
Back to when a summer seemed to last forever...
...before I thought the passage of time would ever end.
Fig. 3: The results of the test.

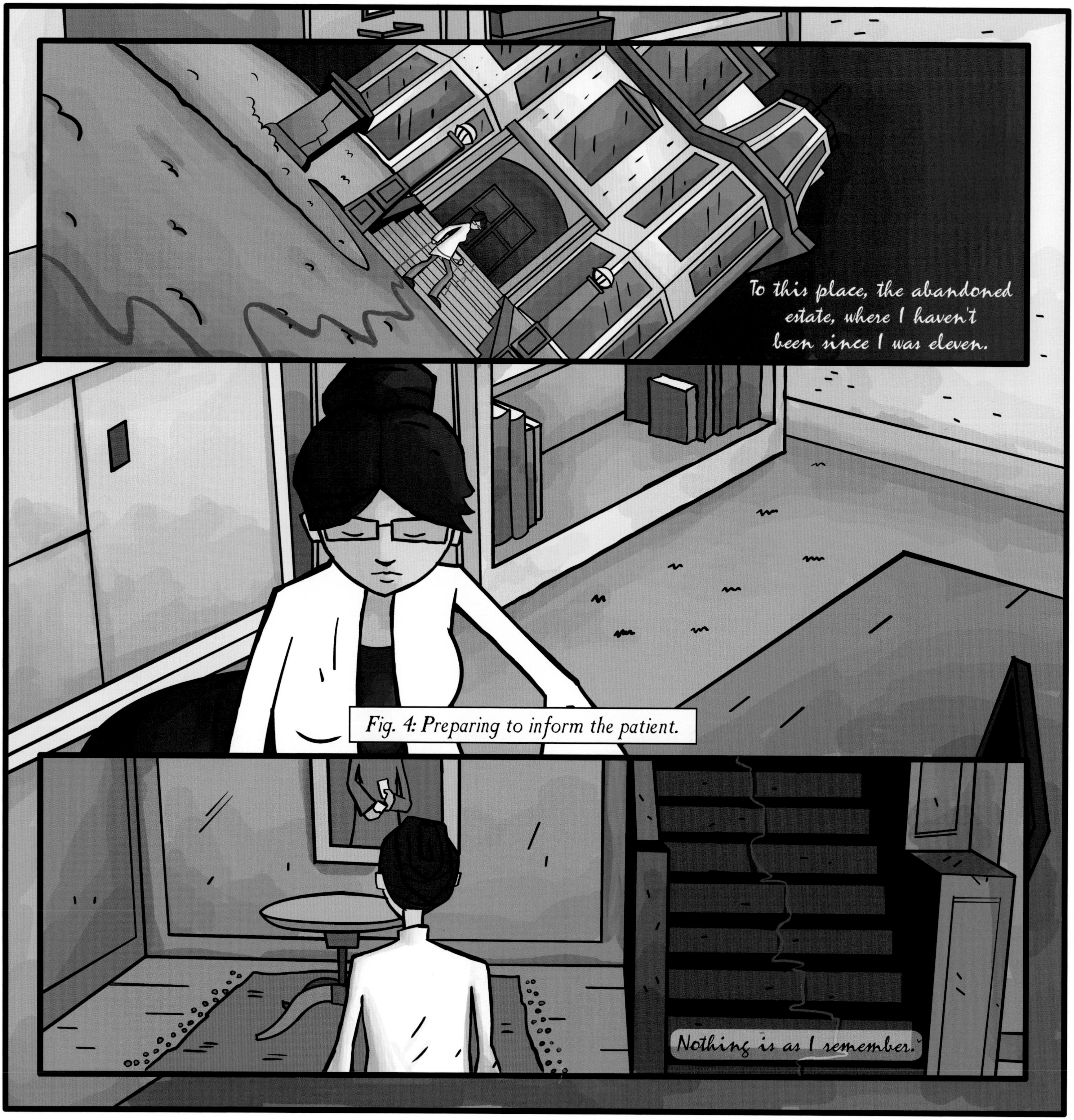
To this place, the abandoned estate, where I haven't been since I was eleven.
Fig. 4: Preparing to inform the patient.
Nothing is as I remember.

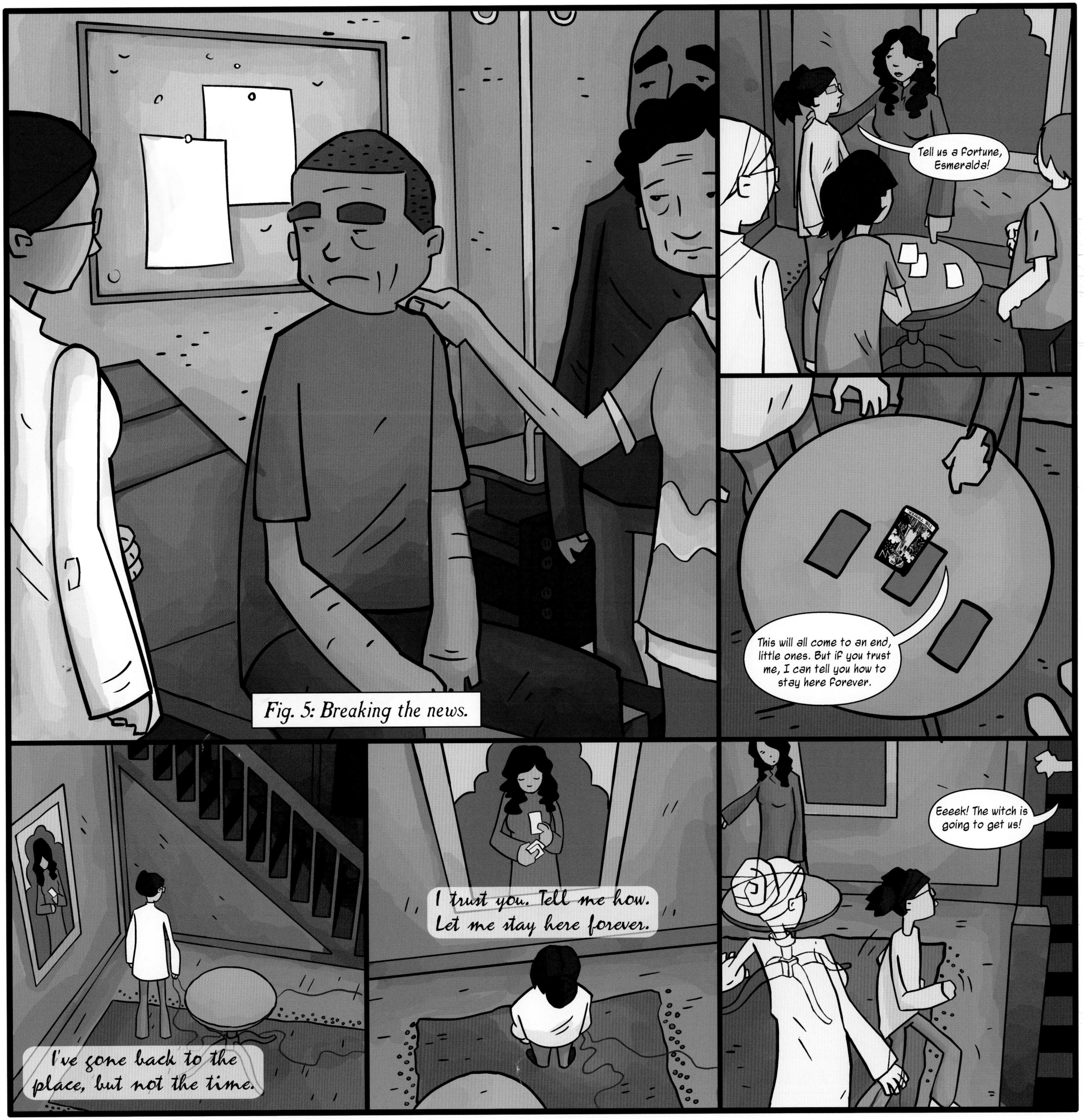
Fig. 5: Breaking the news.
Tell us a fortune, Esmeralda!
This will all come to an end, little ones. But if you trust me, I can tell you how to stay here forever.
I've gone back to the place, but not the time.
I trust you. Tell me how. Let me stay here forever.
Eeeek! The witch is going to get us!

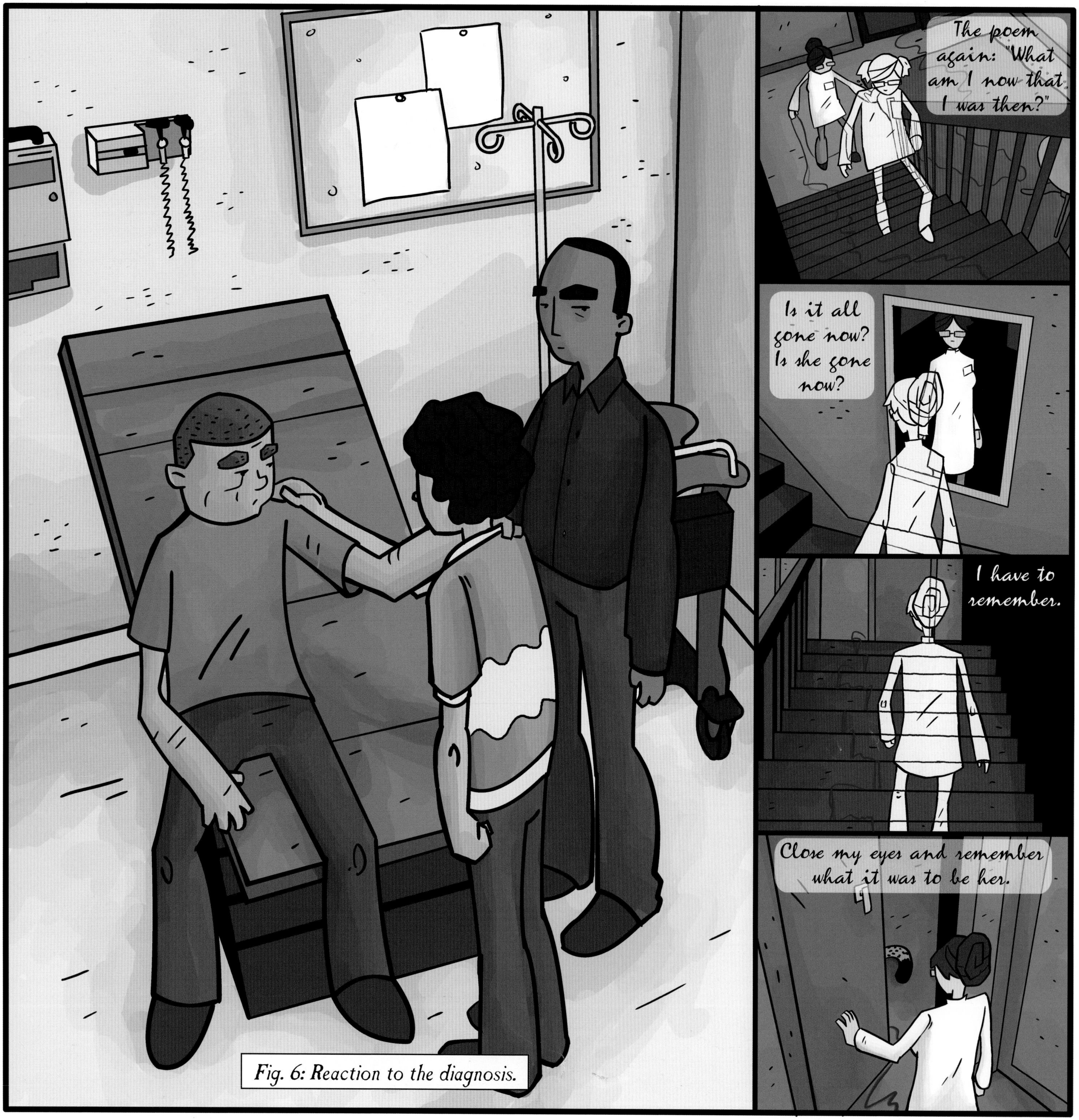
The poem again: "What am I now that I was then?"
Is it all gone now? Is she gone now?
I have to remember.
Close my eyes and remember what it was to be her.

Fig. 6: Reaction to the diagnosis.

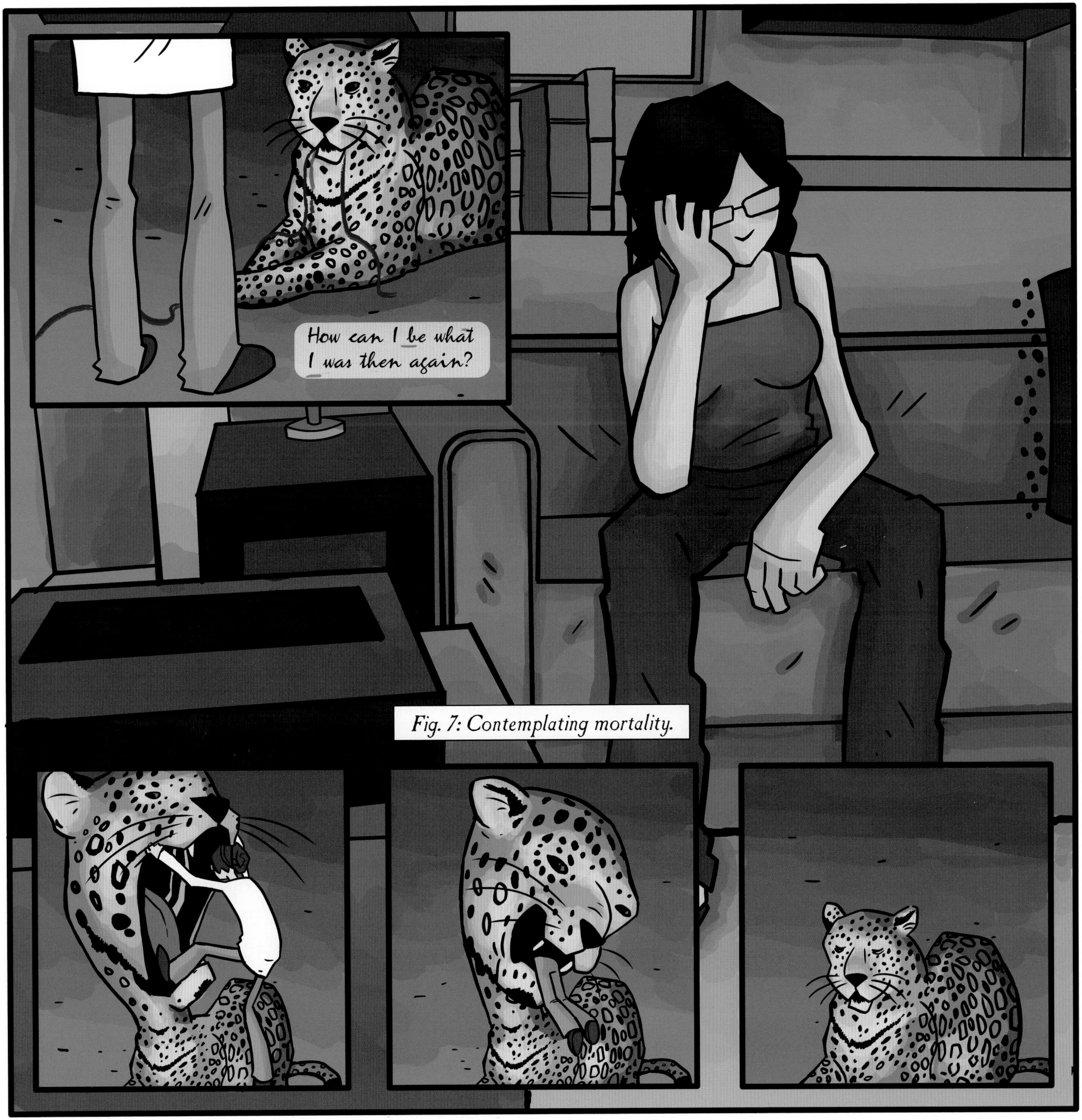
How can I be what I was then again?
Fig. 7: Contemplating mortality.

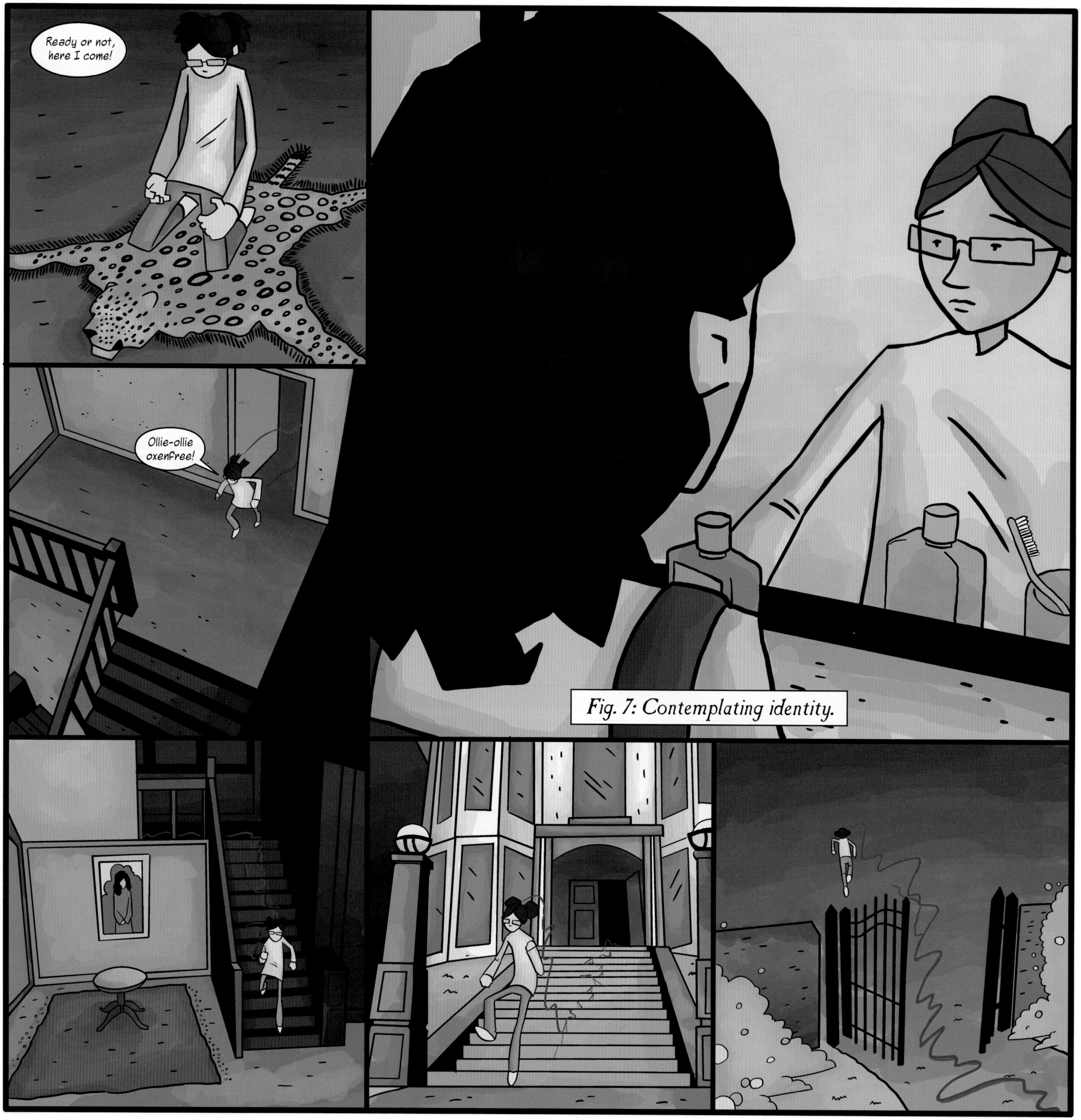
Ready or not, here I come!
Ollie-ollie oxenfree!
Fig. 7: Contemplating identity.

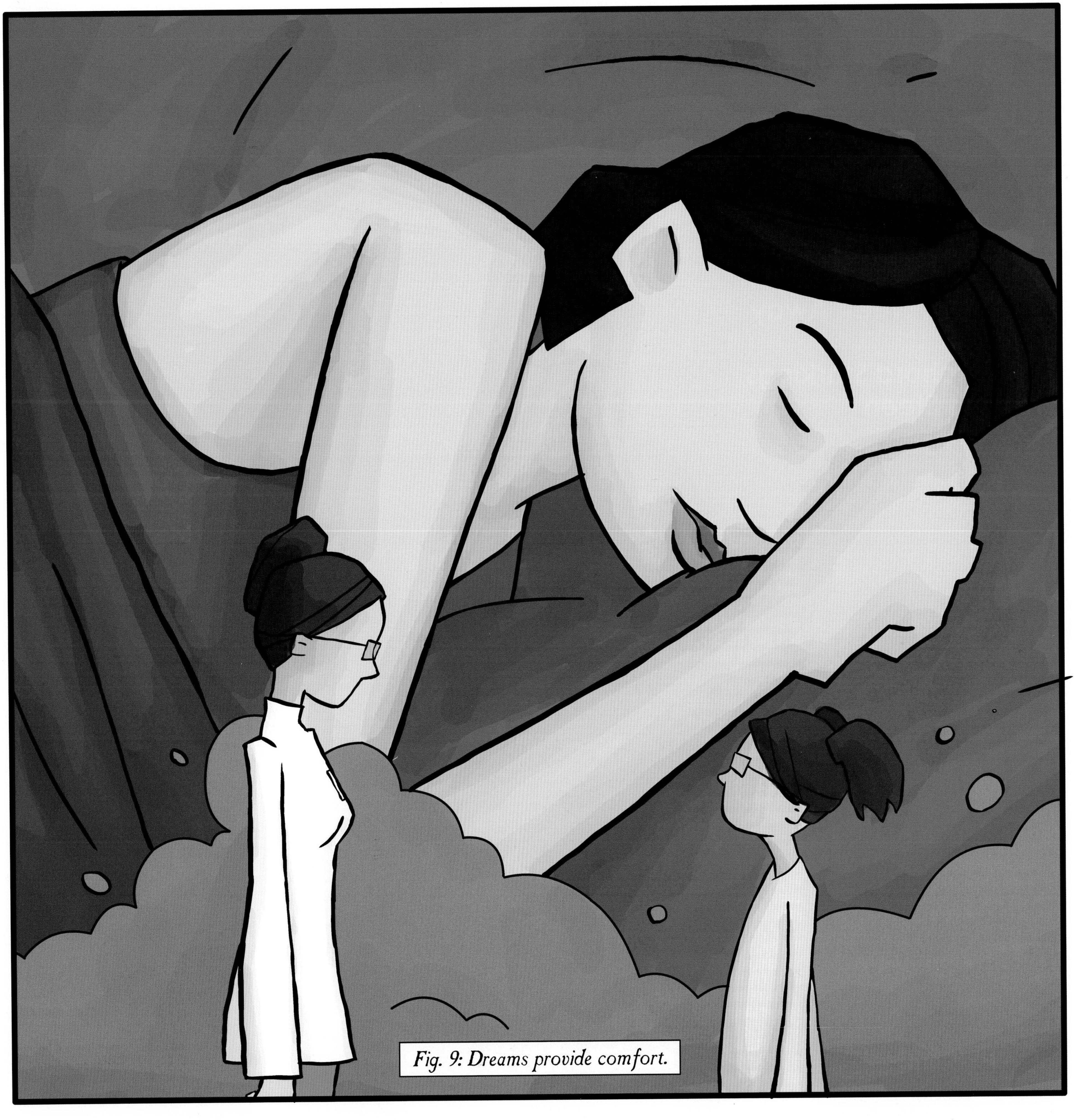

Fig. 9: Dreams provide comfort.

IT WON'T BE LONG NOW

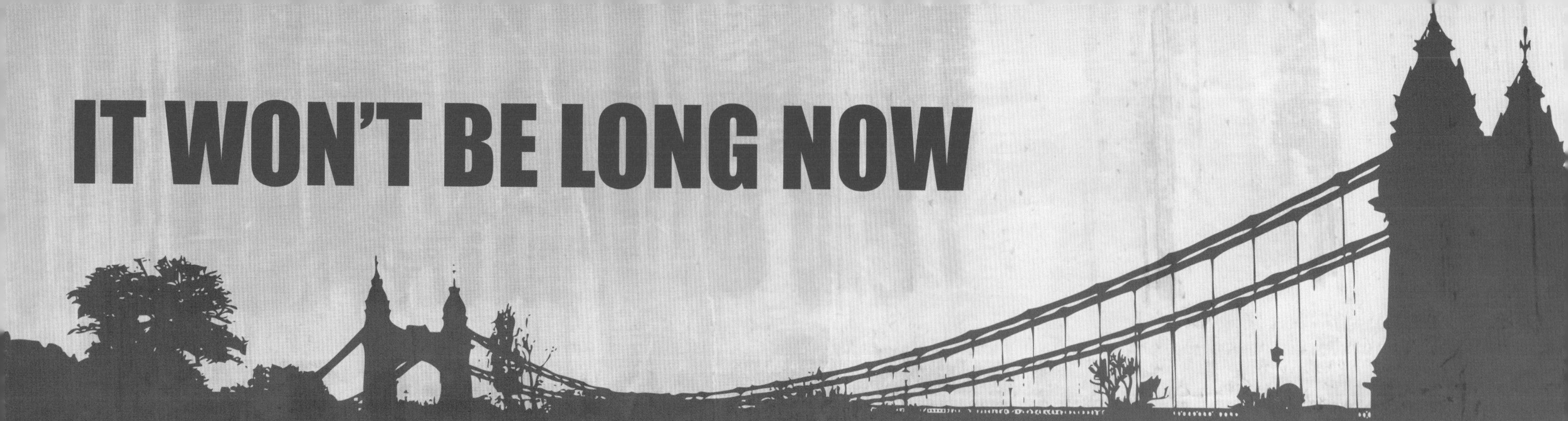

featured on **A Week Away**

story by **Richard Starkings**
art by **Rob Steen**

this shop
sells everything
you ever
really need
i'm standing
looking up
at the sign
above this...

24 months ago
the paintwork was perfect
the writing fashionable
the name it seemed so funny
24 months ago
it had so much potential
but maybe that was in my head

all the people
who've done extra hours for me and
all the people
who keep things ticking over
they're just friends really
it won't be long
but when i'm in the money
i'll say thank you
it won't be long
i'm pretty sure that it won't be long now
it's the best it's been now

this shop
is all i ever wanted
it's quiet now but
all the signs are good
i've dropped my prices
i've increased my hours
saved
borrowed
done without

all my time and money
have gone into this and
i believe the tide has turned
wooooaaaaaah!
this shop is me
this shop is this country
it's insignificant but it
seems so important
if
it won't be long
in your heart you
don't really expect me
it won't be long
to succeed in this then
what
exactly
do you
expect
me to do?

this shop is me
this shop is this country
it won't be long
i spent so much time looking
i can no longer see
if
it won't be long
in your heart you
don't really expect me
it won't be long
to succeed in this then
what exactly
do you expect from me?
do you expect from?
sometimes i feel so down
it won't be long now
can't you see it hurts?
it's the best it's been now

this
shop
sells everything

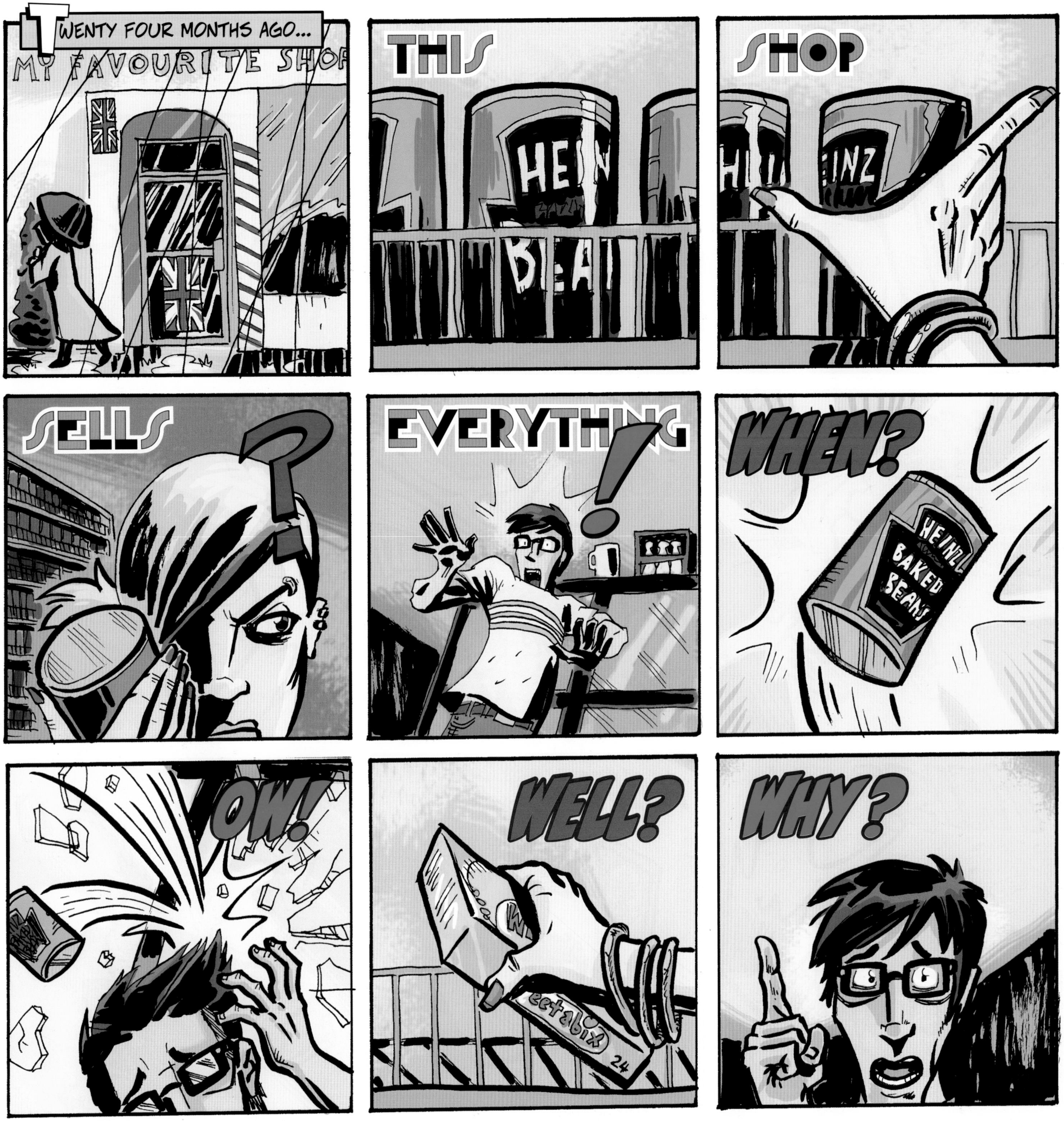
TWENTY FOUR MONTHS AGO...
MY FAVOURITE SHOP
THIS
SHOP
SELLS
EVERYTHING
WHEN?
HEINZ BAKED BEANS
OW!
WELL?
WHY?

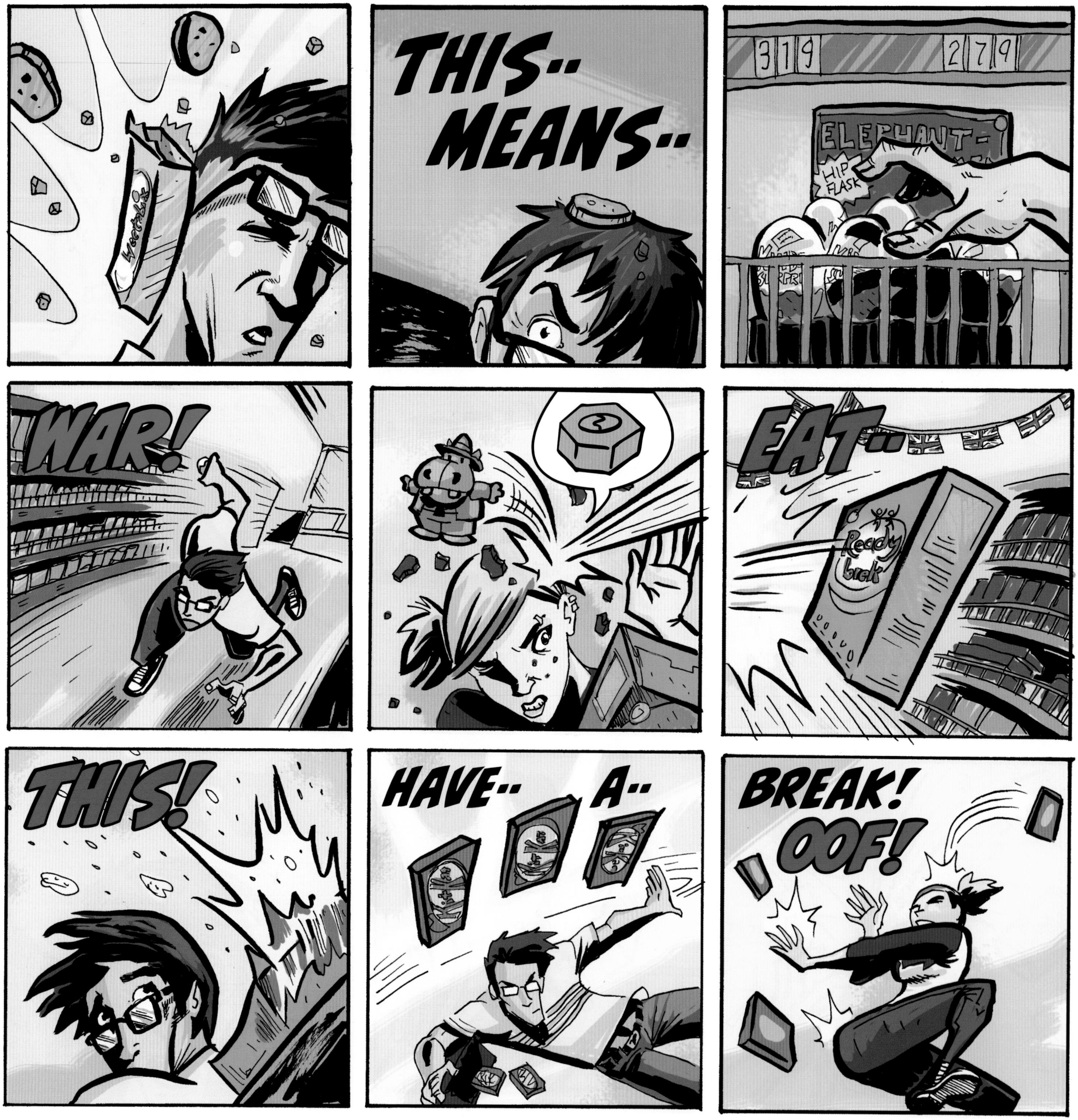
THIS..
MEANS..
WAR!
EAT..
THIS!
HAVE..
A..
BREAK!
OOF!

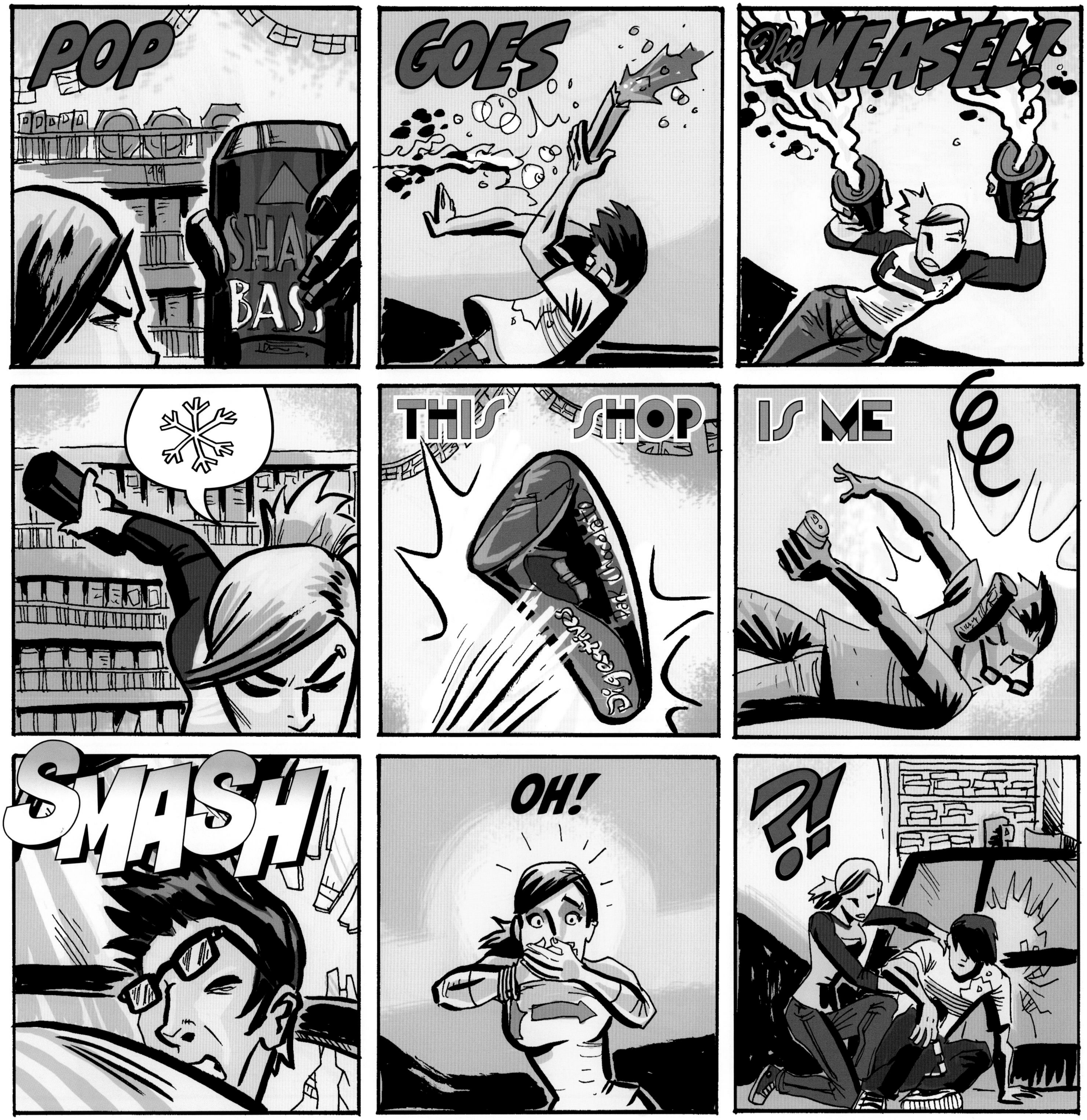
POP
GOES
The WEASEL!
THIS SHOP IS ME
SMASH
OH!
?!

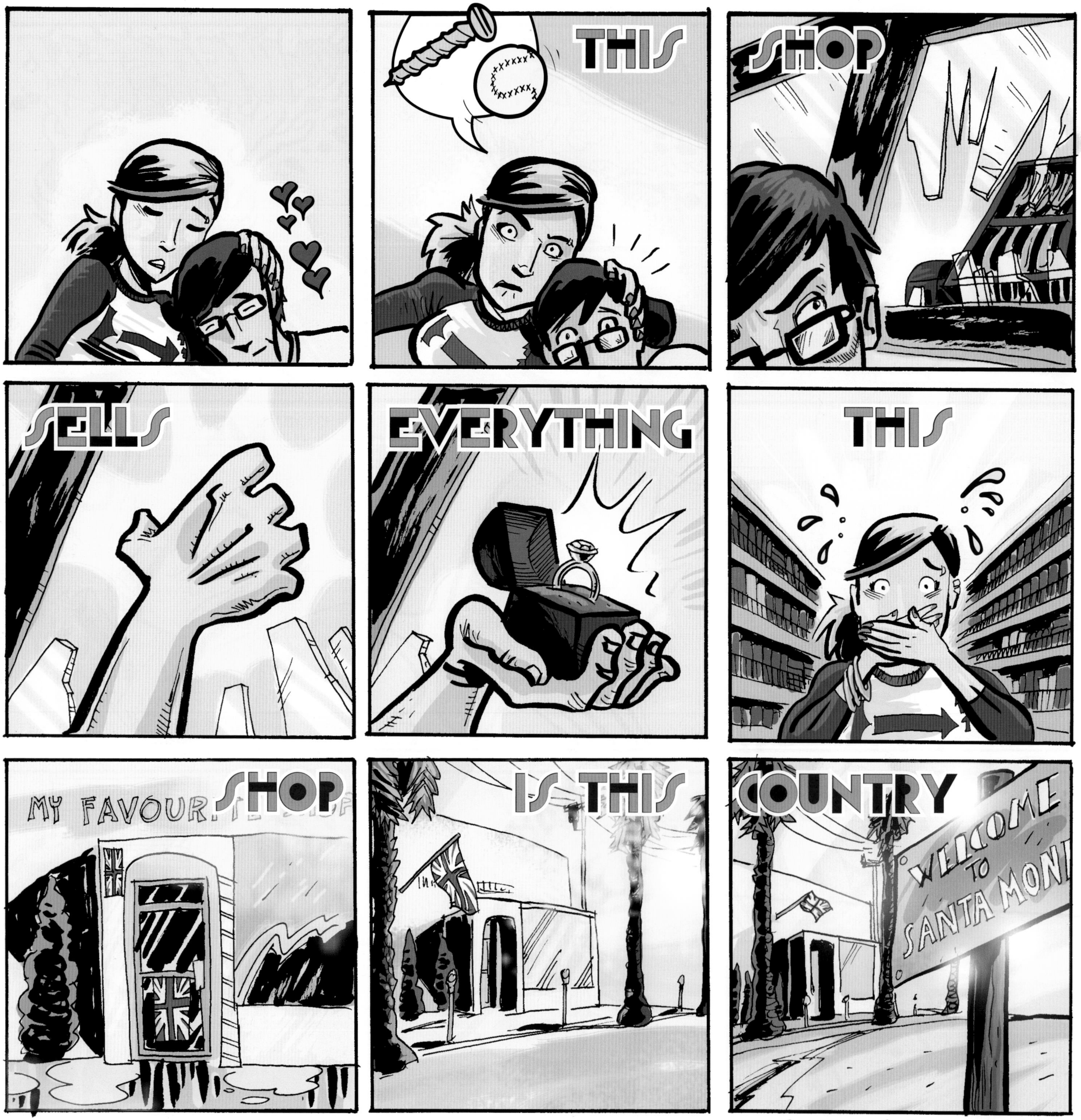
THIS
SHOP
SELLS
EVERYTHING
THIS
MY FAVOUR
SHOP
IS THIS
COUNTRY
WELCOME
TO
SANTA MONI

Starkings & Tindall 2008

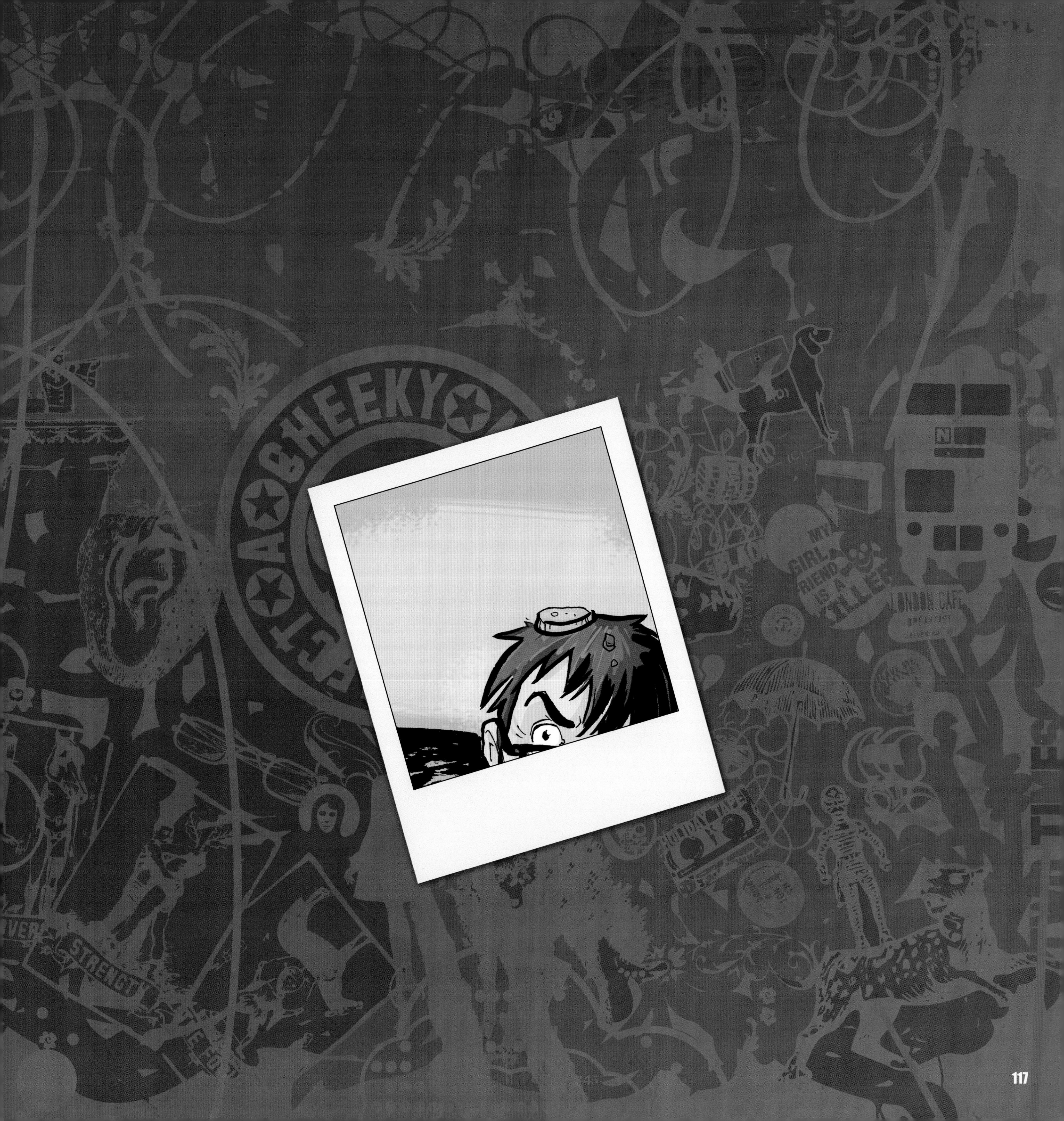
A CHEEKY
MY GIRL FRIEND IS A

MEET MR. MARSDEN

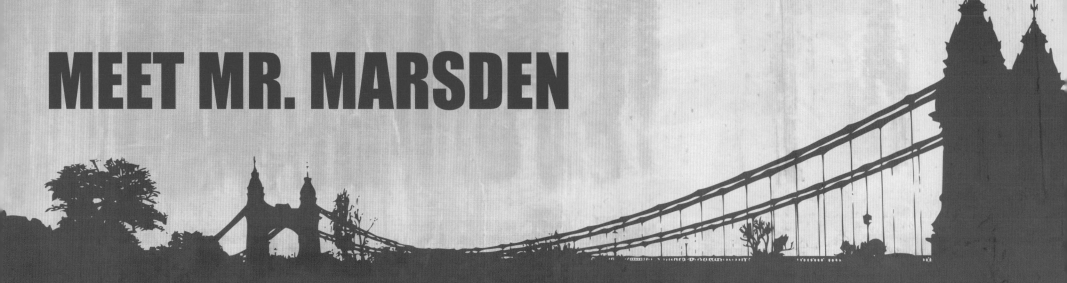

featured on **A Leopard and Other Stories**

story by **Brian Joines**
art by **Bob Rivard**
letters by **Michael David Thomas**

seventy one christmases
eighteen hundred train journeys
four relationships
a hundred and thirty thousand cups of tea
two marriages
one affair
twelve hundred bags of crisps
one near death experience
eight hundred and fifty tubes of toothpaste
one death experience

stop buying records once
lose your virginity once
get born once
be a godfather once
fall utterly and completely in love once
read "lord of the rings" once
meet Mr Marsden once
paint eleven ceilings
read three thousand magazines
buy four hundred lottery tickets
spend one weekend in wales
have eleven close friends
spend one million seven hundred thousand pounds
keep nineteen diaries
watch six thousand films
write two hundred and twenty postcards

seventy birthdays
one lover
two fathers
forty nine bags
one religion
one loss of religion

two real regrets
a hundred and five pairs of shoes
a hundred and the thousand telephone calls
three gardens
twenty two thousand pints of beer
four hundred and twenty pairs of socks

stop believing in father christmas once
lose your parents once
change your politics once
realise you won't go into space once
win ten pounds on the lottery once
go to communion once

lose three close friends
keep four new year resolutions
spend a hundred and eighty thousand hours asleep
go to six weddings
go to seven funerals
fill seven thousand bags of rubbish
visit eleven countries
buy eighteen umbrellas
take seven thousand photographs

watch your favourite film six times
put your clocks back sixty three times
look at the stars four hundred times
watch tv twenty six thousand times
go to hospital four times
meet you four hundred times
think about sex one million three hundred thousand times
make love two thousand five hundred times
go to the office christmas party thirty four times
change your car seven times

write a letter a hundred and eighty times
see "it's a wonderful life" four times
shave eight thousand seven hundred times
sit down five hundred and seventy thousand times
eat japanese food fourteen times
breathe five hundred and ninety five million times
leave hospital four times
buy "all mod cons" two times
be disappointed with your new year's eve fifty eight times
rent a flat five times

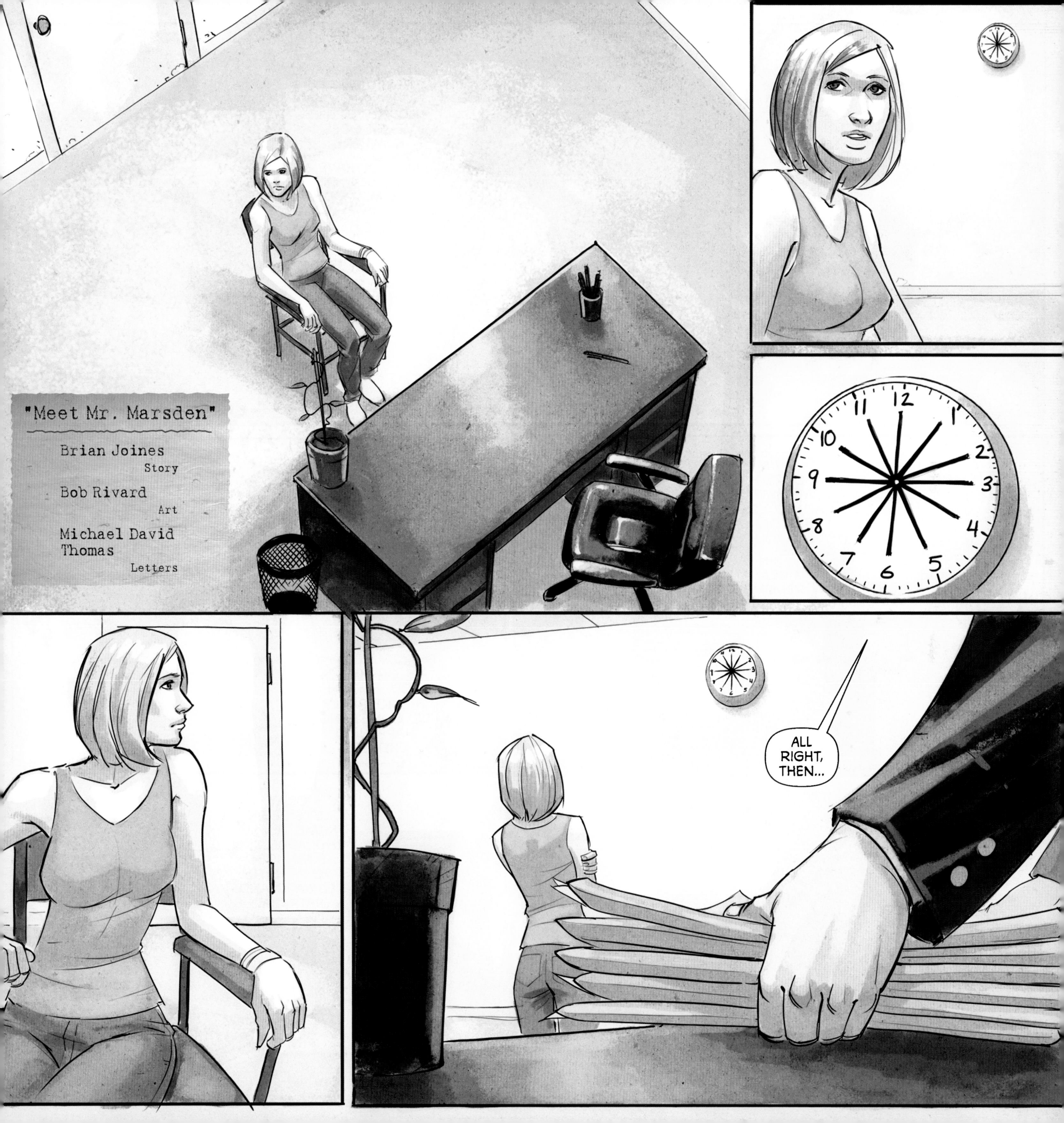
"Meet Mr. Marsden"
Brian Joines
Story
Bob Rivard
Art
Michael David Thomas
Letters
ALL RIGHT, THEN...

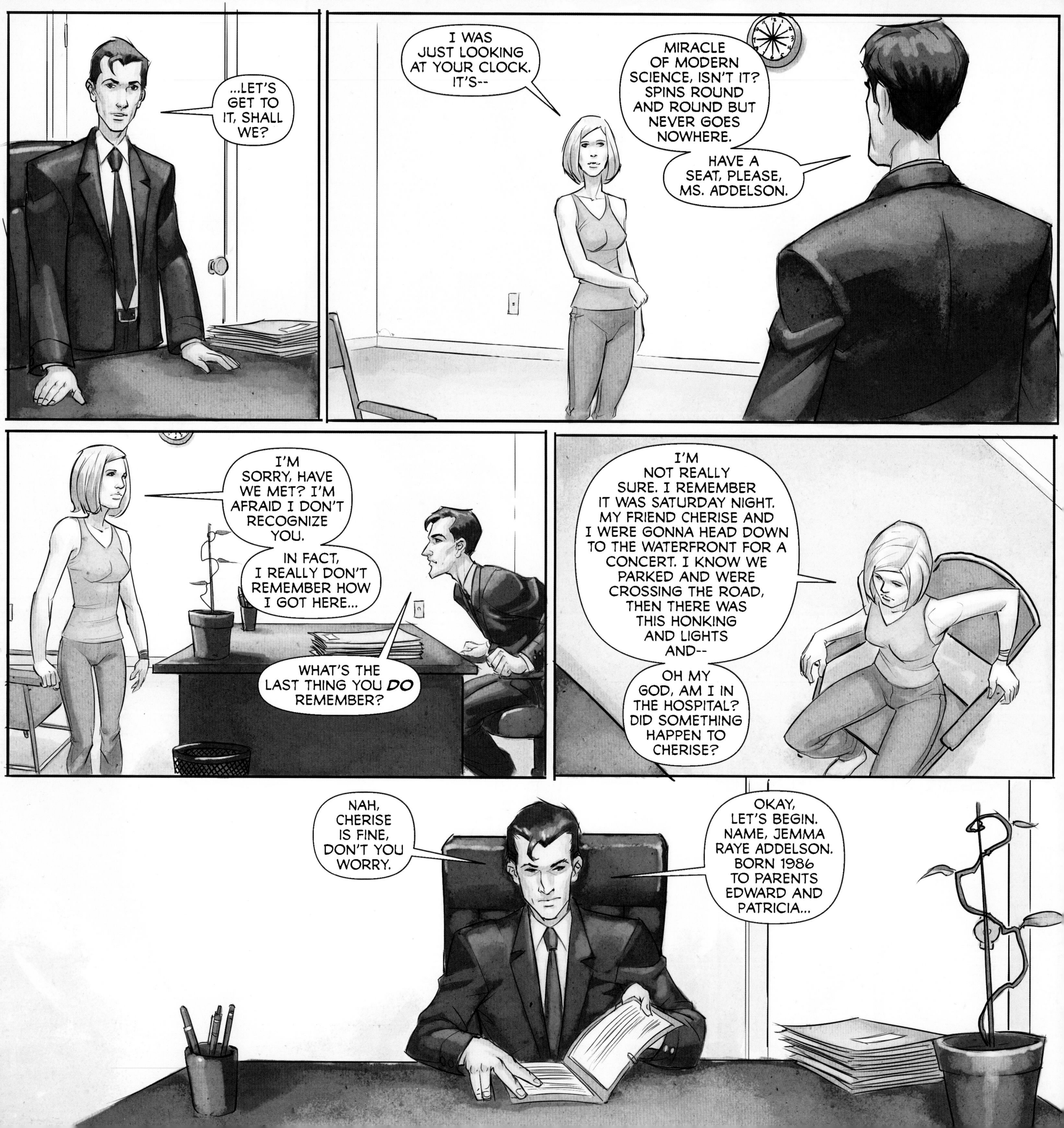
...LET'S GET TO IT, SHALL WE?
I WAS JUST LOOKING AT YOUR CLOCK. IT'S--
MIRACLE OF MODERN SCIENCE, ISN'T IT? SPINS ROUND AND ROUND BUT NEVER GOES NOWHERE.
HAVE A SEAT, PLEASE, MS. ADDELSON.
I'M SORRY, HAVE WE MET? I'M AFRAID I DON'T RECOGNIZE YOU.
IN FACT, I REALLY DON'T REMEMBER HOW I GOT HERE...
WHAT'S THE LAST THING YOU ***DO*** REMEMBER?
I'M NOT REALLY SURE. I REMEMBER IT WAS SATURDAY NIGHT. MY FRIEND CHERISE AND I WERE GONNA HEAD DOWN TO THE WATERFRONT FOR A CONCERT. I KNOW WE PARKED AND WERE CROSSING THE ROAD, THEN THERE WAS THIS HONKING AND LIGHTS AND--
OH MY GOD, AM I IN THE HOSPITAL? DID SOMETHING HAPPEN TO CHERISE?
NAH, CHERISE IS FINE, DON'T YOU WORRY.
OKAY, LET'S BEGIN. NAME, JEMMA RAYE ADDELSON. BORN 1986 TO PARENTS EDWARD AND PATRICIA...

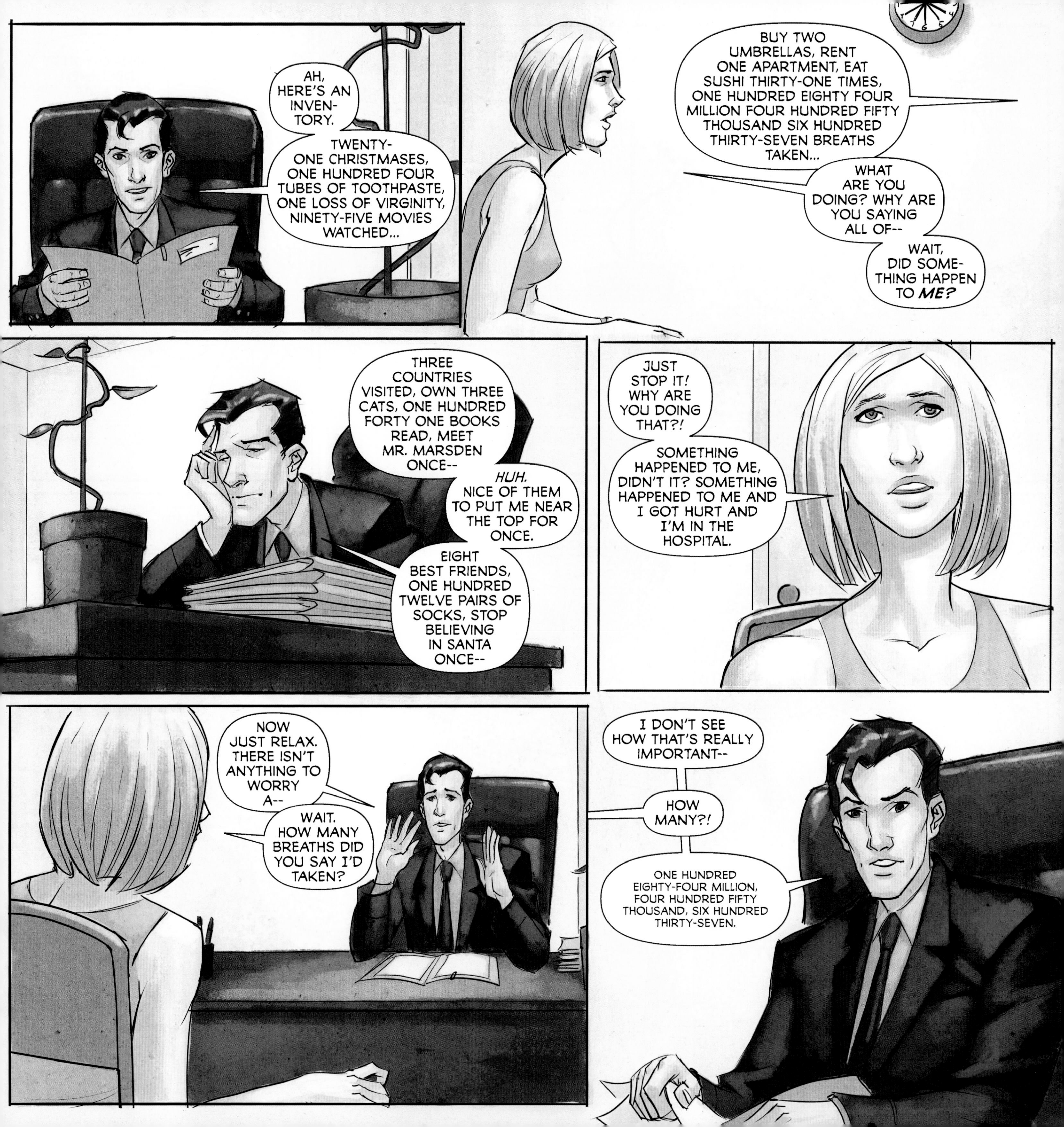
AH, HERE'S AN INVENTORY.
TWENTY-ONE CHRISTMASES, ONE HUNDRED FOUR TUBES OF TOOTHPASTE, ONE LOSS OF VIRGINITY, NINETY-FIVE MOVIES WATCHED...
BUY TWO UMBRELLAS, RENT ONE APARTMENT, EAT SUSHI THIRTY-ONE TIMES, ONE HUNDRED EIGHTY FOUR MILLION FOUR HUNDRED FIFTY THOUSAND SIX HUNDRED THIRTY-SEVEN BREATHS TAKEN...
WHAT ARE YOU DOING? WHY ARE YOU SAYING ALL OF--
WAIT, DID SOMETHING HAPPEN TO *ME?*
THREE COUNTRIES VISITED, OWN THREE CATS, ONE HUNDRED FORTY ONE BOOKS READ, MEET MR. MARSDEN ONCE--
HUH. NICE OF THEM TO PUT ME NEAR THE TOP FOR ONCE.
EIGHT BEST FRIENDS, ONE HUNDRED TWELVE PAIRS OF SOCKS, STOP BELIEVING IN SANTA ONCE--
JUST STOP IT! WHY ARE YOU DOING THAT?!
SOMETHING HAPPENED TO ME, DIDN'T IT? SOMETHING HAPPENED TO ME AND I GOT HURT AND I'M IN THE HOSPITAL.
NOW JUST RELAX. THERE ISN'T ANYTHING TO WORRY A--
WAIT. HOW MANY BREATHS DID YOU SAY I'D TAKEN?
I DON'T SEE HOW THAT'S REALLY IMPORTANT--
HOW MANY?!
ONE HUNDRED EIGHTY-FOUR MILLION, FOUR HUNDRED FIFTY THOUSAND, SIX HUNDRED THIRTY-SEVEN.

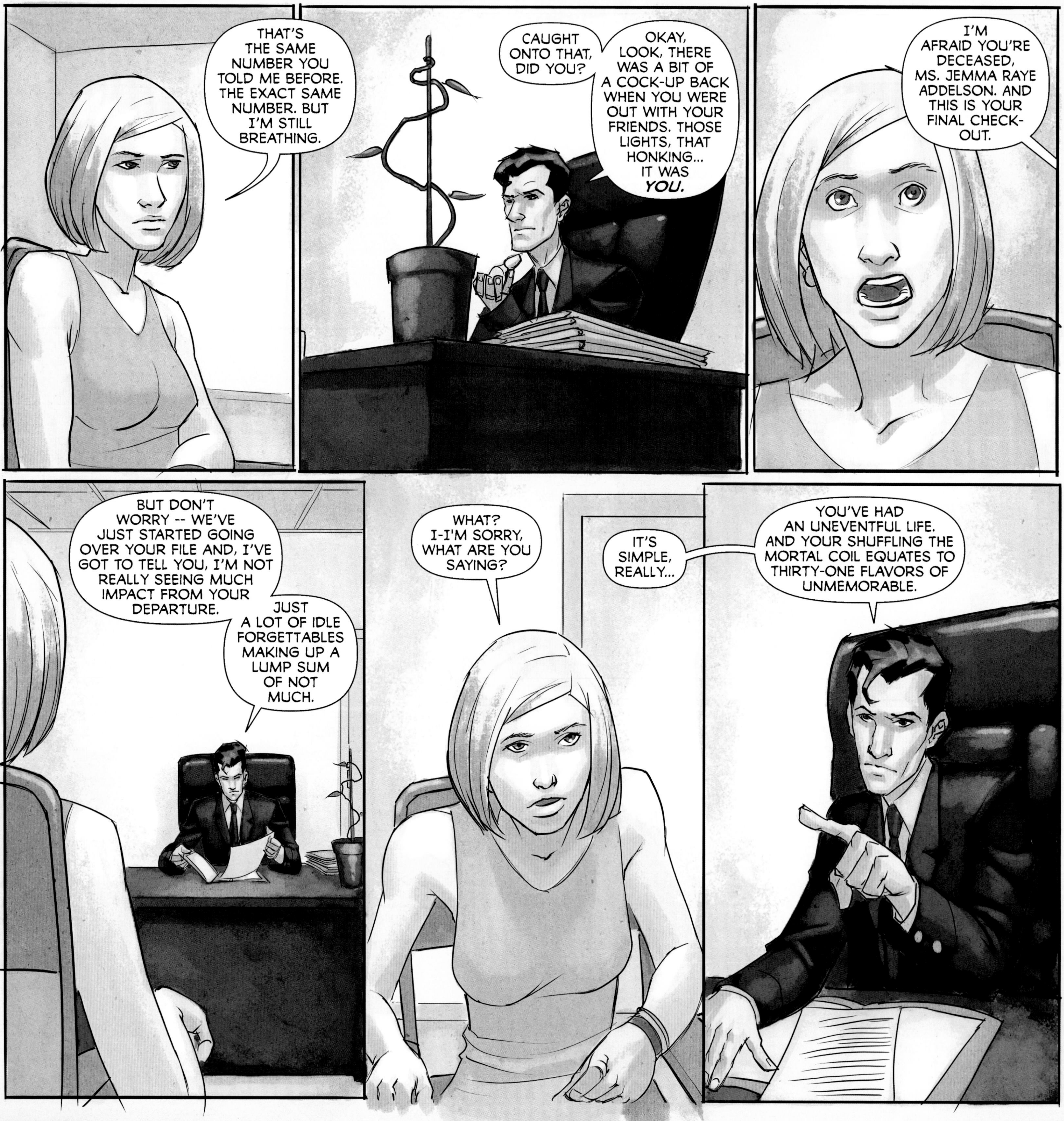
THAT'S THE SAME NUMBER YOU TOLD ME BEFORE. THE EXACT SAME NUMBER. BUT I'M STILL BREATHING.
CAUGHT ONTO THAT, DID YOU?
OKAY, LOOK, THERE WAS A BIT OF A COCK-UP BACK WHEN YOU WERE OUT WITH YOUR FRIENDS. THOSE LIGHTS, THAT HONKING... IT WAS *YOU.*
I'M AFRAID YOU'RE DECEASED, MS. JEMMA RAYE ADDELSON. AND THIS IS YOUR FINAL CHECK-OUT.
BUT DON'T WORRY -- WE'VE JUST STARTED GOING OVER YOUR FILE AND, I'VE GOT TO TELL YOU, I'M NOT REALLY SEEING MUCH IMPACT FROM YOUR DEPARTURE.
JUST A LOT OF IDLE FORGETTABLES MAKING UP A LUMP SUM OF NOT MUCH.
WHAT? I-I'M SORRY, WHAT ARE YOU SAYING?
IT'S SIMPLE, REALLY...
YOU'VE HAD AN UNEVENTFUL LIFE. AND YOUR SHUFFLING THE MORTAL COIL EQUATES TO THIRTY-ONE FLAVORS OF UNMEMORABLE.

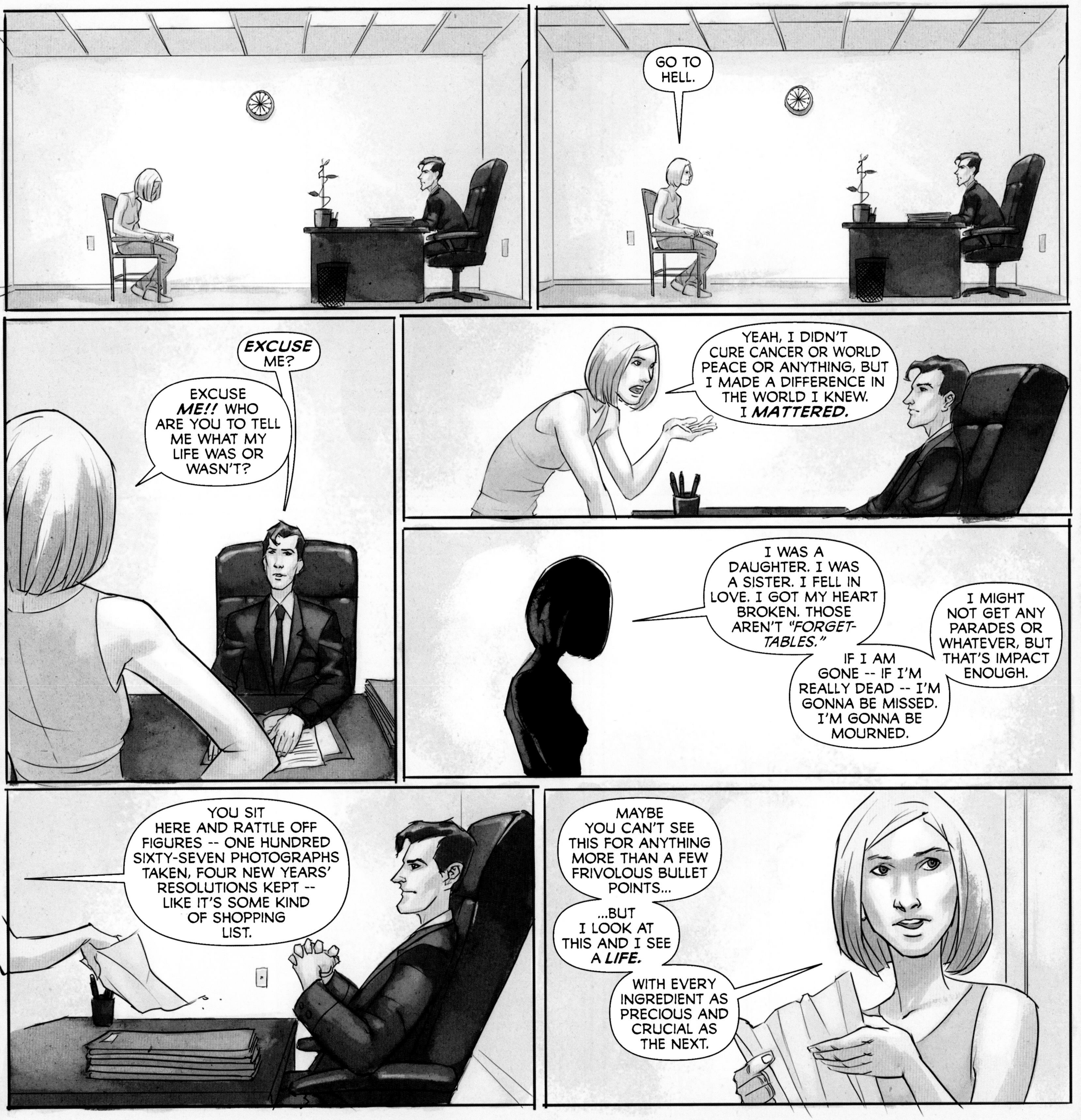
GO TO HELL.
EXCUSE ME?
EXCUSE *ME!!* WHO ARE YOU TO TELL ME WHAT MY LIFE WAS OR WASN'T?
YEAH, I DIDN'T CURE CANCER OR WORLD PEACE OR ANYTHING, BUT I MADE A DIFFERENCE IN THE WORLD I KNEW. I *MATTERED.*
I WAS A DAUGHTER. I WAS A SISTER. I FELL IN LOVE. I GOT MY HEART BROKEN. THOSE AREN'T *"FORGETTABLES."*
IF I AM GONE -- IF I'M REALLY DEAD -- I'M GONNA BE MISSED. I'M GONNA BE MOURNED.
I MIGHT NOT GET ANY PARADES OR WHATEVER, BUT THAT'S IMPACT ENOUGH.
YOU SIT HERE AND RATTLE OFF FIGURES -- ONE HUNDRED SIXTY-SEVEN PHOTOGRAPHS TAKEN, FOUR NEW YEARS' RESOLUTIONS KEPT -- LIKE IT'S SOME KIND OF SHOPPING LIST.
MAYBE YOU CAN'T SEE THIS FOR ANYTHING MORE THAN A FEW FRIVOLOUS BULLET POINTS...
...BUT I LOOK AT THIS AND I SEE A *LIFE.*
WITH EVERY INGREDIENT AS PRECIOUS AND CRUCIAL AS THE NEXT.

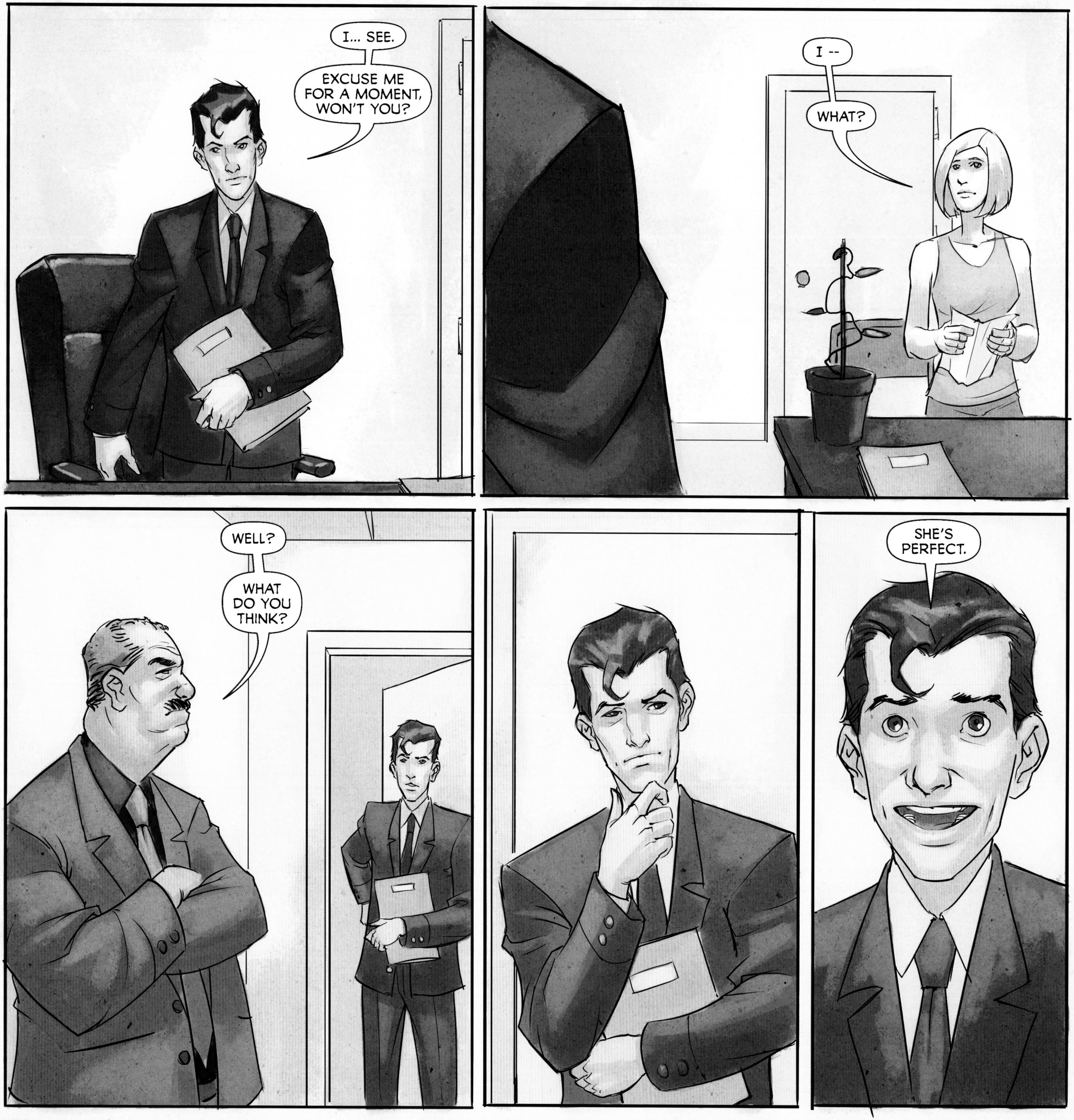
I... SEE.
EXCUSE ME FOR A MOMENT, WON'T YOU?
I --
WHAT?
WELL?
WHAT DO YOU THINK?
SHE'S PERFECT.

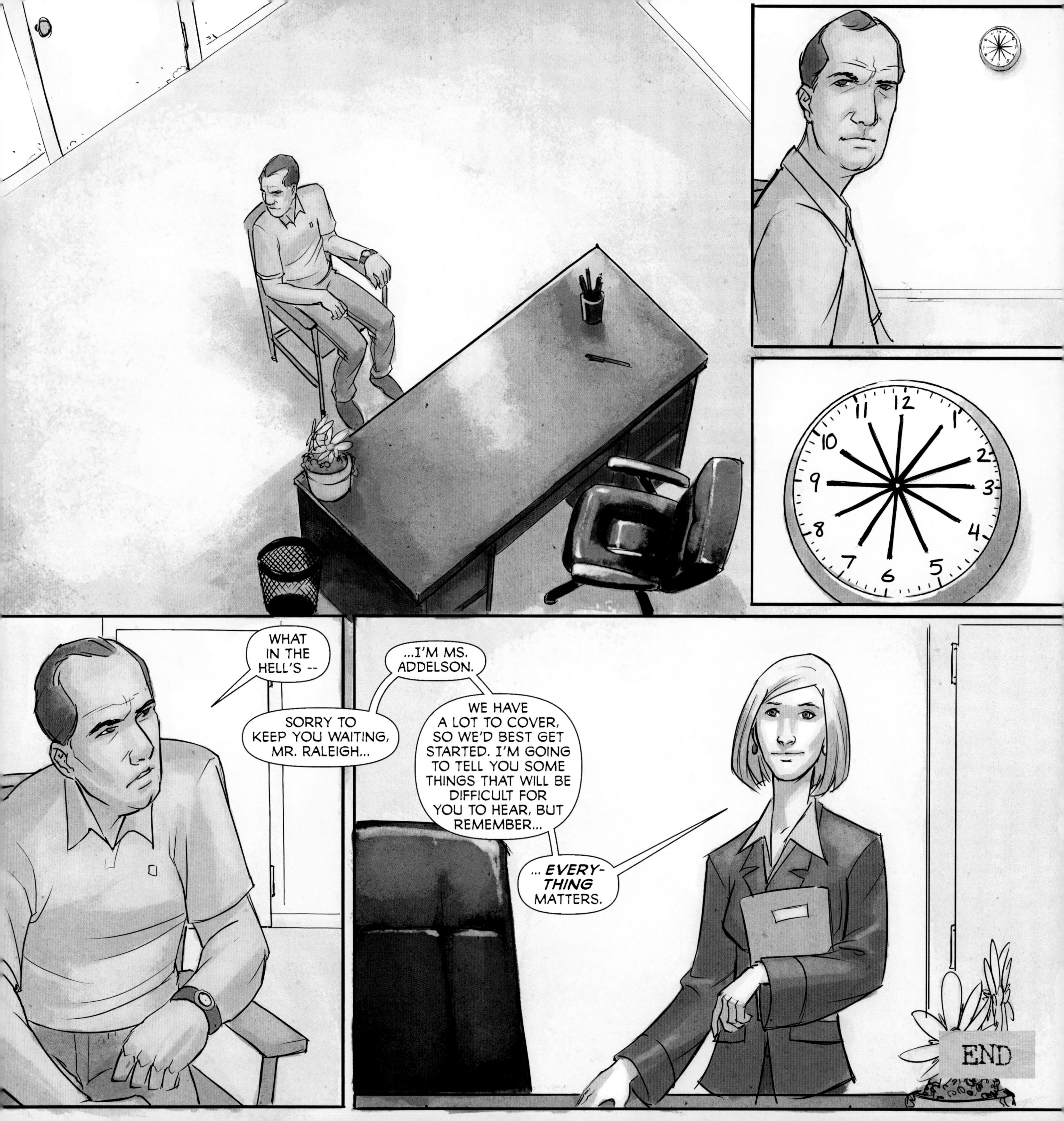

WHAT IN THE HELL'S --
SORRY TO KEEP YOU WAITING, MR. RALEIGH...
...I'M MS. ADDELSON.
WE HAVE A LOT TO COVER, SO WE'D BEST GET STARTED. I'M GOING TO TELL YOU SOME THINGS THAT WILL BE DIFFICULT FOR YOU TO HEAR, BUT REMEMBER...
... *EVERYTHING* MATTERS.
END

I WENT AWAY

featured on **Oklahoma**

by **Marc Ellerby**

the first time i went away
i wrote to you every day
i told you everything i was doing
you'd ring me in the morning
you'd page me in the night
i missed you so much i couldn't sleep without you
and i'd swear
the way i feel
is going to last forever

when i came home
on the third weekend
i was so glad to see you
everything was perfect
everything felt right
and nothing had changed

the second time i went away
i didn't want to go
but we agreed i had to get on with my life
so i slept in every morning
i went out every night
until there were days when i hardly even thought of you
but i'd sear
the way i feel
is going to last forever

when i came home for christmas
i slept for a day
i felt nervous to see you
and all through the holidays
it seemed we'd grown apart
i felt i'd changed but you'd stayed the same

the last time i went away
i think i knew it was over
so i went out and got drunk with my new friends
that was years ago
i've only seen you twice since then
once at a party and once in the street
now i don't know where you are
your family moved away
oh i don't even know what you are doing
but i'm sad and i miss you
and i'd kind of like to see you
and i swear
the way i feel
is going to last forever
forever

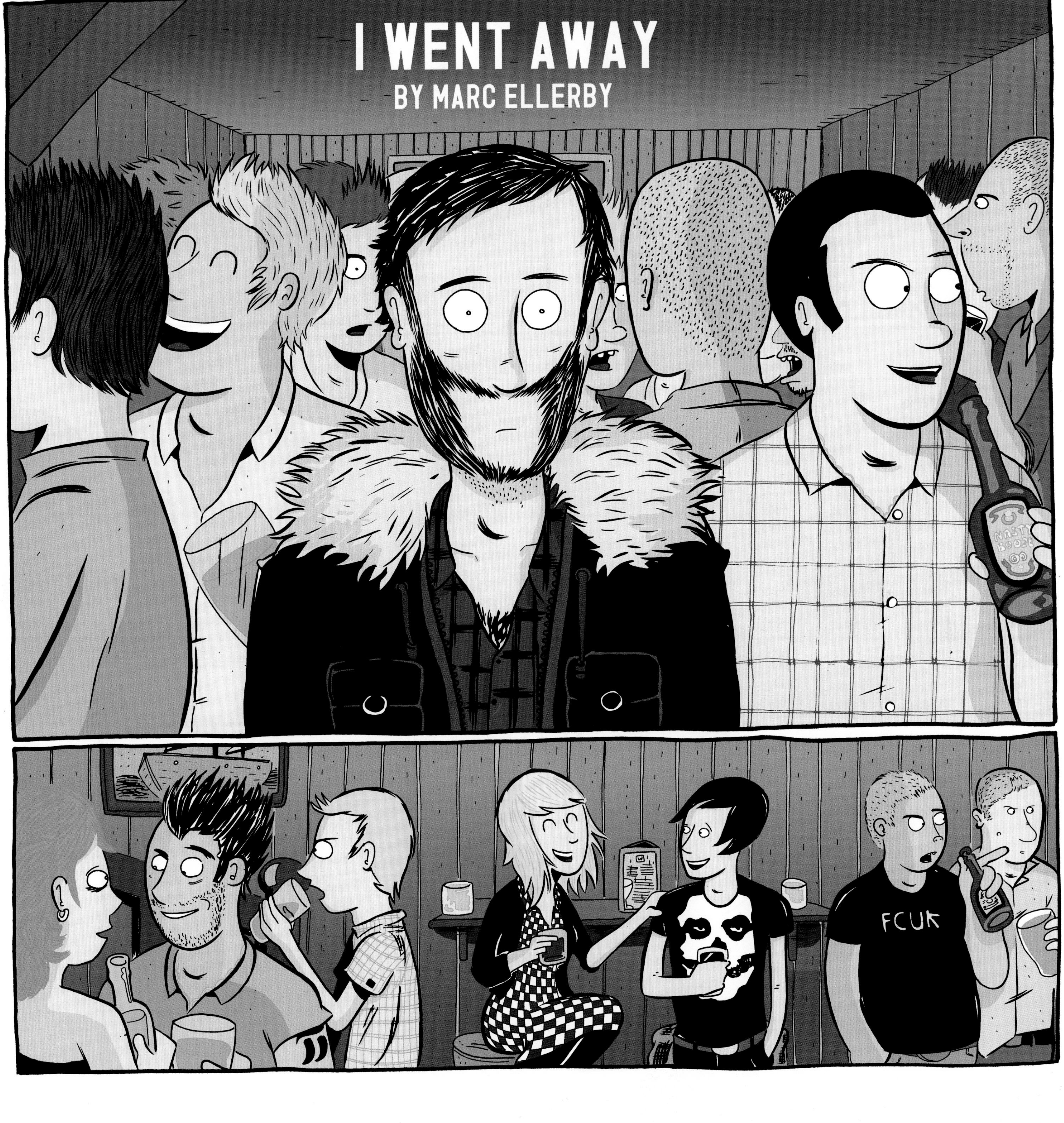
I WENT AWAY
BY MARC ELLERBY
FCUK

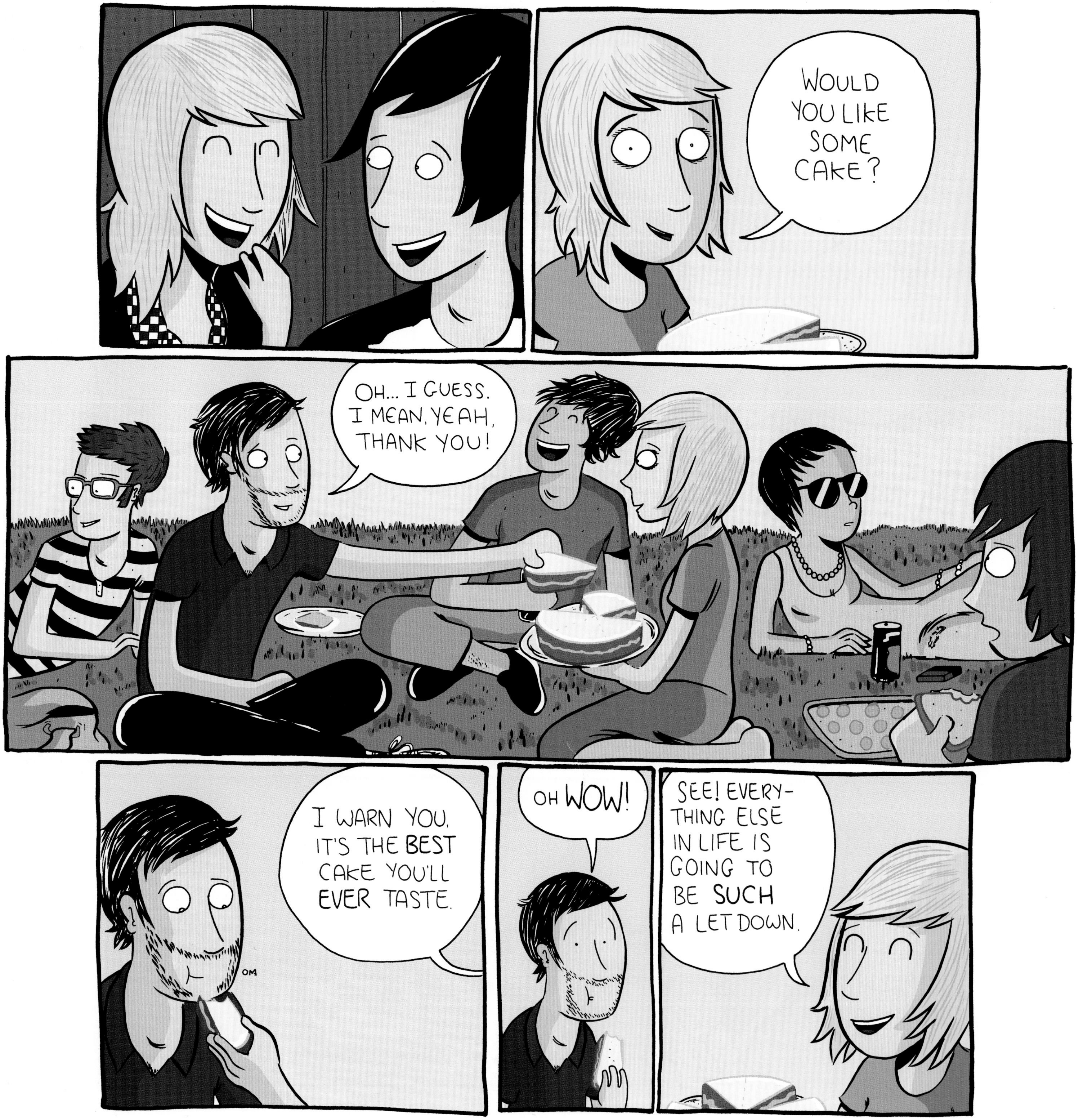
WOULD YOU LIKE SOME CAKE?
OH... I GUESS. I MEAN, YEAH, THANK YOU!
I WARN YOU. IT'S THE BEST CAKE YOU'LL EVER TASTE.
OM
OH WOW!
SEE! EVERY-THING ELSE IN LIFE IS GOING TO BE SUCH A LET DOWN.

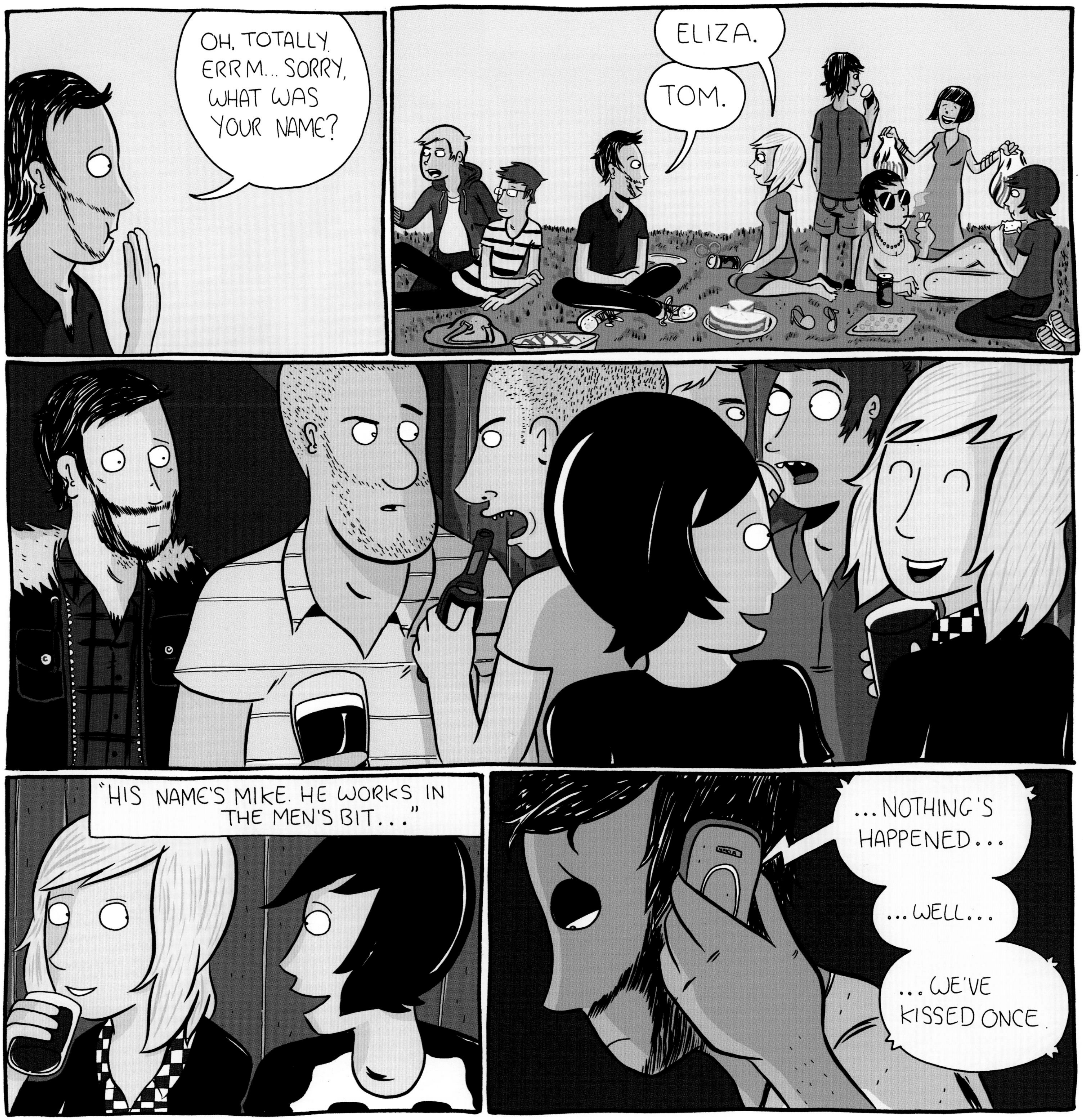
OH, TOTALLY. ERRM... SORRY, WHAT WAS YOUR NAME?
ELIZA.
TOM.
"HIS NAME'S MIKE. HE WORKS IN THE MEN'S BIT..."
...NOTHING'S HAPPENED...
...WELL...
...WE'VE KISSED ONCE.

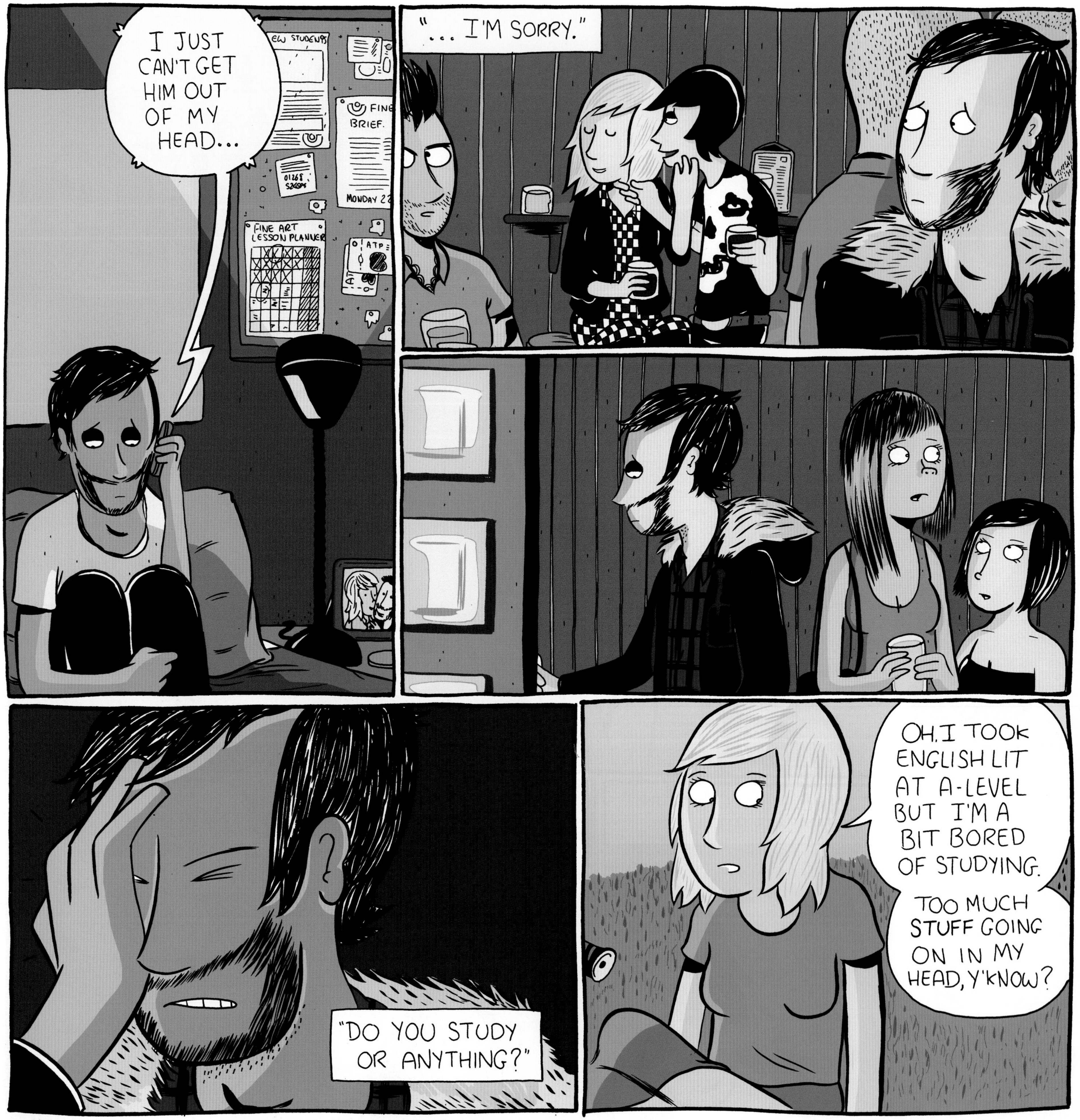
I JUST CAN'T GET HIM OUT OF MY HEAD...
"... I'M SORRY."
"DO YOU STUDY OR ANYTHING?"
OH. I TOOK ENGLISH LIT AT A-LEVEL BUT I'M A BIT BORED OF STUDYING.
TOO MUCH STUFF GOING ON IN MY HEAD, Y'KNOW?

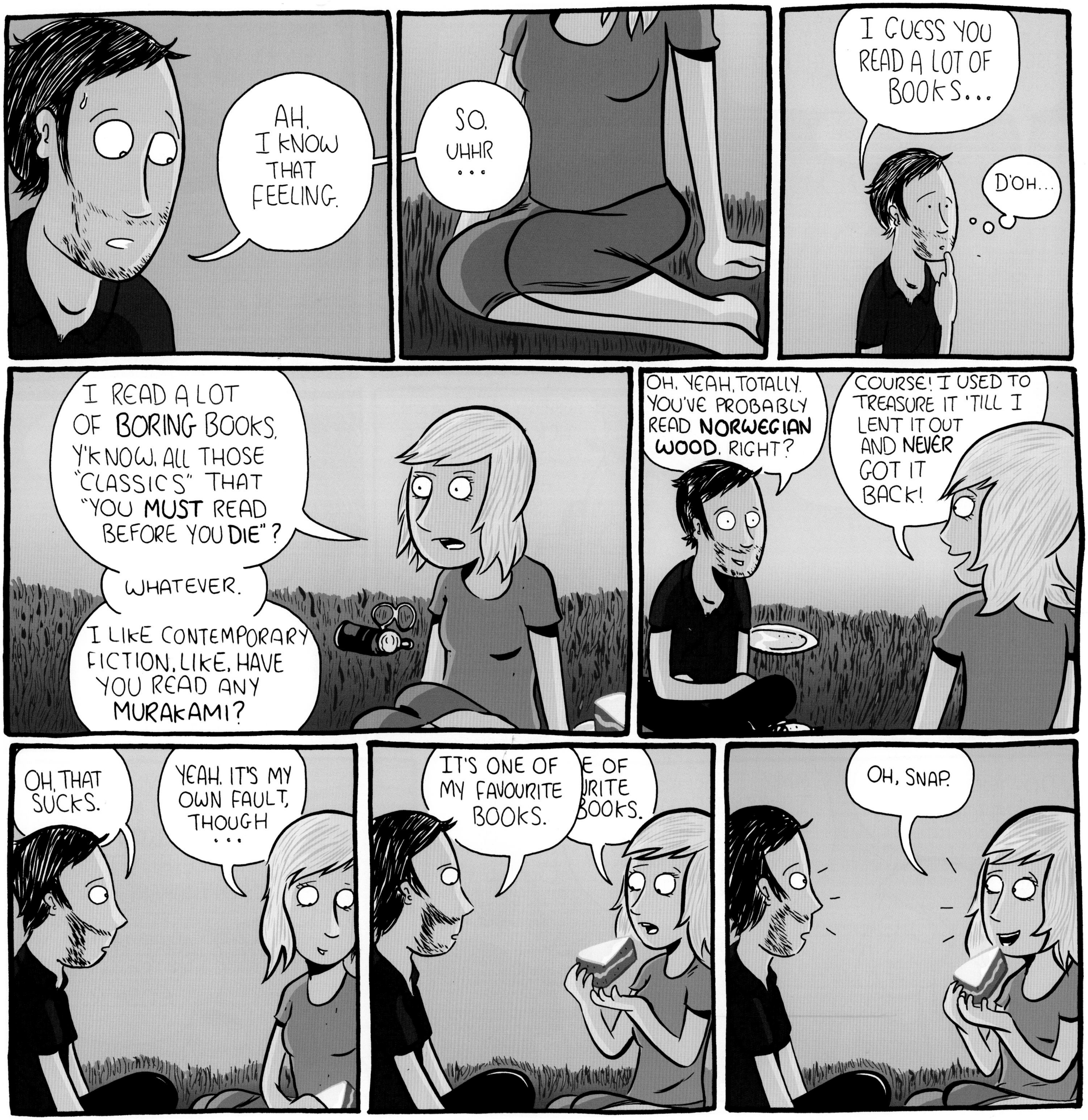
AH, I KNOW THAT FEELING.
SO, UHHR . . .
I GUESS YOU READ A LOT OF BOOKS...
D'OH...
I READ A LOT OF BORING BOOKS, Y'KNOW, ALL THOSE "CLASSICS" THAT "YOU MUST READ BEFORE YOU DIE"?
WHATEVER.
I LIKE CONTEMPORARY FICTION, LIKE, HAVE YOU READ ANY MURAKAMI?
OH, YEAH, TOTALLY. YOU'VE PROBABLY READ NORWEGIAN WOOD, RIGHT?
COURSE! I USED TO TREASURE IT 'TILL I LENT IT OUT AND NEVER GOT IT BACK!
OH, THAT SUCKS.
YEAH, IT'S MY OWN FAULT, THOUGH . . .
IT'S ONE OF MY FAVOURITE BOOKS.
E OF URITE BOOKS.
OH, SNAP.

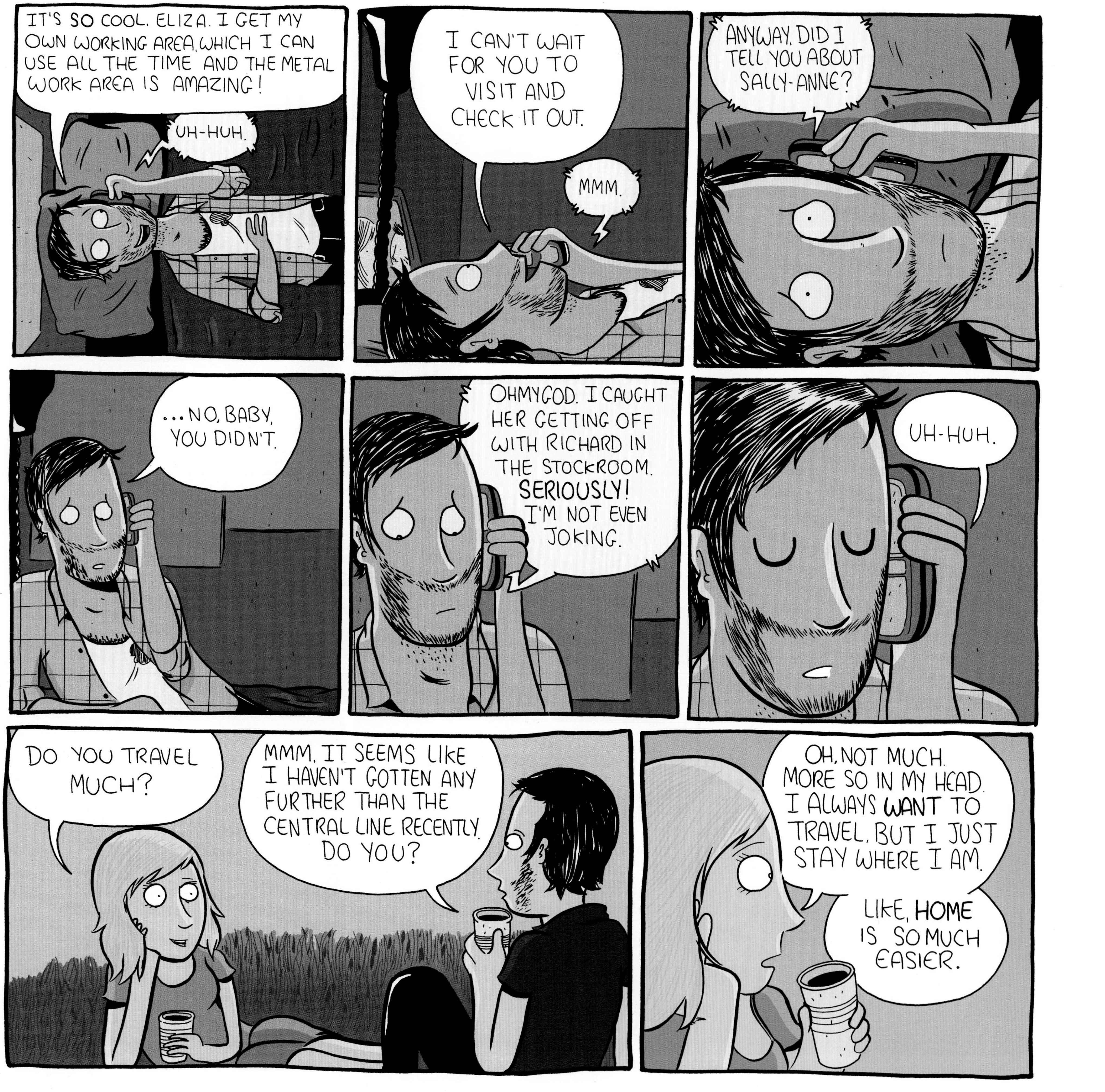
IT'S SO COOL, ELIZA. I GET MY OWN WORKING AREA, WHICH I CAN USE ALL THE TIME AND THE METAL WORK AREA IS AMAZING!
UH-HUH.
I CAN'T WAIT FOR YOU TO VISIT AND CHECK IT OUT.
MMM.
ANYWAY, DID I TELL YOU ABOUT SALLY-ANNE?
...NO, BABY, YOU DIDN'T.
OHMYGOD. I CAUGHT HER GETTING OFF WITH RICHARD IN THE STOCKROOM. SERIOUSLY! I'M NOT EVEN JOKING.
UH-HUH.
DO YOU TRAVEL MUCH?
MMM, IT SEEMS LIKE I HAVEN'T GOTTEN ANY FURTHER THAN THE CENTRAL LINE RECENTLY. DO YOU?
OH, NOT MUCH. MORE SO IN MY HEAD. I ALWAYS WANT TO TRAVEL, BUT I JUST STAY WHERE I AM.
LIKE, HOME IS SO MUCH EASIER.

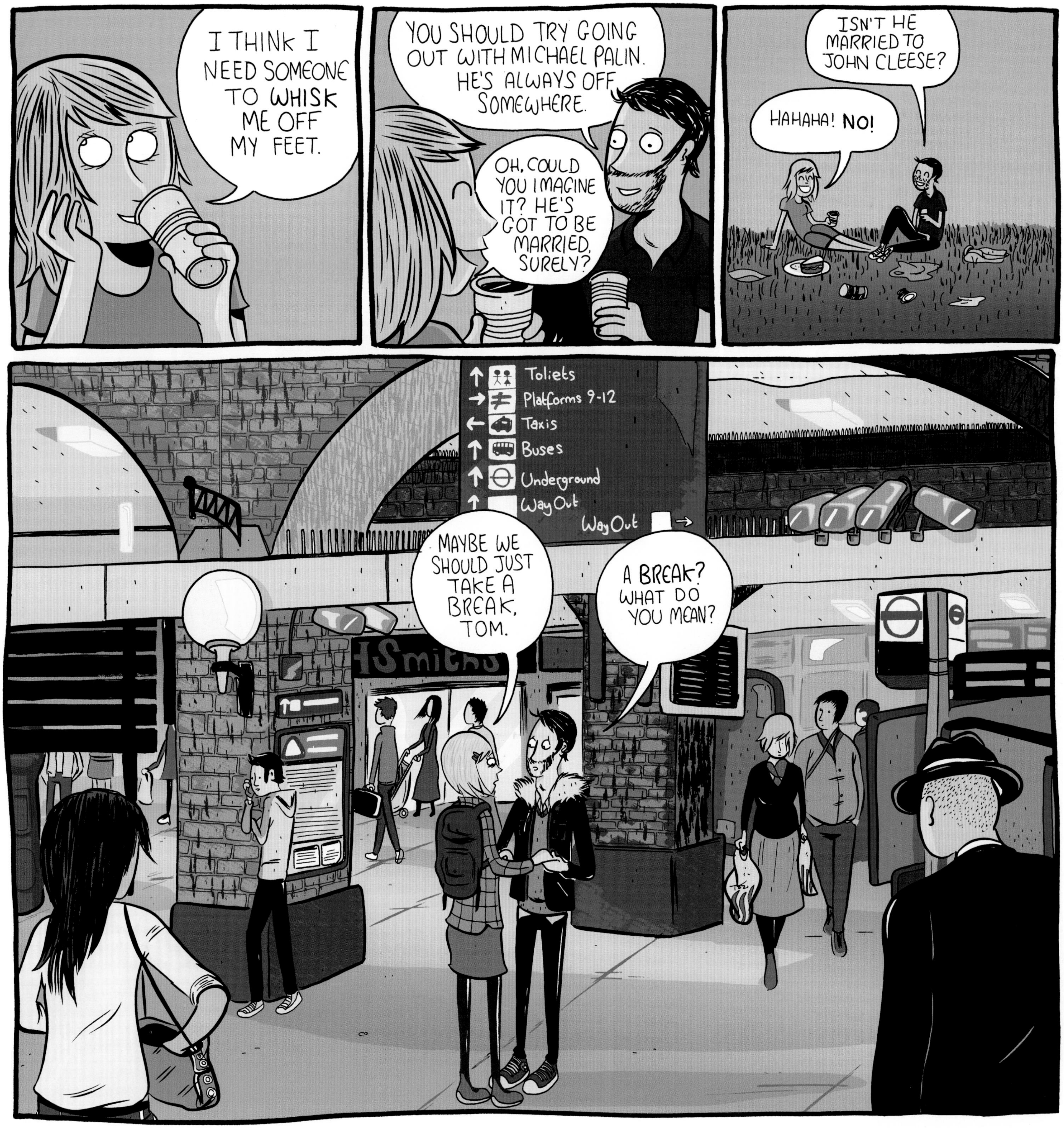
I THINK I NEED SOMEONE TO WHISK ME OFF MY FEET.
YOU SHOULD TRY GOING OUT WITH MICHAEL PALIN. HE'S ALWAYS OFF SOMEWHERE.
OH, COULD YOU IMAGINE IT? HE'S GOT TO BE MARRIED, SURELY?
ISN'T HE MARRIED TO JOHN CLEESE?
HAHAHA! NO!
Toliets
Platforms 9-12
Taxis
Buses
Underground
Way Out
Way Out
MAYBE WE SHOULD JUST TAKE A BREAK, TOM.
A BREAK? WHAT DO YOU MEAN?

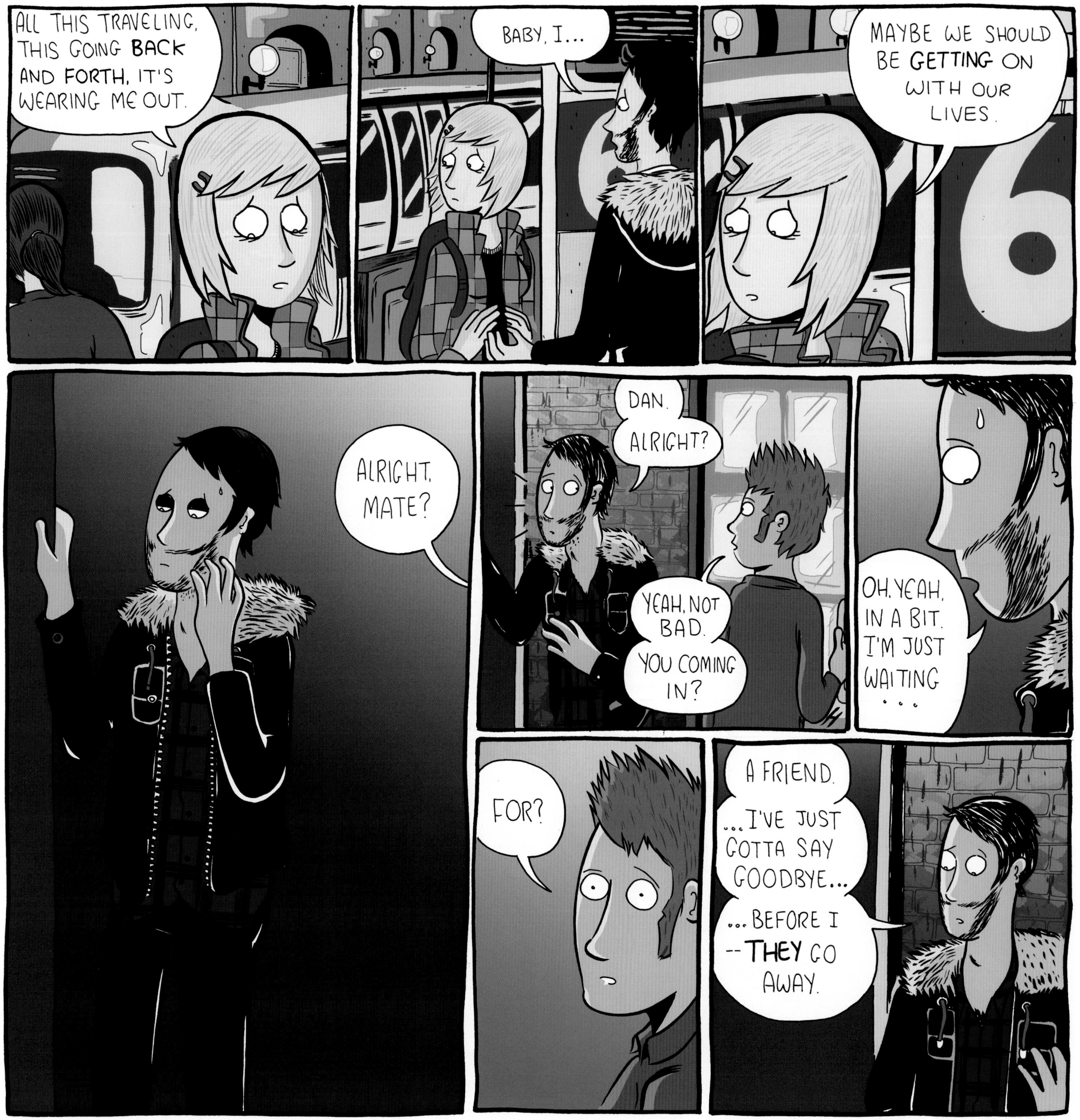
ALL THIS TRAVELING, THIS GOING BACK AND FORTH, IT'S WEARING ME OUT.
BABY, I...
MAYBE WE SHOULD BE GETTING ON WITH OUR LIVES.
ALRIGHT, MATE?
DAN.
ALRIGHT?
YEAH, NOT BAD.
YOU COMING IN?
OH, YEAH, IN A BIT. I'M JUST WAITING...
FOR?
A FRIEND.
...I'VE JUST GOTTA SAY GOODBYE...
...BEFORE I --THEY GO AWAY.

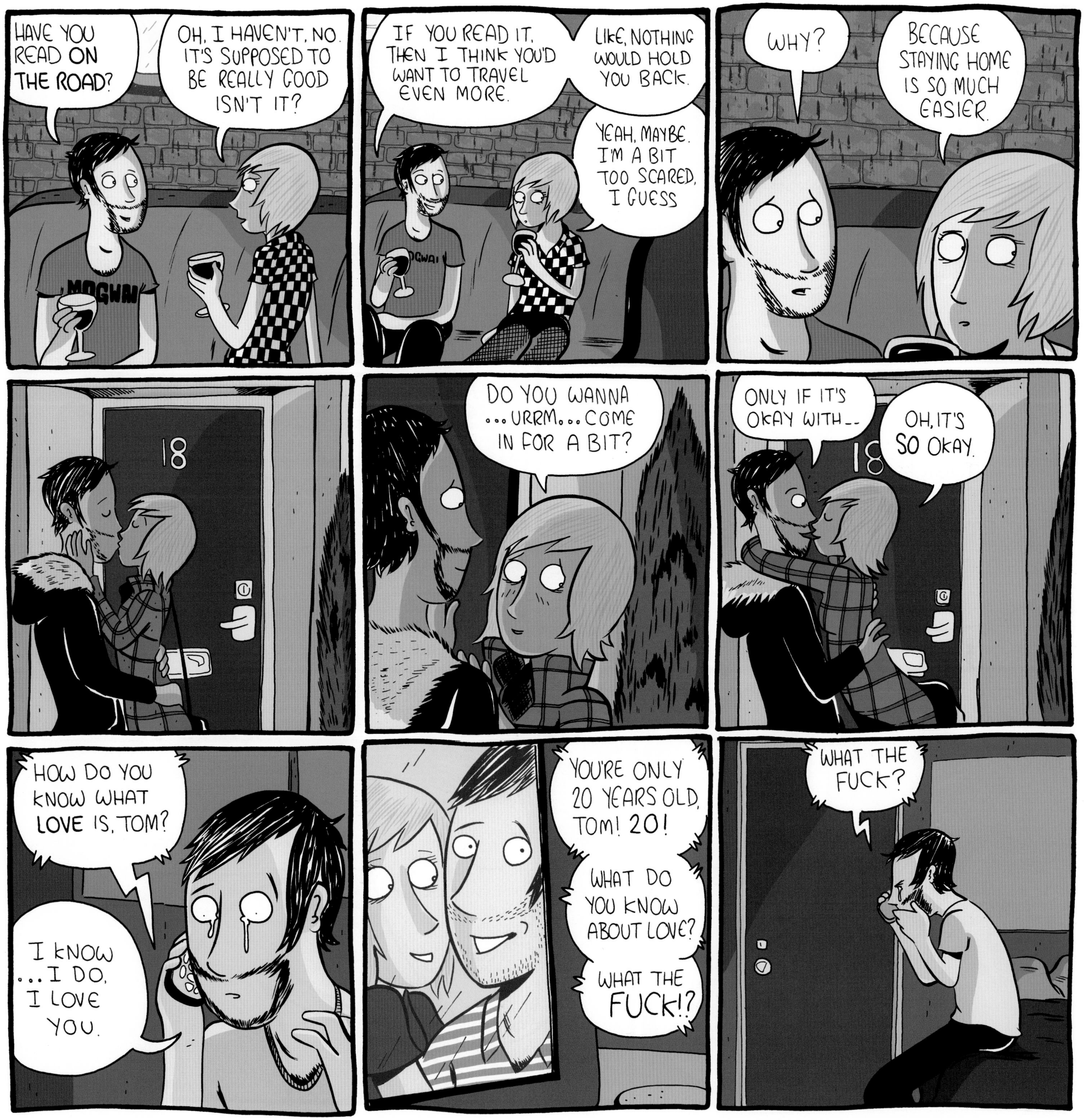
HAVE YOU READ ON THE ROAD?
OH, I HAVEN'T, NO. IT'S SUPPOSED TO BE REALLY GOOD ISN'T IT?
MOGWAI
IF YOU READ IT, THEN I THINK YOU'D WANT TO TRAVEL EVEN MORE.
LIKE, NOTHING WOULD HOLD YOU BACK.
YEAH, MAYBE. I'M A BIT TOO SCARED, I GUESS
WHY?
BECAUSE STAYING HOME IS SO MUCH EASIER.
18
DO YOU WANNA ...URRM... COME IN FOR A BIT?
ONLY IF IT'S OKAY WITH--
OH, IT'S SO OKAY.
HOW DO YOU KNOW WHAT LOVE IS, TOM?
I KNOW ... I DO, I LOVE YOU.
YOU'RE ONLY 20 YEARS OLD, TOM! 20!
WHAT DO YOU KNOW ABOUT LOVE?
WHAT THE FUCK!?
WHAT THE FUCK?

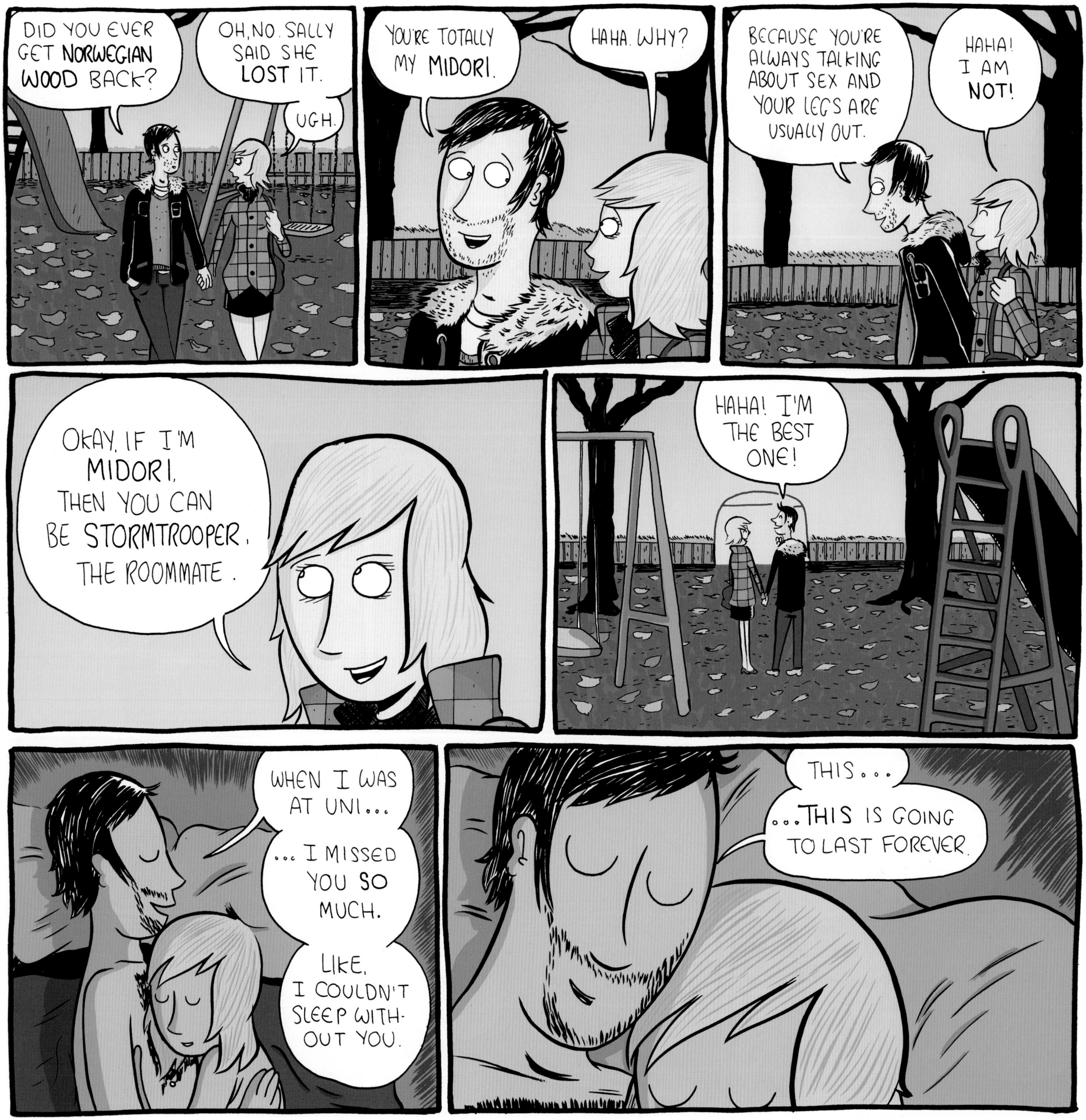
DID YOU EVER GET NORWEGIAN WOOD BACK?
OH, NO. SALLY SAID SHE LOST IT.
UGH.
YOU'RE TOTALLY MY MIDORI.
HAHA. WHY?
BECAUSE YOU'RE ALWAYS TALKING ABOUT SEX AND YOUR LEGS ARE USUALLY OUT.
HAHA! I AM NOT!
OKAY. IF I'M MIDORI, THEN YOU CAN BE STORMTROOPER, THE ROOMMATE.
HAHA! I'M THE BEST ONE!
WHEN I WAS AT UNI...
... I MISSED YOU SO MUCH.
LIKE, I COULDN'T SLEEP WITH-OUT YOU.
THIS...
...THIS IS GOING TO LAST FOREVER.

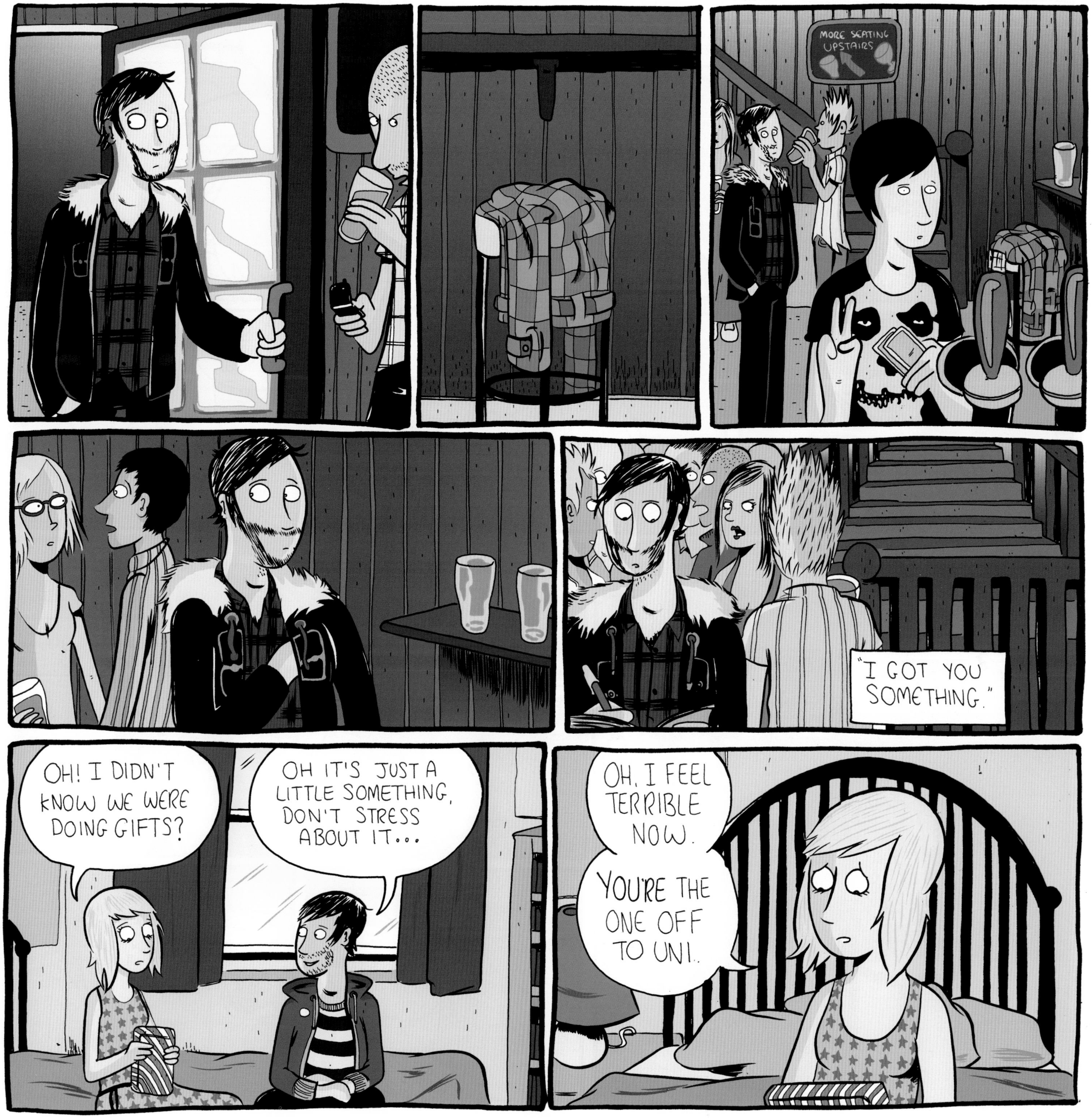
MORE SEATING UPSTAIRS
"I GOT YOU SOMETHING."
OH! I DIDN'T KNOW WE WERE DOING GIFTS?
OH IT'S JUST A LITTLE SOMETHING, DON'T STRESS ABOUT IT...
OH, I FEEL TERRIBLE NOW.
YOU'RE THE ONE OFF TO UNI.

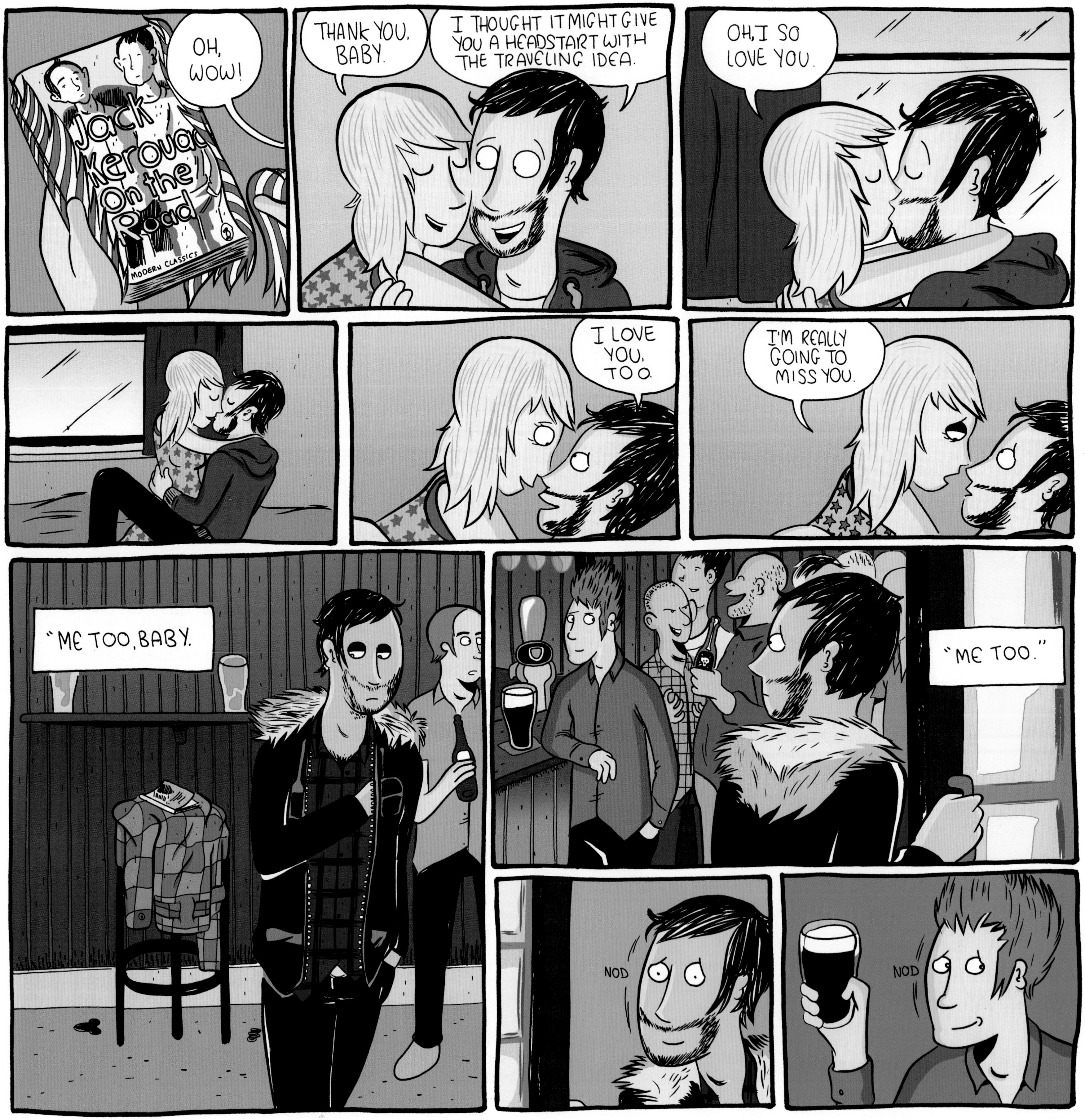
Jack Kerouac On the Road
MODERN CLASSICS
OH, WOW!
THANK YOU, BABY.
I THOUGHT IT MIGHT GIVE YOU A HEADSTART WITH THE TRAVELING IDEA.
OH, I SO LOVE YOU.
I LOVE YOU, TOO.
I'M REALLY GOING TO MISS YOU.
"ME TOO, BABY.
"ME TOO."
NOD
NOD

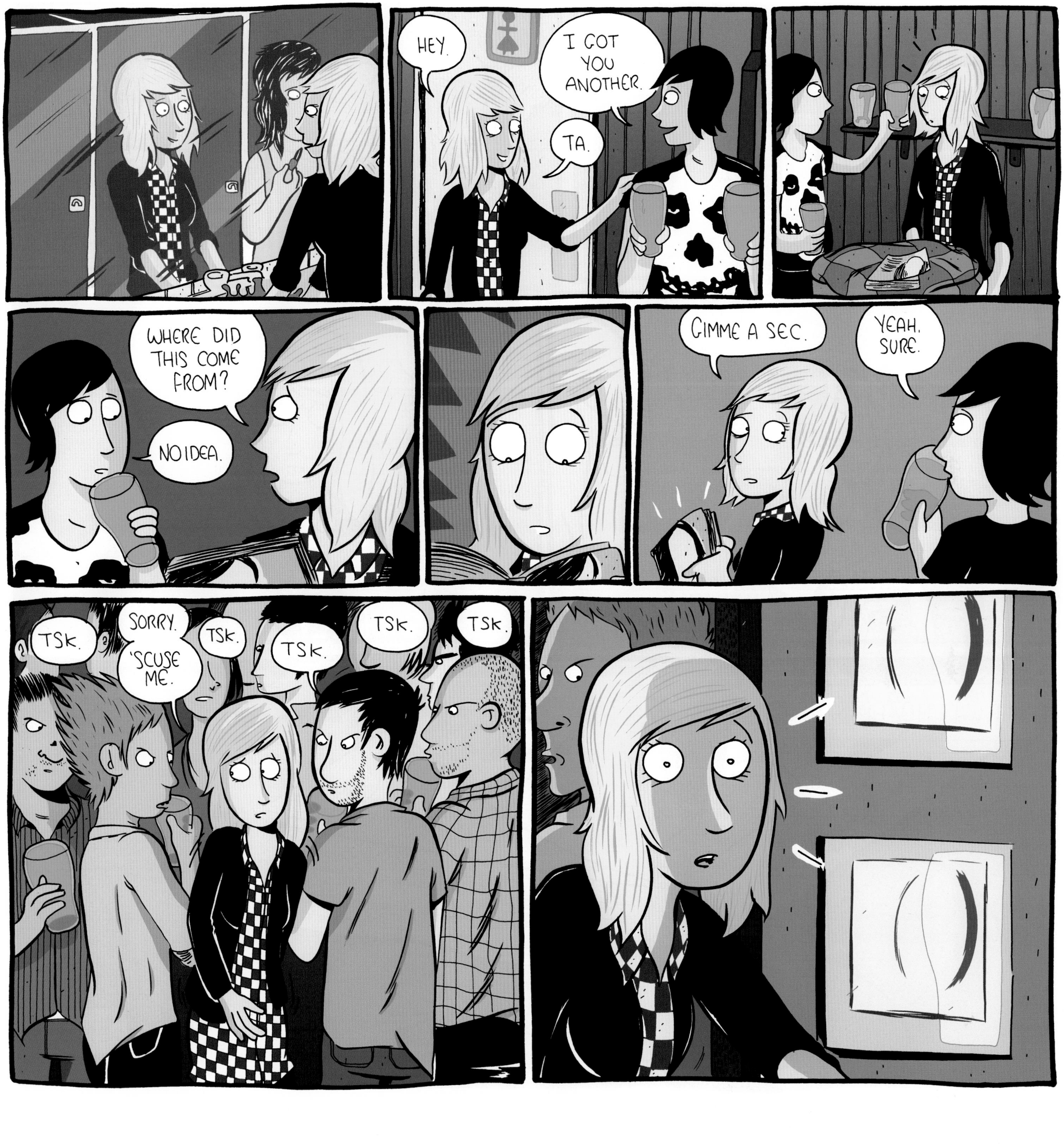
HEY.
I GOT YOU ANOTHER.
TA.
WHERE DID THIS COME FROM?
NO IDEA.
GIMME A SEC.
YEAH. SURE.
TSK.
SORRY.
'SCUSE ME.
TSK.
TSK.
TSK.
TSK.

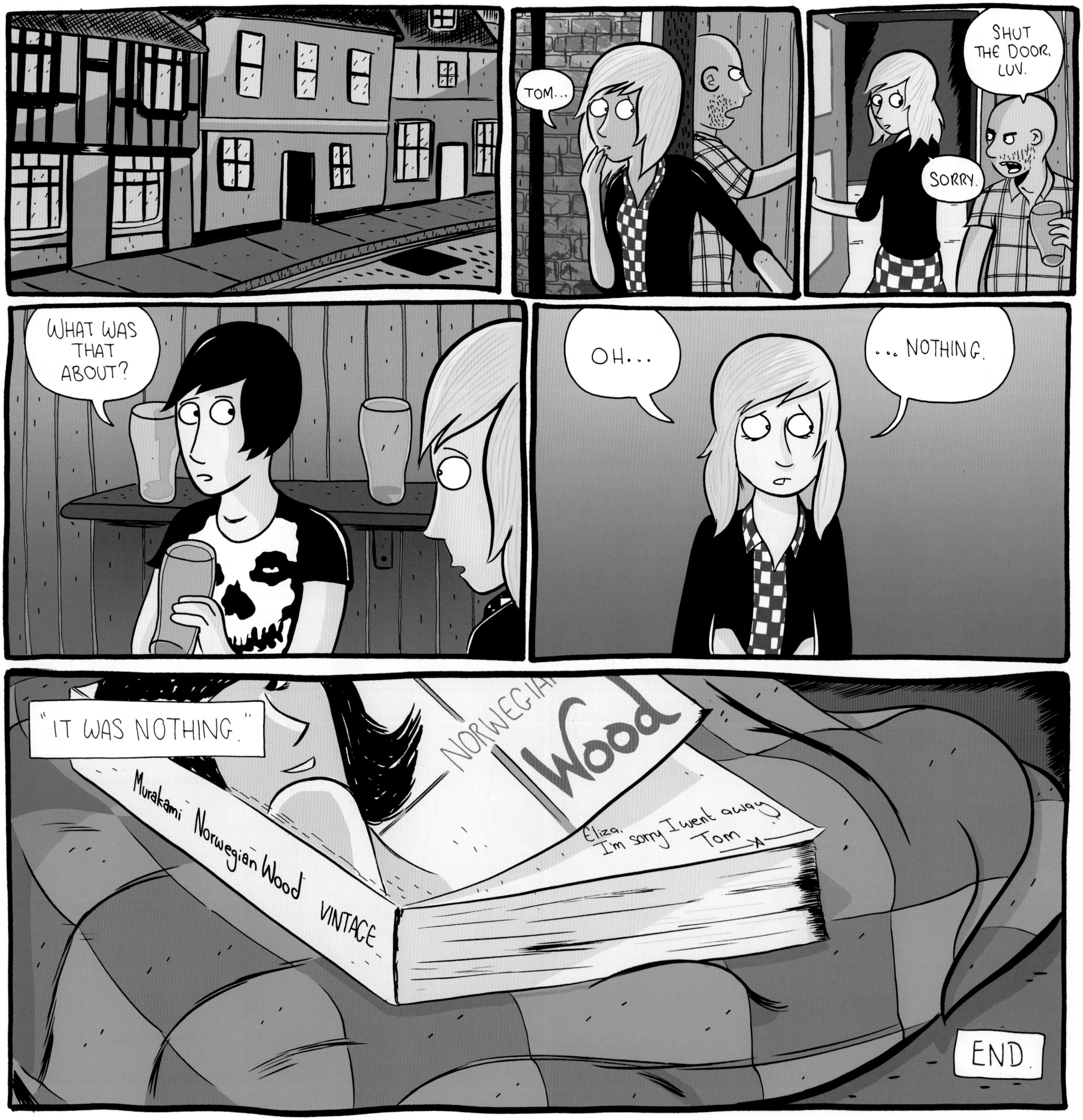

TOM...
SHUT THE DOOR, LUV.
SORRY.
WHAT WAS THAT ABOUT?
OH...
...NOTHING.
"IT WAS NOTHING."
NORWEGIAN Wood
Murakami Norwegian Wood VINTAGE
Eliza, I'm sorry I went away Tom x
END.

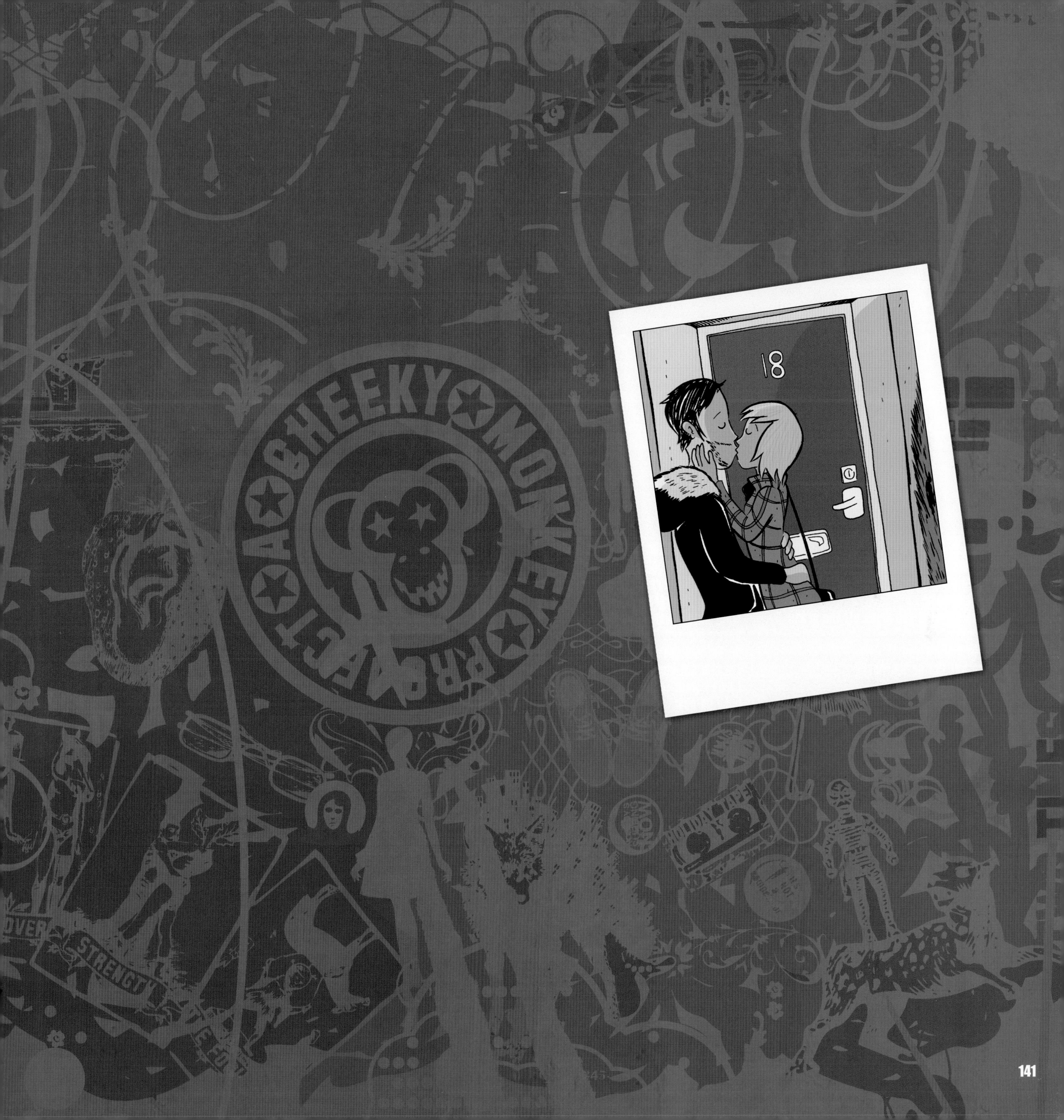
A CHEEKY MONKEY PROJECT
18

A BENCH IN THE PARK

featured on **Songs for the Color Yellow**

story by **Tony Lee**
art by **Kevin Colden**

on a bench in the park
in the grounds of the college
is a bronze plaque
bearing your name
and as the morning sun dries off the grass
i will sit here
and try to picture you
you were sat flat on the floor

i didn't understand your illness
i only knew it made me feel awkward
and you so happy
so at one with the world
a shaved head and a clear smile
how could you be
so at peace with everything
to have seen so much so young

the holidays were long
and when we came back
you were gone

alison kay gave me some words
but i didn't want to sing them

i said i didn't want
to cheapen your memory
but really i just didn't want to face
what had happened to you

i will move at the chime of the clock
but now the clock has stopped
and i'm still here
in these 16 years
what have i learned?
have i learned the strength that you had then?
as the sun goes down
i'm still sat here
i didn't want to sing it then
but i do now
the only time i really spoke to you
you were sat flat on the floor

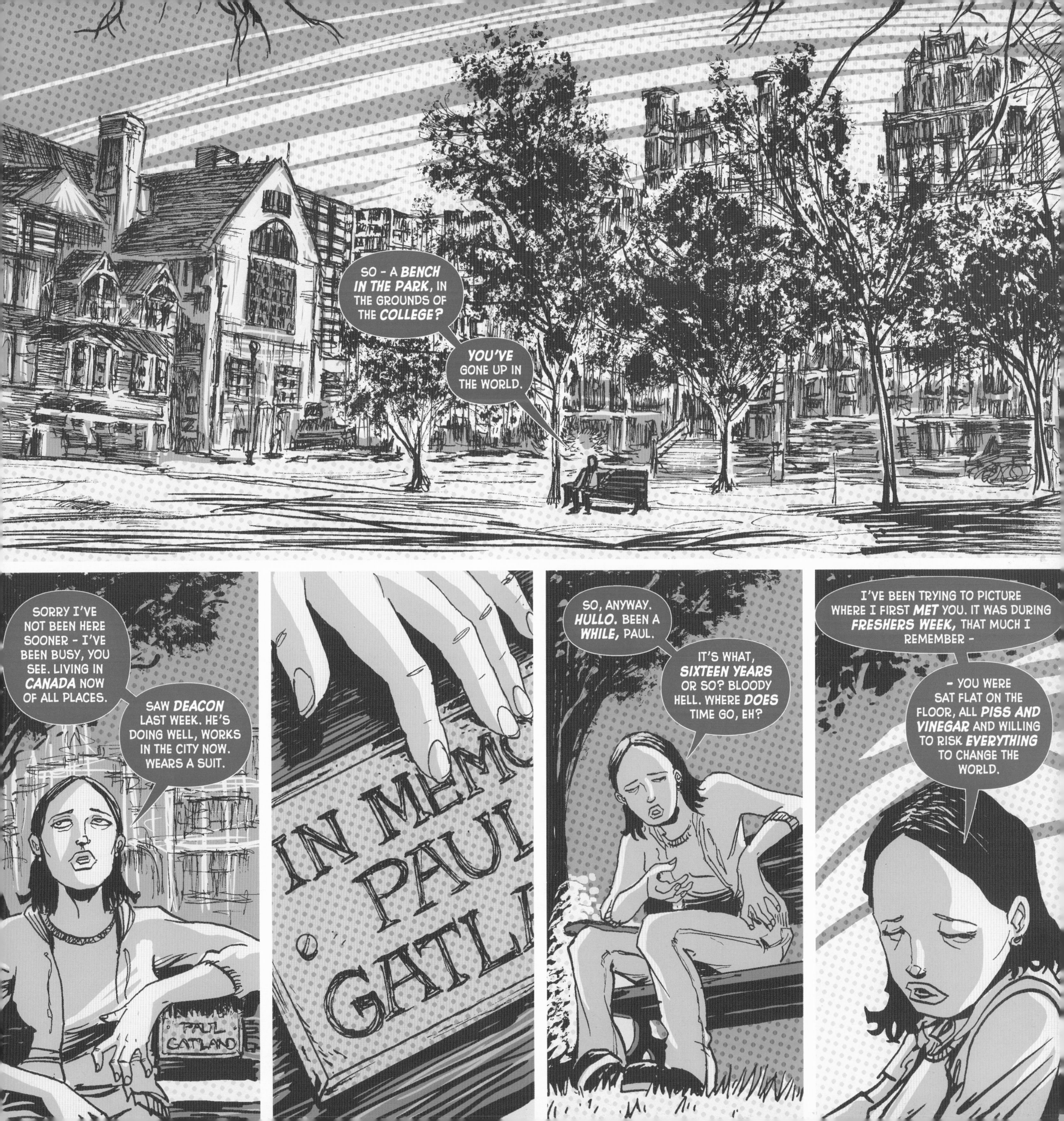
SO - A BENCH IN THE PARK, IN THE GROUNDS OF THE COLLEGE?
YOU'VE GONE UP IN THE WORLD.
SORRY I'VE NOT BEEN HERE SOONER - I'VE BEEN BUSY, YOU SEE. LIVING IN CANADA NOW OF ALL PLACES.
SAW DEACON LAST WEEK. HE'S DOING WELL, WORKS IN THE CITY NOW. WEARS A SUIT.
PAUL GATLAND
IN MEMO
PAUL
GATL
SO, ANYWAY. HULLO. BEEN A WHILE, PAUL.
IT'S WHAT, SIXTEEN YEARS OR SO? BLOODY HELL. WHERE DOES TIME GO, EH?
I'VE BEEN TRYING TO PICTURE WHERE I FIRST MET YOU. IT WAS DURING FRESHERS WEEK, THAT MUCH I REMEMBER -
- YOU WERE SAT FLAT ON THE FLOOR, ALL PISS AND VINEGAR AND WILLING TO RISK EVERYTHING TO CHANGE THE WORLD.

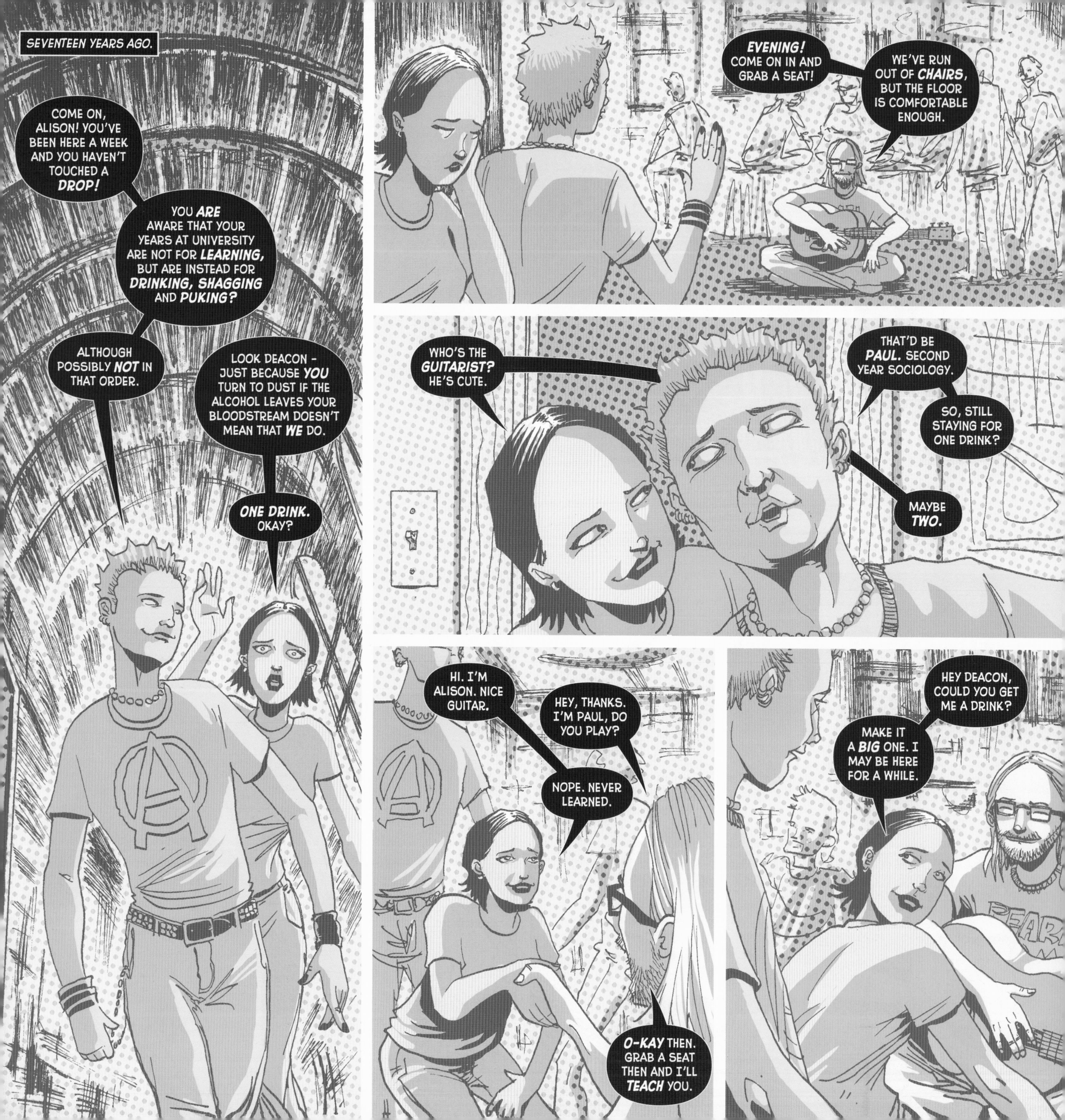
SEVENTEEN YEARS AGO.
COME ON, ALISON! YOU'VE BEEN HERE A WEEK AND YOU HAVEN'T TOUCHED A DROP!
YOU ARE AWARE THAT YOUR YEARS AT UNIVERSITY ARE NOT FOR LEARNING, BUT ARE INSTEAD FOR DRINKING, SHAGGING AND PUKING?
ALTHOUGH POSSIBLY NOT IN THAT ORDER.
LOOK DEACON - JUST BECAUSE YOU TURN TO DUST IF THE ALCOHOL LEAVES YOUR BLOODSTREAM DOESN'T MEAN THAT WE DO.
ONE DRINK. OKAY?
EVENING! COME ON IN AND GRAB A SEAT!
WE'VE RUN OUT OF CHAIRS, BUT THE FLOOR IS COMFORTABLE ENOUGH.
WHO'S THE GUITARIST? HE'S CUTE.
THAT'D BE PAUL. SECOND YEAR SOCIOLOGY.
SO, STILL STAYING FOR ONE DRINK?
MAYBE TWO.
HI. I'M ALISON. NICE GUITAR.
HEY, THANKS. I'M PAUL, DO YOU PLAY?
NOPE. NEVER LEARNED.
O-KAY THEN. GRAB A SEAT THEN AND I'LL TEACH YOU.
HEY DEACON, COULD YOU GET ME A DRINK?
MAKE IT A BIG ONE. I MAY BE HERE FOR A WHILE.

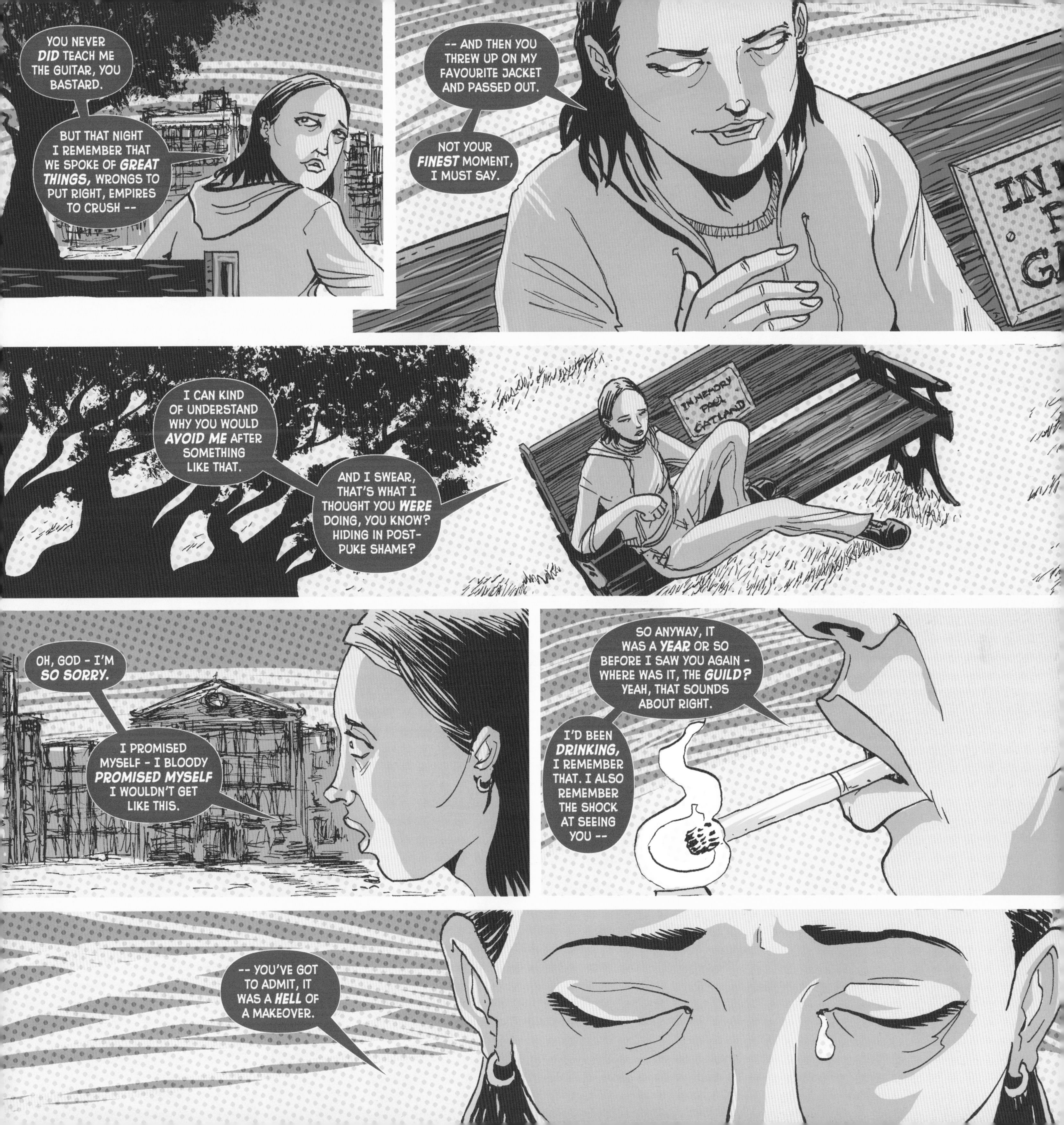
YOU NEVER DID TEACH ME THE GUITAR, YOU BASTARD.
BUT THAT NIGHT I REMEMBER THAT WE SPOKE OF GREAT THINGS, WRONGS TO PUT RIGHT, EMPIRES TO CRUSH --
-- AND THEN YOU THREW UP ON MY FAVOURITE JACKET AND PASSED OUT.
NOT YOUR FINEST MOMENT, I MUST SAY.
I CAN KIND OF UNDERSTAND WHY YOU WOULD AVOID ME AFTER SOMETHING LIKE THAT.
AND I SWEAR, THAT'S WHAT I THOUGHT YOU WERE DOING, YOU KNOW? HIDING IN POST-PUKE SHAME?
IN MEMORY PAUL GATLAND
OH, GOD - I'M SO SORRY.
I PROMISED MYSELF - I BLOODY PROMISED MYSELF I WOULDN'T GET LIKE THIS.
SO ANYWAY, IT WAS A YEAR OR SO BEFORE I SAW YOU AGAIN - WHERE WAS IT, THE GUILD? YEAH, THAT SOUNDS ABOUT RIGHT.
I'D BEEN DRINKING, I REMEMBER THAT. I ALSO REMEMBER THE SHOCK AT SEEING YOU --
-- YOU'VE GOT TO ADMIT, IT WAS A HELL OF A MAKEOVER.

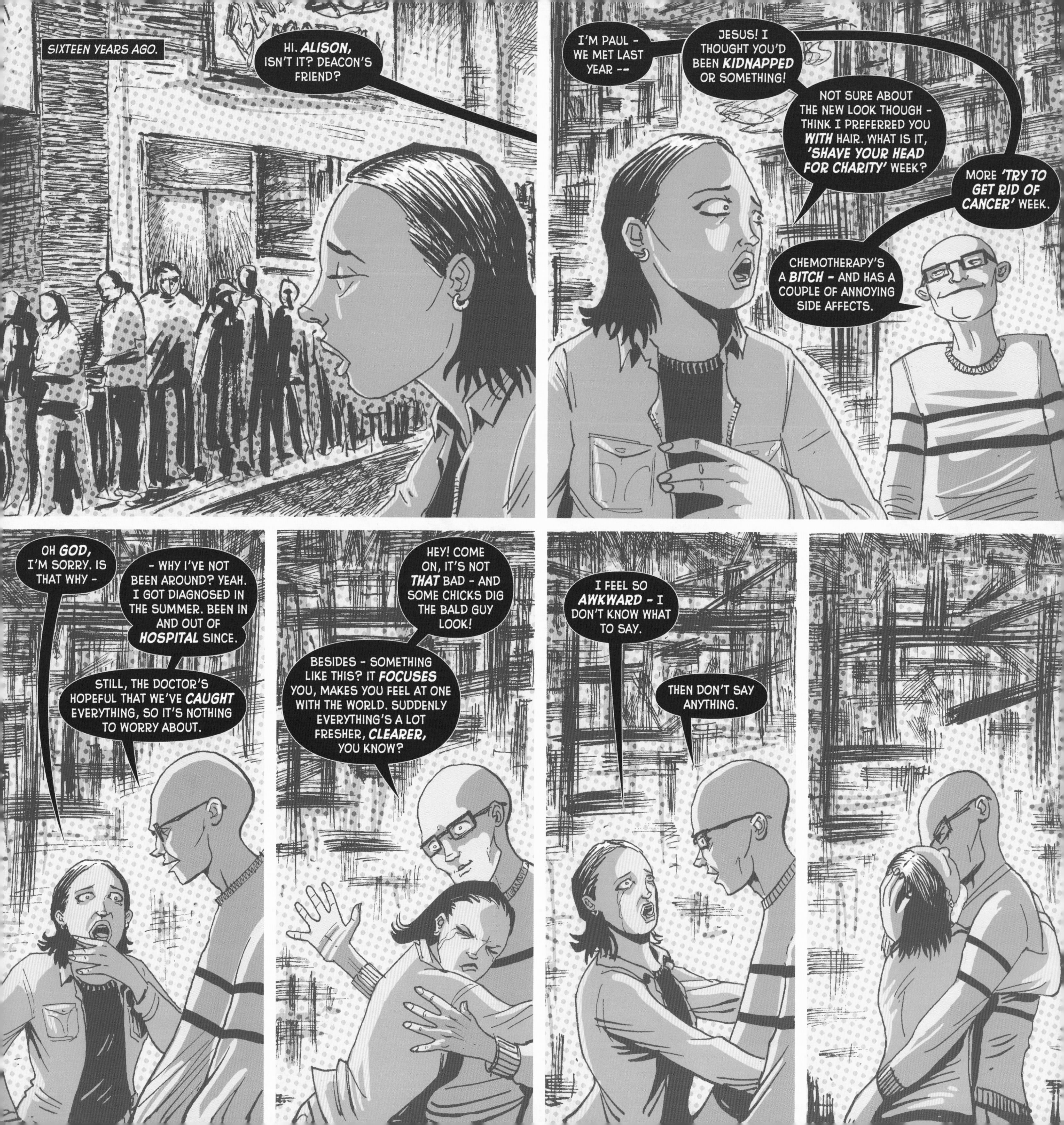
SIXTEEN YEARS AGO.
HI. ALISON, ISN'T IT? DEACON'S FRIEND?
I'M PAUL - WE MET LAST YEAR --
JESUS! I THOUGHT YOU'D BEEN KIDNAPPED OR SOMETHING!
NOT SURE ABOUT THE NEW LOOK THOUGH - THINK I PREFERRED YOU WITH HAIR. WHAT IS IT, 'SHAVE YOUR HEAD FOR CHARITY' WEEK?
MORE 'TRY TO GET RID OF CANCER' WEEK.
CHEMOTHERAPY'S A BITCH - AND HAS A COUPLE OF ANNOYING SIDE AFFECTS.
OH GOD, I'M SORRY. IS THAT WHY -
- WHY I'VE NOT BEEN AROUND? YEAH. I GOT DIAGNOSED IN THE SUMMER. BEEN IN AND OUT OF HOSPITAL SINCE.
STILL, THE DOCTOR'S HOPEFUL THAT WE'VE CAUGHT EVERYTHING, SO IT'S NOTHING TO WORRY ABOUT.
HEY! COME ON, IT'S NOT THAT BAD - AND SOME CHICKS DIG THE BALD GUY LOOK!
BESIDES - SOMETHING LIKE THIS? IT FOCUSES YOU, MAKES YOU FEEL AT ONE WITH THE WORLD. SUDDENLY EVERYTHING'S A LOT FRESHER, CLEARER, YOU KNOW?
I FEEL SO AWKWARD - I DON'T KNOW WHAT TO SAY.
THEN DON'T SAY ANYTHING.

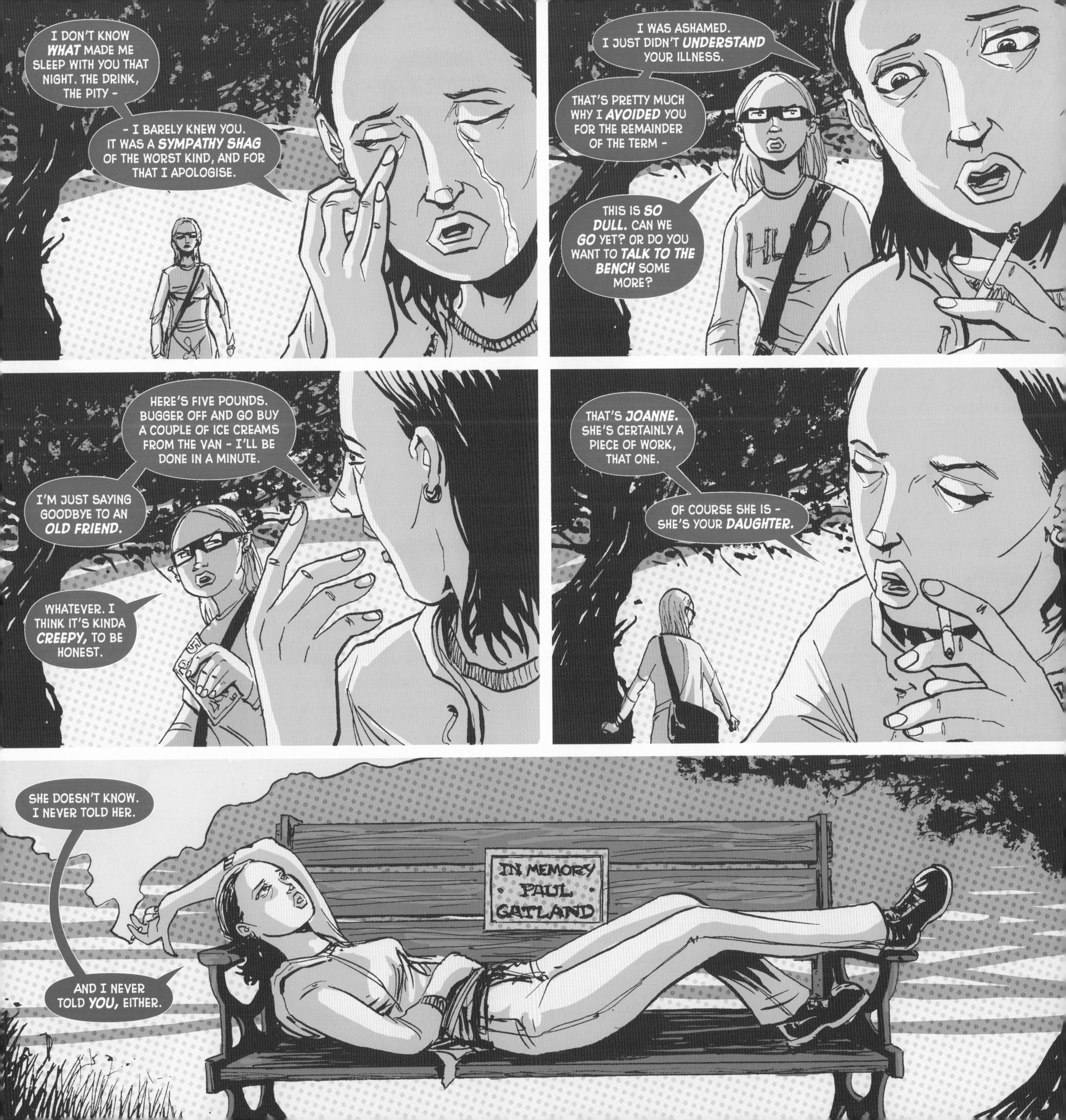
I DON'T KNOW WHAT MADE ME SLEEP WITH YOU THAT NIGHT. THE DRINK, THE PITY -
- I BARELY KNEW YOU. IT WAS A SYMPATHY SHAG OF THE WORST KIND, AND FOR THAT I APOLOGISE.
I WAS ASHAMED. I JUST DIDN'T UNDERSTAND YOUR ILLNESS.
THAT'S PRETTY MUCH WHY I AVOIDED YOU FOR THE REMAINDER OF THE TERM -
THIS IS SO DULL. CAN WE GO YET? OR DO YOU WANT TO TALK TO THE BENCH SOME MORE?
HERE'S FIVE POUNDS. BUGGER OFF AND GO BUY A COUPLE OF ICE CREAMS FROM THE VAN - I'LL BE DONE IN A MINUTE.
I'M JUST SAYING GOODBYE TO AN OLD FRIEND.
WHATEVER. I THINK IT'S KINDA CREEPY, TO BE HONEST.
THAT'S JOANNE. SHE'S CERTAINLY A PIECE OF WORK, THAT ONE.
OF COURSE SHE IS - SHE'S YOUR DAUGHTER.
SHE DOESN'T KNOW. I NEVER TOLD HER.
IN MEMORY PAUL GATLAND
AND I NEVER TOLD YOU, EITHER.

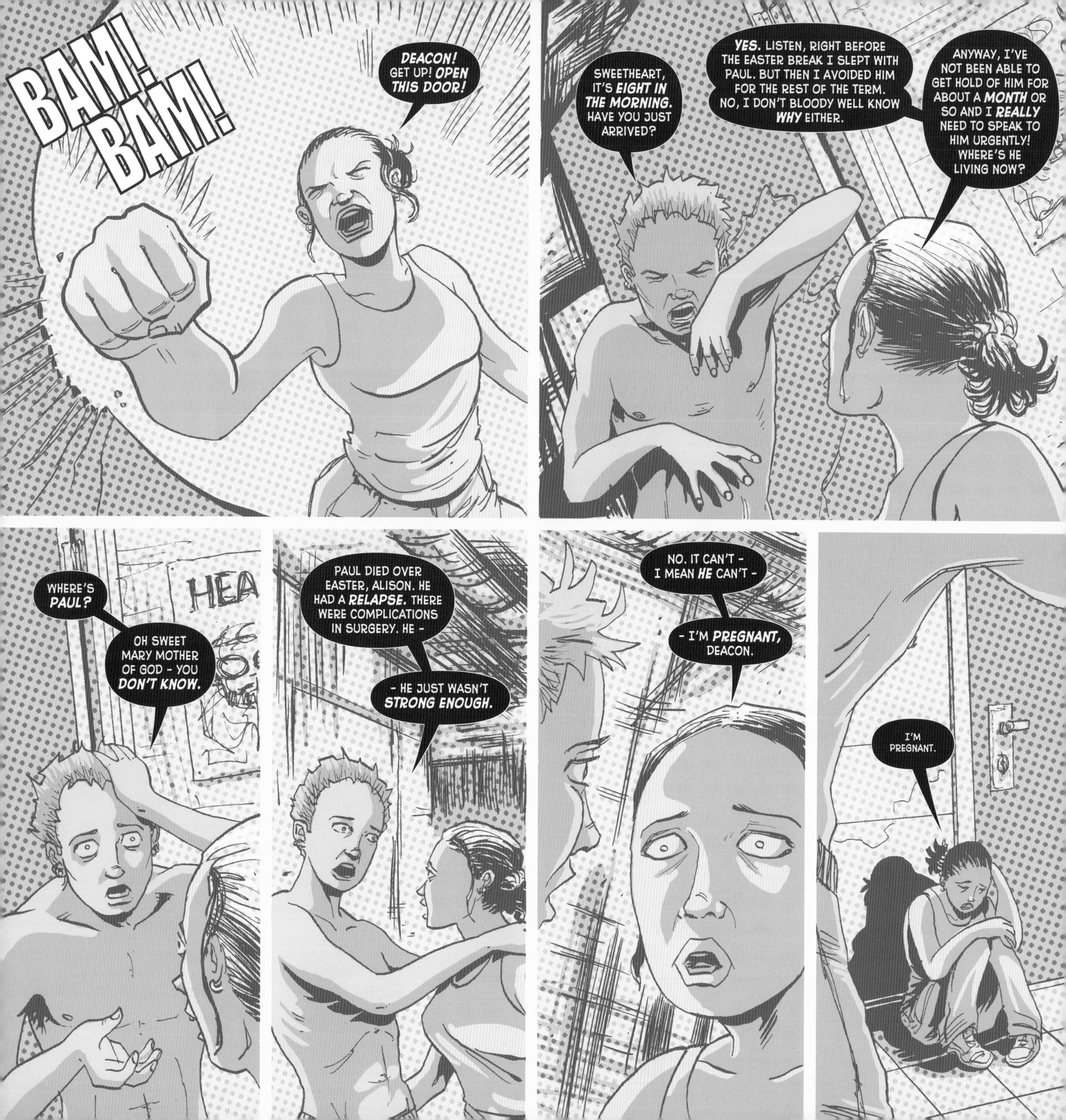

BAM! BAM!
DEACON! GET UP! OPEN THIS DOOR!
SWEETHEART, IT'S EIGHT IN THE MORNING. HAVE YOU JUST ARRIVED?
YES. LISTEN, RIGHT BEFORE THE EASTER BREAK I SLEPT WITH PAUL. BUT THEN I AVOIDED HIM FOR THE REST OF THE TERM. NO, I DON'T BLOODY WELL KNOW WHY EITHER.
ANYWAY, I'VE NOT BEEN ABLE TO GET HOLD OF HIM FOR ABOUT A MONTH OR SO AND I REALLY NEED TO SPEAK TO HIM URGENTLY! WHERE'S HE LIVING NOW?
WHERE'S PAUL?
OH SWEET MARY MOTHER OF GOD - YOU DON'T KNOW.
HEA
PAUL DIED OVER EASTER, ALISON. HE HAD A RELAPSE. THERE WERE COMPLICATIONS IN SURGERY. HE -
- HE JUST WASN'T STRONG ENOUGH.
NO. IT CAN'T - I MEAN HE CAN'T -
- I'M PREGNANT, DEACON.
I'M PREGNANT.

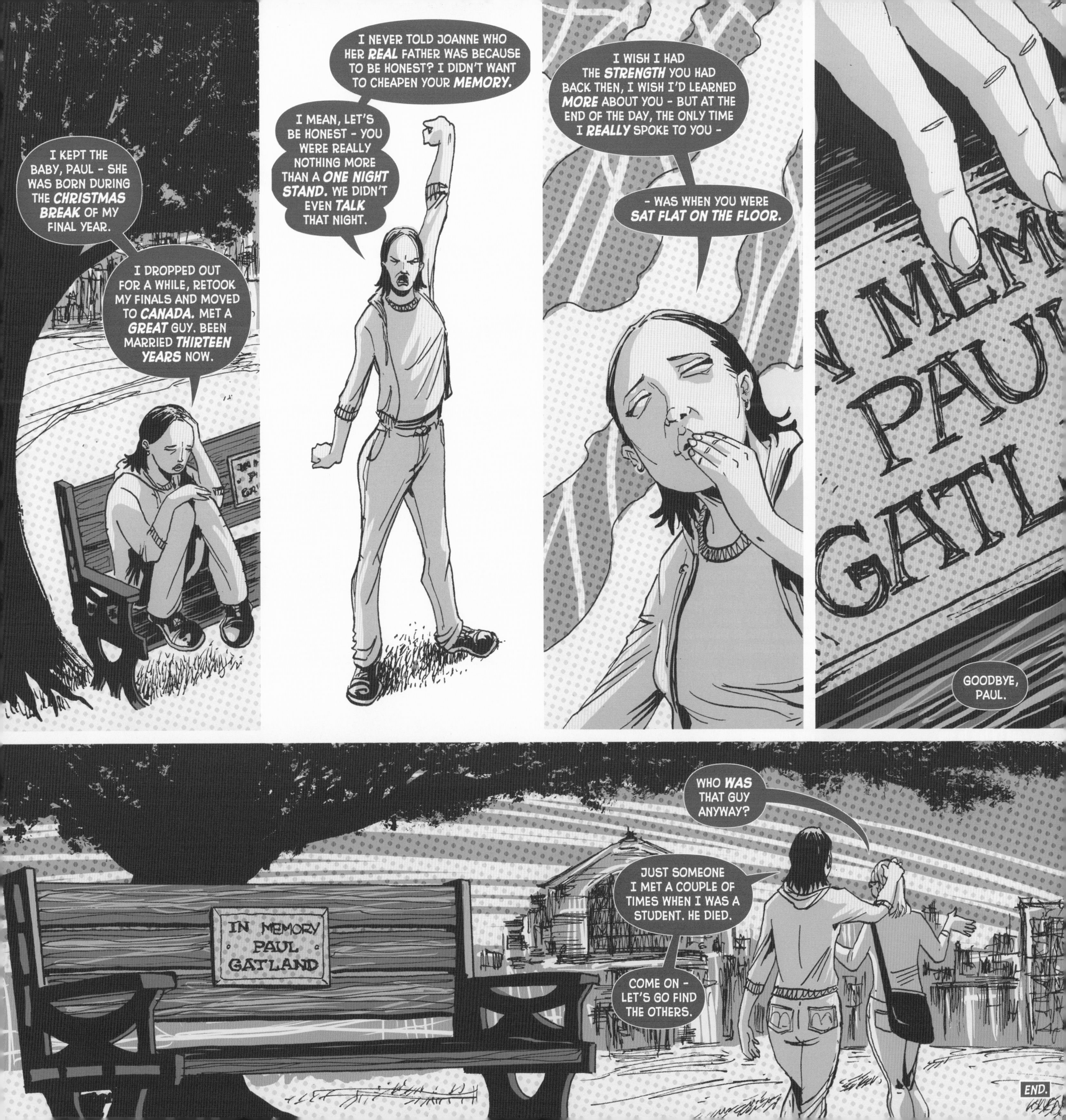
I KEPT THE BABY, PAUL - SHE WAS BORN DURING THE CHRISTMAS BREAK OF MY FINAL YEAR.
I DROPPED OUT FOR A WHILE, RETOOK MY FINALS AND MOVED TO CANADA. MET A GREAT GUY. BEEN MARRIED THIRTEEN YEARS NOW.
I NEVER TOLD JOANNE WHO HER REAL FATHER WAS BECAUSE TO BE HONEST? I DIDN'T WANT TO CHEAPEN YOUR MEMORY.
I MEAN, LET'S BE HONEST - YOU WERE REALLY NOTHING MORE THAN A ONE NIGHT STAND. WE DIDN'T EVEN TALK THAT NIGHT.
I WISH I HAD THE STRENGTH YOU HAD BACK THEN, I WISH I'D LEARNED MORE ABOUT YOU - BUT AT THE END OF THE DAY, THE ONLY TIME I REALLY SPOKE TO YOU -
- WAS WHEN YOU WERE SAT FLAT ON THE FLOOR.
GOODBYE, PAUL.
IN MEMORY PAUL GATLAND
WHO WAS THAT GUY ANYWAY?
JUST SOMEONE I MET A COUPLE OF TIMES WHEN I WAS A STUDENT. HE DIED.
COME ON - LET'S GO FIND THE OTHERS.
END.

THE RESERVOIR

featured on **Shirley Lee**

story by **Charles Brownstein**
art by **Frederick Noland**

never knew you loved
jacques tati
never knew you did
impressions
of john wayne
and jacques tati
i knew you had a temper
which you passed onto me

when i was a boy
yorkshire sunday mornings
we'd drive out and walk
round the reservoir
and i'd talk to you
and you'd listen to me
and no matter what
you'd always support me

the last time i saw you
you were so ill
i said that my music
might just turn out well
and you laughed at me
as if to say
"firstly, you're a fool
and secondly, that would be lovely"

the side of a hill
in the belgian rain
a view over town
in the belgian sunshine
that's where you lie now
for almost four years
i've been missing you so
for almost four years

wish i could see you again
just one final time
walk round the reservoir with you
one last sunday morning
tell you what's been happening in my life
and tell you my plans
and you'd give me that smile
because somehow, then there would be
hope
there would be hope...

but most of all
i'd like to see
your impression
of jacques tati

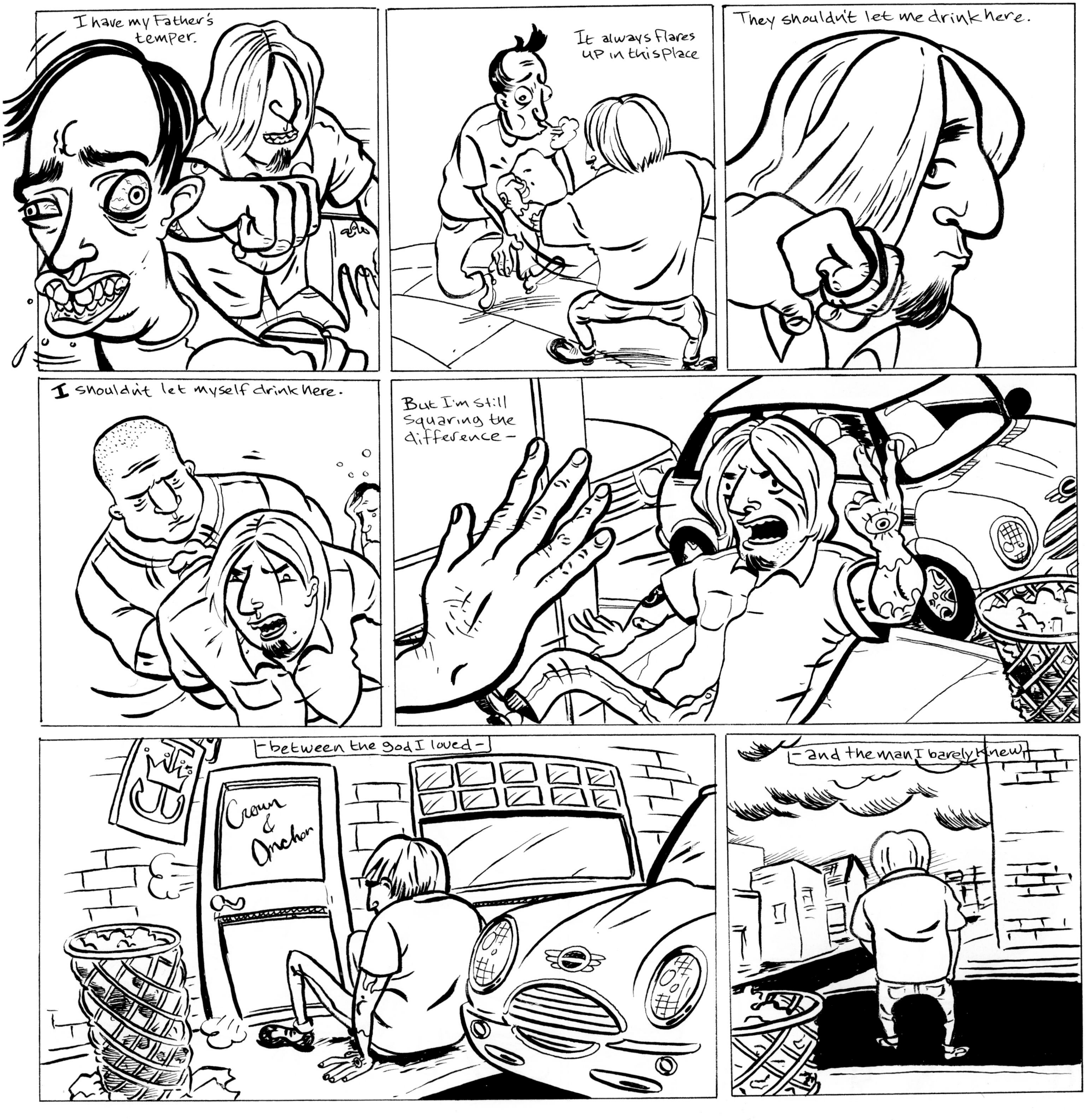
I have my Father's temper.
It always flares up in this place
They shouldn't let me drink here.
I shouldn't let myself drink here.
But I'm still squaring the difference -
- between the god I loved -
Crown & Anchor
- and the man I barely knew -

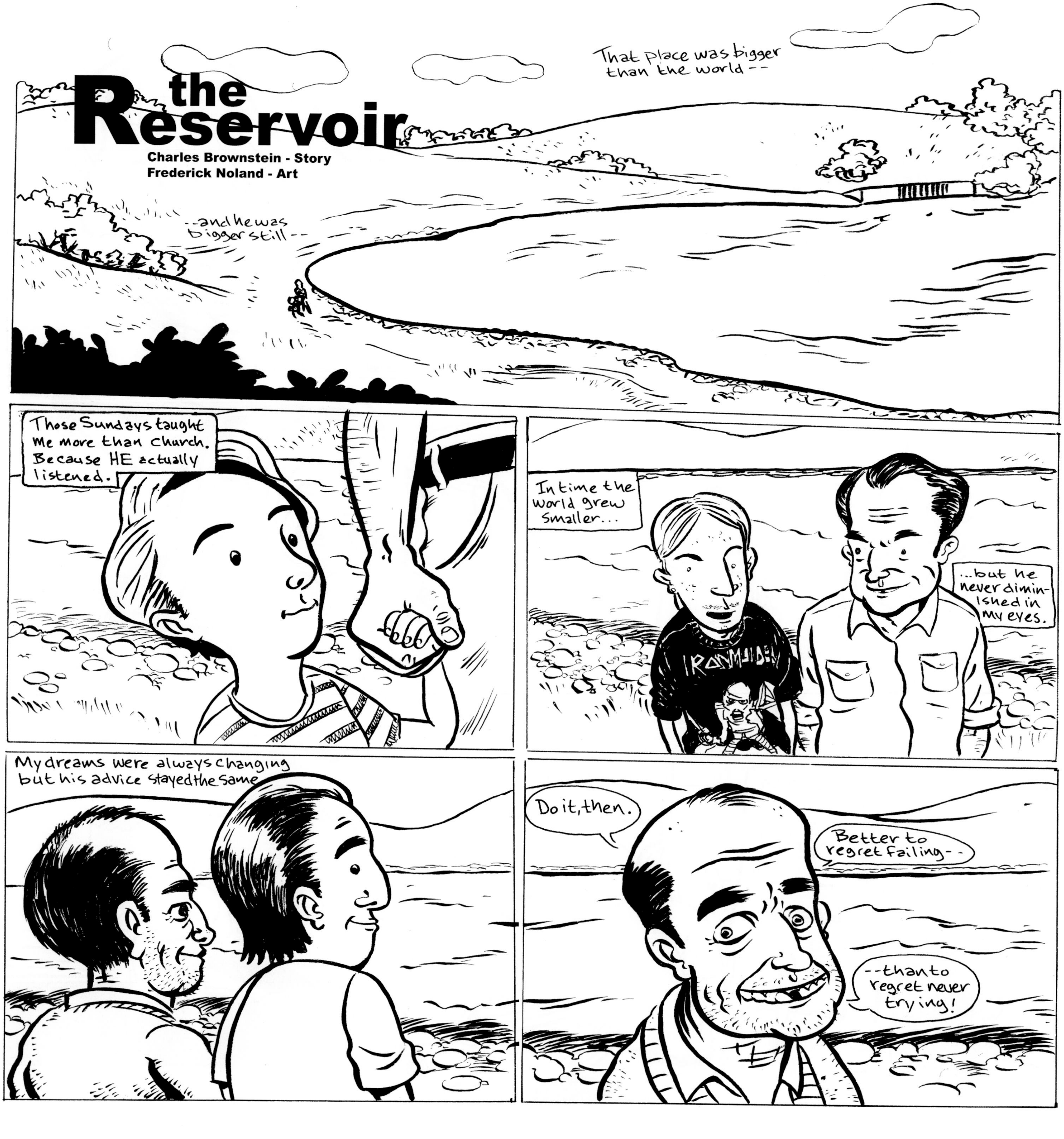
the Reservoir
Charles Brownstein - Story
Frederick Noland - Art
That place was bigger than the world --
--and he was bigger still--
Those Sundays taught me more than church. Because HE actually listened.
In time the world grew smaller...
...but he never diminished in my eyes.
My dreams were always changing but his advice stayed the same.
Do it, then.
Better to regret failing--
--than to regret never trying!

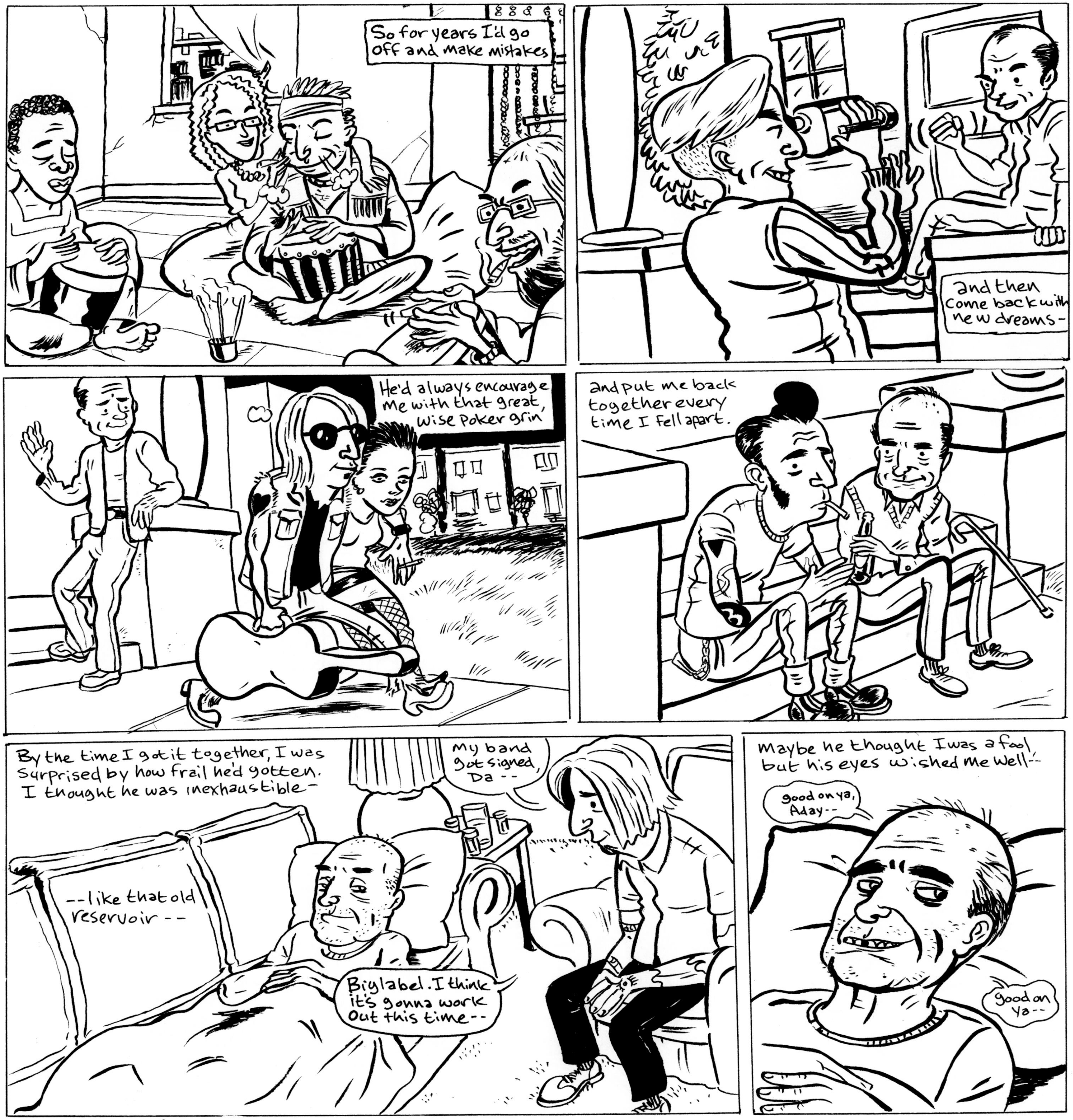

So for years I'd go off and make mistakes
and then come back with new dreams -
He'd always encourage me with that great, wise poker grin'
and put me back together every time I fell apart.
By the time I got it together, I was surprised by how frail he'd gotten. I thought he was inexhaustible -
--like that old reservoir --
My band got signed, Da --
Big label. I think it's gonna work out this time --
Maybe he thought I was a fool, but his eyes wished me well--
good on ya, Aday --
good on ya --

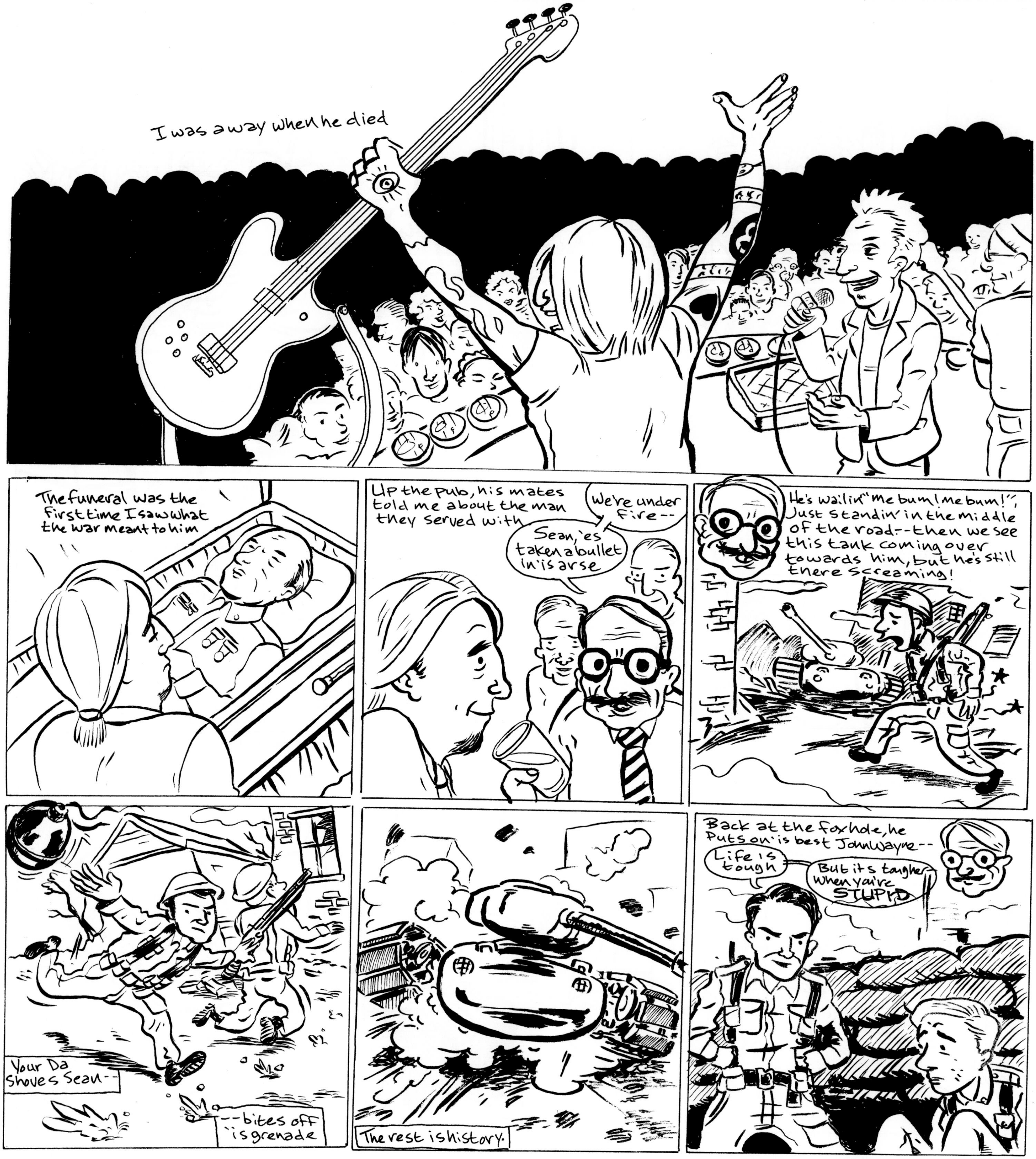
I was away when he died
The funeral was the first time I saw what the war meant to him
Up the pub, his mates told me about the man they served with
We're under fire--
Sean, 'es taken a bullet in 'is arse
He's wailin' "Me bum! Me bum!", Just standin' in the middle of the road--then we see this tank coming over towards him, but he's still there screaming!
Your Da shoves Sean--
--bites off 'is grenade
The rest is history.
Back at the foxhole, he puts on 'is best John Wayne--
Life is tough
But its tougher when you're STUPID

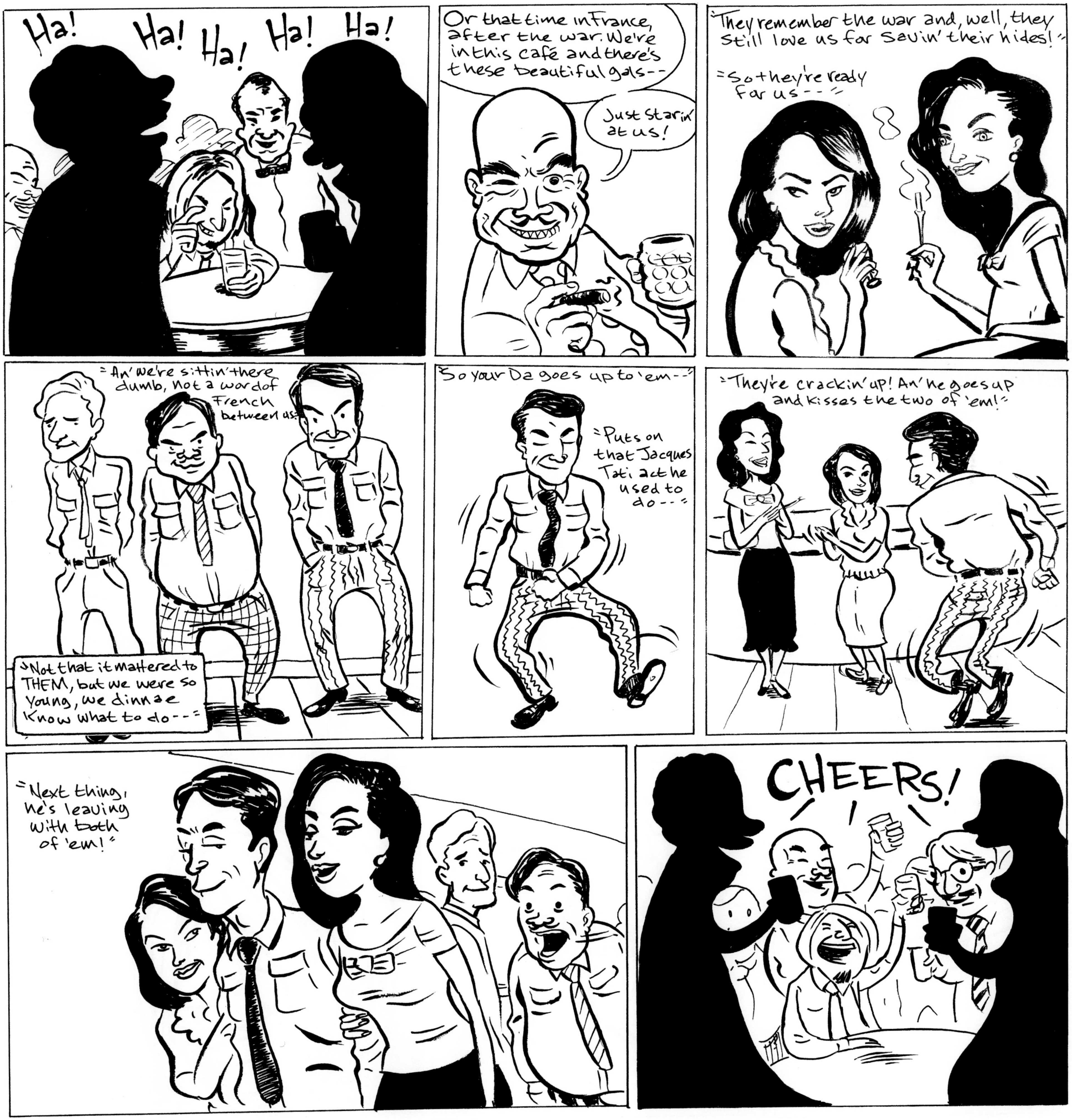
Ha! Ha! Ha! Ha! Ha!
Or that time in France, after the war. We're in this café and there's these beautiful gals--
Just starin' at us!
"They remember the war and, well, they still love us for savin' their hides!"
"So they're ready for us--"
"An' we're sittin' there dumb, not a word of French between us."
"Not that it mattered to THEM, but we were so young, we dinnae know what to do--"
"So your Da goes up to 'em--"
"Puts on that Jacques Tati act he used to do--"
"They're crackin' up! An' he goes up and kisses the two of 'em!"
"Next thing, he's leaving with both of 'em!"
CHEERS!

Four years, Da. Four years you've been gone.
All those Sundays at this reservoir. I told you all my dreams, all my mistakes.
I never thought to ask about yours
This place is much smaller now.
I wish I could walk around it with you once more
I wish I could hear your stories. Your voice.
See that poker grin
Most of all...
I'd love to hear your tale about those girls who loved Tati

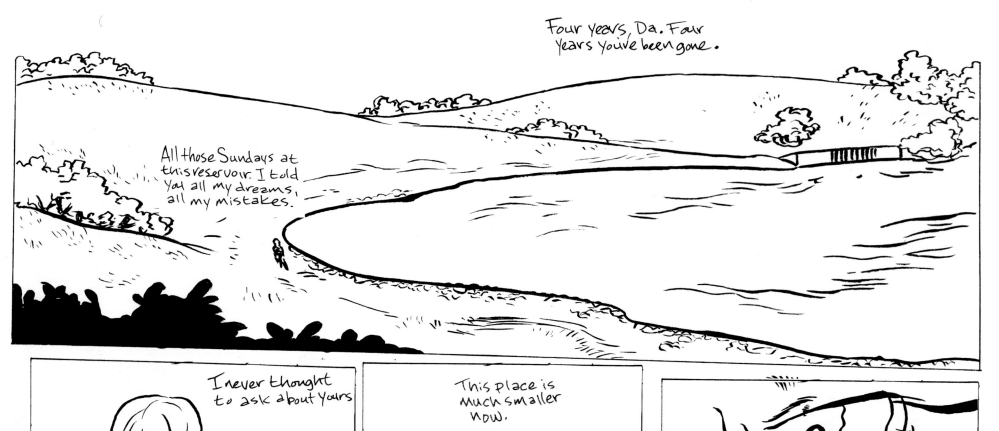

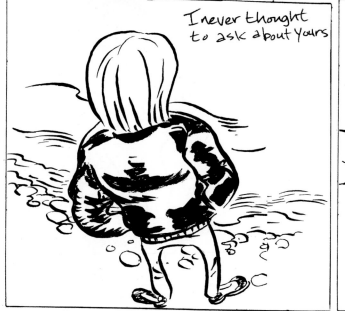

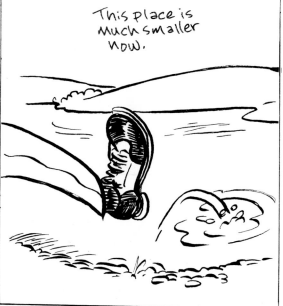

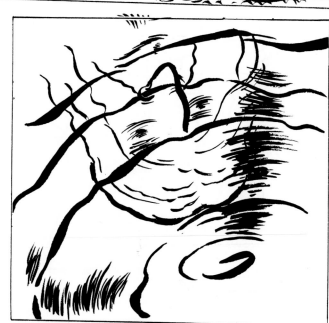

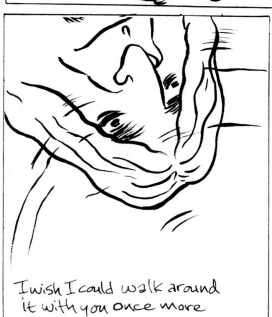

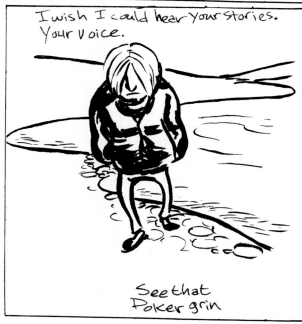

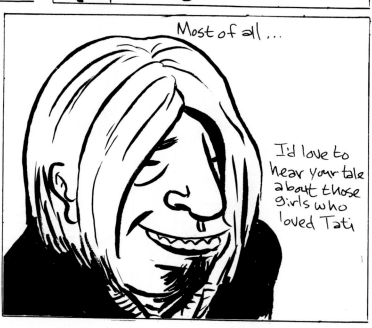

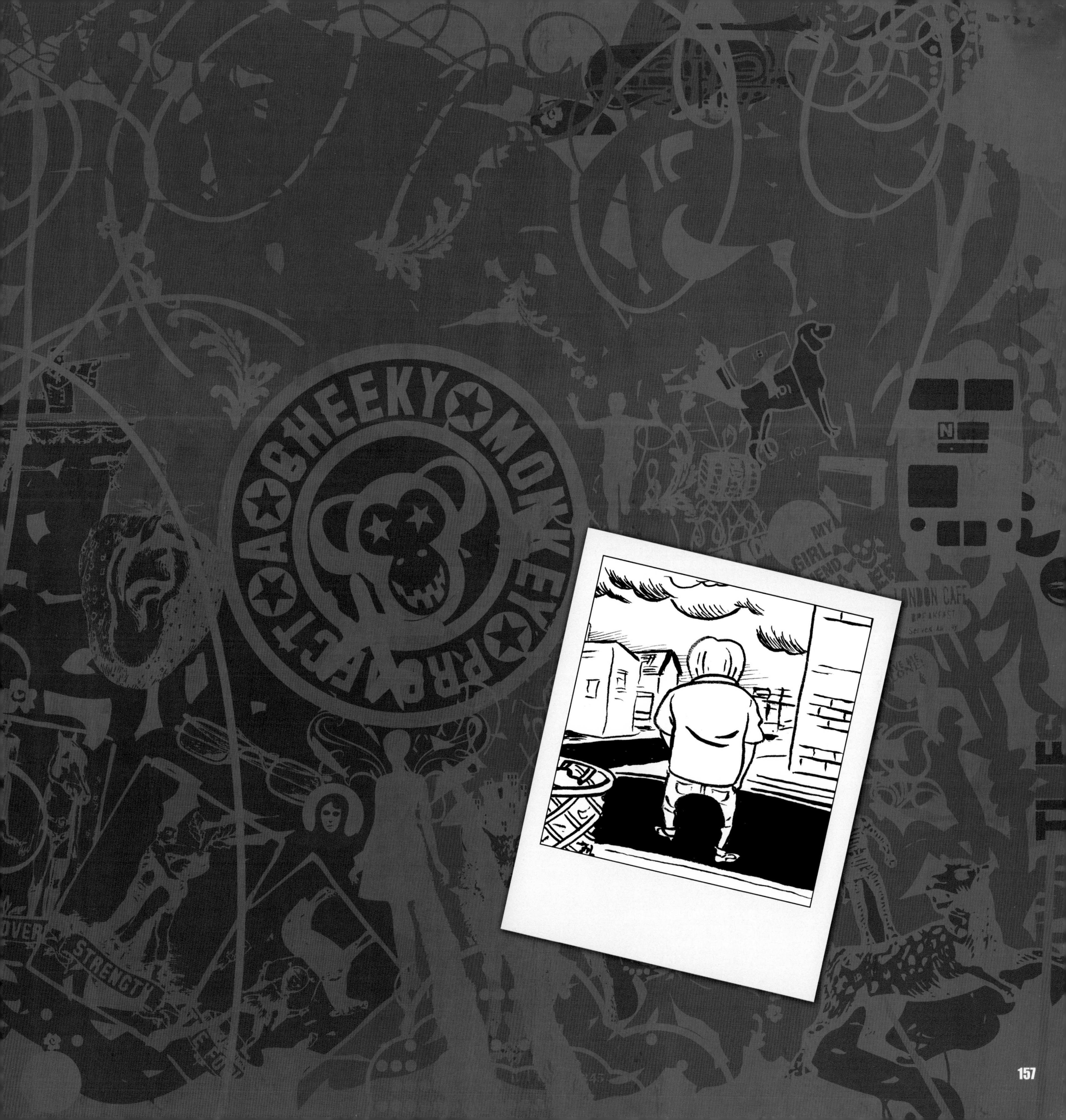
A CHEEKY MONKEY PROJECT
LONDON CAFE
BREAKFAST
STRENGT
OVER

LEFT ALONE AMONG THE LIVING

featured on **My Missing Days**

by **Chynna Clugston-Flores**
lettering by **Drew Gill**

thursday morning on my way into work
i suddenly started asking myself all these questions
it started raining
it started raining really hard
so i ducked into a cafe
she brought me coffee
and the questions poured down over me
like, what do you value?
do you really care about your job?
it's not like you work in a hospital or something
would it really make any difference
if you didn't go in today?
or tomorrow?
i mean, would they even notice?
is it just the money that matters?
is it that important that you have enough
to choose what you do
what you eat
what you drink
what couldn't you live without?
and what wouldn't you miss at all?

i could tell by your voice
on the answerphone
it was bad news
didn't ring back straight away
carried on with what i was doing
for another five minutes
without this news in my life

you're not crying for him
you're crying for yourself
you're full of guilt
for still being here

well you're left behind among the living
left alone among the living

it takes a tragedy
to appreciate
how much you've lost
what someone means to you
are you square with the people
that you care for?
if you lost them today
would there be things left over?
things you wanted to say

i could tell by your face
when you got home
you hadn't heard the news
didn't say straight away
carried on as though things were normal
for another five minutes
without this news in your life

you're not crying for him
you're crying for yourself
holding on to the world
as it spins so fast
and you're left behind among the living
you're left alone among the living
left alone among the living
just save your tears for the living

the hours went by and i just sat there
watching the rain and trying to figure out
what really matters?
what do you value?

your privacy?
your health?
your free time?
and what about religion?
do you even think about that any more?
or is a football team more important to you now?
and your possessions
you could easily live without most of them
but could you live without acquiring more?
and what about your lover?
are they more important to you
at the expense of your friendship with others?
and your family?
you don't see them as often as you'd like
what couldn't you live without?
and what wouldn't you miss at all?
so she brought more coffee
and the questions kept coming
kept buzzing

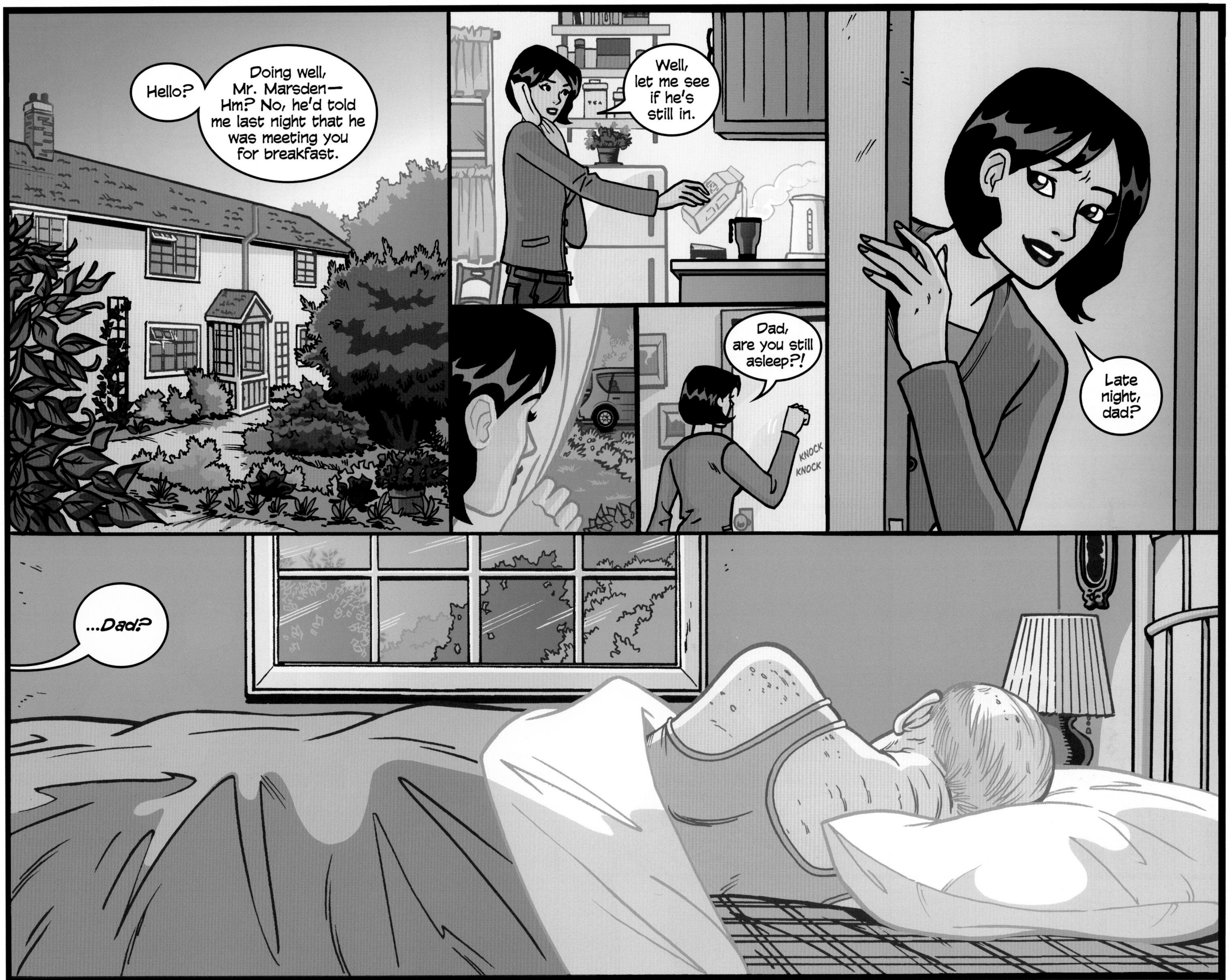
Hello?
Doing well, Mr. Marsden— Hm? No, he'd told me last night that he was meeting you for breakfast.
Well, let me see if he's still in.
Dad, are you still asleep?!
KNOCK KNOCK
Late night, dad?
...Dad?

Left Alone Among The Living

Art, paraphrasing and colors by Chynna Clugston

Lettering by Drew Gill

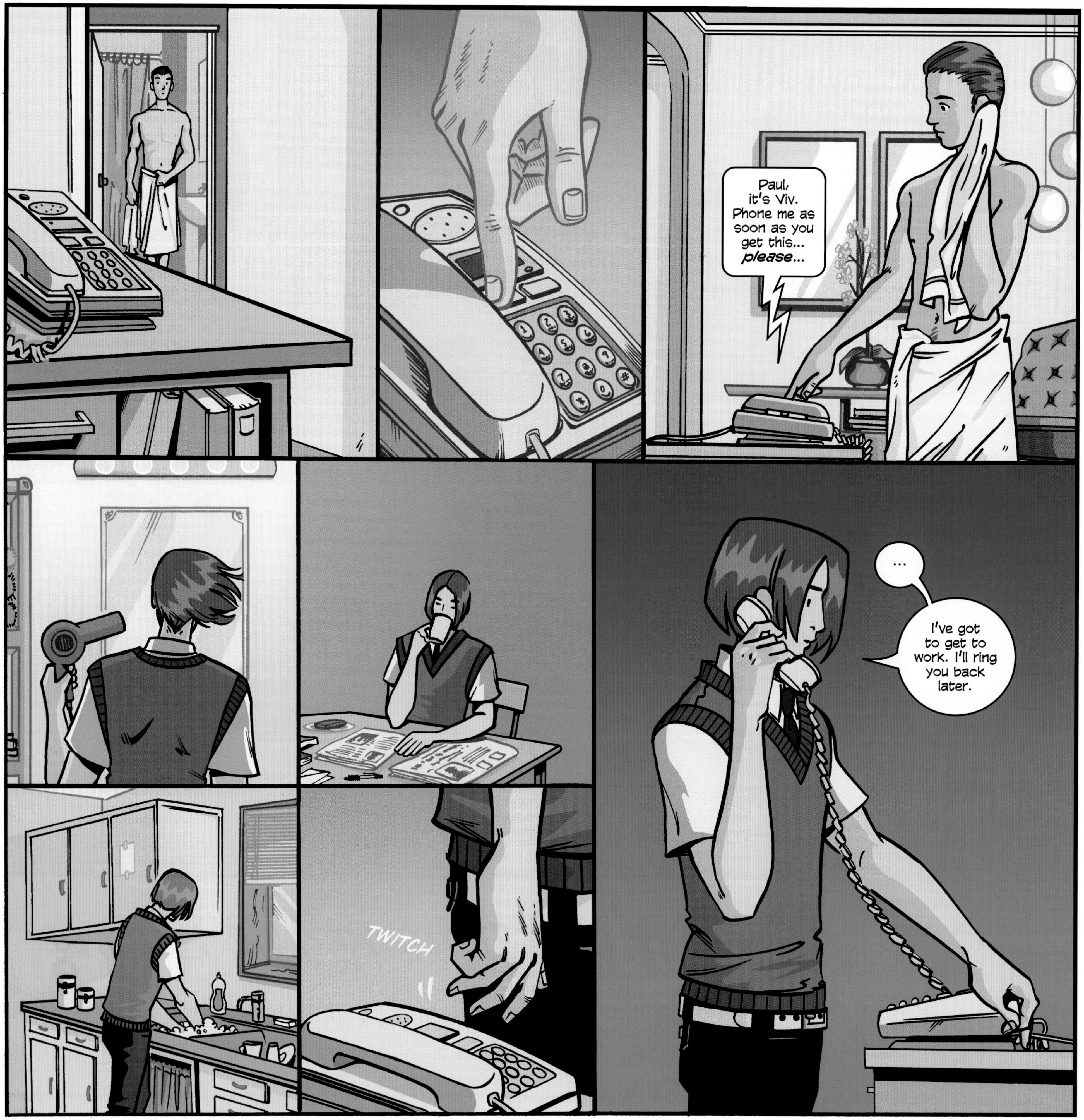
Paul, it's Viv. Phone me as soon as you get this... *please*...
...
I've got to get to work. I'll ring you back later.
TWITCH

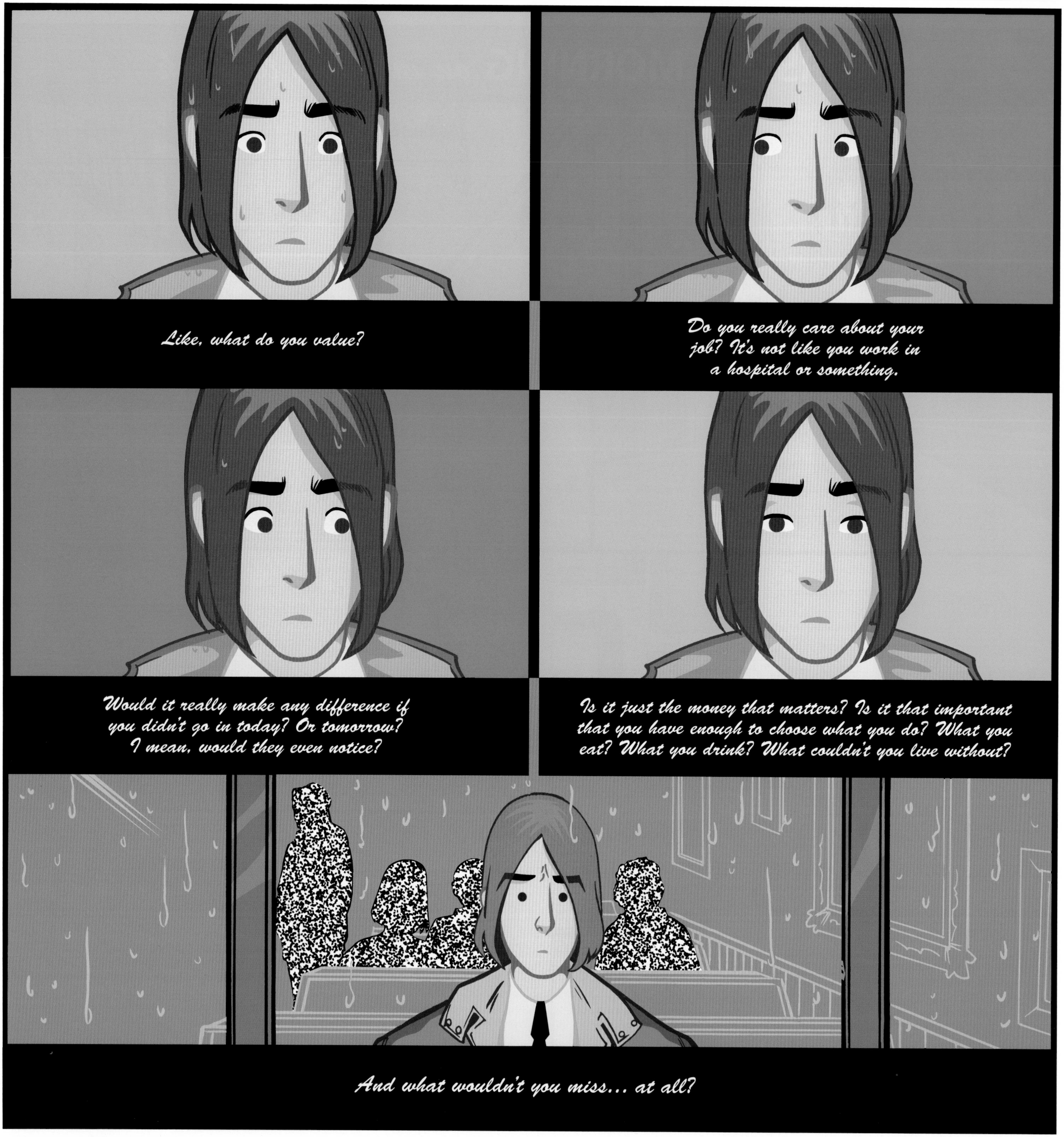
Like, what do you value?
Do you really care about your job? It's not like you work in a hospital or something.
Would it really make any difference if you didn't go in today? Or tomorrow? I mean, would they even notice?
Is it just the money that matters? Is it that important that you have enough to choose what you do? What you eat? What you drink? What couldn't you live without?
And what wouldn't you miss... at all?

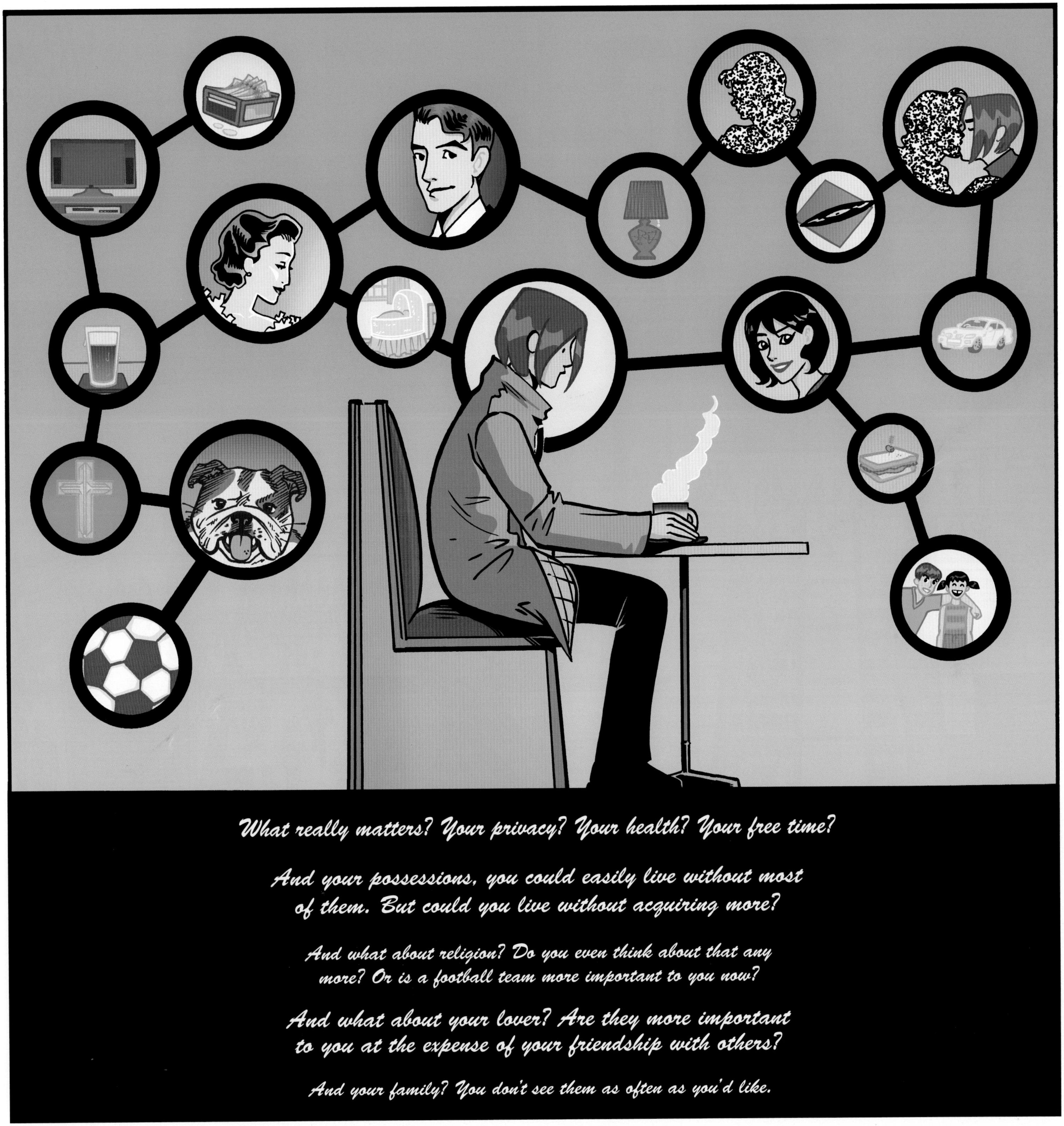
What really matters? Your privacy? Your health? Your free time?
And your possessions, you could easily live without most of them. But could you live without acquiring more?
And what about religion? Do you even think about that any more? Or is a football team more important to you now?
And what about your lover? Are they more important to you at the expense of your friendship with others?
And your family? You don't see them as often as you'd like.

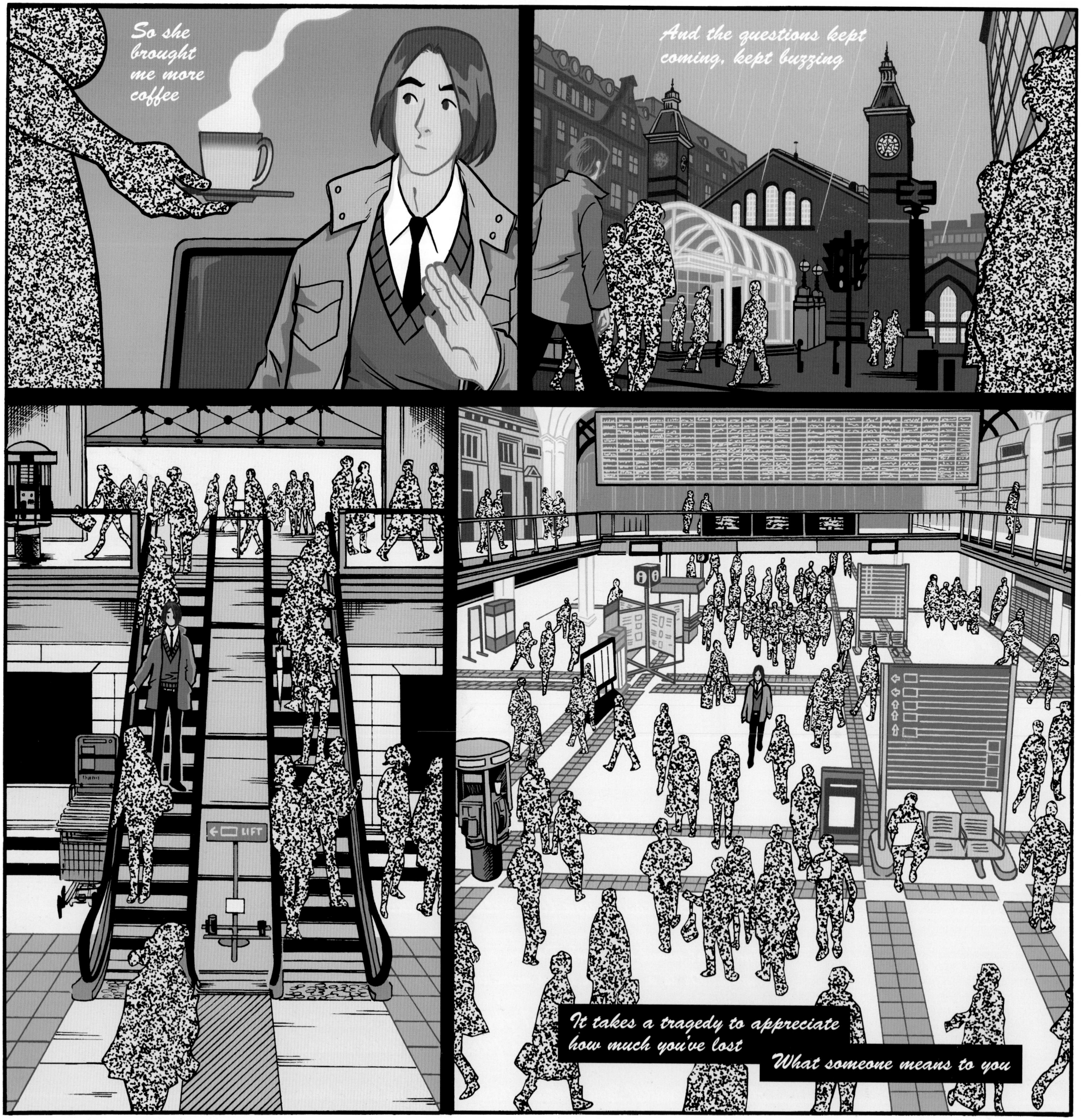
So she brought me more coffee
And the questions kept coming, kept buzzing
LIFT
It takes a tragedy to appreciate how much you've lost
What someone means to you

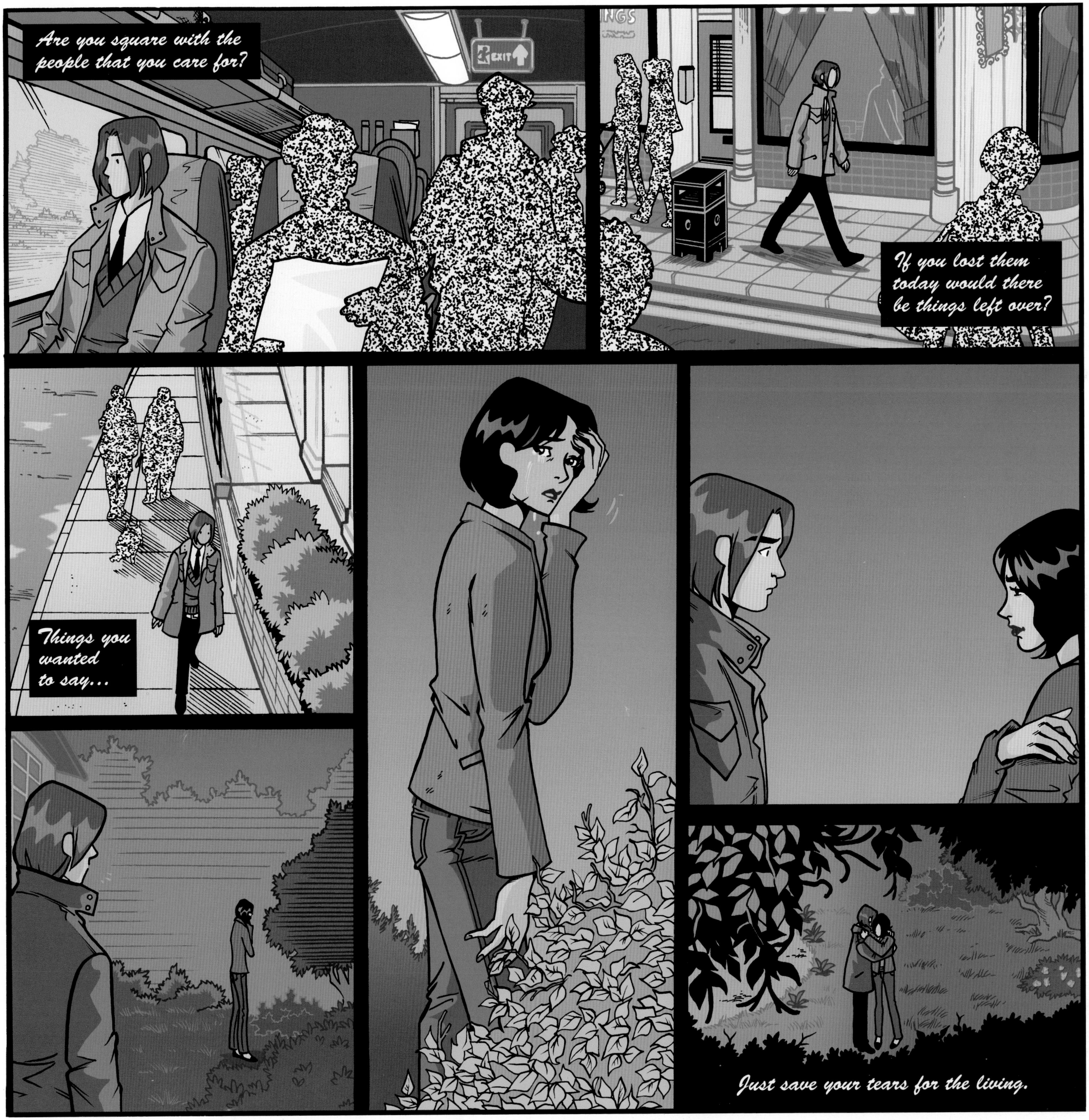
Are you square with the people that you care for?
EXIT
If you lost them today would there be things left over?
Things you wanted to say...
Just save your tears for the living.

THE FIRST TIME YOU SAW SNOW

featured on **Shirley Lee**

story by **Jamie S. Rich**
art by **Kelley Seda**

On a bench in the park in the grounds of the college
Is a bronze plaque bearing your name
And as the morning sun dries off the grass
I will sit here and try to picture you
You were sat flat on the floor

I didn't understand your illness, I only knew it made me feel awkward
And you so happy, so at one with the world
A shaved head and a clear smile...
How could you be so at peace with everything
To have seen so much so young

The holidays were long and when we came back
You were gone

Alison Kay gave me some words but I didn't want to sing them
I said I didn't want to cheapen your memory
But really I just didn't want to face what had happened to you

I will move at the chime of the clock
But now the clock has stopped and i'm still sat here
In these 16 years what have i learned?
Have i learned the strength that you had then?
As the sun goes down I'm still sat here
I didn't want to sing it then, but I do now
The only time I really spoke to you
You were sat flat on the floor

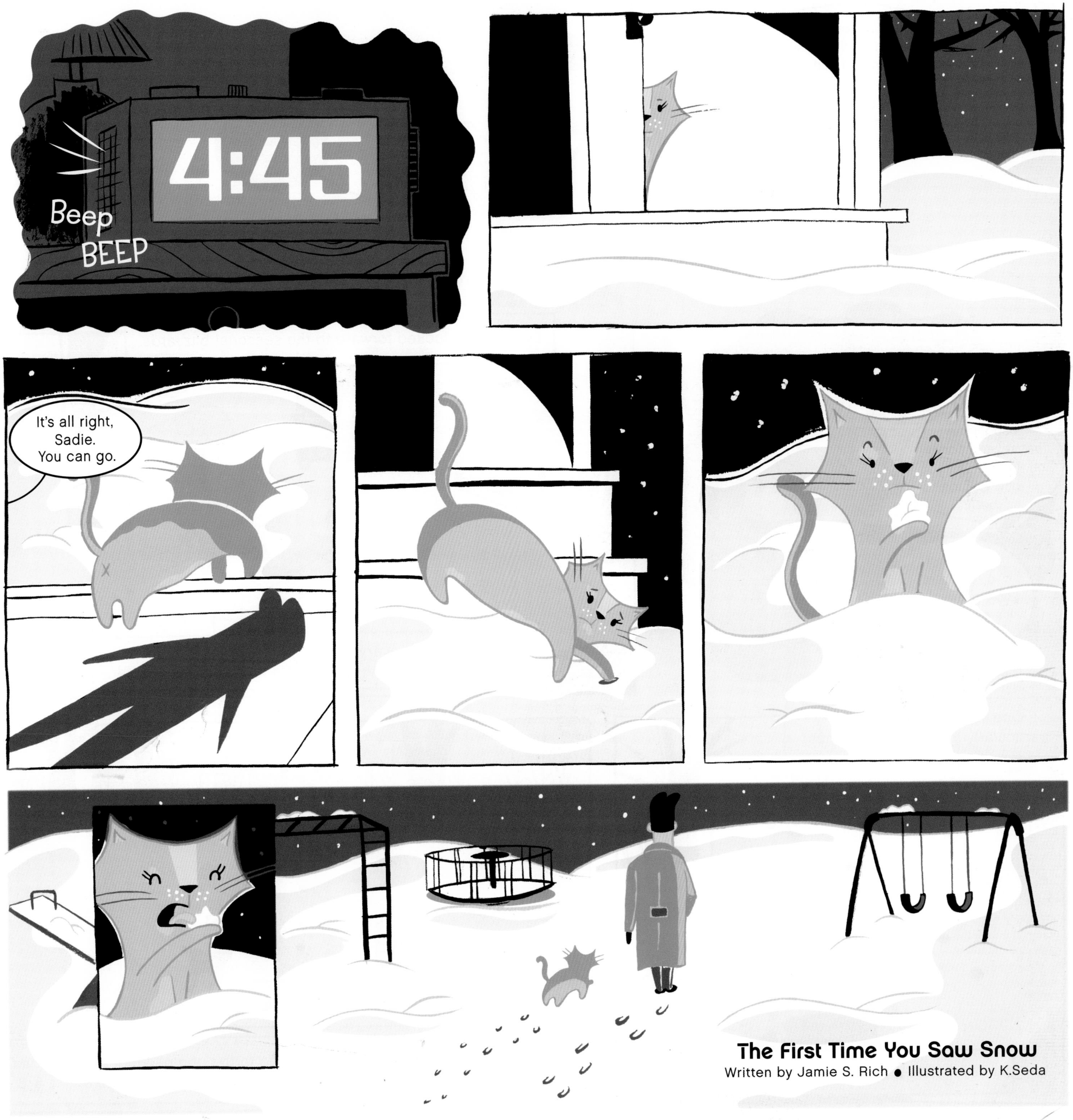
4:45
Beep
BEEP
It's all right, Sadie. You can go.
The First Time You Saw Snow
Written by Jamie S. Rich • Illustrated by K.Seda

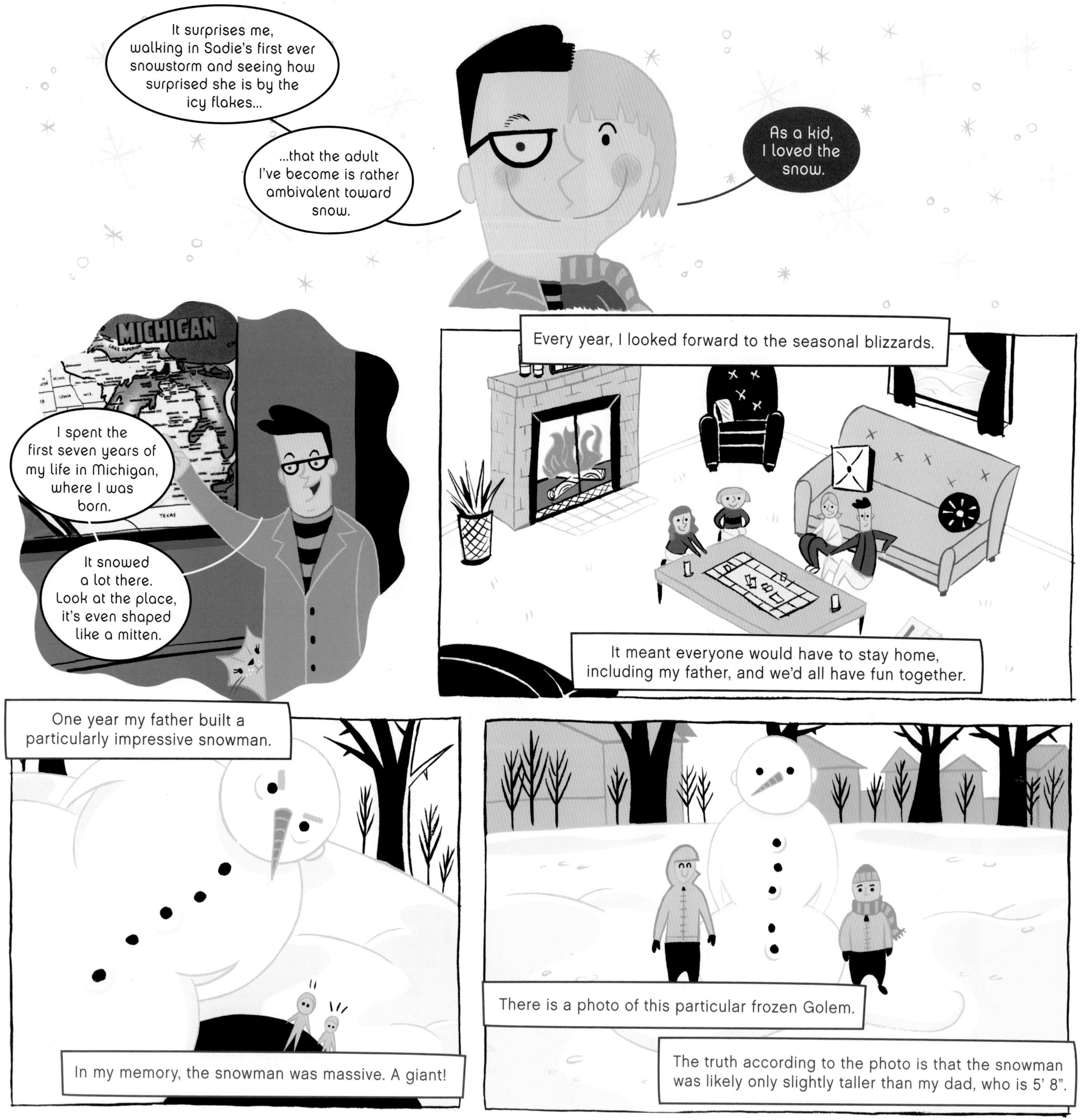

It surprises me, walking in Sadie's first ever snowstorm and seeing how surprised she is by the icy flakes...
...that the adult I've become is rather ambivalent toward snow.
As a kid, I loved the snow.
MICHIGAN
I spent the first seven years of my life in Michigan, where I was born.
It snowed a lot there. Look at the place, it's even shaped like a mitten.
Every year, I looked forward to the seasonal blizzards.
It meant everyone would have to stay home, including my father, and we'd all have fun together.
One year my father built a particularly impressive snowman.
In my memory, the snowman was massive. A giant!
There is a photo of this particular frozen Golem.
The truth according to the photo is that the snowman was likely only slightly taller than my dad, who is 5' 8".

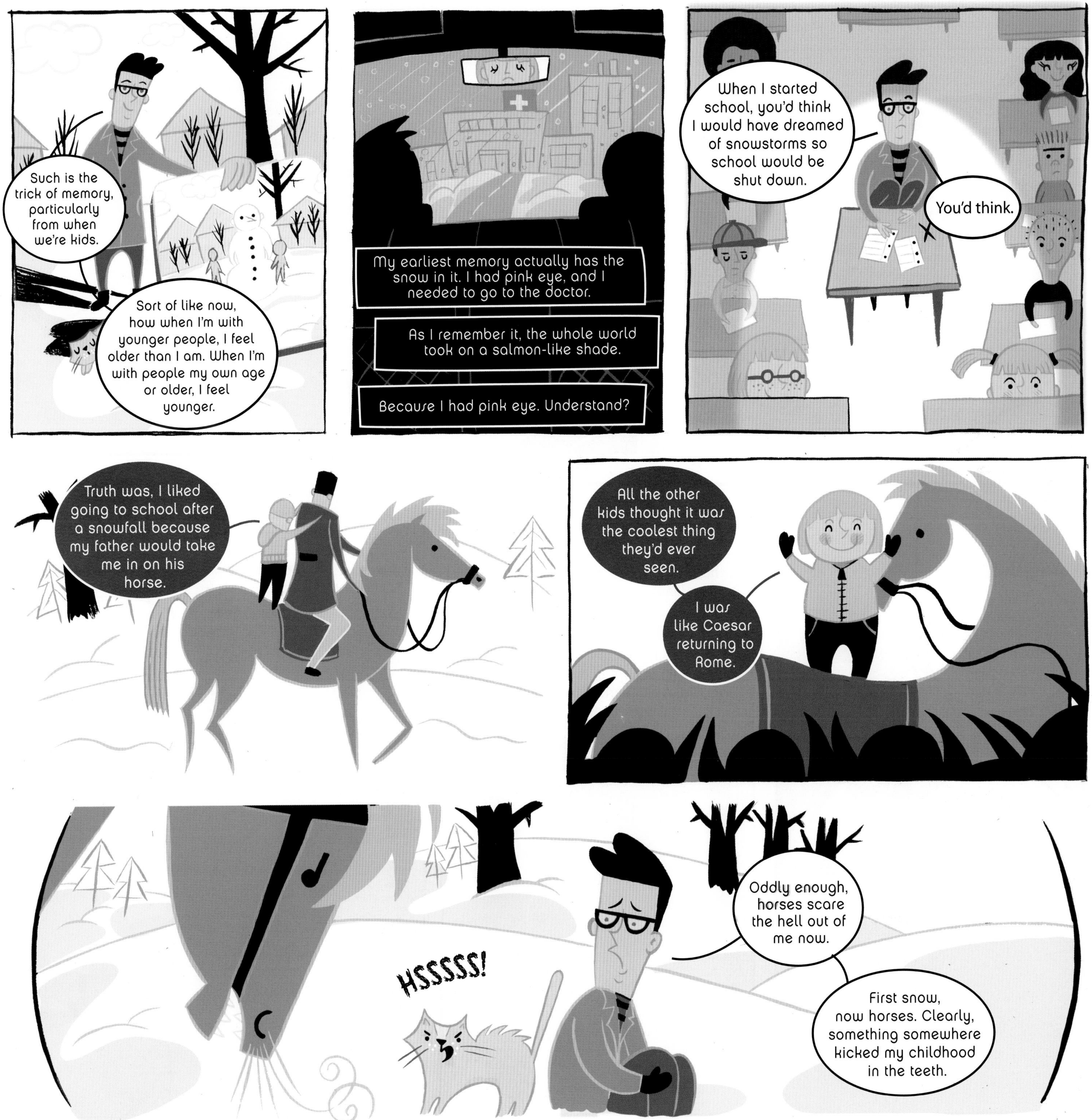

Such is the trick of memory, particularly from when we're kids.
Sort of like now, how when I'm with younger people, I feel older than I am. When I'm with people my own age or older, I feel younger.
My earliest memory actually has the snow in it. I had pink eye, and I needed to go to the doctor.
As I remember it, the whole world took on a salmon-like shade.
Because I had pink eye. Understand?
When I started school, you'd think I would have dreamed of snowstorms so school would be shut down.
You'd think.
Truth was, I liked going to school after a snowfall because my father would take me in on his horse.
All the other kids thought it was the coolest thing they'd ever seen.
I was like Caesar returning to Rome.
HSSSSS!
Oddly enough, horses scare the hell out of me now.
First snow, now horses. Clearly, something somewhere kicked my childhood in the teeth.

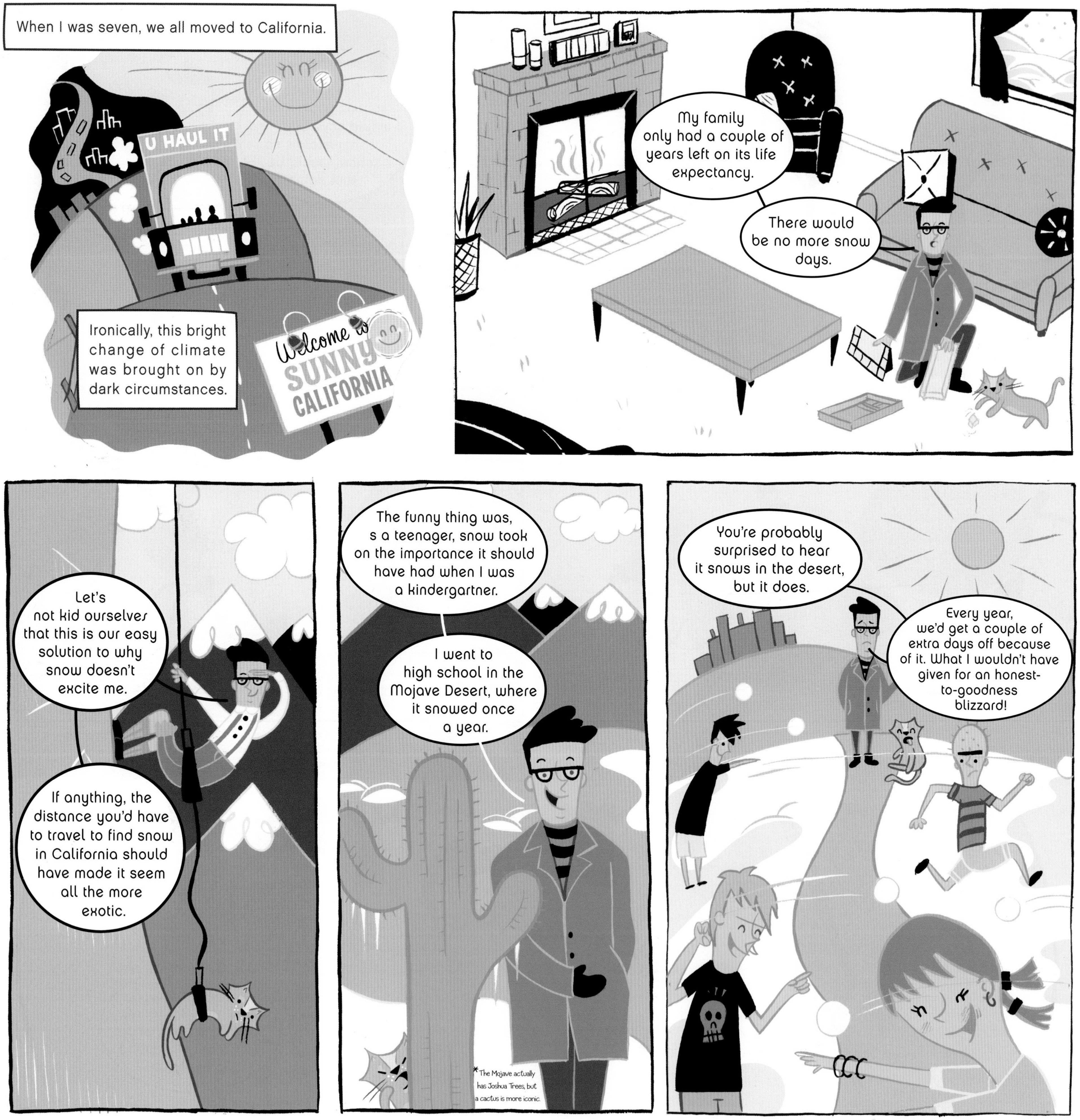
When I was seven, we all moved to California.
U HAUL IT
Welcome to SUNNY CALIFORNIA
Ironically, this bright change of climate was brought on by dark circumstances.
My family only had a couple of years left on its life expectancy.
There would be no more snow days.
Let's not kid ourselves that this is our easy solution to why snow doesn't excite me.
If anything, the distance you'd have to travel to find snow in California should have made it seem all the more exotic.
The funny thing was, s a teenager, snow took on the importance it should have had when I was a kindergartner.
I went to high school in the Mojave Desert, where it snowed once a year.
*The Mojave actually has Joshua Trees, but a cactus is more iconic.
You're probably surprised to hear it snows in the desert, but it does.
Every year, we'd get a couple of extra days off because of it. What I wouldn't have given for an honest-to-goodness blizzard!

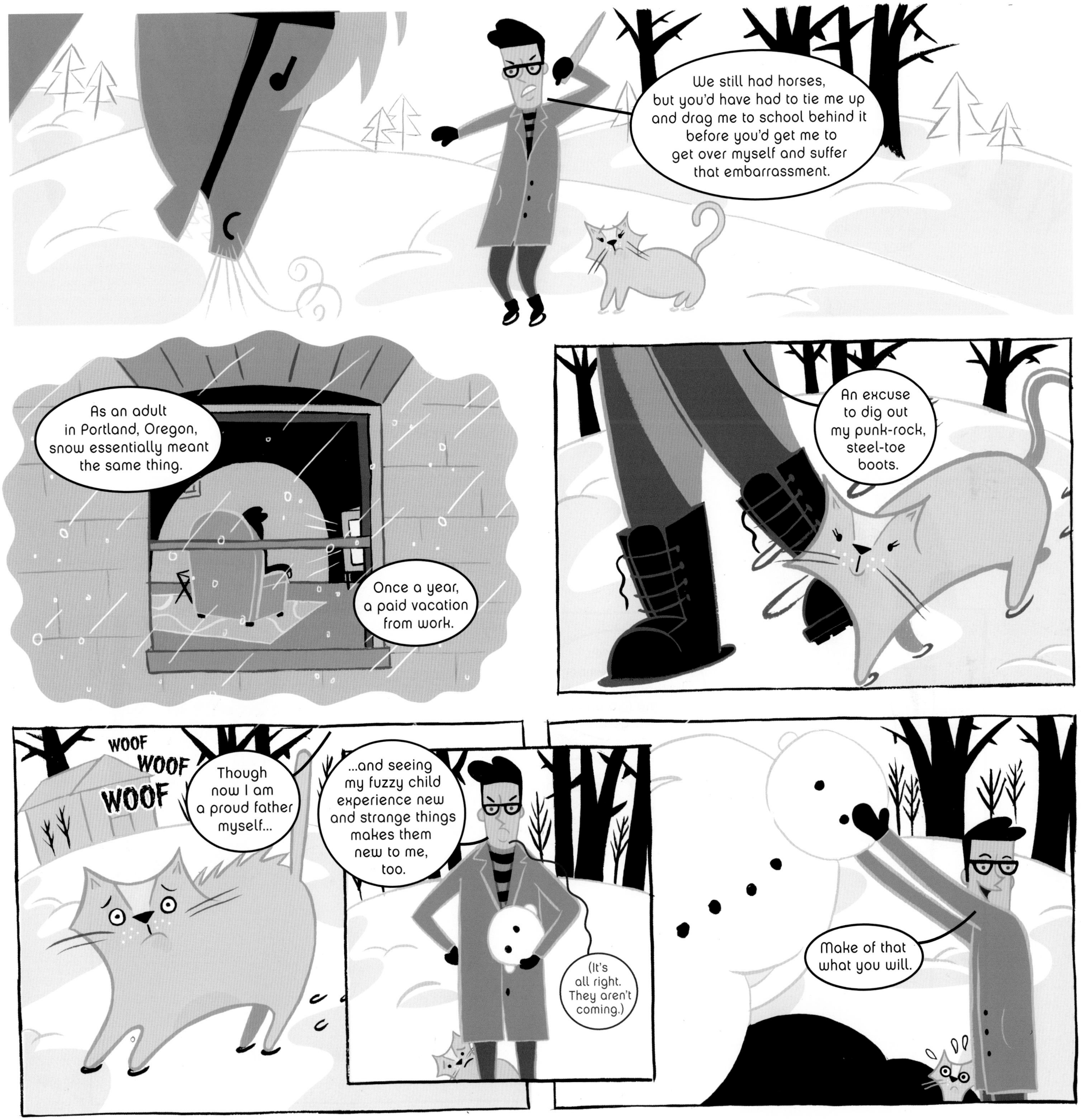
We still had horses, but you'd have had to tie me up and drag me to school behind it before you'd get me to get over myself and suffer that embarrassment.
As an adult in Portland, Oregon, snow essentially meant the same thing.
Once a year, a paid vacation from work.
An excuse to dig out my punk-rock, steel-toe boots.
WOOF
WOOF
WOOF
Though now I am a proud father myself...
...and seeing my fuzzy child experience new and strange things makes them new to me, too.
(It's all right. They aren't coming.)
Make of that what you will.

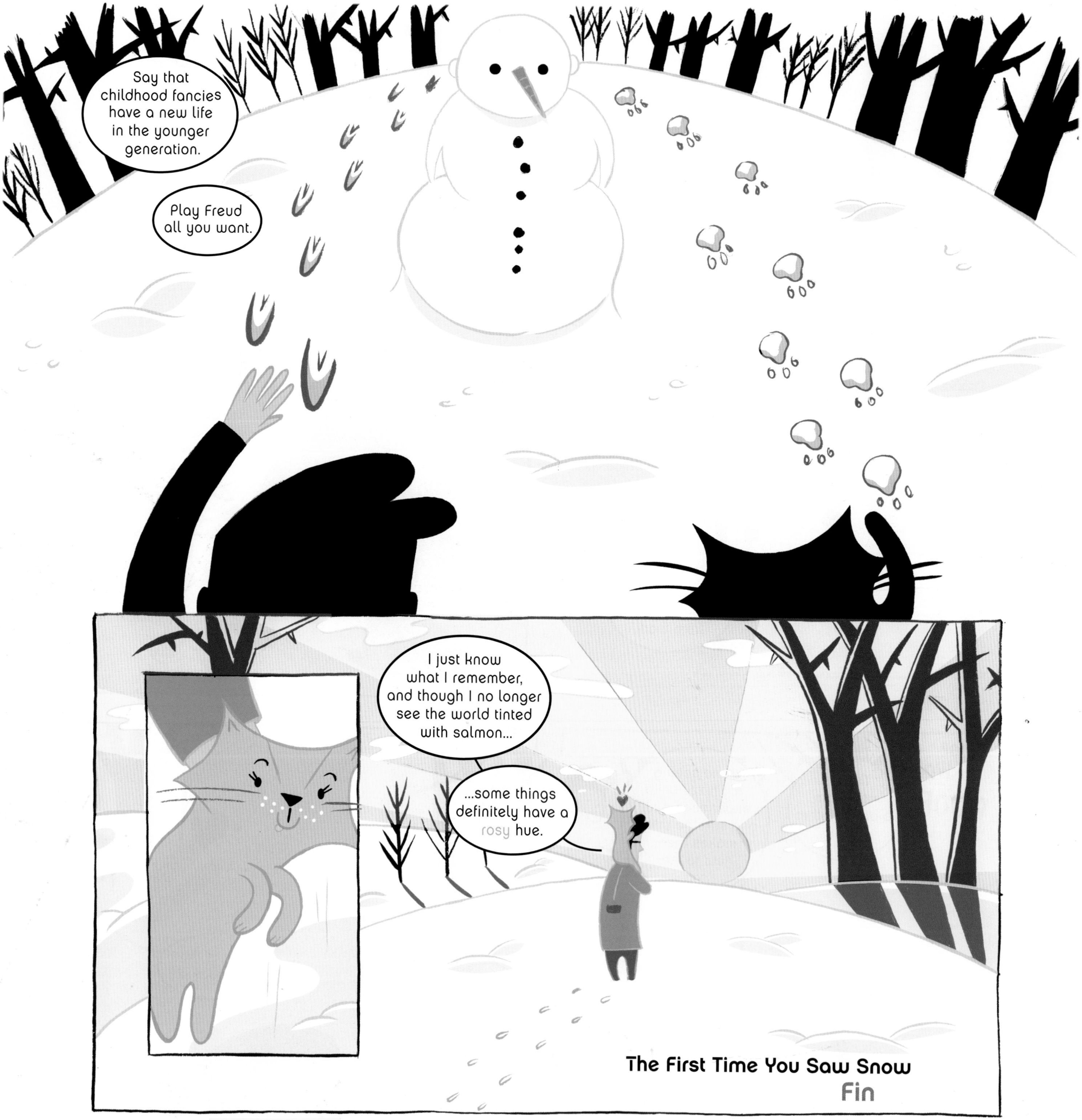
Say that childhood fancies have a new life in the younger generation.
Play Freud all you want.
I just know what I remember, and though I no longer see the world tinted with salmon...
...some things definitely have a rosy hue.
The First Time You Saw Snow
Fin

MORE MUSIC ANTHOLOGIES by IMAGE COMICS

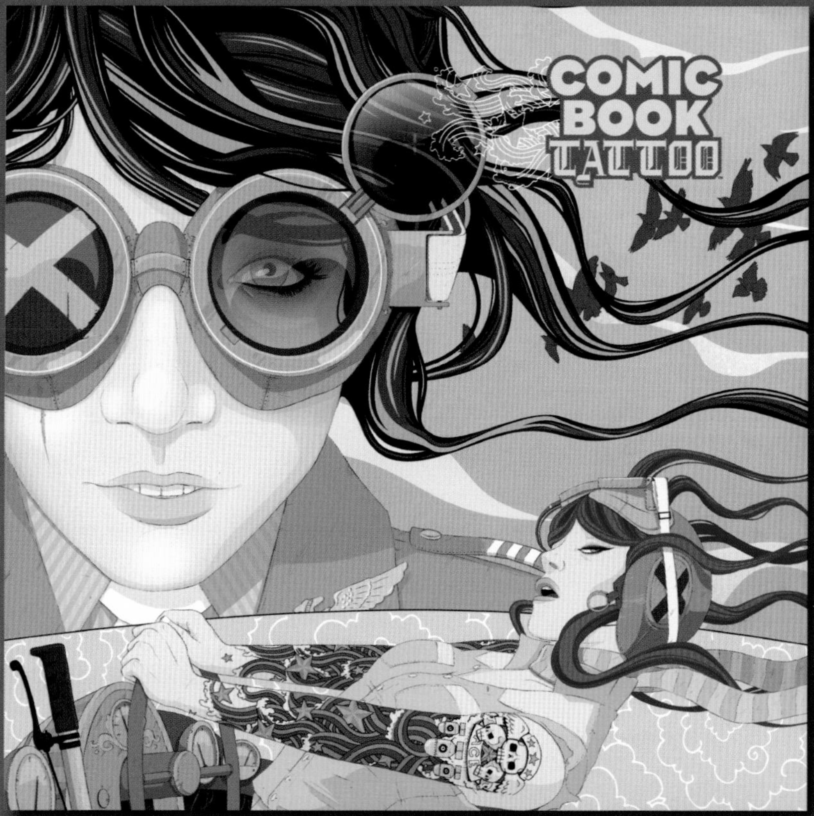
COMIC BOOK TATTOO

COMIC BOOK TATTOO

INSPIRED BY THE SONGS OF TORI AMOS!
Over 80 of the best creators from every style and genre, have contributed over 50 stories to this anthology featuring stories inspired by the songs of multi-platinum recording artist, TORI AMOS. Featuring an introduction by NEIL GAIMAN, with stories by creators such as CARLA SPEED McNEIL, MARK BUCKINGHAM, C.B. CEBULSKI, NIKKI COOK, HOPE LARSON, JOHN NEY REIBER, RYAN KELLY and many, many others, COMIC BOOK TATTOO encapsulates the breadth, depth and beauty of modern comics in this coffee table format book.

480 pages in Full Color!

HARDCOVER • $49.99 USD
ISBN: 978-1-58240-965-8

SOFTCOVER • $29.99 USD
ISBN: 978-1-58240-964-1

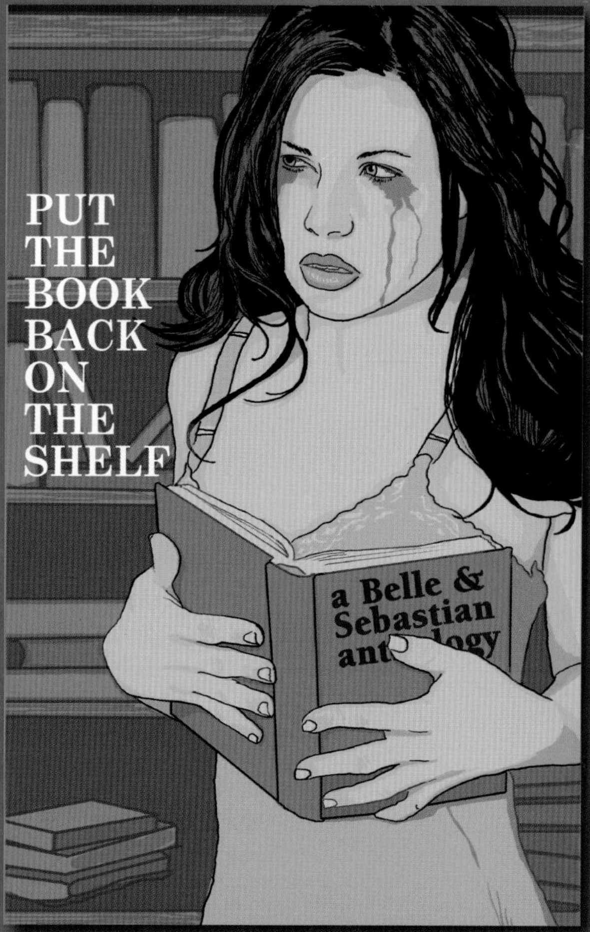
PUT THE BOOK BACK ON THE SHELF
a Belle & Sebastian

PUT THE BOOK BACK ON THE SHELF

Combining colorful lyrics and fulll-bdied melodies, Belle and Sebastian's infectious brand of indie pop has made the Scottish band cult and critical favorites the world over. PUT THE BOOK BACK ON THE SHELF is a collection of stories by independent comic creators who have put their own spins on a cross section of Belle and Sebastian's songs, crafting narratives inspired by the band's music.

192 pages in Full Color!

$19.99 USD
ISBN: 978-1-58240-600-8

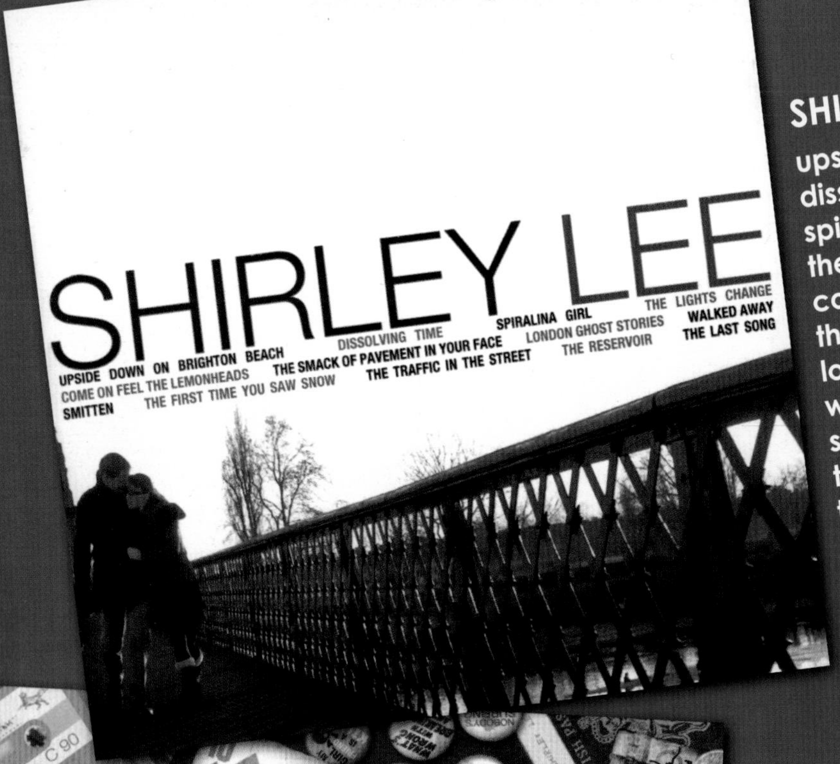
SHIRLEY LEE
UPSIDE DOWN ON BRIGHTON BEACH
DISSOLVING TIME
SPIRALINA GIRL
THE LIGHTS CHANGE
COME ON FEEL THE LEMONHEADS
THE SMACK OF PAVEMENT IN YOUR FACE
LONDON GHOST STORIES
WALKED AWAY
SMITTEN
THE FIRST TIME YOU SAW SNOW
THE TRAFFIC IN THE STREET
THE RESERVOIR
THE LAST SONG

SHIRLEY LEE (2009)

upside down on brighton beach
dissolving time
spiralina girl
the lights change
come on feel the lemonheads
the smack of pavement in your face
london ghost stories
walked away
smitten
the first time you saw snow
the traffic in the street
the reservoir
the last song

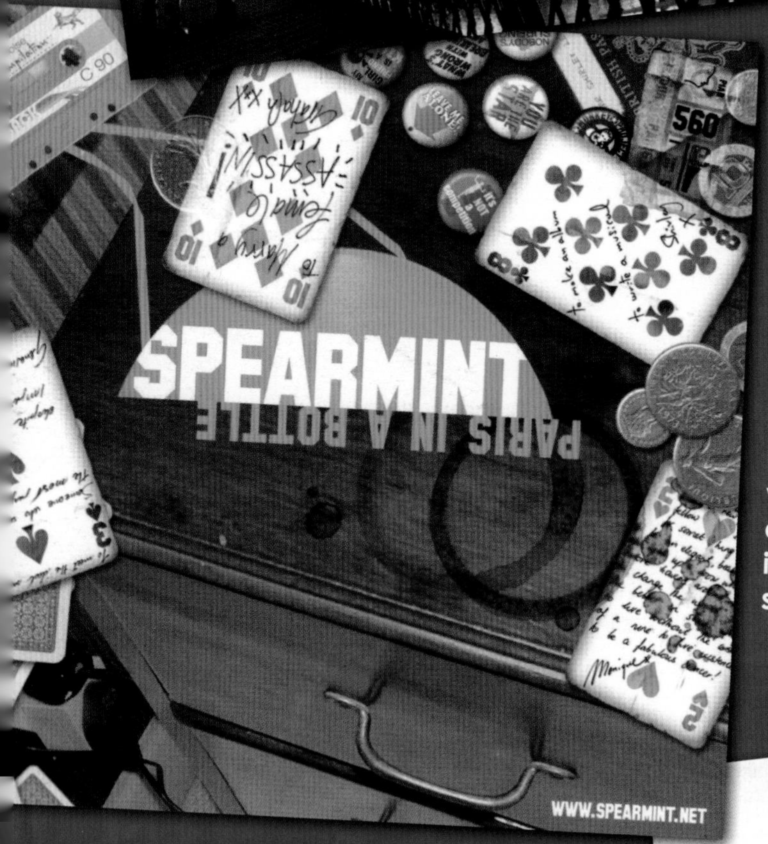
SPEARMINT
PARIS IN A BOTTLE
WWW.SPEARMINT.NET

PARIS IN A BOTTLE (2006)

first time music
tuesday morning
leave me alone
psycho magnet
my girlfriend is a killer
wednesday night
the competition
the space
what's wrong with breaking up anyway?
in a bottle
saturday rain

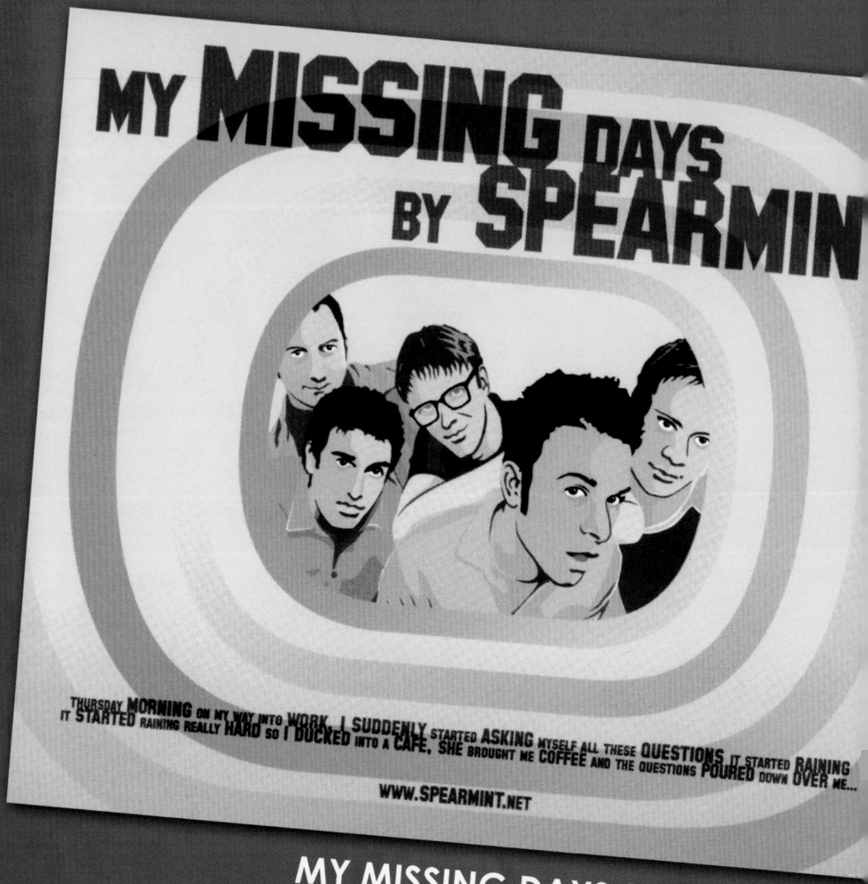
MY MISSING DAYS
BY SPEARMIN
THURSDAY MORNING ON MY WAY INTO WORK, I SUDDENLY STARTED ASKING MYSELF ALL THESE QUESTIONS, IT STARTED RAINING
IT STARTED RAINING REALLY HARD SO I DUCKED INTO A CAFE, SHE BROUGHT ME COFFEE AND THE QUESTIONS POURED DOWN OVER ME...
WWW.SPEARMINT.NET

MY MISSING DAYS (2003)

a happy ending
left alone among the living
enough for me
giving it away
time is now
my missing days
don't get me started
mike's wall
i didn't buy you flowers
the book
perhaps you were sleeping
the start of it all

A LEOPARD AND OTHER STORIES (2004)

a leopard
the beautiful things
say something else
vince's holiday tape
the whole summer long
i invented someone
death of a scene
you were always happy
this is a souvenir
bad souvenirs
the last bus home
nothing
we dyed the bathroom green
meet mr marsden

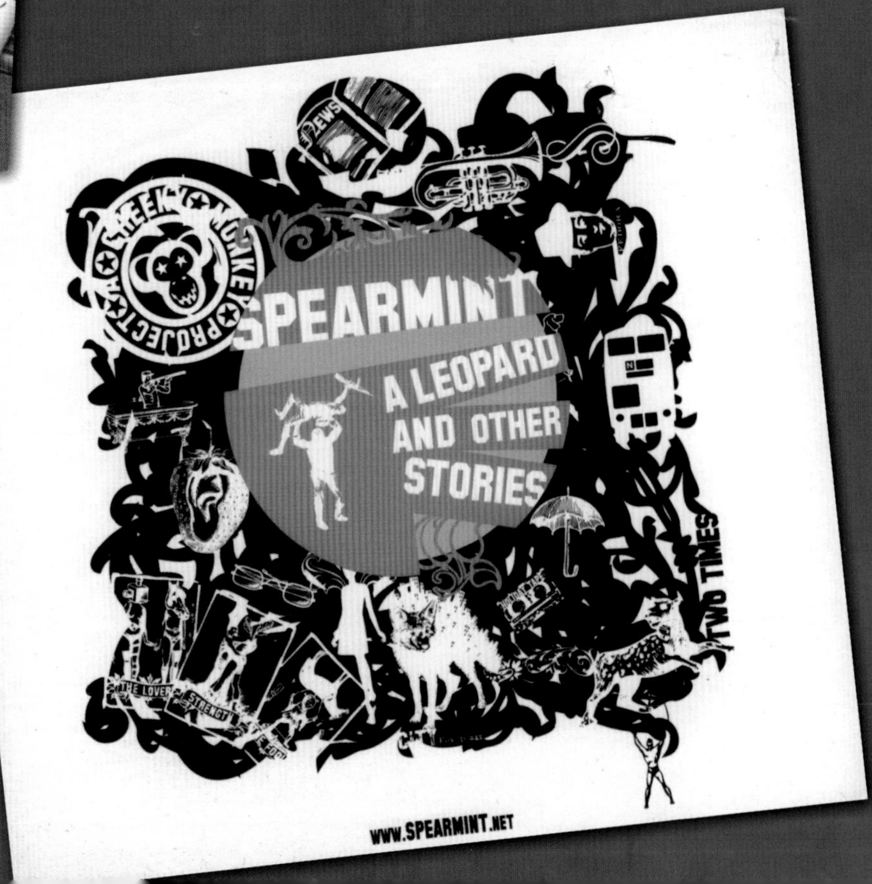
SPEARMINT
A LEOPARD AND OTHER STORIES
WWW.SPEARMINT.NET

ALBUMS BY SPEARMINT & SHIRLEY LEE

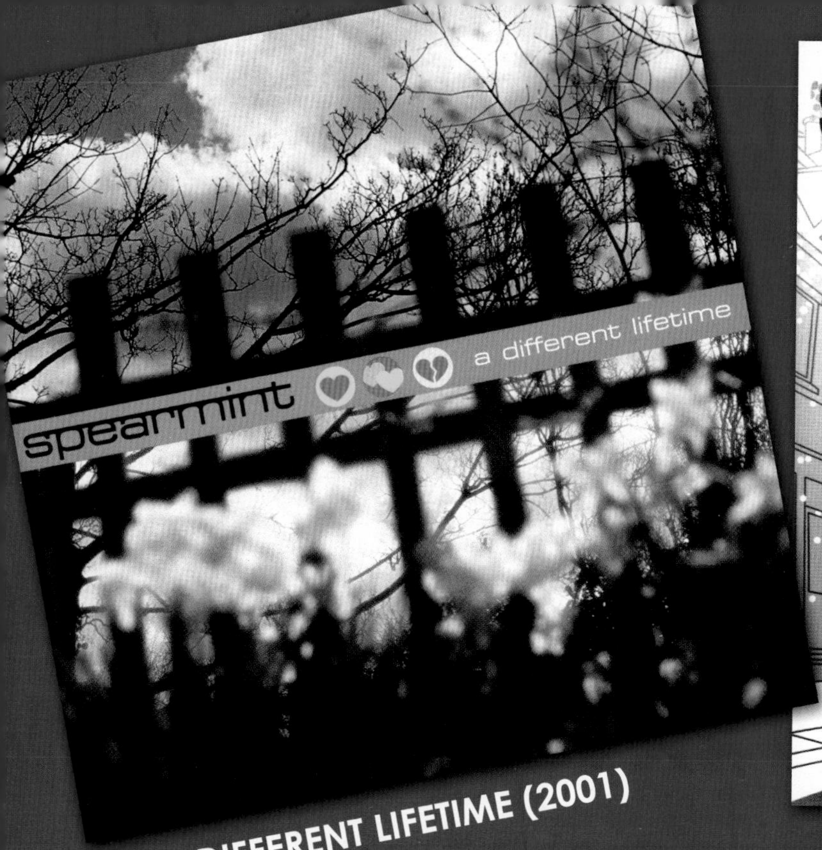
spearmint
a different lifetime

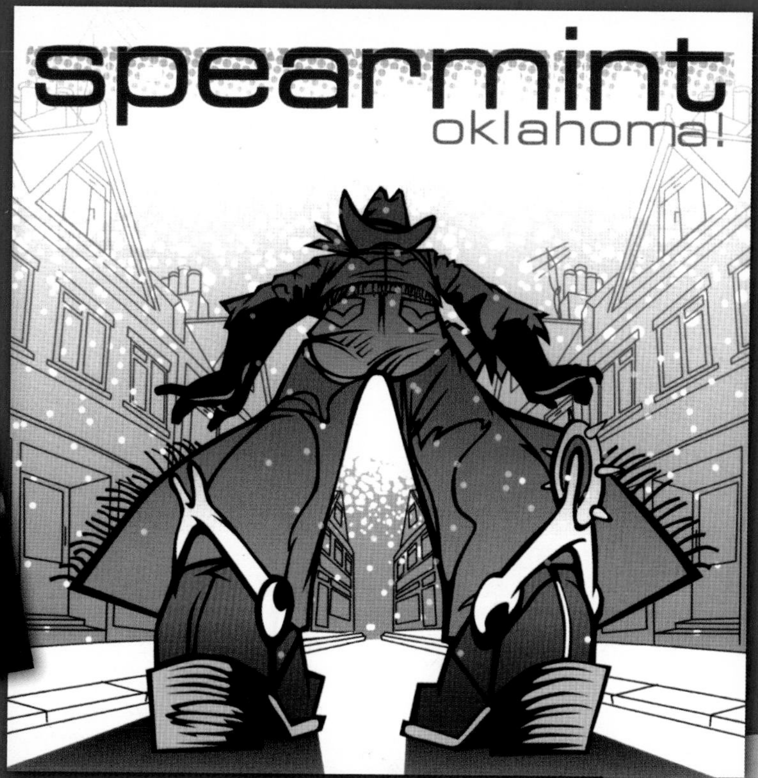
spearmint
oklahoma!

OKLAHOMA! (2000)

oklahoma!
leaves
the good of the family
i went away
the locomotion
new year song
happy birthday girl
vivian
howling christmas

A DIFFERENT LIFETIME (2001)

it will end
distant star
stealing beauty
julie christie!
suddenly
scottish pop
wrapped up together
the moment in my mind
go
the flaming lips
solace
a different lifetime
single again
"i'm so sorry..."
"... you are forgiven"

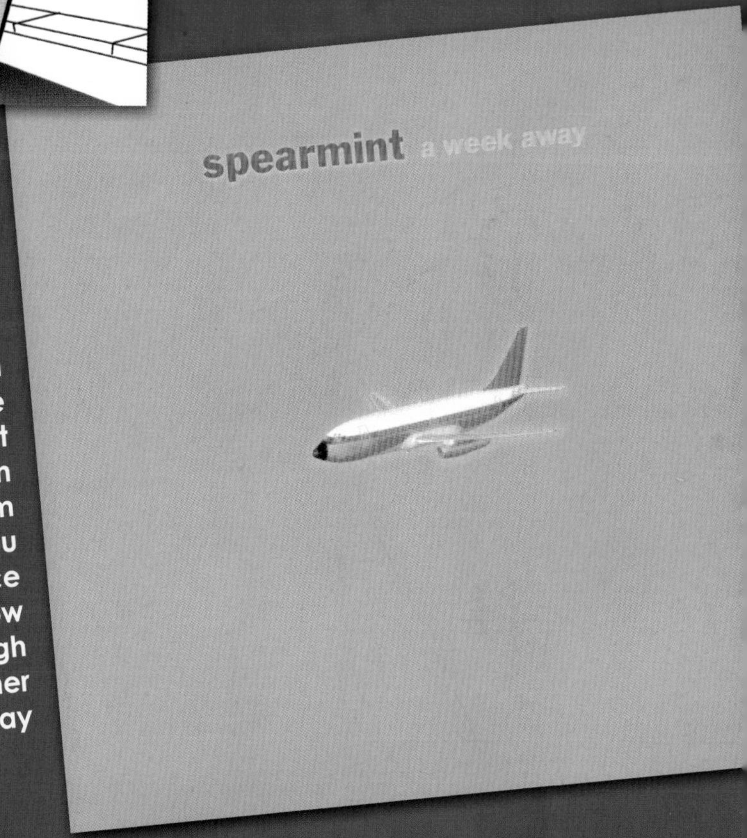
spearmint a week away

A WEEK AWAY! (1999)

a week away
isn't it great to be alive
sweeping the nation
a third of my life
we're going out
start again
best ballroom
you carry this with you
a trip into space
it won't be long now
making you laugh
you are still my brother
saturday

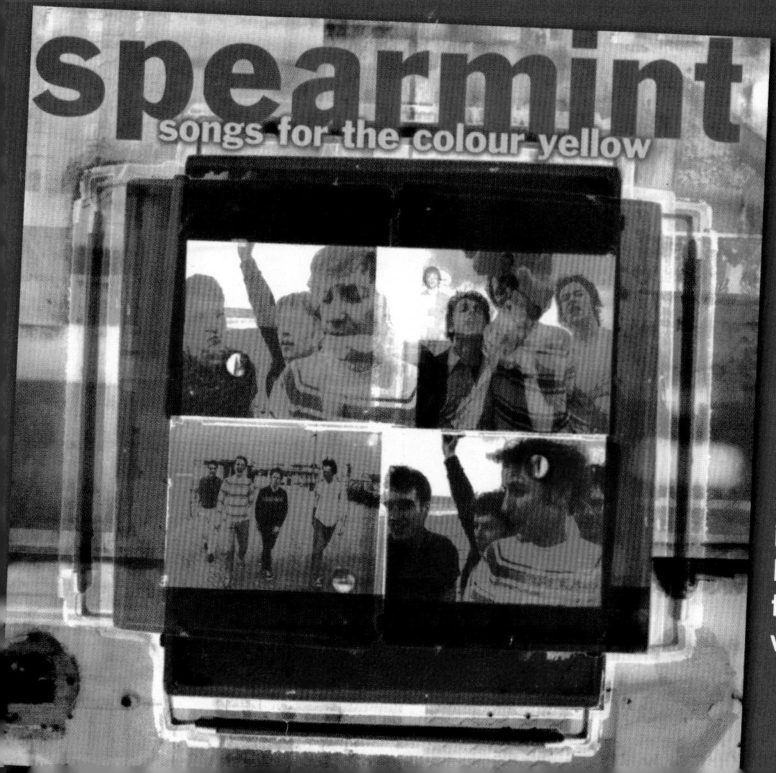
spearmint
songs for the colour yellow

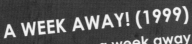

SONGS FOR THE COLOUR YELLOW (1998)

goldmine
a bench in a park
this is green, this is grey
song for the colour yellow
scared of everything
slips away
do you remember me?
sky
best friends
at this moment
i can't sleep
bee gee
the other seven
when i get out of here

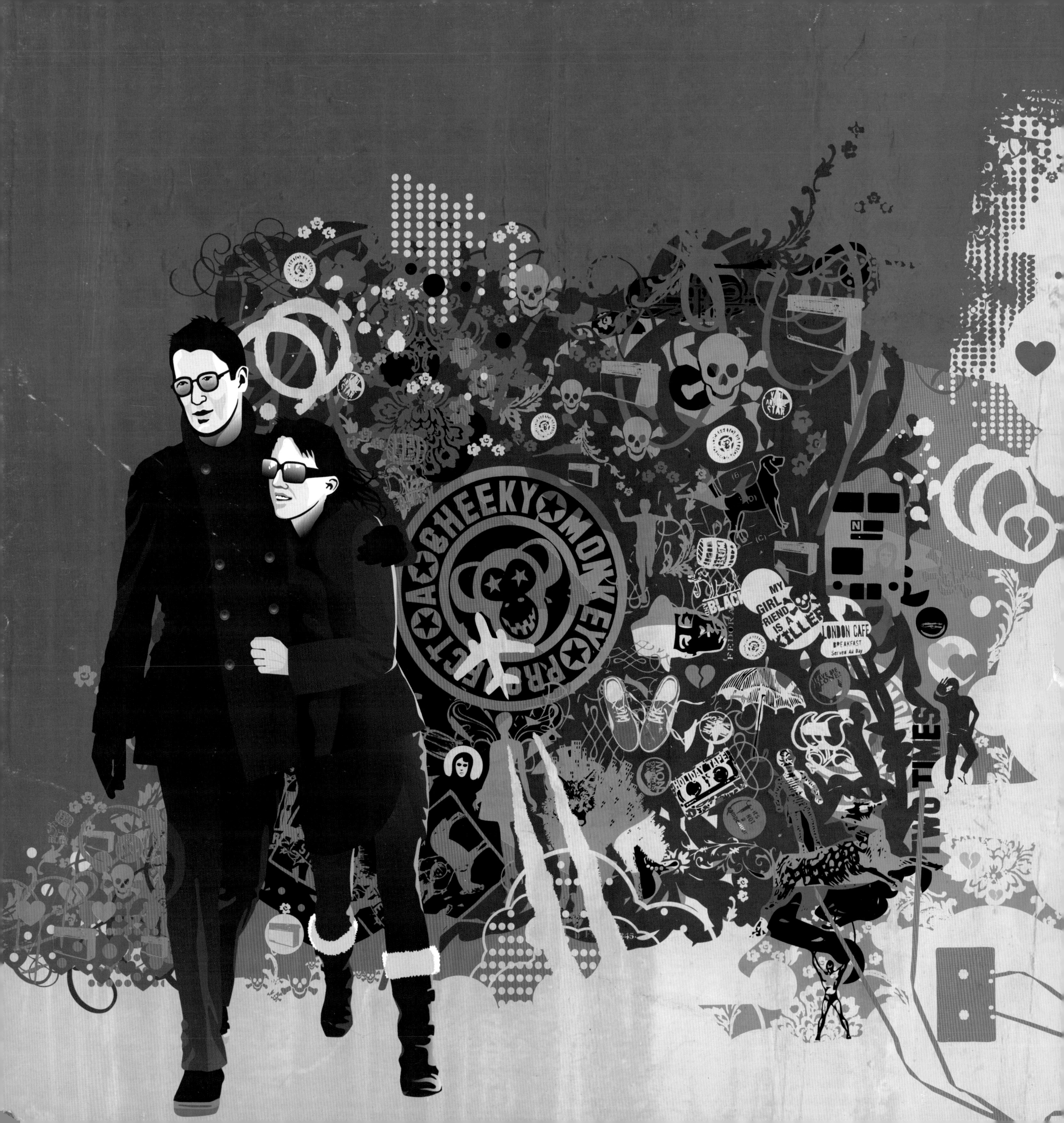
A CHEEKY MONKEY PROJECT
MY GIRL FRIEND IS A KILLER
LONDON CAFE
BREAKFAST
Served All Day
BLACK
FEDORA
HOLIDAY TAPE
TWO TIMES